parenting empires

parenting empires class, whiteness, and the moral economy of privilege in latin america ana y. ramos-zayas

Duke University Press   *Durham and London*   2020

© 2020 DUKE UNIVERSITY PRESS. All rights reserved
Designed by Courtney Leigh Baker
Typeset in Premier Pro by Westchester Publishing Services

Library of Congress Cataloging-in-Publication Data
Names: Ramos-Zayas, Ana Y., [date] author.
Title: Parenting empires : class, whiteness, and the moral economy of
privilege in Latin America / Ana Y. Ramos-Zayas.
Description: Durham : Duke University Press, 2020. | Includes
bibliographical references and index.
Identifiers: LCCN 2019034191 (print) |

LCCN 2019034192 (ebook) |
ISBN 9781478007746 (hardcover) |
ISBN 9781478008217 (paperback) |
ISBN 9781478009252 (ebook)
Subjects: LCSH: Parents, White—Brazil—Rio de Janeiro. |
Parents, White—Puerto Rico—San Juan. | Parenting—Brazil—
Rio de Janeiro. | Parenting—Puerto Rico—San Juan. | Elite (Social
sciences)—Brazil—Rio de Janeiro. | Elite (Social sciences)—
Puerto Rico—San Juan. | Whites—Race identity—Brazil—Rio
de Janeiro. | Whites—Race identity—Puerto Rico—San Juan. |
Privilege (Social psychology)—Brazil—Rio de Janeiro. | Privilege
(Social psychology)—Puerto Rico—San Juan. | Wealth—Moral
and ethical aspects—Brazil—Rio de Janeiro. | Wealth—Moral
and ethical aspects—Puerto Rico—San Juan. | Ipanema (Rio de
Janeiro, Brazil)—Social conditions. | San Juan (P.R.)—Social
conditions.
Classification: LCC HQ755.8 .R355 2020 (print) | LCC HQ755.8
(ebook) | DDC 305.809/08—dc23
LC record available at https://lccn.loc.gov/2019034191
LC ebook record available at https://lccn.loc.gov/2019034192

COVER ART: Family outing, Itacar, Brazil. © Lorenna
Morais / EyeEm. Courtesy of the artist and Getty Images.

To never forgetting . . .

4,645 deaths in Puerto Rico
1964 and its aftermath in Brazil

contents

acknowledgments

My interests in parenting, sovereignty, and the Latin American elite emerged in uneven, roundabout ways, at the unexpected intersections of personal and academic paths. The fieldwork for *Parenting Empires* began after a decade of learning about the lives of working-class Brazilian migrants and US-born Puerto Ricans in Newark, New Jersey, as well as following Brazilian and Puerto Rican youths on their return to their parents' ancestral lands. As a new parent, increasingly moving in various parenting circles in Brazil, Puerto Rico, and the United States, I came to realize how much parenting ambitions and sovereign aspirations mirrored each other. For Latin American elites, like those profiled in this book, closeness to power turns parental ambitions and sovereignty aspirations into everyday practices of place making, affective inequalities, and inner-world dispositions. This is what I hope to document here in this ethnography, a work spanning more than six years and enabled by many people.

I am thankful to the individuals whose voices appear in this ethnography. They generously gave me their time and emotional labor, introduced me to their lives and loved ones, and shared interior worlds and everyday routines with me over my years of fieldwork in Brazil and Puerto Rico. Some unexpected friendships formed during the making of this ethnography, as interlocutors became unwitting collaborators and allowed me to witness vulnerable moments in their lives and to examine their ongoing ambivalence about their privileged place in the world. Following anonymity and confidentiality promises, I will not mention these interlocutors by name. I want to assure them, however, that I appreciate their willingness to allow me into their journeys, as they aimed to resolve the dissonance and multiple conflicts caused by the presumably noble task of advocating on behalf of their children, their neighborhoods, and their countries.

During moments when I was not physically in the field, I worked as a faculty member at CUNY-Baruch College, where I occupied the Valentín Lizana y Parragué Endowed Chair in Latin American Studies, and at the CUNY Graduate Center, where I was affiliated with the Center for Latin American, Caribbean, and Latino Studies (CLACLS) and the Critical Social Psychology Department. At the Graduate Center, I am grateful to Michelle Fine, Setha Low, and the faculty in the Critical Social Psychology program, who welcomed me into the Psychology Department despite my training in anthropology; to Dana-Ain Davis, director of the Center for the Study of Women and Society, whose understanding of the unrealized potential of anthropology keeps me hopeful; to Arlene Torres, who remains committed to identifying issues of discrimination against Latinx faculty throughout CUNY; and to the CLACLS staff for so enthusiastically embracing my work. At Baruch, I want to thank Sandra Nieves, administrative assistant in the Black and Latino Studies Department. Sandra was always honest and kind, showing the greatest dignity, even when wealthy South American donors criticized her Nuyorican working-class Spanish and did not want her included at the lunch table. She made tough years in a tough place more bearable, and I will always be very thankful for that. Over the years, I have benefited from the unwavering support of Katherine S. Newman, my former dissertation advisor and the best example of what mentoring should look like. I also appreciate Micaela di Leonardo's candid guidance and occasional tough love over the past several decades.

In the fall of 2016, and after nearly two decades teaching at public institutions, I accepted a position at Yale University, where I am currently professor of American studies; women's, gender, and sexuality studies; and ethnicity, race, and migration. I thank the colleagues in each of these exceptional programs, as well as those affiliated with the Center for the Study of Race, Indigeneity, and Transnational Migration and La Casa. I want to single out the leadership of Alicia Camacho-Schmidt, Inderpal Grewal, Matthew Jacobson, and Stephen Pitti. I always knew I would meet bright minds and gifted teachers in this new adventure, but the fact that I also encountered warmth, solidarity, commitment to social justice, and humility has been a marvelous surprise. The ethnographer in me also appreciates the opportunity to work alongside Aimee Cox, Kathryn Dudley, and Eda Pepe to invigorate and "re-enchant anthropology" at Yale and beyond. My students at Yale are similar to the extraordinary students I met during my years at Rutgers and CUNY: they are energetic working-class, first-generation students of color, some undocumented, who possess a unique conviction and dedication to issues of social justice. Regardless of the institutions I inhabit, those graduate and undergraduate students still make me feel like the luckiest person in the world when I walk into the classroom, whether at Rutgers, CUNY, or Yale.

The Whiteness in the Americas workshop served as intellectual home for this project over the past five years. I am especially thankful to the unwavering support, brotherly warmth, and incisive intellectual engagement of workshop co-organizer and compadre Carlos Vargas-Ramos. I am immensely grateful for his feedback, encouragement, and support, as I am for those I received from WIA members Jillian Báez, Hal Barton, Ulla Berg, Hugo Cerón-Anaya, Milagros Denis, Zaire Dinzey-Flores, Melissa Fischer, Henry Franqui-Rivera, Daniel HoSang, Aldo Lauria-Santiago, Hilda Lloréns, Katherine López, Airín Martínez, Geisa Mattos, Tshombe Miles, Suzanne Oboler, Yadira Pérez, Edgar Rivera Colón, Patricia Silver, Stanley Thangaraj, Juan Usera, and Anahí Viladrich. Rubén Gaztambide-Fernández, John Jackson, and Shamus Khan were guest speakers at different WIA events and have served as important interlocutors for this project. Victoria Stone and Ana María Becerra took care of the administrative tasks and helped planned the Whiteness in the Americas conference, inspired by the workshop, at the CUNY Graduate Center in 2014. In addition to finishing each other's sentences (at times literally), I want to give special thanks to dear sister-friend, coauthor extraordinaire, and intellectual kindred spirit Ulla Berg, who has kept us internationally plugged in as we traveled to Buenos Aires, Paris, Bogotá, and Cali to crush the boundaries of US academia. Rachel Sherman and Patricia de Santana Pinho provided incisive readings and comments that were instrumental in helping me think through some impasses I faced along the way. Likewise, the students in Branquitude and Anti-Racismo, a course I co-taught with Geísa Mattos at the Universidade de Ceará in Fortaleza, provided the final push and inspiration that got me even more deeply connected with this project. The Whitney and Betty MacMillan Center for International and Area Studies at Yale provided funding for final follow-up trips to Brazil and Puerto Rico.

I have presented portions of this book at several US and international forums, but the two that stand out were organized by the Brazilian activist group Brazilian Resistance against Democracy Overthrow in New York (BRADO-NY) and by the Women's Studies program at Jawaharlal Nehru University (JNU) in New Delhi. Debarati Sen and Mallarika Sinha Roy orchestrated the visit to JNU, where I got asked a question that I am still pondering: Can we rescue self-care and wellness from the realm of privilege? At the BRADO event, among working-class Brazilian migrants in the NYC area, the question that stood out was, Can we rescue Brazil from its seemingly impending spiral into fascism? I am not sure I have addressed either of these audience questions adequately here, but I am still thinking about both, and there is another project in the pipeline that engages some of those lingering political projects beyond this current book. I want to thank the scholars, activists, and participants that attended these two events.

Valêria Araújo, Ana María Becerra, and Tiffany Medina entered my life when I was desperate for help with several tasks—from transcribing numerous Spanish and Portuguese interviews to putting together illustrations and maps to searching newspaper archives in Brazil, Puerto Rico, and beyond. I am convinced that there is nothing these young women cannot do. In their other lives, they are talented musical composers, graphic artists, travel bloggers, scrapbookers, dedicated moms, and the center of gravity for their families and communities. I admire their dedication to finding their life passions and am happy to consider them the younger sisters I never had. Jeannette Zaragoza De León, Oscar Blanco-Franco, and Thomas Abraham took some of the photos in this ethnography, and Francisco Javier Sánchez located important archival documents related to El Condado. Thanks to all of them for coming to the rescue!

Although I have worked with editor Gisela Fosado and editorial associate Alejandra Mejía for only a few months, their professionalism, enthusiasm, energy, and resourcefulness have helped me understand what all the fuss about Duke University Press is about. Ellen Goldlust, book project editor at Duke, provided needed reassurance and came to my rescue a few times in the final stages of this project. I feel privileged to entrust this manuscript to them and the rest of the production staff and editors at Duke.

My family, nuclear and extended—by birth, marriage, or choice—is my world. As an only child, I have a special love for my siblings-in-law, Premila Hoon and Peter Abraham, and their partners, Harry Baden-Powell and Lavinia Abraham. Along with our nephews, Jayant Hoon and Alok Abraham, and my amazing stepson, Christopher Abraham, they make our intercontinental households feel less distant. Likewise, the Fernandes, D'Souzas, Farias, and Alnemris in New Jersey and Pennsylvania allow us to come together for all holidays and treat us to the most delicious Indian cooking and hospitality. I am always, every day, grateful for my comadres Ana María Becerra and Aixa Cintrón, for Aixa's partner, Julia Burch, for my nieces, Ino and Amelia Cintrón-Burch, and for my nephews, the wonder twins Michael and Daniel Patino-Becerra, and for my siblings-by-choice, Carmen Benet, Oscar Blanco-Franco, Clara Castro-Ponce, and Raúl Perales. Julia Burch receives a special shout-out for reading (twice!) this whole thing and making critical editorial suggestions.

My close-knit family in Puerto Rico—my mom, Ana Hilda; my dad, Vicente; my aunts and uncles, Manuel and Yolanda, and Magaly and Javier— are the motivation for everything I do. During the time of writing this ethnography, Hurricane Maria virtually destroyed our island and revealed the stark social inequalities we always knew existed. The few days when we had not heard from my parents were dreadful, and the number of months without electricity were unbearable. If this was scary for my family members, who live in solid buildings in the metropolitan area of Santurce, I can only imagine the desperation of Puerto Ricans in poorer, more rural regions of the country. If "Puerto Rico Se Levanta," as the slogan goes, then *levantarse* will only happen when we heal the lingering trauma, critically examine the colonial context that led us here, and become able to imagine a future in our own terms. Coincidently, around the same time of Hurricane Maria, another type of threat and trauma took over Brazil, as a Far Right government swept the country and fascism reared its ugly head. Those ongoing processes of trauma and healing tacitly underscore this ethnography.

My life partner, Thomas Abraham, was at least as affected by the hurricane and how Puerto Ricans were treated in its aftermath as I was. Indian by birth, he has adopted Puerto Rico as a home he loves. He took us to marches, organized collections of provisions, proposed student *brigadas*, delivered food and water filters in Yabucoa, and was a caring son to my parents during these frightening times, as well as being a great support to my extended family for the last decade. His integrity, the way he shows up and stands up for others, his brilliance, modesty, and how he is as a parent continues to have me asking: How did I get so lucky? Perhaps our best joint project, and the source of our own parenting dramas and anxieties, is our spunky, mischievous, witty son, Sebastián Abraham-Zayas. Barely two years old at the time of my first fieldwork trip, Sebastián used his Spanish to communicate with the Portuguese-speaking teachers and kids at his daycare in Brazil and adapted to various fieldwork demands in Puerto Rico. He became a participant observer of the Ipanema and El Condado lagoons and beaches, of neighborhood parks and playgrounds, and a lover of *sucos de manga, brigadeiros,* and *empanadillas de pizza*, all without missing an ethnographic beat.

Finally, I dedicate this project to those Brazilians and Puerto Ricans, friends, relatives, and strangers, who continue to imagine what we could become, precisely by never forgetting. This is what the 4,645 deaths in Puerto Rico and 1964 and its afterlife in Brazil means in the dedication page of this book.

I

Parenting Empires and the Moral Economy
of Privilege in Brazil and Puerto Rico

In March 2016, the photo of a dark-skin and uniformed *babá* (nanny), walking behind a white Brazilian couple while pushing twin toddlers in a stroller through Ipanema, captivated the Brazilian media. The couple, sporting the colors of the Brazilian flag, and the nanny were participating in one of the early marches protesting Partido dos Trabalhadores (PT, or Workers' Party), which a few months later would lead to the impeachment of democratically elected president Dilma Rousseff. The nanny in the photo was eventually identified as forty-five-year-old Maria Angélica Lima, who served as *babá folguista* (weekend nanny) for the children of Carolina Maia Pracownik and her husband, Claudio Pracownik, the vice president of finance for the Flamengo, one of Rio's soccer teams.

The irony behind the photo of a wealthy Ipanema family bringing their nanny along to a demonstration against the PT, a party that for more than a decade had been responsible for, among other things, establishing legislation to protect the labor rights of nannies and domestic workers, was not lost to some. Media interviews with Carolina, the employer, and Angélica, the nanny, followed. "I went to the streets with my whole family, and I would go again! If this country seems good to others, it is not good for us. We went to protest against all this embarrassing corruption," stated Carolina, who claimed to be "shocked and scared" by the violence of critics who viewed her as the classic *dondoca* (snobbish, superficial woman). Carolina defended her decision to ask Angélica to wear the all-white nanny uniform, a source of polemic in Ipanema at the time: "There is a 'dress code' for many professions: doctors, nurses, doormen. . . . Why wouldn't nannies, now a regulated profession, wear white, transmitting peace to the children they care for? That argument

FIGURE 1.1. Uniformed nanny accompanying Ipanema couple and their children on an anti–Workers' Party demonstration, March 2016. Photo: João Valadares / Correio Brazilienze / Da Press

about discrimination is unacceptable. As they say: prejudice is in the eye of the beholder." As part of a response posted on her Facebook page and reprinted in other news media, Carolina stated, "My children recognize my smell, the warmth of my hug, my smile of approval. . . . In our home, the discussion is affectionate and the arguments are intelligent and stimulating" ("Patroa de foto polêmica" 2016). In the months following this demonstration, Brazil saw intensifying polarization over issues that were broad, diverse, and internally contradictory, culminating in dueling marches for and against the impeachment of President Dilma Rousseff in 2015 and the imprisonment of former president Luiz Inácio "Lula" da Silva as part of the Lava Jato "anticorruption" investigation (chapter 2).

More than 5,000 kilometers (3,242 miles) from Rio's political demonstration, in El Condado, an affluent neighborhood in San Juan, Puerto Rico, Tony Fortuño Vernet remarked, "Living in El Condado is also a huge part of how we parent." Mariblanca Giusti, Tony's wife, further noted, "Not everybody can create a good environment for their children, expose them to nature, be outdoors, rather than sit them in front of a screen. In El Condado you have that healthier, active lifestyle integrated into your daily life." As Tula, a dark-skin Dominican woman, who served simultaneously as housekeeper and nanny, walked by, Mariblanca remarked, "Which is what I tell Tula, because her grandchildren live in front of the TV. You need to take them out, to the park, outdoors!" Tula responded something like "I try, I try, but they don't listen to me," as she carried an armload of laundry. Mariblanca and Tony looked almost like siblings: they were both tall, athletic, and permanently tanned. Over the years of my fieldwork, they insisted that these obvious indicators of material wealth and a luxurious lifestyle "meant nothing" to them. What mattered to them was their emotional growth and spiritual journeys, as they worried about their country and raising their children. Mariblanca explained, "When I became pregnant with [my first child], I also became interested in Eastern spirituality, got certified in yoga. I wanted to turn my life around. Our country is in crisis, and it is partly a crisis of values. This demands a transformation, from all of us, from within."

The moral economy of wealth, implied in Mariblanca's remarks, challenged modernist ideals of increased technological and industrial development, the centrality of materialism and consumption, and an unconditional value of all things Western. As minimalist consumers, parents like Mariblanca embodied a version of national austerity politics and an austerity subjectivity; they drew from a neoliberal narrative of austerity to decry the evils of "irresponsible" consumption of their subordinates, and connected it to discussions around the national debt, social welfare, and the environment. These ethos of being down to earth (*pessoas despojadas* in Ipanema and *gente sencilla* in El Condado) was strongly linked to changing legal and hemispheric perspectives on race and "diversity" and a general distaste for mass-market consumer behavior. While domestic work in Brazil and Puerto Rico, and throughout the world, has undergone significant transformations over the last century, its present social form in Ipanema, El Condado, and perhaps other elite liberal neighborhoods was powerfully shaped by evolving practices of "parenting" that granted moral virtue to even the most profoundly unequal affective relations with subordinates.

There are multiple lenses through which one could examine the Ipanema photo and the conversation in El Condado. In this ethnography, I place the magnifying glass on the white wealthy parents who resided in arguably two of the most upscale neighborhoods in Brazil and Puerto Rico, respectively. Through a moral economy built on affective practices, anticonsumption, and antimaterialist discourse; psychological cultivation; child-centered environments; and everyday interpretations of national crises and the need for austerity, these Latin American urban elites altered their neighborhoods and cities, as they effected change in physical landscapes, structures of feeling, and processes of integration, segregation, and surveillance. More significantly, though, these upper-class Latin American parents—like Brazilian and Puerto Rican national elites of the past—were collaborators with the dictums of US empire. *Parenting Empires* shows how the parenting subjectivities and practices of urban elites in Brazil, Puerto Rico, and possibly in liberal urban centers across Latin America and the Global South forged child-centered sociabilities and national affects, and provided moral justifications for inequality that complement US political, financial, and military hemispheric interventions.

Parenting Empires may not be what most readers would imagine an ethnography of empire, colonialism, or sovereignty to look like. However, the project is concerned with pushing beyond conventional imaginings of empire and sovereignty to understand how hemispheric forms of control and influence get solidly entrenched in the fabric of daily life, parental aspirations, and routines. As agents of empire, the upper-class parents in this ethnography engaged in spaces and circuits of affinity and sociability that produced forms of personhood rooted in aesthetics of affect and morality, which effectively dovetailed with projects of austerity and perspectives on "crisis" and "corruption" in Brazil, Puerto Rico, and the Americas more broadly.

In this book, I endeavor to see how Brazilian and Puerto Rican elites inhabited their privilege and strove to make ethical and moral sense of racial and social inequalities that were inherently immoral. I use "parenting empires" in the title as both concept and verb. As a concept, the term labels the processes by which practices attached to the contemporary parenting of elites in the Americas intersected with national and hemispheric ideas of empire and sovereignty. As a verb, "parenting" serves as an action generative of empires; it indicates that forms of empire in the twenty-first century are in fact ideologically nurtured in child-centered ways that have unique moral appeal. Partly nurtured from a failed consolidation of sovereignty and US hemispheric reach, these forms of empire recast elite ideals into normative and commonsensical relational standards that effectively foreclosed alternative grassroots critique and narratives. (After all, who could challenge that children are any country's future? Or that parents should care about their children more than about other people's children? Or that being "mindful," having high "emotional intelligence," and investing in children's cultural cultivation are good things?)

As *Parenting Empires* demonstrates, the moral economies of privilege underscoring sovereignty and parenting prove particularly effective in granting currency to US hemispheric implementation of a "war on corruption" in the region and providing moral grounding to neoliberal austerity projects. Wealth and inequality, even under authoritarian governments, still requires a moral logic. Parenting—with all its neoliberal intensities, aspirations, languages, claims to expertise and science, and emphasis on inner-world cultivation—has become an effective, morally legitimate imperial formation.

Studying Privilege in the Americas

As Michel Pinçon and Monique Pinçon-Charlot remark, "Poverty allows itself to be scrutinized, cataloged, described.... Wealth, on the other hand, is little explored by sociologists who do not seem to venture into noble neighborhoods" (2007, 22–23); in a Lacanian sense, wealth is unrepresentable, or more precisely, it is the invisible tableau on which other things are situated for representation. While most research on the global inequality gap tends to focus on the lives of the poor, some recent scholarship has taken up anthropologist Laura Nader's (1974) challenge to "study up," extending the ethnographic gaze to those populations who have benefited from these global economic trends. Contemporary studies of elites in the Americas have examined how status, whiteness, and class take shape through elite collaborations and various forms of engagement with empire and nation building. One strand of this bibliography, in relation to Rio de Janeiro, includes Jerry Dávila's *Diploma of Whiteness: Race and Social Policy in Brazil, 1917–1945* (2003) and Zephyr Frank's *Dutra's World: Wealth and Family in Nineteenth-Century Rio de Janeiro* (2004), and in relation to Puerto Rico as a whole, Teresita Levy's *Puerto Ricans in the Empire: Tobacco Growers and US Colonialism* (2014) and Julian Go's *American Empire and the Politics of Meaning: Elite Political Cultures in the Philippines and Puerto Rico during US Colonialism* (2008).[1] From a historical perspective, these works discern early iterations of elite family life, wealth, and race in relation to questions of national sovereignty. *Parenting Empires* brings these historical overviews on colonial elite and populist collaborations to the present, examining the unique ways in which neoliberalism has altered what Latin American and Caribbean collaborations with US economic expansionism look like.

Another line of this bibliography of Latin American elites draws from urban studies and sociology to examine relationships of class and race, privileging living arrangements and the built environment as analytical lens. Centering on the proliferation and segregationist appeal of gated communities, Teresa Caldeira's *City of Walls: Crime, Segregation, and Citizenship in São Paulo* (2000) and Zaire Dinzey-Flores's *Locked In, Locked Out: Gated Communities in a Puerto Rican City* (2013) are exceptional works, which combine urbanism with understandings of democracy, citizenship, and race in the cities of São

Paulo, Brazil, and Ponce, Puerto Rico, respectively.[2] Building on these ideas, *Parenting Empires* aims to critically analyze not the Latin American elites that choose to self-segregate (or segregate the poor, in some of the cases Dinzey-Flores describes), but rather those that claim to want their children to feel at ease among "all sorts of people," and who are critical of walls and gates. The study pushes for a perspective on elites as heterogeneous and not always easily corresponding to popular images of the powerful. It makes the claim that such a perspective could yield a more complete (and complicated) understanding of how power, class, and race manifest in built and natural environments, and operate to sustain forms of white supremacy that are hardly transparent or easily detectable. This ethnography, thus, focuses on the upper classes that chose to settle in traditional upper-class neighborhoods, claiming that such neighborhoods were more accepting, open, and democratic, and who, in fact, viewed residents of gated communities as provincial, constitutive outsiders.

Dynamics of conspicuous consumption, a focus on the body and physical appearance, and luxurious and aspirational lifestyles are at the center of anthropological studies of Latin America and Caribbean middle and upper classes. Alexander Edmond's *Pretty Modern: Beauty, Sex, and Plastic Surgery in Brazil* (2010), for instance, compellingly analyzes the complex and relatively democratic world of plastic surgery and body politics in Rio de Janeiro, where domestic workers and the poor have also come to view cosmetic procedures as a vehicle to social mobility and work opportunity, and a proxy for modernity. Likewise, Maureen O'Dougherty's *Consumption Intensified: The Politics of Middle-Class Daily Life in Brazil* (2002) masterfully documents how in the mid-1980s, at the peak of Brazil's greatest inflation, the middle and upper-middle classes in fact intensified their consumption. These sectors came to primarily define themselves in terms of their privileged consumption (and the media continually addressed these middle-class Brazilians as consumers), and consumption in fact became a symbol of racial, cultural, and moral superiority; parents had to be more flexible in the jobs they were willing to take, while putting stakes in their children's expensive private education as a social mobility project. Moreover, in the context of Barbados, and possibly applicable to other Caribbean nations, Carla Freeman's *Entrepreneurial Selves: Neoliberal Respectability and the Making of a Caribbean Middle Class* (2014) examines how an entrepreneurial middle class reworks the Caribbean cultural model of reputation and respectability in alignment with postcolonial neoliberal demands of flexibility and self-making. The figure of the entrepreneur embodies not only financial aspirations, but also the very reworking of personhood and intimacy. While *Parenting Empires* recognizes that consumption, body work, and entrepreneurial ventures were enduring cultural practices among the Ipanema and El Condado upper classes, and the ethnography is inspired by some of this scholarship, it extends consumption beyond the easily observable realm of monetary transactions and body projects to the realm of interiority and its inconspicuous forms. Practices associated with Eastern religions, spirituality, psychology, and wellness, some of which actually rendered conspicuous consumption suspect, were important status markers and parenting subjectivities in Ipanema and El Condado.

While research on Latin American upper classes and racial privilege is rare, possible exceptions include Jennifer Roth-Gordon's *Race and the Brazilian Body: Blackness, Whiteness, and Everyday Language in Rio de Janeiro* (2017) and Jessé Souza's *A elite do atraso: Da escravidão à Lava Jato* (2017).[3] Roth-Gordon proposes the term "comfortable racial contradiction" (2017, 1) to highlight how structural racism that privileges whiteness exists alongside a deeply held pride in Brazil's history of racial mixture. From a sociolinguistic perspective, she argues that individuals from Rio's shantytowns and middle classes read one another's bodies for racial signs. They determine the amount of whiteness or blackness a body displays, based on specific phenotypic features as well as cultural and linguistic practices, speech, and slang. Roth-Gordon compellingly examines the minutiae of the linguistic strategies deployed by residents of Rio de Janeiro's poor communities, as they engage in forms of cultural production and territorial claims over the neighborhood. Her discussion of white upper-class Rio residents resonated with some of the language and parenting practices I noticed in Ipanema, though not with those I witnessed among the upper classes of El Condado, as I examine in this volume. This is one of those instances in which the South-South comparative ethnographic angle becomes critical in understanding that it is largely the diversity in elite socialization practices that effectively sustains power inequality in the Americas.

Adopting a political economic and historical framework, Jessé Souza traces how the language of corruption has become a cultural fact inseparable from elite perspectives on Brazilian governmentality, or the country's presumed inability to reach the marks of a modern democracy. As Souza argues, contemporary Brazilian elites have consistently rejected populism, and the country's intellectuals have situated corruption exclusively in the realm of the nation-state, thus effectively absolving financial and corporate sectors from blame for the country's various crises. The national government, therefore, becomes entirely responsible for rampant corruption. This perspective situates the genesis of social and racial inequality, fiscal debt, and governmentality crises entirely outside the financial and corporate sectors, which at times are often viewed as the saviors of corrupt government through various privatization projects. As Souza demonstrates, the discourse of corruption has predictably served forms of governmentality that have benefited the upper classes—from the imposition of military governments to the impeachment of democratically elected ones. Fostering the belief that corruption is a social fact unique to Brazil, these upper classes reinforce a US historical narrative of Latin American backwardness.

As is the case among Puerto Rico's upper classes, Brazilian elites rarely approached corruption as a critique of US and foreign intervention or corporate greed. The deployment of corruption as a rallying point into which the upper classes draw alliances with the middle class, furthermore, enforces narratives of dysfunction and pathology onto the lower, often racialized, populations.[4] This application of a corruption narrative to explain Brazilian failure of governance similarly applied to Puerto Rico during the time of my fieldwork. Puerto Rico's upper and middle classes almost exclusively associated corruption with the island's government and public institutions, as opposed to white-collar crimes of their own class; they harbored the view that privatization and giving tax incentives to foreign investors would eliminate corruption and believed that austerity was the only way out of the country's debt crisis. This has never, of course, been an exclusive narrative of the upper classes. Yet, the upper and upper-middle classes in Ipanema and El Condado placed child-centered practices and deployed a moral economy of wealth to position themselves as innocent bystanders, frequently absolved from the downward spiraling of the nation.

While *Parenting Empires* enters in conversation with this remarkable, if partial, body of literature on Latin American and Caribbean elites, the clearest debates for this volume belong to a US-based scholarship more explicitly concerned with urban upper classes, liberalism, parenting, and the moral economy. Two of these works, which I engage with in greater depth in later chapters, are Rachel Sherman's *Uneasy Street: The Anxieties of Affluence* (2017) and Elizabeth Currid-Halkett's *The Sum of Small Things: A Theory of the Aspirational Class* (2017). Sherman examines the "anxieties of affluence" among wealthy New Yorkers, while Currid-Halkett alludes to "the aspirational class of inconspicuous consumers." Both works show how US urban elites, particularly in their role as parents, instill and reproduce ideas about how to occupy privilege legitimately. Dilemmas related to money and identity, and the challenges of striking a balance between giving children material resources and opportunities without spoiling them, for instance, were ultimately conflicts about how to render one's wealth moral and legitimate, especially at a moment of extreme economic inequality.

This contemporary US work on elites has extended the boundaries of studying up beyond analyses of conspicuous consumption, leisure, and luxurious lifestyles to investigations of psychological, affective, and wellness orientation among elites. These studies note that since the 1899 publication of Thorstein Veblen's *Theory of the Leisure Class*, the sociological classic that introduced the phrase "conspicuous consumption" and described the frivolity of the upper class, the power of material goods as symbols of status has diminished with their wider accessibility. As a result, US and European upper classes have altered consumption habits away from extravagant displays and excessive expenditures to more subtle, less materialistic forms of inconspicuous consumption, which are also emblematic of elites' conflictive attitudes toward the quality, identities, and display of wealth.[5]

Another important body of US-based studies of elites has centered, ethnographically, on boarding schools as totalizing institutions for adolescent socialization. Two seminal works that examine capital beyond economic advantage are Shamus Khan's *Privilege: The Making of an Adolescent Elite at St. Paul's School* (2012) and Rubén Gaztambide-Fernández's *The Best of the Best: Becoming Elite at an American Boarding School* (2009). Khan views privilege as a sense of self and a mode of interaction that advantages upper-class students. He identifies "ease"—the ability to comfortably inhabit most social settings, both those considered to be "above" and "below" oneself in an enduring social hierarchy—as the core of such class privilege in the United States. Likewise, Gaztambide-Fernández illuminates how elite boarding schools emphasize the importance of being a "good person," even though these enactments of goodness—through volunteerism, for instance—necessitated marginalized others who lacked the material resources to themselves undertake similar goodness actions. The broader social context for elite schooling and privatized education in First World and emerging economies has significantly changed over the last half century. With the spread of democratic processes and meritocratic ideologies, social elites are no longer the historically closed circles created by inherited or ascribed sociological status, reinforced by intermarriage and exclusive social circuits. This shift has fostered greater uncertainty, anxiety, and strategy around the intergenerational transfer of privilege, as parents develop strategies to position children advantageously for educational opportunity starting earlier and earlier. Importantly, Pierre Bourdieu's classic work argued that parents' backstage investments orchestrated the child's individual achievement of such status by meritocratic means, "so that the educational system seems to award its honors solely to natural qualities" (1984, 254). This individualized achievement could then be formally confirmed and validated by educational credentials. A significant, and perhaps counterintuitive, finding of this scholarship is that greater institutional openness or inclusion (i.e., the liberal alternative of a diverse student body and curriculum), in and of itself, does not yield greater social equality or radically challenge structural inequalities.

The US-based sociological and ethnographic work outlined here unfolds in a context where social class has historically been undermined by the language of the American Dream, meritocracy, intergenerational upward mobility, and hard work. This US foundational language, while not entirely absent in Ipanema and El Condado, operated very differently in relation to class and racial hierarchies in Brazil and Puerto Rico. *Parenting Empires* examines elite gestures toward social and racial openness, but rather than focusing on the world of adolescents and schools, it analyzes how experimentations with inclusion in Ipanema and El Condado were situated in the realm of parenting and its child-centered sociability, practices, and idioms.

The Perils and Politics of Parenting

I do not propose the concept of "parenting empires" in the title of this ethnography as an arsenal of practices exclusively implicating parents and their children. Instead, parenting empires is a form of sociability and relatedness that positioned child-centeredness in terms of how the upper classes in two Latin American affluent neighborhoods worked through relationships across racial and class lines, altered urban practices and the built environment, crafted a sense of personal depth and interiority currency, and adapted a national language of austerity and corruption to neighborhood governance. Working within theories of the moral economy, I analyze how political economic and historical practices intersected with a person's moral value, increased investment in reflexivity and personal growth, and led to the virtual demise of structural explanations for inequality. In countries infamous for having draconian austerity measures and the highest levels of social inequality in the world, investments in forms of "immaterial" advantages were hardly immaterial. These moral dilemmas, embodiments of privilege, inner-world aesthetics, and concern with a progressive self-fashioning often provided the impetus for civic neighborhood action, institutional and spatial privatization, and exclusionary practices that did not require encroaching walls or country club memberships.

In *Parenting Empires,* the concept of parenting is a social phenomenon that provides a productive analytical lens to how other liberal democratic concepts— like sovereignty, empire, corruption, or crisis—and hierarchies of class and race get recast when privilege is examined in all its moral and affective complexities.

Over the last fifty years, we have witnessed a powerful global convergence of ideas and practices regarding child rearing and parenting. In Philippe Aries's 1960 study of privileged French parenting, he shows that there was already tremendous investment in the child in the sixteenth through the eighteenth centuries. Unlike those early iterations of family life and childhood, however, contemporary parenting culture is built on tensions between the call to individual fulfillment of the late twentieth century and the altruistic expectations around resources given to children. A term that became prominent in the 1950s in a language used by psychologists, sociologists, and social work practitioners in North America, "parenting" does not have a perfect Spanish or Portuguese translation, though I did occasionally hear the terms *crianza* (to raise a child) in Puerto Rico and *parentalidade* (assuming the role of a parent) in Brazil. Nevertheless, parenting, a phenomenon with its own vocabulary, practices, and rules, serves as conduit to processes otherwise associated with sovereignty and governance, including surveillance and policing in the elite neighborhoods in this ethnography.

Ellie Lee, Jennie Bristow, Charlotte Faircloth, and Jan Macvarish's edited volume, *Parenting Culture Studies* (2014), and Inderpal Grewal's *Saving the Security State: Exceptional Citizens in Twenty-First Century America* (2017) offer exceptional examinations of child rearing in connection to public debate, moral panics, and policymaking in Europe and the United States, respectively. These works view parenting not primarily as a site of intergenerational social reproduction, but as one of governmentality (see also Cecello and Kholoussy 2016). Covering political developments in Europe and North America, Lee et al. (2014) analyze the reasons why the minutiae of how parents raise their children—how they feed them, talk to them, play with them, or discipline them—have become routine sources of public debate and policymaking. *Parenting Culture Studies* situates parental determinism in the wider context of risk consciousness and the demise of social confidence about the future. The edited volume focuses on various ways in which explicit parenting support policy entered European political agendas during the early 1990s and produced a "turn to parenting," with its experts, new terms, instruments, and institutions.

Tracing the changing relations between the US state and its citizens in an era marked by the decline of US geopolitical power, endless war, and increasing surveillance, Inderpal Grewal (2017) demonstrates how the private domestic space of American women has been expanded, so that idealized mother-subjects have come to play critical roles in the privatization of welfare, surveillance, and security in an array of everyday forms (e.g., gated communities, shopping malls, suburbs). During the US war on terror, these "security moms" were invested in obsessive surveillance and projected state terror onto criminalized foreigners and racialized domestic populations. Rather than harboring an expansive view of violence, which might include a common feminist concern with issues of domestic violence, US security moms viewed the home as a fortress against "Islamic terrorists," "illegal aliens," and racial and criminalized Others. Evidenced in the propensity of white mothers to call the police on Black and Brown (male) bodies, for instance, this increased anxiety engendered distrust and competitiveness; it is centered more on individuality and less on community belonging. Ultimately, these maternal super-citizen subjects sustained and gave moral value to neoliberal agendas and economic policy that otherwise led to government retrenchment and the virtual elimination of social justice and welfare concerns.

Parenting Empires draws inspiration from these analyses, which view parenting not as part of a psychological realm of parental anxieties, neuroses, depressions, narcissisms, or paranoia, but as practices that are often pawns of and complicit with broader nation-state projects. In complicated Global South contexts, like Ipanema and El Condado, sovereignty, austerity, and national crises were attributed to, or heavily imposed on, racialized and socially marginalized populations, whose very parenting was rendered suspect. Global processes that converge in the Caribbean and Latin America trouble the claim that national governments have supreme control over their internal affairs and that other states cannot intervene, under exception of threat or obligation of alliance. It has been widely demonstrated that in Latin America and the Caribbean, the sovereign nation is a myth or an aspirational model at best. This impossibility of sovereignty, and even the uneven desire for sovereignty, in fact turns other social formations as proxies, to do what sovereignty promises but fails to deliver. As I highlight throughout this book, moral dilemmas among elites are important not because of the anxiety and inner conflicts they might cause these upper-class populations but because these dilemmas were impetus for increased surveillance and privatization actions with direct material repercussions on racialized and stigmatized Others, like Dominican immigrants in El Condado and migrants from the impoverished Brazilian Northeast in Ipanema.

Parenting produced an intimate public sphere in which sovereignty became the sum of the private acts and values of individual subjects; it effectively situated social action around inequality away from concentrations of congealed wealth and toward culture and intimate conduct, feelings, and morality. A shrinking welfare state and severe austerity measures have become morally justified through new positions of active and responsible citizenship, including forms of parenting empires. Having absorbed this profound significance, parenting is imagined to be both the cause of, and solution to, all social ills and structural inequality.

Parenting Empires: A Theoretical Framework

In this South-South comparative ethnography, I propose the framework of parenting empires to trace dynamics of race and class privilege as they acquired materiality and psychological depth through the built environment, landscapes, child-centered sociabilities, and the regulation of affective expectations that Ipanema and El Condado upper classes had of themselves and their subordinates. This framework proposes that these dynamics in fact communicate the goals of US hemispheric reach and enlist the collaboration of national elites in processes of empire and colonial control. The theoretical framing of parenting empires is built on three cornerstones, each doing some of the work the concept proposes: the salience of "child-centered nodules of urbanism" and sites of adult sociability and relatedness; the dedication to crafting an "interiority currency," a particular form of inner-world cultivation, which I propose is a white elite project fundamental to Latin American and Caribbean white supremacy; and the moral justification of wealth through the everyday productions of "austerity subjectivities" and narratives around government corruption.

CHILD-CENTERED NODULES OF URBANISM

A cornerstone of parenting empires in Ipanema and El Condado were the "child-centered nodules of urbanism," as I refer to the neighborhood-based physical or social locations where adults involved in the care of children came together, sometimes crossing class, regional, ethnic, and racial lines. These were prosaic spaces of urban encounters—and sites of Foucauldian panoptic force—that occasionally opened up new perspectives about segregation and (dis)assemblies of collective life. Child-centered nodules of urbanism gave spatial forms to the elite sociability on which parenting empires were built. These were embodied sites of locating unrest, fear, austerity, and making judgment on individuals, families, and neighborhood transformations. Neoliberal discourses of choice, responsibility, and aspiration gained moral currency and got played in everyday routines around children, yet only certain social subjects were able to mobilize their interest to achieve a legitimate subject-position in these spaces. Imperfectly modular and at times amorphous, these were spaces whose density, history, and public or semipublic quality contribute to imprinting them onto local urban aesthetics, routines, and ideologies around child rearing, even when children were not physically present or when such spaces were not explicitly designated as "child-friendly spaces." Affective dispositions, aspirational language, and anxieties about safety, opportunity, and distinction acquire materiality in these nodules.

Some of these nodules were perhaps predictable: playgrounds, school campuses, parks and plazas, enrichment classes (swimming, beach volleyball, kayaking, languages), puppet theaters, and children's sections in local bookstores. Others were not explicitly associated with children but still played significant roles in the children's socialization and in parental self-fashioning: popular bakeries and ice cream parlors, speech or occupational therapy lectures, cafés and restaurants, country and sports clubs, pregnancy/postpregnancy yoga and Pilates. "Nature" and "outdoors," such as the neighborhoods' respective beachfront, the Rodrigues de Freitas Lagoon in Ipanema and the Condado Lagoon in El Condado, and corresponding adjacent national parks were also child-centered nodules associated with shifting and arbitrary understandings of healthy living, fitness, spirituality, and body care.

These child-centered nodules are founded on gradated variations and degrees of sovereignty and disenfranchisement, on multiple criteria for inclusions and sliding scales of basic rights. As parenting becomes the most intimate terrain where empires are constructed and entitlements are embodied, child-centered nodules do the spatial work of redrawing categories of subject and citizen, fostering elaborate nomenclatures that distinguish between *favelados*, *títeres*, foreign billionaires who get tax exemptions, national elites, and internal and transnational immigrants (e.g., *nordestinas/os, dominicanas/os*). They produced scales of differentiation and affiliation that exceeded a clear division between ruler and ruled (Wright 2015).

As socially produced and made productive in social practices, child-centered nodules of urbanism were characterized by the contradictory, conflictual, and ultimately political character of their very process of production. Henri Lefebvre's work—with its focus on the role representation plays in the production of space—aids our understanding of contemporary urban processes and the "feel" that places like Ipanema and El Condado have on the national (and even international) imaginaries (Lefebvre 1991, chapters 2 and 3).[6] In segregated cities, where zones of poverty are ubiquitous in the landscapes of the wealthy, as is the case in San Juan and Rio de Janeiro, child-centered nodules of urbanism provided, ironically, one of the few spaces in which forms of subaltern "resistance" were experimented with, largely because these were oftentimes public spaces shared by paid and unpaid caregivers.

FIGURE 1.2. El Condado, aerial view of field site. Photo: Oscar Blanco

Participating in child-centered nodules of urbanism was not merely about individuals interacting with their surroundings, but about being intimately—not just transactionally—involved with hierarchies of power. Parenting was a neoliberal subjectivity that was particularly effective in the privatization of public spaces and in subjecting those spaces to surveillance, policing, and exclusion. I trace the process of how inner, personal, and moral conflicts, more frequently articulated through a language of parenting, became engines for collective exclusionary neighborhood practices.

INTERIORITY CURRENCY: EMOTIONAL DEPTH, COGNITIVE AESTHETICS, AND PERSONHOOD

A second cornerstone of parenting empires considers ever-increasing commitments to projects of the self, Eastern spirituality, and personal growth. Such projects are certainly contemporary staples of neoliberal personhood, a profitable "happiness industry" (Davies 2015), and the commodification of feelings worldwide (Hochschild 1979; Illouz 2007) and are not unique to Brazil and Puerto Rico. In Ipanema and El Condado, however, such interiority projects were also fundamental to the solidification and legitimation of white privilege. While early twentieth-century Brazilian and Puerto Rican intellectual elites

FIGURE 1.3. Ipanema, aerial view of field site. Photo: Luiz Eduardo Lages, http://luizeduardolages.com/turfindx.htm

viewed various modalities of "racial democracy" (e.g., *mestiçagem* in Brazil, *mulataje* in Puerto Rico) as an intrinsic national trait, contemporary Ipanema and El Condado elites cultivated inner-world aesthetics that allowed them to preserve their white privilege while sustaining, questioning, and being ambivalent about the tenets of racial democracy. Thus, virtually every interlocutor, in both Ipanema and El Condado, recognized racism and racial discrimination in their countries, while also proposing inner-world cultivation as a site where these social inequalities would presumably be ironed out. They imagined how socially subordinate and marginalized populations could reach personal fulfillment by working on spiritual development and self-regulating to overcome whatever "unfortunate" life situation they faced.

The upper-class and upper-middle-class parents I met were dedicated not just to "being themselves," but to doing the work of *becoming* a certain kind of individual recognized for her or his ability to understand, discuss, and enact the world of emotional depth and interiority.[7] Debates about whether the self was "found" or "made," and other philosophical stances about one's inner quests, personal journeys, and metaphysical and existentialist concerns were intertwined with recommendations for life coaches, therapists, Buddhist meditation centers, yoga retreats, Kardecismo and *espirita* groups (in Brazil), and various healers, gurus, and relationship experts (see chapters 4 and 5).[8] These debates were not very different from those common among upper-class parents in the United States or the United Kingdom; what was different was how these practices were entangled with neighborhood governance, expectations of social relations across class and race, and approaches to sovereignty and austerity.

As a cornerstone of parenting empires, such interiority currency is productive in illustrating the social effects of notable changes from conspicuous to inconspicuous forms of consumption (or the conspicuous consumption of socially worthy things) among Ipanema and El Condado elites. In these neighborhoods, explicit luxury and superficial displays of wealth were no longer unambiguous signals of respectability, modernity, or personal worth, as they may have been a generation before (chapter 6). Importantly, far from making the world more egalitarian, this shift in fact entrenched modern elites' racial and class privilege even more effectively than conspicuous consumption habits ever did (cf. Currid-Halkett 2017; Sherman 2017b).[9]

I use "interiority currency" to highlight a form of capital that, unlike the inculcated cultural capital Bourdieu discusses, or even Michèle Lamont's (1992) symbolic moral capital, never gets to be viewed as second nature or perfectly achieved.[10] For interiority to constitute a form of capital, it had to be actively and continuously pursued, worked on, and never fully realized. Upper-class Ipanema and El Condado parents viewed their inner world not as "just who you are," but as who you are *and* could become, as a work-in-progress rooted in commitment, dedication, and hard work, and therefore accessible to anyone willing to do that work. Interiority currency was realized not only through outward body display, cosmetic, behavioral, or even spiritual, but through the continuous critical and conscious pursuit of an understanding and management of one's interior growth or path. Targeting areas for personal improvement and growth, cultivating the emotional intelligence to navigate complex affective entanglements and social situations, focusing on transforming the "outside world" through self-awareness, and the very decision to pursue this path as a life quest were at the center of this interiority currency. Under these forms of self-cultivation was a demand for an ordered futurity, where hierarchies were not so obstructive, and desires were uncorrupted by the weight of historical guilt and violence.[11]

Over the last few decades, scholars have written about "therapeutic culture" (Illouz 2008, 30), the self-help industry, "entrepreneurial selves" (Freeman 2014), "regimes of the self" (Rose 1996b, 81–82), and "street therapists" (Ramos-Zayas 2012), in which "therapy is not just an adjustment device but an expression of generalized reflexivity" (Giddens 1991, 180). Increasingly in the Global South, parents deployed therapeutic language and treatments to relate to their children, thus engaging in emotional coaching and becoming reliant on child development experts to vindicate child-rearing decisions.[12] The tenacity of distinctly therapeutic notions and the mainstreaming of ordinary psychological anxieties of the upper- and upper-middle classes into a broader emotional micro-public sphere (cf. Illouz 2007) served as tools through which the upper classes developed relational expectations of subalterns and the "psychological narrativity" (Tobin 1995, 234) that they used in child-centered nodules of urbanism.[13] Tracey Jensen (2010) argues that parenting is the most recent of the intimate realms into which emotional capitalism is stretching, and on which ideologies of individualism get cemented.[14] Therapeutic style, language, and communication furthermore shaped elite expectations of how relationships, not just interactions, with racialized and social subordinates ought to be conducted and evaluated, as well as what that said about them as elites.

Focusing on parenting—and the highly politicized and deeply moralistic set of rules, ideologies, and impositions that accompany it—allows for a clearer view of how structures of power are rendered legibly, acquire social significance, and get codified in the realm of emotion, affects, and sentiments.[15] Parenting empires provide a framework to trace how child-centered sociabilities have become the social lynchpin between affect, morality, and politics in everyday life.

AUSTERITY SUBJECTIVITIES, CORRUPTION, AND THE MORAL ECONOMY OF PRIVILEGE

The third main theoretical cornerstone of parenting empires focuses on the social networks of child-centered care that upper-class parents enlisted. The adults enlisted in these networks—namely, members of the extended family and domestic workers—served as proxies for a broader political economy of the Global South, including the colonial, transnational, and imperial histories of Brazil and Puerto Rico. It was through these networks of child-centered care that a national rhetoric of "corruption" and a focus on austerity acquired everyday grounding and immediacy.

Although technically, Brazil is a sovereign nation and Puerto Rico a US territory, both countries have often found themselves questioning their ability to have their democratic political choices respected. Since colonial logic dictates that empires must incorporate colonial subjects to obscure dehumanization (Mendez and Germann 2018), Puerto Ricans, including elites, were included in the social structures of the United States, albeit as "delinquent citizens" (Ramos-Zayas 2004). Since the first decade of this century, the specific path adopted by Brazilian elites to interact with central economies was to transform the country into an international platform for financial valorization (Almeida 2016). The impeachment of a democratically elected president in Brazil in

2016, like the Federal Control Board imposed by the US Congress to oversee the Puerto Rican government, suggested a lack of democratic value and political autonomy.[16] In the posh living rooms of Ipanema and El Condado, residents speculated about how such national crises and political divisions would affect personal safety, close relationships, and their children's future and quality of life, as well as contemplating when to exert discretionary powers, as citizens of their specific neighborhoods, to punish transgressions, and when to make the customary exception from the law. Discussions around "corruption" and "the merits of austerity" became the threads to how parenting empires legitimated social inequality, privatization of national resources, and foreign intervention. Parenting empires in the affluent neighborhoods in this ethnography were premised on a moral economy of privilege and wealth.

As I was discussing this project with US and Latin American scholars, it became clear how terms like "colonialism," "empire," and "sovereignty" had a currency, legibility, and quotidian character in the Global South that may not quite resonate in Global North contexts. This could arguably be because in Brazil, Puerto Rico, and perhaps other countries in the Global South, sovereignty has become precarious, even untenable, and increasingly associated with everyday relationships across domains of class, race, and local geographies, rather than confidence in the state, democracy, or political autonomy. The presumed failure to achieve the normative ideal of national sovereignty—what Michel-Rolph Trouillot (2002) terms the North Atlantic Universal—is furthermore associated with a state of unachieved (or underachieved) modernity. But even in Brazil, understandings of sovereignty are integrated into a future, a popular orientation toward a commitment to "the children" and "future generations." Neither Brazil nor Puerto Rico can be understood without examining the critical role that US imperialism has played in Latin America and the Caribbean over the twentieth century.[17]

The question of pursuing a "moral" way of being wealthy in countries of astonishing economic inequalities is interwoven with imperial and colonial projects and sovereign aspirations. Arguably better than other adult subjectivities, parenting provided an effective grounding to how elites rendered their wealth and racial privilege legitimate. Among wealthy Latin American and Caribbean populations, a new form of global, cosmopolitan parenting operated as the affective underside of a moral economy of wealth. Through parenting, morality acquired materiality, concreteness, and rhetorical currency; anticorruption and proausterity measures were tangled with parental aspirations, socialization practices, and neighborhood expectations. A rhetoric of fiscal responsibility accompanied the implementation of austerity policies, as panacea for economic crises, attributed to "excessive spending" or a necessary response to irresponsible fiscal management in previous administrations. Fiscal discipline was positioned as the solution to the current crisis of capitalism, whereby the correct response to the precarious future was to shrink the state and condense public spending. Even though austerity as fiscal remedy hardly works, with many economies moving into, or having already moved into, second stages of recession, austerity continues to enjoy moral appeal in Ipanema and El Condado (Jensen and Tyler 2012).

In Brazil and Puerto Rico, financial crises, caused by the banking and financial sectors and colonial and neocolonial projects, were attributed to "unsustainable" levels of public debt and social spending. Austerity architects, and the Ipanema and El Condado residents that supported them, put financial crises, like those affecting Brazil and Puerto Rico over the period of my research, to ideological and moral work; they claimed that various forms of social safety nets, and the commitment by some governments to support its citizens via the provision of welfare, had become too costly. *Parenting Empires* aims to illuminate how Brazilian and Puerto Rican elites straddled links between geopolitical centers of power and local manifestations of that power. A child-centered politics of care intersected with how operations of sovereignty, austerity, and corruption materialized in the everyday life of neighborhoods and acquired moral legitimacy through the parenting practices of Latin American elites.

Methodologies: How I Got "There" and What I Did

Do you ever suddenly find it strange to be yourself?
—Clarice Lispector

In Clarice Lispector's metafictional novel *Un sopro de vida* (A breath of life), the Brazilian writer appears fascinated by the ambiguity between main character and narrator, creator and created, representations of others and presentations of self. Hers is a meditation on life, personhood, and time, not too different from the process of ethnographic writing and reflexivity. When I set out to do fieldwork on affluent Latin American neighborhoods, parenting, and US hemispheric influence and empire, I began to recognize how each of these relational concepts, like all affective entanglements, was both magnetic and repellent. This recognition demands a discussion not only of methodology, but also of self-positioning and epistemology.

Coming of age in the middle- and working-class areas of Santurce, Puerto Rico, in the 1980s, my perspectives on wealth were concretely spatial. At the time of my fieldwork, Santurce had been referred to as the Puerto Rican Williamsburg, a vibrant urban community of young artists, university activists, hip chefs, and internationally recognized muralists. When I was growing up, however, residents of the nearby affluent neighborhoods of El Condado and Miramar viewed Santurce as a predominantly Dominican immigrant enclave and stigmatized the area accordingly. "Calle Cerra? That's where all the prostitutes used to be!" my dad, who grew up in Santurce, declared when I enthusiastically mentioned that there was a new vegan restaurant on that very street.

I attended a private Catholic school that, by Puerto Rican standards, was remarkably diverse socioeconomically and ethnically. I had classmates who had recently arrived from the Dominican Republic and classmates who were the children of 1960s Cuban exiles; students who hailed from working-class areas, like Barrio Obrero, to upper-middle-class areas of Isla Verde. We all knew there were affluent neighborhoods, some close to where we lived, and others farther. We knew that everyone recognized a handful of schools as "the best schools," and that ours was not one of them but was also not as "bad as a public school." We knew that individuals who lived in wealthy neighborhoods and attended the best schools dated and hung out at the Caparra Country Club and Casa Cuba, places that remained almost mysterious to me until I began this project. Certainly, "studying up" in El Condado would have been easier, at least initially, if I had been able to activate personal alumni networks from high schools or contacts from private country club rosters. Likewise, had I studied in a public school instead of a Catholic school, or had I grown up outside the metropolitan area of San Juan, the neighborhoods, schools, and country clubs I came to associate with the upper and upper-middle classes in this ethnography may not have had the same meaning or name recognition.

While on their own these facts might have made for a compelling narrative about my relative lack of privilege, this would be an incomplete story. After I graduated from high school, I ended up attending undergraduate and graduate Ivy League institutions in the United States, each increasing the professional credentials and cultural and social capital that in fact personally connects me to the individuals I would come to meet in this study. Along with my light skin, my own investment in "interiority" projects, and Yale professorship (arguably the ultimate form of symbolic capital in the world of global hyperparenting), being the mother of a young child and member of a married heterosexual couple further facilitated my relationships with Puerto Rican and Brazilian interlocutors. In Ipanema, the fact that I had lived in New York most of my adult life, my connections to US higher education, and English fluency triggered parental imaginaries of studying abroad and Ivy League college admissions for their children. In El Condado, my "proper Spanish" was valued even more highly than my English fluency, particularly at a time when "Spanglish," Dominican-accented Spanish, and even English were viewed as threatening to national cultural sovereignty. These forms of embodied, cultural, social, and symbolic capital often overrode economic differences and allowed my interlocutors to imagine what our relationship could become and the networks or interests we could share.

In conventional anthropological parlance, I was a "native ethnographer" in Puerto Rico. My connection to Brazil, on the other hand, was more informal (e.g., attending Brazilian friends' weddings) and academic. I had conducted ethnographic research among Brazilian migrants in Newark, New Jersey, from 2001 through 2010 (Ramos-Zayas 2012) and had lived in Belo Horizonte, Minas Gerais, for several months in 2006, while doing research on youth and return migration. Nevertheless, I had come in late to Brazilian studies and Brazilian anthropology. While I felt tremendous support, encouragement, and collegiality from Brazilian academics in the United States, Brazil, and elsewhere, that was not always the case among a few white male senior scholars who appeared invested in forms of US academic dominance and gatekeeping.[18]

I had visited most regions of Brazil for academic conferences, vacations, and to see friends, but it was not until I began this project, in 2012, that I developed an enduring and powerful connection with Rio de Janeiro. This connection was both strongly visceral and deeply embarrassing, as I frequently caught myself drawn to some of the very essentialist qualities of the place that I was trying to peel off; there was also something almost eerily similar between Rio and places I knew from my childhood in Puerto Rico. While nobody ever gave me suggestions about how to approach fieldwork in Puerto Rico, I still recall a close Brazilian friend and colleague advising, "To do research in Ipanema, you need to be lighter. Go with the flow, and tone down that dark humor and cynicism of yours. Rio is not São Paulo. It is not New York." Her recommendation, and Clarice Lispector's quotation, would come to mind often over the time of my fieldwork, though I often felt I would have benefited from guidance on approaching El Condado too.

I found it strange, to follow Lispector's words, to be my Puerto Rican self in Ipanema. I remained profoundly aware of how, in Brazil, Puerto Rico was virtually invisible, even in discussions about Latin America or the Caribbean. When I would introduce myself as being from Puerto Rico, I would often have to add a qualifier like, "an island in the Caribbean, near Cuba," or resort to the popular icons, like Ricky Martin or Menudo. Once "Despacito" became a global musical sensation, many interlocutors told me that they could appreciate the song more because they had met me, the only Puerto Rican they knew. Once cursory explanations of Puerto Rico's relationship to the United States were out of the way, further processes of what I came to view as intra–Latin American body politics came into play. At five foot three, I had never been as aware of my height as I was among Ipanema's upper classes. Height became, to my surprise, a way in which upper-class South Americans of European background came to racialize many other Latin American populations. Most of the individuals I interviewed in Brazil were quite tall, and several of them spontaneously mentioned that the reason "most Brazilians are tall" and "most (other) Latin Americans are short" had to do with the particular racial mixing in Brazil, the strong European influence, rather than the "indigenous look" they associated with Central and northern parts of South America. These conversations about body aesthetics took multiple shapes (no pun intended) in El Condado and Ipanema, where female bonding often happened around discussion of plastic surgeries, nutrition, fitness, and cosmetic treatments.

My fieldwork consisted of eight months each in Ipanema and El Condado, spanning a period of five years, from 2012 through 2017. These months corresponded to US academic calendar breaks (June–August; December–January; and brief interludes, like spring break). The ethnographic purist in me had difficulty accepting that I would not be uprooting my family to spend an uninterrupted consecutive period of at least a year in each place. After all, as an anthropologist, I was trained to view participant observation not only as the foundation of ethnographic research, but also as a measure of anthropological authenticity. The more the anthropologist pushes the boundaries of her comfort zone and sacrifices for the field, the more "authentic" she becomes and, presumably, the more reliable her data are. And yet, there was no roughing it in an ethnography of upper classes in beachside neighborhoods, at least not in any traditional sense.

Over the eight months I spent respectively in Ipanema and El Condado, I attended extended family gatherings (birthdays, anniversaries, graduations, funerals); parent-sponsored lectures in neighborhood bookstores, university campuses, and private homes; and philanthropic and civic events in the interlocutors' communities. More often, however, I shared everyday routines. I accompanied individuals to Pilates and yoga, to children's sports events, to cosmetic clinics and spas, and spent time in homes, work sites, the beach, cafés, and restaurants. Conducting some audio-recorded walkabouts through areas of the neighborhood that interlocutors claimed as part of these routines allowed me to compose cognitive and social maps, and to better understand the personal significance of landmarks, landscapes, and the built environment. Interlocutors shared visual biographies, like family videos, photographs, and meaningful artwork or inherited jewelry, and demonstrated their own engagement with space through home décor and solar panels, and interests in photography, landscaping, design, and architecture. I met most of the Ipanema residents at local beachfront playgrounds and through the daycare that my son attended during our first summer in Brazil; in El Condado, I used a snowballing approach that involved contacting three El Condado families who were friends of friends and having them introduce me to their respective social networks.

In addition to the data gathered through participant observation, social mapping, and visual biographies, I conducted numerous structured and semistructured interviews. In Brazil, I conducted multiple interviews with a total of thirty-nine individuals, consisting of eight fathers, fifteen mothers, four grandparents, six private school and crèche (daycare) staff, and six nannies. I held focus groups with several other people, mostly nannies, extended family members, store clerks, and parents from areas outside Ipanema who were regular participants in beach playground events. I interviewed Ipanema parents who were involved in collaborative efforts with the municipal police and attended monthly police briefings given to Ipanema residents. In Puerto Rico, I conducted repeated interviews with thirty main interlocutors: twelve mothers, ten fathers, three nannies, two private school teachers, and three Calle Loíza community activists involved in child-centered urban development projects. Additionally, I conducted focus groups with parents affiliated with each of two private schools, one in El Condado (St. John's School) and one in Miramar (Academia del Perpetuo Socorro). Although the Academia del Perpetuo Socorro is technically not in El Condado but in the adjacent neighborhood of Miramar, the parents affiliated with El Condado and these schools overlapped quite a bit, a revelation yielded from social mapping. Hence, in the El Condado sample, I interviewed a few families who lived in the Miramar area; and in Ipanema, I included a few residents of the adjacent neighborhood of Leblon. Most of the focus groups and interviews were conducted in Portuguese or Spanish. Two exceptions were a portion of an interview in which a Brazilian mother asked me to switch to English so her young son, who was playing nearby, would not understand. In Puerto Rico, even among Spanish-dominant, island-born individuals, interviews were characterized by high levels of code switching between English and Spanish; in fact, I was stunned by what appeared to me to be a new sociolinguistic phenomenon, which was even more pronounced among school-age children (see chapter 5). Although I had help transcribing the audiotapes, I did all the translations myself.

In between periods of being in the field, I maintained connections and communication with interlocutors through various social media sites, as well as by email, phone, and Skype. On a few occasions, I got together with interlocutors from Brazil and Puerto Rico when they came to New York City on vacation, or when we coincided in other US cities, like Philadelphia, DC, and Boston, where they would come for work, vacations, or to take their children on school-related sports events or college tours. This long-distance ethnographic data in fact yielded a valuable panoramic overview of the field and interlocutors. The time I spent physically away from the field was not idle or unproductive. Quite the contrary. Those times were critical to developing a closeness and mutual imaginaries that were personally rewarding, ethnographically helpful, and empirically valuable.

I was aware that several interlocutors had Googled my name or requested me as a "friend" on Facebook shortly after meeting. There they could see family photos, occasional political statements, and my own idiosyncratic selection of articles and memes. This socially mediated information accelerated (or slowed down) the pace of the ethnographic relationship. For instance, two El Condado residents whom I had known for several months—both Puerto Rico–raised Cuban women—disliked an article and comment I posted when the United States resumed diplomatic relationships with Cuba, under President Obama. I was able to reconnect with one of these women but never heard back from the other. The only way for me to confirm whether this distancing had to do with the Facebook post was to test my hypothesis with a third woman who was also friendly with the woman avoiding me. To my surprise, while it was true that these women had not liked my Cuba post, the main reason why one of them had continued to avoid me was that she felt betrayed because I had remained in touch with an ex-boyfriend of hers after they had broken up. Her ex-boyfriend remained in my sample throughout. While social media provided valuable insight into the events in people's lives, and even about their aspirational lives and sense of self, I also recognized that these data needed to be tested and triangulated. Facebook, Skyping, WhatsApp groups, and texting enabled a continuous, if imperfect, alternative to some of the logistic limitations of multisited comparative research. Moreover, Facebook helped me to develop kin charts, where I was able to trace connections through friend lists, distinguishing between friends and acquaintances, and considering the frequency and quality of specific interactions.[19] While definitely an imperfect tool, these Facebook kin charts helped me corroborate, challenge, and triangulate data from other sources; identify issues and questions I wanted to pose in person; and consider forms of fictive kinship (Stack 1974) that more traditional ethnographic methods might have missed.

Notes on Epistemology and Terminology: Who These People Are

I must try and break through the clichés about Latin America. Superpowers and other outsiders have fought over us for centuries in ways that have nothing to do with our problems.
—Gabriel García Márquez

Some epistemological and terminological aspects of this ethnography merit explicit acknowledgment and clarification. First, the neighborhood, more than simply one of many possible units of analysis, is the scale and focus I use to inspect the state. I treat the state as a composite operating under singular historical and political economic conditions, and the affluent neighborhoods as significant components of such composites. Significantly, neighborhoods gain immediacy and moral quality through normative tropes like "family," "parenting," and "children." Neighborhoods like Ipanema and El Condado, and the child-centered nodules of urbanism that constituted them, allowed parents to imagine a unique childhood and life trajectory for their children, as well as a desirable parental identity for themselves.

Second, throughout this ethnography, I use terms like "upper class," "upper-middle class," "elite," and "affluent" to showcase aspects of class subjectivity. Instead of emphasizing social determinism in a classical Marxist sense, I approach class as it was subjectively experienced, managed, and attached to specific structural processes or how it influenced those processes. Similarly, I use "privilege" to indicate elite positionalities that were not circumscribed to economic capital but that indicated other sources of power, most notably whiteness. When relevant, I retain the languages of class that permeated popular culture in Puerto Rico and in Brazil. In Puerto Rico, class appeared in the quotidian usage of racialized status terminology, like *cafre*, *comemierda*, and *guaynabito*, which I discuss later in this ethnography. In Brazil, a cultural narrative of class emerged likewise through frequent references to *arrumadas/os*, *dondocas*, *piruas*, or *moleque*. In Brazil, however, unlike in Puerto Rico, sociological and policy class rubrics employed by the government were also frequently used, notably the A-B-C-D-E designator, where each letter stands for an income bracket (*faina de renda*). I rarely heard the term "elite" as a self-referent or an emic category; classed identities and racial pronouncements in Ipanema and El Condado were more coded, implicit, and relational. I want to underscore that each voice that appears in this volume is relevant not for its representativeness, but as the outcome of regional, historical, and personal processes that, taken together, reflected some imperfect patterns and social fabrics.

Another important epistemological element of this ethnography is that, when I declare its comparative aspect, I am comparing not objects, people, or essences, but processes of meaning construction, relationships among persons, situations, events, frameworks, and discourses in material political economic contexts that are distinct. My comparative axis consisted of a set of open analytical questions posed differently in each neighborhood, rather than predefined entities, so as not to overshadow contextually significant variables. I am not just portraying the lives of affluent individuals in Brazil and Puerto Rico but also comparing the structural conditions, hemispheric dynamics, and processes of agency that contributed to shaping practices of parenting, privilege, and urbanism in two neighborhoods in different parts of the world. In choosing Brazil and Puerto Rico, moreover, I retain a comparative angle that was not mediated, as is usually the case in transnational, global, or multisited studies, by a direct comparison with the United States. The processes under analysis in this ethnographic project decenter the United States as intellectual, epistemological, and methodological center, while seriously engaging with its colonial and imperial reach across the Latin American and Caribbean region.[20]

This takes me to a leading question often raised: "Why Puerto Rico and Brazil?" Puerto Rico and Brazil are vastly different, in the size of their land, population, and economy; they are different in colonial history, economic influence and status, global political presence (or absence), and even language. A Portuguese-speaking country, Brazil had the fifth largest population and eighth largest economy in the world in 2010, while Puerto Rico, a US territory where Spanish is the main language, lacked international political representation and faced significant population decline. And yet, Brazil and Puerto Rico shared a national mood of bewildered anxiety about their respective political and economic futures, austerity policies, privatization of industries and institutions, and governmental corruption over the time of my fieldwork. They each served as global stage for discussions about the Zika epidemic and pregnancy avoidance; in Puerto Rico, this public health crisis was magnified as a result of Hurricane Maria, a devastating category-4 hurricane, which brought forth US neglect and invigorated discussions of US colonialism in Puerto Rico. Each country also consistently ranked among the top ten most unequal countries in the world.[21] Distrust of the government, fears related to economic insecurity and crime, a weakened or eroded sovereignty, and fiscal debt and governmentality crises serve as broader background to neighborhood life in Ipanema and El Condado.

Nodules of Latin American and Caribbean tourism and tax exemption havens to foreigners, Ipanema and El Condado witnessed the influx of foreign developers and oil corporation billionaires, who often settled with their families alongside local Brazilian and Puerto Rican national elites, shaped the international private school market, and became unwitting interlocutors for domestic claims to sovereignty. Adjacent to some of the most impoverished areas of Rio de Janeiro and San Juan, Ipanema and El Condado are not simply the Latin American neighborhoods of postcards, tourist advertising campaigns, and high-end retail.

Behind these iconic images, Ipanema and El Condado are residential neighborhoods where the Brazilian and Puerto Rican upper classes, especially those who fashioned themselves as progressive, socially conscious, and cosmopolitan, chose to raise their children. Rather than viewing residents of these neighborhoods as representative of liberal elites, however, I view the spaces they inhabit as representative of such liberal elitism in their respective countries. The privileged unit of analysis here is the neighborhood, while moving across a scale of mutually constitutive imaginaries, including the individual, family, household, nation, and beyond. It could be argued that Ipanema and El Condado have more in common with each other than Brazil and Puerto Rico have in common with each other. Yet I do believe that US hemispheric control—of which parenting has become an imperial formation—mediated Brazil's expectations of Ipanema and Puerto Rico's connection to El Condado in similar ways.

It is also important to underscore that, in this ethnography, I view Puerto Rico as a self-standing social and cultural entity, not exclusively or primarily as an extension of the US mainland. This is a deliberate effort to push against academic conventions that have deployed Puerto Rico's "exceptionalism" to justify its frequent exclusion from both Latin American studies and mainstream scholarship in American studies. While Puerto Rico is decidedly a colony of the United States, the United States has formal or informal imperial relations with many nations, even some that are technically considered sovereign, like Brazil. Following Ann Stoler's "degrees of imperial sovereignty" (2006), I place Brazil and Puerto Rico in a continuum, not in entirely different universes, in their relationship with US imperialism in the American hemisphere. The realignment of Puerto Rico and Brazil, and other parts of the Global South, as part of the same US imperial landscape is productive for understanding contemporary circulation of geopolitical configurations, including fascist tendencies, austerity policies, and parenting trends. Moreover, viewing Puerto Rico as a self-standing entity allows me to foreground the emic perspective of El Condado interlocutors (in all their upper-class privilege and cosmopolitan aspirations), who overwhelmingly viewed Puerto Rico as linguistically, culturally, and socially distinct from the United States, or who, at the very least, were strategic about how they situated Puerto Rico in relation to the US mainland, the rest of the Caribbean, and Latin America as a whole. On a macro level, US colonization of Puerto Rico constrained the island's economic development, trade, and political representation on a global stage, and El Condado interlocutors were clear about this, as they were about the ease of travel conferred by US citizenship. In the everyday parenting lives of elites, however, these constraints did not figure prominently; as long as they stayed on the island, their lives were hardly different from those of other Latin American elites (and they arguably shared more in common than they shared with US elites in terms of values, perspectives on sophistication, aesthetic dispositions, and cultural capital).

A final epistemological and methodological question that underscored this research almost from the beginning, which colleagues and friends frequently asked when I presented earlier versions of this work, was, "Who are these elites?" This was not a question of how representative these elites were but of who their counterparts might be—in their respective neighborhoods, countries, and internationally, or at various historical moments. This was a question that rose from the difficulty in categorizing them, either in traditional sociological rubrics (e.g., old/new money, intellectual/political/corporate) or through popular images. The Ipanema family attending the anti-PT march at the beginning of this chapter resonates with the most recognizable and iconic global image of "the Latin American elite"; they are not different from the superficial wealthy family at the center of Rubén Blades and Willie Colón's 1978 song "Plástico," or more recently, Teatro Breve's comedy series *Las Real Housewives de Miramar*. Nevertheless, the demographics for which these images stand, and the interlocutors in this ethnography, defy such facile categorization.

Most of the parents in this ethnography came of age in the 1980s and 1990s and, in the Brazilian case, viewed themselves as part of a "lost generation," unsure of itself and, until becoming parents, unsure of its role in the future of the nation (Maia 2012, 43). These upper-class parents in Puerto Rico and in Brazil had virtually lost faith in their respective national governments. Since corruption was so firmly grounded in a political elite, the imperialist US "war on corruption" against both Brazil and Puerto Rico, projects to encourage foreign interests and capital, and other questionably neoliberal and austerity practices made sense to them. Nevertheless, and perhaps unlike European and US urban or progressive elites (e.g., Sherman 2017a), Ipanema and El Condado elites continued to value cultural nationalist practices, even when they were generally sympathetic to US imperial, corporate, and colonial influences.

Interlocutors in the El Condado sample led virtually the same lives that their own parents and even grandparents had led; they attended the same schools and clubs, grew up in the same neighborhoods, had the same occupations, knew the same families, married people they knew since childhood, and had dense social networks. I have never seen a more perfect example of what classical sociology has called "social reproduction" than what I witnessed in El Condado. In Ipanema, interlocutors followed more diverse social paths; some had grown up in Ipanema, whereas others had moved there as adults; none of them had attended the same schools, though some of their children did go to a handful of local private schools; some of them had inherited wealth and recognizable surnames, but others were the first in their families to pursue higher education and had earned their wealth. A few of the Ipanema interlocutors had experienced tremendous social mobility in their lifetime and invariably attributed such mobility to merit and personal effort (see Rockman 2014); many others, including a couple of El Condado interlocutors, had experienced a combination of paths to wealth, as well as downward and upward mobility trends over generations.

At times, in different parts of this ethnography, I propose that Ipanema and El Condado elites are a new type of elite, thus suggesting a historical or generational distinction in what constitutes being an elite in Latin America and the Caribbean. This is because, unlike older generations who unapologetically displayed and inhabited their wealth, the contemporary elites at the center of this ethnography were often aware of how wealth was globally associated with corruption and frivolous consumption. The broadening of a social sphere, coupled with these elites' determination to disavow such corruption and frivolity, further encouraged their continuous moral justifications and interiority projects. Unlike in their parents' or grandparents' generations, discussed in chapter 6, these contemporary elites felt they needed to justify their privilege, and they engaged in practical, psychological, and rhetorical projects to render their status and wealth moral.

The interlocutors in *Parenting Empires* tended to fashion themselves as politically and socially "progressive," and they viewed other Puerto Rican and Brazilian elites, including others in their neighborhoods but more frequently those who lived in gated communities or traditional upper-class US-style suburbs, as more conservative and less cosmopolitan. Importantly, though, even these characterizations were fluid, and from the beginning of my research in 2012 through its official end in 2017, I witnessed what some Brazilians have called the "Right coming out of the closet" phenomenon. Some of the Puerto Rican and Brazilian elites in this ethnography gradually adopted more conservative political stances; tacit acceptance of the US-imposed Fiscal Control Board in Puerto Rico and explicit support of the impeachment of Dilma Rousseff in Brazil were examples of this shift. A possible reading of this is that they were socially progressive but fiscally or politically conservative all along, but this was not always the case. Rather, they explained the crises in their respective countries largely in terms of the inherent corruption of politicians, almost to the exclusion of any other factors (e.g., financial sector, foreign interests).

On a final ethical note, concerns with confidentiality and anonymity are at the center of most ethnographic research. "Everybody knows each other here," claimed an El Condado parent when I assured him that I would use pseudonyms. The possibility of changing the names of the neighborhoods, the schools, the social clubs, and the other identifying landmarks and institutions at the center of my interlocutors' lives was a strategy to protect anonymity that was suggested to me in one of the preliminary presentations of this work. While I do use pseudonyms for individuals, I decided against anonymizing places for several reasons, including the fact that I am sympathetic to Rubén Gaztambide-Fernández's call for academics to adopt a "radically un/ethical position" when researching elites.[22] This un/ethical position might help us address difficulties articulating a structural, distributional critique, rather than an individualistic, behavioral one, "that no one deserves to have so much while others have so little, regardless of how nice or hardworking or charitable they are" (Sherman 2017b, 25), and, indeed, they were nice, hardworking, and charitable.

"I don't think I could deal with the snobbishness and First World problems of these people," my husband once remarked, echoing what other colleagues would also tell me upon learning of my research. And yet, that is the irony about researching "up": most of my interlocutors had the ability to be engaging, profound, laid back, and quite charming. I entered their spaces with the practiced ease of someone who hangs out in places similar to the ones frequented by Ipanema and El Condado elites. As an academic mom, it is not uncommon for me to spend time at neighborhood coffee shops with my laptop in the middle of a weekday, or to be (painfully) familiar with the world of playdates and concerted child cultivation.

I felt a sincere friendship and personal connection with many of the interlocutors in this ethnography, including Maribel Seijo, an El Condado resident. Talking with Maribel was like talking with some of my closest academic friends—both fun and intellectually stimulating without pretension. Toward the official end of my fieldwork, in 2017, I was convinced that Maribel could tell that I was puzzled about her life choices; at the most basic level, I could not understand how she did not get bored staying at home, by herself, most of her weekdays. Sure, she attended Pilates classes, had lunch with friends she knew since elementary school, and was a member of a long-standing book club. Still, I found myself asking her, on several occasions, if she had ever thought of going back to work or considering graduate school or even volunteering. She would answer that, even when she thought about it, there had never been a financial need to motivate her, nor had she identified a clear "path" or "passion" for herself.

I interviewed a few mothers and fathers who considered parenting as a space for creative expression; they spent time building sophisticated architectural models with their children, hosting sleepovers, and decorating Pokémon cupcakes; planning elaborate princess birthday parties or seeking the best party planners and venues; who looked forward to going to a designer's atelier to see a daughter getting fitted for a formal gown. Maribel was not one of those parents. Her lack of a sense of competency baffled me: "I haven't put up that frame, because [my husband] has been very busy"; "We haven't finished planting those pots because I will need help holding the plant while I put in the dirt"; "I will wait until the weekend so that [my daughter] can come with me to take the dog to the vet." I came to interpret these common attitudes toward the mundane as a low threshold for discomfort. Sure, nobody likes to have to juggle heavy grocery bags in one hand and a barely folded stroller in the other, but oftentimes, for my interviewees, these levels of mundane discomfort were not even entertained. I found myself mourning the lives that some of these individuals, with all their resources, could have enjoyed had they better managed their tolerance for discomfort—the discomfort of work politics; the discomfort of doing things because you have to, not because you want to; the discomfort of daring to take risks and enduring rejection and failure. These instances, to me, highlighted the importance and inescapable ordinariness of affect, something central to an ethnographic praxis that is always funny and traumatic, poignant and mundane, about how anthropologists and their informants can embody a fully affective subjecthood during the ethnographic encounter.

At a rational level, the sadness I experienced toward Maribel, a wealthy, resourceful, and reasonably happy woman, was paternalistic, condescending, and misplaced. It also gave currency to what John Jackson (2010) calls a shift from ethnographic authenticity to ethnographic sincerity, which requires us to ask what sociocultural knowledge through immersion might leave in its wake and urges us to treat subjects/informants more robustly, as fully embodied and affective interlocutors. As difficult as it was at times, I really tried to move beyond my impulse to judge elites in ways I could not imagine doing with the working-class interlocutors of my previous research, though I am not sure I always succeeded.

My interlocutors' practices of inquiry, familiarity with parenting language and expertise, and search for a form of relatedness in which their authority was established frequently challenged the analytic forms and methodological tools I brought to the field. It demanded acute attention to how individuals' perspectives manufactured political discourses and influence. Access to considerable material resources made a great deal of difference in the knowledge El Condado and Ipanema parents produced, the weight such knowledge production carried, and how I analyzed, produced, and conveyed my own knowledge about them. Daily political intrigues, discussions of corruption, indignity about top-down colonial and imperial impositions, and perspectives on a national crisis were neither abstract nor overly deterministic of the social field these elites inhabited. Personal actions and mobilization around the welfare of elite children provided El Condado and Ipanema parents, even those who did not belong to an official or elected political elite, an everyday language that aimed to break through forms and foreclosures imposed by broader national conditions and international agendas. The parents I met in Brazil and Puerto Rico had a clear, thorough understanding of their privileged worlds and charmed lives, of the social dramas they had to navigate, and of the kind of politics that would better serve their aspirations and interests.

The singularity of each fieldwork relationship is not simply established once but is continuously renegotiated through the course of the research, reflecting, and writing processes. This book is the result of an ethnographic fieldwork through which, in response to Clarice Lispector, I did "find it strange to be myself."

Book Overview

I view this ethnography as implicitly divided into three main sections, two chapters each, in addition to this introduction and the epilogue. In the first section, I situate each neighborhood's "child-centered nodules of urbanism" in the history, built environment, and urban planning of Ipanema (chapter 2) and El Condado (chapter 3), and in the political economy of Brazil and Puerto Rico. In these two chapters, I examine Ipanema and El Condado in contradistinction to affluent suburban and poor urban communities in Brazil and Puerto Rico, as well as to the foreign billionaires settling with their families in the neighborhoods. Chapter 2, "The Feel of Ipanema: Social History and Structure of Feeling in Rio de Janeiro, " considers the social history and cultural narratives around Ipanema as a global, sensual, and aesthetically privileged neighborhood, while also examining how governance through parenting unfolded.

Chapter 3, "Parenting El Condado: Social History and Immaterial Materiality in San Juan," traces practices of parenting through the social history of El Condado and the adjacent traditional upper-class neighborhood of Miramar. An argument here is that all affluent urbanism is, necessarily, child centered. I show how child rearing has become almost inseparable from elite lifestyles, the cultivation of adult friendships, and the "feel" of a place. I also highlight parallels in my fieldsites by noting how, just as the upper-class suburb of Barra da Tijuca and Rio's favelas were constitutive outsiders to Ipanema, the suburb of Guaynabo and poor areas of Santurce served a similar symbolic function for El Condado parents.

In the second section of the ethnography (chapters 4 and 5), I examine interiority currency—the cultivation of psychological depth, emotional vocabularies, and spiritual formations among the elite. Gaining mastery over one's inner world, in all its presumed elasticity and potential for expansion, was at times a compensatory strategy for the national political instability and economic crisis that characterized Brazil and Puerto Rico during the time of my fieldwork. In chapter 4, "Whiteness from Within: Elite Interiority, Personhood, and Parenting," I examine how a tendency to psychologize the social (and a socialization of the psychological) manifested as a search for *afinidade* (affinity) in Ipanema and for *personas sencillas* (down-to-earth people) in El Condado. Ipanema and El Condado elites were invested in shifting the sociological field from the material to the metaphysical, in ways that altered local sociabilities and granted legitimacy to widening racial and class inequalities in both countries. Attributing certain therapeutic qualities to nature, being outdoors, and beachfront landscapes; deploying Orientalist narratives and genealogies; presenting an evolved masculinity as evidence of gender equality; and situating capitalist achievements in a language of miracles were critical tools for cultivating interiority currency as a white privilege project.

In chapter 5, "Schooling Whiteness: Adult Friendships, Social Ease, and the Privilege of Choosing Race," I examine how schools served as eminent spaces of parenting empires. In relation to school choice, discussions of religious versus secular culture, native-language education versus English-dominant instruction, and forms of relatedness forged contemporary versions of noblesse oblige. I argue that Ipanema and El Condado parents actively worked through their children's schools, and memories of their own schooling, as they aimed to render their wealth as moral, deserved, and altruistic; more significantly, though, these experiences of schooling were central to various racial aesthetics and misrecognitions that arose as parents struggled over how much to expose their children to social and racial inequality.

The third and final section of the ethnography considers how parenting empires fostered familial and affective expectations of care across ethnic, regional, and racial lines, as Ipanema and El Condado parents enlisted other adults—namely, extended family members and domestic workers—to solidify everyday child-centered routines, socialization, and austerity ideologies. Within this moral economy of wealth, elites positioned themselves in relation to ethnoracial and regional Others, while also translating neoliberal state politics into austerity subjectivities. In chapter 6, "The Extended Family: Intimate Hierarchies and Ancestral Imaginaries," I examine how the grandparents' generation provided financial support and ancestral connections to highly valued ethnic heritages. A traditional Latin American cultural trope, the extended family served as a leading affective vessel through which Ipanema and El Condado parents explored resentment, gratitude, trauma, insecure adulthood, and ambivalence toward life choices, on the one hand, while securing racial and class privilege through connection to a family lineage and financial resources on the other.

In chapter 7, "Affective Power Inequalities: Childcare Workers and Elite Consumptions of Blackness," I examine the relationship between elites and domestic workers, particularly nannies. I identify the ways in which parents produced racialized intimacy and difference—simultaneous affective attachment and sociological detachment—with Dominican domestic workers in El Condado, and with dark-skin nannies from the Brazilian Northeast in Ipanema. I draw on distinct cultures of domestic work in Brazilian and Puerto Rican societies to analyze the formulation of whiteness in reference to *nordestinas* (women from the Brazilian Northeast) and *dominicanas* (women from the Dominican Republic). The epilogue revisits the framework of parenting empires and analyzes the relation between national draconian austerity measures and the US war on corruption in the Americas, while also considering the issue of judgment in research about Latin American and Caribbean elites.

2

The Feel of Ipanema

Social History and Structure of Feeling in Rio de Janeiro

O Brasil não será feliz enquanto todos não puderem morar em Ipanema. (Brazil will never be happy until everyone gets to live in Ipanema.)—Antônio Carlos Jobim

At each end of Ipanema's beachfront—near Copacabana, on the northeast, and Leblon, on the southwest—are cordoned-off sections separated from the rest of the beach.[1] Brightly colored toy castles, pirate ships, baby pools, and plastic slides catch the attention of joggers, volleyball players, ambulatory vendors, families, tourists, and other beachgoers on one of the most glamorized beaches in the world. These play areas—known among locals as IpaBebê and BaixoBebê—have been features of Zona Sul parenting culture since the 1990s, but they are easy to miss in the magnificence of the landscape.

Each play area is adjacent to one of the many kiosks along the Ipanema beachside, where patrons get coconut water and snacks. Two particular kiosks stand out from those that are fixed features of Ipanema's *calçadão* because they have designated stroller-parking areas and diaper-changing tables. Whereas other Ipanema kiosks may attract beach volleyball and soccer coaches or personal trainers and their clients, for instance, the kiosks near the play areas are bustling sites where stylish parents and uniformed nannies orchestrate various social interactions around children and one another, at times in perfectly choreographed fashion. As a mother holds a baby, a dark-skin and uniformed nanny pushes the stroller; knowing when to enter the scene, the nanny parks the stroller and swiftly, in a hardly noticeable way, gets the baby from the mother. If I look briefly away, I will miss when this happens or how the nanny ended up playing in the sand with the baby, while the mother asks the kiosk worker to pour the water from a coconut into the baby's bottle. I do notice when a tall, athletic father, sporting exercise gear, who has been playing for a few minutes with his toddler, says good-bye to the baby, who is now in the nanny's arms. The father goes off for a jog. These beachside play areas had become important nodules of child-centered urbanism in Ipanema at the time of my fieldwork.

I came to view nodules of child-centered urbanism as physical and social spaces deliberately created and sustained on an elite ideology of "in the name of the children" but that were in fact mostly about adult sociability, governance, and practices of class and racial inequality in intimate contexts. Child-centered nodules of urbanism were never spaces in which children of upper-class families were on their own; ultimately, one could argue, these were generative spaces of *adult* relatedness and urban lifestyle among the upper classes and the individuals they employed. These spaces were largely about adult social self-fashioning and functioned around specific feeling rules and performances, which relied on the ability of the upper class not only to embody ease and a sense of entitlement, but also to showcase a form of affective sociability with subaltern populations. IpaBebê and BaixoBebê were main entry points in this ethnography.

In October 2013, IpaBebê made the front page of *Journal do Rio* and *O Globo*, two leading Brazilian newspapers, because the beach playground had been on the way of an *arrastão* (sweep, or dragnet). "It was such an obvious attempt to terrorize all beachgoers and especially our parents and children," noted Verônica Igel Botelho, one of the parents who, in the early 2000s, had sought a municipal license to cord off the beach area and register it as a not-for-profit group. Verônica described how, during the arrastão, "four *moleques* [brats] passed running by, trying to steal from us. They weren't able to steal anything, and the municipal guard went running after them and eventually caught them." In a pattern that appeared to have repeated itself nearly every summer since 1992, people ran because they saw others run, and soon there was a hysterical scramble to get away from some kind of unknown danger. Groups of poor teenagers took advantage of the panic to grab valuables that were left behind and, in some cases, to mug wealthy beachgoers. Fernando Coutinho Leite, another one of the parents who had been involved in IpaBebê for over a decade, furthermore noted: "Once the arrastão happened, we had to get together and take a stand, because everyone was so terrified, and we wanted to calm our own neighbors down. A wave of panic is not good."

As stated in local newspapers:

> The scene was frightening. The mothers who were on the Ipanema beach, in front of the Hotel Fasano, early Friday afternoon, used the sticks of

the barracks to try to defend their children in an arrastão that began on Arpoador and ended on Posto 8. That beach strip has a high concentration of small children, since that's where IpaBebê is located. One of the mothers who was on the beach at the time of the incident commented: "We were all with the children in the beach and the wave of chaos started. Everyone stood up, ran, grabbed the babies and felt desperate. I stood up and held onto the side of the barrack, and told other parents to do the same. There was no time to escape. Four guys ran by, stealing everything. I gave a shack [di uma barracada]. Then four municipal guards followed." (Guimarães and Bastos 2013)

The municipal guard's intelligence unit highlighted the need for collective community-police collaboration to handle disturbances, such as the one IpaBebê had experienced, and similar ones attributed to robberies on bus routes transporting "petty thieves who robbed in small groups" from the *subúrbios* (poor communities) in the Zona Norte to the wealthier Zona Sul beach area.[2] As a spokesperson for the municipal police stated, "What has happened is that a multitude of people, consisting mostly of minors, take the bus to commit crimes. . . . We are putting together a record for each one of them" (Araujo and Remalho 2017).

Gabriela Braga Vellozo, Fernando's wife, added, "We have great respect for the police, but it was also necessary that the governor, the chief of police, the general commander of the municipal police, and the Ministério Público felt the pressure and give importance to this wave of terror." Silvana Vilella Mattos, a tall, stylish white Brazilian woman in her early fifties, who was also very involved in IpaBebê, was instrumental in forging tighter connections with municipal authorities and developing strategies to deal with "an unfortunate situation," which came to be referred to as "terrorism" in some parenting blogs (Motta 2013). The specter of public disorder consolidated Ipanema parents' fears, while also leading to a heightened collaboration between parents and the municipal and military police (Godfrey and Arguinzoni 2012). Over the years of my fieldwork, upper-class Ipanema parents continuously demanded increased police presence and governmental control of public space.

Fernando, Gabriela, Verônica, and Silvana were among the many Ipanema residents who, as parents, exerted considerable influence on local authorities and undertook various forms of local governance through child-centered spaces of urbanism. As a result of the incident described, and the newspaper articles that followed, the connections between government security agencies and Ipanema residents—particularly Ipanema parents—strengthened over

FIGURE 2.1. One of the Ipanema beachfront kiosks where one can get coconut water and some local snacks. This one is named Pais e Filhos (Parents and Children). Photo by the author

the years of my fieldwork. Eventually, several bus routes from Zona Norte and Zona Oeste to Zona Sul were redirected or altogether suspended on weekends. They still operated during the week, as many Zona Sul families depended on them to transport their domestic workers and nannies.[3] Members of IpaBebê, along with other neighborhood associations, scheduled regular meetings with units of the municipal police and the mayor's office to "trace a strategy for sunny days."

This chapter considers the social history and cultural narratives around Ipanema as a global, sensual, and aesthetically privileged neighborhood, while also examining how governance and sociabilities through parenting sustained class and racial hierarchies—in fact, awarded moral legitimacy to child-centered nodules of urbanism, a central tenet of parenting empires.[4] First, I briefly outline upper-class understandings of Brazilian national politics during the time of my fieldwork. Second, I discuss the development of the Atlantic beachfront section of Rio de Janeiro since the early 1900s, when Villa Ipanema, as Ipanema was known at the time, was developed specifically to attract elite carioca (from Rio) families and foreigners. I consider the transition from single-family homes to collective condominium living; the fostering of beach sociability, for which Rio's Atlantic coast is notorious worldwide; and the particularities of the new Ipanema upper classes. Moreover, I examine Ipanema's structure of feelings (Williams 1977) and how the area generated sentiments, emotions, and affects that often unified its elite residents in a common socializing project of belonging and entitlement. Finally, I return to the child-centered spaces of urbanism to discuss how parenting empires supplied the moral justifications for policing, regulation, and real estate decisions and carried specific repercussions for racial and class relations in the neighborhood.

Brief History of Brazil

In July 2015, Verônica Igel Botelho, Beatriz Pisollo Itamar, and I met at a café near the Pilates studio where Verônica and I met for classes in Ipanema. Verônica commented that she had noticed how one of the Pilates instructors had posted on Facebook "something like 'Of course, these Zona Sul people are against Dilma, against the PT. . . . They are the elite' this and that." Verônica reported the comment to the owner of the Pilates studio, who reportedly told the instructor, a tall dark-skin young man who would commute from a working-class neighborhood in the Zona Oeste, "Listen, you can be as disgusted as you want with that 'elite' you talk about, but those 'Zona Sul people' you're talking about are your clients!" Verônica went on to mention that the trainer had to apologize. Beatriz, who was relatively sympathetic to the Workers' Party social programs, vaguely mentioned, "This political antagonism is new to Brazil. The country is in an economic crisis and terribly divided. People you used to know, old friends, reveal themselves in a way, displaying a lot of aggressiveness. I don't even know how to explain it. Maybe it has to do with having more access to information, social media. But even empregadas, you know, [would say] 'I'm going to vote for Dilma.' I asked her why. 'Because she gives me the Bolsa Família.' Of course, that's why! But where is her responsibility as a citizen?" Although Bolsa Família constituted only 2 percent of the government's total spending, it was a high-profile program that narrowed the inequality gaps between lower and middle classes (Rockman 2014; Walkerdine 2003). Fernando Coutinho Leite remarked on the limitation of the actual mobility provided by Bolsa Família: "We thought we were finally, after all these years, developing, growing, being global players, because even the lower classes were doing well. But we have failed to make that jump that all developed countries go through, and this impacts workplace relations, personal relations. Because those people may have moved up socially, but they don't have the level of education in terms of human interaction." Bolsa Família was the linchpin of the middle- and upper-class critique of Lula da Silva's and then Dilma Rousseff's governments.

Vera Ferreira de Oliveira, who had grown up in a working-class neighborhood in Niteroi before coming to university in Rio, was an example of how many Ipanema residents came to evaluate the Brazilian government over the years of my fieldwork. Married to a wealthy longtime Ipanema resident and the mother of one son, Vera had worked for various multinational companies in the fields of accounting and marketing. She noted, "Lots of people are dependent on Bolsa Família. The rich are rich and don't have to worry. It is the middle class, like us, who are suffering, with the high taxes, we are financing the lives of the poor." The fluidity of her definition of the "middle class" became even more evident when she explained, "We know a couple, two doctors, he is a surgeon, with his own office around here. You'd think they would be at a much higher economic scale, but they're not. Why are people not making as much money?" And she added, "Here you have a snowball effect. Because if I lose my job, I will have to let go of the empregada. So then the empregada won't have money to support herself. What will happen with her kid? Probably her kid is going to get into illegal activity, stealing, trafficking. And that's what I've seen already. The other day they killed someone in the metro station. Now you can't even use your iPad or cell phone on the metro. The violence is getting closer and closer."

In 2010, Dilma Rousseff declared her intent to continue her predecessor's social welfare programs, including the expansion of Bolsa Família and Fome Zero. While conducting fieldwork, I witnessed part of Dilma's first term, her election to a second term, and her eventual impeachment—a neoliberal coup that was widely celebrated in Ipanema and the Zona Sul—in 2016. In 2013, Dilma's approval rates hovered higher than any other Brazilian president in the postmilitary era, but a wave of localized urban protests voicing discontent with transportation, health, and quality education struck certain areas of the country, most notably Rio de Janeiro and São Paulo. The day after the 2014 Brazilian elections, when the PT won another term, several Ipanema parents contacted me seeking information about housing and schools in the United States; they expressed how intolerable it would be to remain in Brazil, given the electoral outcome.[5] They joined anti–Workers' Party demonstrations and foregrounded "corruption" as a main rallying point in their opposition to the electoral results.

Although hundreds of government politicians were implicated in a complex and vast network of money laundering and patronage, which came to be popularly known as Operação Lava Jato (Operation Car Wash), the scandal's most visible casualty was Dilma. On August 31, 2016, the Senate voted to remove her from the presidency. During the summer of 2016 and in the months after, mass protests and counter-protests—in favor of and against the PT government and its policies—dominated Brazilian society. Dilma was accused of issuing various illegal and unconstitutional decrees that extended credit to finance certain PT staple programs, like Bolsa Família and Social Security. The second much larger scandal concerned Brazil's state-owned oil company Petrobras. Throughout the PT's four-term tenure, the first two under Lula (2002–10) and the last two under Dilma (2010–16), Brazil operated under the assumption that, because of the increase in oil prices and the uncovering of extensive offshore gas and oil reserves in 2007, Brazilian-owned oil company Petrobras would be the engine of Brazil's future economic growth. In the sprawling investigation behind Operation Car Wash, authorities uncovered a scheme whereby Petrobras executives accepted bribes from politicians in exchange for overpriced contracts that favored construction companies (Greenwald, Fishman, and Miranda 2016). Considered by some as the largest corruption scandal in Brazil's contemporary history, the laundering scheme extended to close to five hundred people at every level of the Brazilian government and from every major political party, including Michel Temer, who notwithstanding his shady reputation still assumed power after Dilma was removed from office.[6] Notably, Temer's first cabinet appointments of white upper-class men suggested that his administration would strengthen the entrenched class, racial, and gender hierarchies that have historically characterized Brazilian society (Norvell 2002; Prada 2016; Robinson 2016). Rede Globo, the conservative media conglomerate that dominates Brazilian television and print media and that is noted for its connections to and support of Brazil's military government, effectively drew on hearsay and speculation, which has since been traced to opposition leaders, rather than on evidence (Gindre 2015).

Clearly, corruption and national economic woes rendered Dilma and the PT, and subsequently all politicians, intensely unpopular among all Ipanema classes and groups. What remained critical in this context, though, was that corruption was almost exclusively located in the realm of government and politicians, never deployed in reference to financial sectors or foreign interests, which had in fact directly benefited from such dealings (cf. Souza 2017). Importantly, the number of people participating in anti-PT street protests was minimal, and the protesters belonged to a relatively narrow societal segment, compared to the 54 million people who had voted to reelect Dilma in 2014. Many of the Ipanema parents I met had come of age during the end of the dictatorship in 1985, and some of them seemed to have a rather tenuous attachment to the country's transition to democracy, even tacitly expressing nostalgia for the "order" and "transparency" they attributed to the military period.

In December 2016, despite an approval rate barely reaching 14 percent, Michel Temer's Congress mustered the majority required to approve a series of fiscal reforms that were considered "the harshest austerity measures in the world" (L. Carvalho 2017). Freezing the federal budget for the following twenty years, this cap meant that funding for education, healthcare, pensions, infrastructure, and other government programs would remain constant until 2036. In failing to account for any growth in Brazil's population or economy, the spending cap is a slow-motion destruction of the country's welfare state; Brazil's public healthcare system, already precarious, would be underfunded to serve the country's aging population and a disaster for the poor.

I witnessed upper-class Ipanema families going from rejoicing in Dilma Rousseff's 2015 impeachment and tacitly accepting Michel Temer to feeling a sense of despair about what they viewed as Brazil's inability to secure the geopolitical status it had come so close to reaching. They curiously viewed democratically elected Dilma, the imposed Temer government, and subsequently the Jair Bolsonaro government as equivalent. "Corruption" has been an ongoing narrative in Brazil; it has been historically deployed as the excuse for a range of issues, from military takeover in the 1960s to the inability to compete on international financial stages. Nonetheless, the corruption within the Workers' Party specifically led the Ipanema elite to mobilize, possibly for the first time in recent history, to march in their neighborhood streets. As Ann Mische (2018) notes, some Brazilian academics, activists, and members of marginalized communities expressed their fear of the dangerous situation in their country; the parents whose voices appear in this volume demonstrated, for the most part, an opposition to far-right candidate Jair Bolsonaro and participated in #EleNão demonstrations. Once Bolsonaro got elected, the upper-class parents who had so vehemently opposed him in favor of Fernando Haddad became quickly willing to swallow their reservations and adopt a bystander "let's see what happens" position. They were part of "a shrug of the shoulders and back to normal," where life quickly goes back to the ordinariness of their privilege; in that seduction of the ordinary is where the parenting empires at the center of this ethnography flourished.

Fernando Coutinho Leite, one of the IpaBebê founding parents, called the state of Brazil in 2017 "a crisis of values, ethics." He explained, "Because when you see that the issue of corruption is so widely disseminated, you can't just project that onto the government. This is largely a crisis of the self. Brazilians view politicians as either the perpetrators or the saviors but never ask 'What can I change?' Because, you know the story, how every Brazilian thinks that God is Brazilian. So each Brazilian is always waiting for that miracle." When I asked him to elaborate, he added,

> People here move very differently, emotionally, culturally, in every way, from the US. And there are some positive aspects: the happiness, the playfulness, spontaneity, the *jogo de cintura* [movement of the waist, suggesting flexibility], right? But that's precisely the Brazilian problem. We, Brazilians, know we have the capacity to adapt, so we don't plan ahead. As a former colony, we have a strong Portuguese, Indigenous, and Black influence. The African culture is a culture of immediate gratification [*prazer imediato*]. So if I have a moment of happiness, I don't think about the future. We did not inherit a culture of sacrifice, of effort. There was always greater permissiveness in state affairs, a more tenuous line between legal and illegal.

Through structure of feeling, Raymond Williams challenges the idea that the way of thinking attributed to a time or place is hegemonic and argues instead that there must always be an internal dynamic—and I would argue, affective dispositions—by which new formations emerge. Although Fernando referred to Brazil as a whole, Rio de Janeiro's beach neighborhoods, particularly Ipanema, figured prominently in how history is used to explain feelings, dispositions, and affect. This structure of feeling, unlike those Williams masterfully identifies, was grounded on projects of racial formation. The feel of Ipanema and the role of child-centered nodules of urbanism exerted a heteronormative framing of whiteness and privilege, as oftentimes "protecting (white) children and families" became the reason for exerting sovereignty over material, territorial, and affective neighborhood parameters.

Ipanema, Then and Now

Rio de Janeiro has been viewed as the synthesis of Brazil. Sometimes the concrete ecology of Ipanema, the neighborhood's very materiality—its natural landscape, the Dois Irmãos mountains against the extensive beach, the lagoa— served as raw material in metaphysical discussions around wellness and like-mindedness among the individuals whom I met through BaixoBebê and IpaBebê. That this landscape was presumably available to anyone, regardless of racial or class background, contributed to producing the child-centered nodules of urbanism as socially neutral, if not fully democratic, spaces.

Ipanema's spatial dimensions are often said to be unproportional to its symbolic ones.[7] Founded in 1894 as Villa Ipanema, by the 1960s Ipanema had become one of the most prestigious residential areas in Rio de Janeiro, and the most expensive square meter in Brazil. In geographical terms, the neighborhood, affectionately referred to as the Republic of Ipanema, is a narrow strip of land in Rio's Zona Sul, situated between the Atlantic Ocean and the Lagoa Rodrigo de Freitas. It shares borders with Copacabana in the northeast and the neighborhood of Leblon in the south.

A city of former slaves, fishermen, and a subordinate workforce, Rio de Janeiro was transformed at the turn of the twentieth century into the Cidade Maravilhosa of today (Abreu 1987; Tolosa 1996). During the early decades of the 1900s, Rio's mayor Francisco Pereira Passos sought to reinvent Rio as a modern capitalist city and transform it into a "tropical Paris" (Godfrey 1991). The Reforma Passos consisted of a series of projects, including the modernization of the Zona Centro and its port, as well as the expulsion of the lower classes, increasingly composed of recently freed Blacks, to the neighborhoods in the northern area of the city, the subúrbios, and the favelas. Simultaneously, it involved the urbanization and modernization of the southern area of the city, the Zona Sul, valorizing and marketing it to appeal to a carioca elite.[8] As the poor and working poor grew in the Zona Centro, and in connection to European scientific ethos of the time, an "ideology of hygiene" emerged; this ideology projected images of *contágio* (contagion), both moral and physical, onto the lower classes and former slaves, who became associated with laziness and vices, discussed in terms of public health hazards. These concerns with sanitation among the elite gave an urgency to the need for a radical urban reconfiguration, including the search for residential areas outside the Zona Centro of the city.[9]

Viewed as a bucolic, empty canvas sparsely inhabited, on the one hand, and as an area that promised a modernist future and considerable real estate potential, on the other, Rio's Atlantic coastal region was conjured by the carioca elite, national agencies, and corporate developers as the healthier, salubrious, even medicinal alternative to the overcrowded Zona Centro.[10] The inauguration of streetcar lines accelerated Rio's expansion toward Arpoador and the creation of a new neighborhood: Ipanema. By the early 1900s, the Atlantic beachfront sectors of Rio de Janeiro—which currently include the neighborhoods of Copacabana, Ipanema, and Leblon—were added to the city's cartographic and social landscape. The occupation and development of Copacabana and subsequently Ipanema consolidated Rio de Janeiro as a modern city, an enduring symbol of the newly emergent republic and of its dominant classes.[11] To civilize Rio meant to establish the European-inspired patterns of the bourgeoisie, particularly in terms of the legal and social regulation of public spaces championed by Pereira Passos.[12] By the 1920s, the first of many large-scale clearances of poor communities had begun as part of an earth-moving venture to allow Rio to expand against the mountains (Del Rio and Siembieda 2009).[13] Lower-income residences were pushed toward the new favelas in the hills around downtown and, ironically, became a trademark of Rio's urban landscape and postcards thereafter. Several factors that contributed to the consolidation of the beachfront neighborhoods included, first, a change in perspective toward the beach and beachfront sociability; second, a reconfiguration of the built environment, particularly the proliferation of high-rise apartment buildings; third, the emergence of a new elite of salaried professionals; and, finally, the creation of literary, educational, and commercial institutions.

Once viewed as a sort of vacant terrain, where one would see only "children holding the hand of foreign maids or some solitary lovers," Rio's Atlantic coast now had a beachfront aesthetics and a *projeto praiano-civilizatório* (civilizing beach project) (O'Donnell 2013; see also B. Carvalho 2007).[14] Colorful *barracas de lona* (tents) and giant umbrellas prompted comparisons between Rio's Atlantic coast and the beaches of Biarritz and Miami. While beach baths had been viewed as medicinal, and not particularly enjoyable in the 1800s, by the twentieth century, the beach had become a place of leisure that drew from European models of sociability, relatedness to nature, perspectives on the body, fashion, and cosmopolitan self-fashioning.

In addition to the transformation of beach sociability, a second process that consolidated the construction of Ipanema and the other Atlantic beachfront neighborhoods as white elite spaces had to do with changes in the built environment, particularly the proliferation of high-rise buildings. The preference for single-family houses among the Brazilian elite presented some real challenges to the real estate boom in the Zona Sul, and developers needed to find a way of presenting "collective housing" (as apartment buildings were viewed) in a positive light. The transformation in the Zona Sul's built environment required that Ipanema be marketed as an elite *family* neighborhood. The beginning of a touristic industry coincided with local interests in producing this elite family market niche.

In 1922 the newly inaugurated Hotel Copacabana Palace was publicized not only as a luxurious space for foreigners and local elites or even just the face of Rio de Janeiro to the world of tourism. Rather, this first multistory building in the Atlantic beachfront area was also marketed in terms of what it offered to elite carioca *families*. Built on a beachfront area that had been characterized by single-family *palacetes* and bungalows, the construction of the Copacabana Palace ignited a broader trend toward residential high-rises that significantly changed the neighborhood's landscape (cf. O'Donnell 2013, 187). Until then, collective living had been a characteristic of poor dwellers in favelas and subúrbios, not of respectable members of the old elite or of a newly emergent professional class. Public discussions around multilevel buildings, at times contentious, were generally grounded on perspectives of morality and family values. Unlike other collective residential arrangements, like the *cortiços* that Pereira Passos had fought to remove barely two decades prior, which housed former slaves and the urban poor, the apartment buildings were linked to hygiene, civility, luxury, comfort, wealth, and a modern lifestyle, appealing to the elites (Cardoso 2010, 84).[15]

Notwithstanding efforts to interweave the modernity of the high-rises and the natural beauty of the Atlantic beachfront in the consolidation of a tropical civilization, challenges to these real estate goals would soon arise, particularly among a growing number of journalists and intellectuals interested in documenting the development of the area. Asking, "Why would a rich man go to live in a poor man's house?" (Por que foi o rico morar em casa de pobre?), a *Correio da Manhã* journalist echoed other writers of the time. Targeting a growing middle class, advertisements reveal a shift in the real estate market from focusing primarily on large investors (who would buy an entire building) to the sale of residential family units. This shift ultimately led to apartment buildings becoming the leading residential structure in the consolidation of Copacabana and Ipanema as neighborhoods that would attract a population of families, who saw living in these areas as an important step in their social mobility aspirations. Many of these families belonged not to a traditional carioca elite, but rather to a class of former *fazendados* (hacienda owners), or more commonly, an upwardly mobile and newly salaried class of *professionais liberais* (liberal professionals), a social sector increasingly associated with the symbols and values of Latin American modernity.[16]

These professionals were the sons and occasionally daughters of a declining elite, recent immigrants and native-born Brazilians, who were beginning to rub shoulders in commerce, journalism, insurance companies, public employment, banks, factories, and schools. Their lives were taken up by a concern for status, pursuit of success through merit, dependence on patronage, an affinity for respectable employment, a tortured desire for conspicuous consumption, a preoccupation with class, and a desperate desire for moral superiority.[17] They were drawn toward an urban economic arena increasingly defined by market relations and educational credentials.

Behind the objective and aspirational aspects of neighborhood life was the increasing connection between a culture of domesticity and parental ideologies around individual achievement and social status. Books such as Isabela Serrano's *Minha casa* offered housekeeping advice and covered the minutiae of home hygiene—how to deal with home appliances, mend clothes, prepare and conserve food, deal with servants, and rear children (Owensby 1999, 121). Serrano described the refined person in terms of simplicity and "absence of affectation," since "pedantry, artifice, exaggeration bespeak an individual who does not feel at ease in a polite environment and who, as a result, pretends to qualities he does not possess" (1945, 172). In this manual, like in other similar ones, order and discipline were interior traits attained through hard work and dedication rather than through money. What mattered was the psychological state of the individual, not her or his material possessions; Serrano counseled her readers to be "optimistic and try to see the world through the prism of good spirits. Happiness is to be found within, not without" (173).

Beyond obvious racial and class advantages, this symbolic *dona de casa* (housewife) was a partner in a modernizing project through her traditional relationship to the maid; this fierce intimacy with the workings of social difference put housewives in the position of presiding over the process by which children learned hierarchy (Owensby 1999, 125–26). Ideologies of domesticity were ensconced in a tacitly developing connection between social mobility, parenting, and individual achievement.[18] Parenting turned discourses about race and class into everyday practices wherein social inequality was not commonly evident but was always a crucial determinant of sociability, life chances, and area of residence. In parenting practices, race was not treated as a product, as a main or sole analytical category, because it was diffused through other relationships, including deeply affective ones (even those of servitude, as examined in chapter 7). The affective entanglements of parenting, by their very nature and social expectations, often rendered power inequalities difficult to demonstrate.

By the end of the 1950s, Ipanema had followed the same real estate speculation as its neighboring Copacabana. Apartment buildings proliferated at the expense of single-family housing, and population density increased. By the 1970s, the Avenida Vieira Souto, which borders Ipanema's beachfront, became one of the most expensive addresses in Rio de Janeiro, surpassing even the Avenida Atlântica in Copacabana. Ipanema would remain an elite family neighborhood therein, opened to *conversas na calçada* (spontaneous beachfront or street gatherings), unlike Copacabana, which had already become quite popular (and populated).

In addition to beachfront socialization, real estate interest in condominiums, and an emergent class of liberal professionals, the Atlantic beachfront neighborhoods were also defined in terms of new institutions dedicated to profile, represent, and educate its families; local publications, social clubs, and schools were at the forefront of these goals. Although an Ipanema cultural and intellectual elite did not reach its golden age until the 1960s and 1970s, several decades before that, life in the beach neighborhoods had already caught the imagination and interest of an intellectual elite, particularly writers who documented everyday neighborhood history in local journals like *O Copacabana* and, especially, the *Beira Mar*. These writers and intellectuals seemed especially attentive to models of progress and modernity, while trying to distinguish the new elite beachfront neighborhoods from the traditional aristocratic lifestyle of neighboring Botafogo.[19] Théo Filho, *Beira Mar's* editor in chief, aimed to chronicle life in Atlantic beachfront neighborhoods through somewhat pompous description of the moral and professional contributions of specific residents and, more significantly, through the unequivocal centrality of the "family" for the identity and legitimacy of individuals.[20]

A handful of social clubs further affirmed local practices of class socialization and an *espírito de fraternidade* (spirit of brotherhood) among neighborhood individuals, particularly families. These social and sports clubs, rooted in the family as its basic constituency, confirmed the association between morality, intellectual development, and neighborhood identity. This new elite created perspectives on the family that departed from a traditional concern with family surname, inheritance, or lineage. Instead, the focus was on the eminent impact of other forms of cultural and social capital, such as professional and educational credentials, self-regulation (through sports, behavior, manners, or appearance), and the emphasis on sociability between "like-minded" and "progressive" families.

By the 1970s, a different set of actors would take on the task of imprinting the beach neighborhoods, particularly Ipanema, with an enduring, globally circulated structure of feeling. Left-leaning musicians, cinematographers, and writers produced artistic genres that foregrounded Ipanema and viewed its residents and natural beauty as inspiration.[21] These actors engaged in their far-reaching artistic tour de force while ensconced in the military conservatism and repression that characterized Brazil from 1964 through 1985. Noted for its "provincial cosmopolitanism," Ipanema sustained relatively progressive ideological and liberal leanings through Brazil's "transition to democracy" in the 1980s and 1990s (Castro 1999).[22] During Brazil's transition to democracy in the late 1980s and 1990s, Rio began a notable if uneven urban renaissance.[23] After ambitious programs to widen traffic corridors, expand parks and beachfronts, and construct sewage infrastructure through the 1960s and 1970s, a relative civic decline marked the 1980s, when Rio lost its status as national capital to Brasília and its economic leadership to São Paulo. More significant, under the military regime of 1964–85, Rio's political leadership was at odds with the federal government.

When Tom Jobim and Vinicius de Moraes wrote the legendary "Garota de Ipanema" (Girl from Ipanema) in 1962, while sitting at the Bar Veloso, they probably never anticipated the symbolic, material, and social impact this bossa nova phenomenon would have on the neighborhood. Since then, Bar Veloso has been renamed Garota de Ipanema to commemorate the physical space that witnessed the birth of the immortalized masterpiece, and Helô Pinheiro, the muse, became a local celebrity of sorts. Ipanema became a place where people wanted to be noticed (*aparecer, se exibir*), whether through transgressive behaviors, embodied practices, or an inherently relaxed attitude toward even the more pernicious social and political tensions.

Marisol Rodriguez Valle (2005) compares historical and contemporary representations of Ipanema in literary productions of the 1960s and 1970s with contemporary journalistic accounts from 2004. Rodriguez Valle notices two distinct symbolic maps of Ipanema: on the one hand, the bohemian, avant-garde, transgressive Ipanema of the past; on the other, a contemporary Ipanema considered elegant, sophisticated, and athletic. The description of behavior, preferences, and desires of a group of young middle-class (and upper-middle-class) protagonists is evidence that "Ipanema changed the Brazilian way of writing, talking, clothing and perhaps even thinking" (Castro 1999, 11). Dilma Rousseff settled in Ipanema after her impeachment, and a few blocks down from her lived Aecio Neves, who had been her electoral opponent in 2014. Ipanema became associated with a Brazilian intellectual elite. However, what distinguished the Ipanema upper classes of my ethnography was not only the parenting lifestyle the neighborhood afforded but also their explicit rejection of US-style suburbs, particularly Barra da Tijuca, which they sometimes called the Miami of Rio.

Barra da Tijuca was created in the context of the rising global connection between the United States and Brazil that included, for instance, the opening of Ford and General Motors plants in Brazil. The newly rich and upwardly mobile demanded coastal property and were attracted to a US-influenced suburban lifestyle. By the late 1980s, Barra da Tijuca had become Brazil's largest wealthy suburban land development (Herzog 2012, 124). Most Ipanema parents remarked on the prefabricated lifestyle of Barra da Tijuca and blamed Barra residents, who were considered *emergentes* (new-moneyed) for consumption practices that left a negative imprint on the planet and were ultimately tacky or too flashy.

Observers noticed that Barra's suburban culture of leisure and consumerism had "produced an entire generation of children who are incapable of living outside their gated worlds. They have been to Disneyland in Florida but not to downtown Rio, have flown in airplanes or ridden in Mercedes Benz but have no idea how to ride a city bus or take the metro" (Gomes and del Rio 1998, 105). Some Barra parents I met seemed aware of this perception and expressed child-rearing concerns with overprotectiveness. Even dating back to the late 1990s, Barra residents had requested that "community associations contract with psychologists and social workers to help children and adolescents growing up alienated and isolated in fake cities" (Herzog 2012, 132).

Rather than becoming secluded or "feeling trapped" in a Barra da Tijuca building, Zona Sul parents, including those who founded and participated in beachfront or lagoon-side playgrounds like IpaBebê and BaixoBebê, sought to carve out spaces not only for children to play, but for "like-minded" families, and paid caregivers, to socialize. These residential preferences were loaded with ideological, political, and social significance in how Rio's elites assumed its heterogeneity. Moreover, though, the child-centered nodules of urbanism forged in the context of these residential preferences were important, not only as spaces of parental idiosyncrasy, but as elite projects of governance and sovereignty.

Child-Centered Nodules of Urbanism, Governance, and Parenting

Verônica Igel Botelho, along with Fernando Coutinho Leite, his wife, Gabriela Braga Velozo, and Silvana Villela Mattos, were among the dozen or so parents involved in the founding of IpaBebê. They often reminisced about how they had turned a "spontaneous" group of Ipanema families, who would meet on the beach often, into IpaBebê, a municipality-licensed corded-off beach area, where kids and toddlers could play safely. Verônica explained the process in a matter-of-fact way, suggesting the ease of these processes for most well-connected Ipanema residents: "One of us went to the mayor's office; another one went to get the money; another one got donations for the [beach toys]; another one did a web page. When we came to realize it, we had IpaBebê!" Fernando further explained, "There are other beachside groups, BaixoBebê and others, but we are completely different, not for profit. We are just regular parents who have similar values. We reject a consumption-driven society, are civic minded." IpaBebê's cultural and civic events were supported by donations and group discounts from Ipanema business owners and friends of the families. Gabriela also noted that, over the years, they had sought donations from local private schools, gyms, boutiques, and enrichment programs to furnish the play area with toys and to produce children's theater, arts and crafts workshops, and cultural events.

While IpaBebê was parent led, other similar play areas had followed a different trajectory and administrative setup. Founded in 1990 and listed in some Rio de Janeiro "travel with kids" brochures, BaixoBebê emerged as an annex to a beach kiosk near neighboring Leblon. The profit the kiosk generated from selling coconut water and other snacks was used to pay the salary of a play area administrator and upkeep of the area toys. Eloisa Leme Palmeira, the administrator of BaixoBebê at the time of my fieldwork, was a part-time lawyer and longtime Leblon resident. She described these play areas as civic-minded entrepreneurial initiatives intended to create a more family-friendly Ipanema and Leblon. "The goal was to transform the kiosk into a family-oriented point, not a place associated with heavy drinking, smoking," Eloisa explained. "We are not far from Complexo de Alemão [favela] over there, so this beach area always struggled with that, and this was a way to keep the area adequate for little babies, parents, grandparents, by giving the area a family focus." In Eloisa's view, Dona Nilza, the wealthy Ipanema resident who owned the beach kiosk, had

FIGURE 2.2. Playhouses and toys at one Ipanema's beachfront playgrounds. Behind is a view of houses in one of the adjacent poor communities (*comunidades*, or *favelas*). Photo by the author

been a true visionary, finding a way to integrate children into places of adult socialization and yielding a profit from doing it.

IpaBebê and BaixoBebê shared some ideological characteristics and common practices that rendered them child-centered nodules of urbanism, spaces in which parenting empires acquired materiality and through which public spaces became semiprivate, if not totally unavailable to some populations. Like other spatial manifestations of parenting empires, child-centered nodules of urbanism were spaces in which segregation and inequality became legitimate and even moral. Upper-class parental prerogatives, anxieties, and aspirations provided the impetus behind these spaces, their privatization, protection, and governance. In *Toward an Architecture of Enjoyment* (2014), Henri Lefebvre argues that "democratic spaces of leisure" could easily become deceiving traps that create spaces of domination, as the state always strives to domesticate popular joys and turn them into mere satisfaction, which under capitalism becomes the fetishized "illusion of private enjoyment" (5, 70). Child-centered nodules of urbanism fit Lefebvre's characterization of democratic spaces of leisure in that they were also viewed as a positive appropriation of space against "hostile spaces," crime, and insecurity. They also re-created interactions oftentimes associated with the domestic realm—like the relationship between parent and child or a mother and her child's nanny—in a public setting. Ipanema and El Condado, perhaps counterintuitively, were public settings in which liberal, progressive ideals—of inclusivity, open-mindedness, democratic values, cosmopolitanism—carried considerable social capital. Child-centered nodules of urbanism were not rigidly demarcated and at times were quite fluid, their practices more ambiguous; however, some basic characteristics marked a space as a child-centered urban nodule, as opposed to other kinds of spatial configurations.

First, these spaces were highly didactic, as claims to various forms of knowledge and expertise—from folk to scientific, or "expert," knowledge—about child development, socialization, disciplining, and affective needs got circulated, applied, and assessed. In these exchanges, ambivalent feelings around parenting and childcare—joy, anxiety, fear, insecurity—would surface and dissipate. These exchanges of information and expertise around children, notwithstanding their apparent transient or ephemeral quality, contributed a feel or affective energy to the social space.

Despite having completed graduate degrees in law, Silvana's main interest when I met her was bringing together Ipanema parents and child development experts around various child-rearing themes. The mother of a ten-year-old who attended Escola Parque, a pedagogically progressive private school in the nearby neighborhood of Gávea, Silvana had been instrumental in founding a group dedicated to raising awareness about the dangers of hyperconsumption and marketing aimed at children. She would frequently organize book readings and lectures on these topics, sometimes at Livraria Travessa, a spacious and elegant Ipanema bookstore and café, and other times in her luxurious beachfront apartment.

A second characteristic of child-centered nodules of urbanism had to do with the way in which the encounter between personhood and landscape was recast. While the view of Rio de Janeiro's Atlantic coast as a place of health has multiple historical referents, child-centered nodules of urbanism generated a tendency to frame certain settings as having intrinsically therapeutic properties. Parents attributed therapeutic qualities to the Zona Sul landscape in terms of a parenting polity or collectivity.[24] These patterns of human behavior and affective registers, attributed to "nature" and nature-filled settings, were part of the interplay between the self and various localized norms and social expectations (cf. Foucault 1977). This framing generally disregarded variation in individual experiences of those specific environments, experiences that ranged from enjoyment to ambivalence or even fear. Child-centered nodules, therefore, often supported David Conradson's (2005) suggestion that a therapeutic landscape experience is "best approached as a relational outcome, as something that emerges through a complex set of transactions between a person and their broader socio-environmental setting" (338). Cecilia Marcondes, who was proud that her four-year-old daughter had never set foot in a shopping mall, was growing increasingly frustrated with the "issue of homelessness" in Ipanema and decided to do something about it:

> When Alice was about two, I head out at 7 AM to take a stroll with her around Lagoa, and a guy with drool on his dirty face approaches me: "Can you give me some food?" Seven in the morning! This is a time for people to appreciate a beautiful sunrise, not be exposed to that. He started telling me that he had AIDS. I just told him, "Here, go, don't get close to me!" Then he looked at my daughter and said, "She has blue eyes? How can she have blue eyes if you are *morena*?" And I'm thinking, "Oh God, I don't deserve this!" I arrived home hysterical [*aos prantos do jeito, descontrolada*]. I left my daughter with [the nanny] and went to my room to cry about the absurdity of the situation. I denounced it to the UPP [Unidade de Policia Pacificadora, a municipal police unit]. I told them, "I think it is absurd that we pay such a high IPTU [Imposo Predial e Territorial Urbano, a city tax], and when you open your door, all you see is people sleeping on paper on the street, peeing right there. You should remove them." The civil defense came to remove them, and they began screaming. This is a lack of governance, of education. Cariocas sometimes don't call [the authorities], because they don't want to be bothered. They just go to the beach and forget. But when you become a parent that changes. I no longer forget.

For Cecilia, Ipanema should be "magical," "energizing," and a "source of well-being," all phrases used by Ipanema interviewees. The showcasing of nature and all things natural, as expression of interiority and spiritual capital, was a means through which a desired cosmopolitanism became realized. The built environment—the doorman buildings, ample and luxurious apartments—was hardly ever alluded to in conversations, except when it had to do with moving or renovations; those spoke for themselves. Likewise, the lack of material currency of shopping malls and conspicuous consumption in Ipanema, something at times explicitly associated with the lower classes and tacitly associated with the dark-skin residents of comunidades, appeared almost in tandem with the increased currency of "the natural"—nature and the outdoors, organic foods and fabrics, but also recyclable objects. There is a transformation or

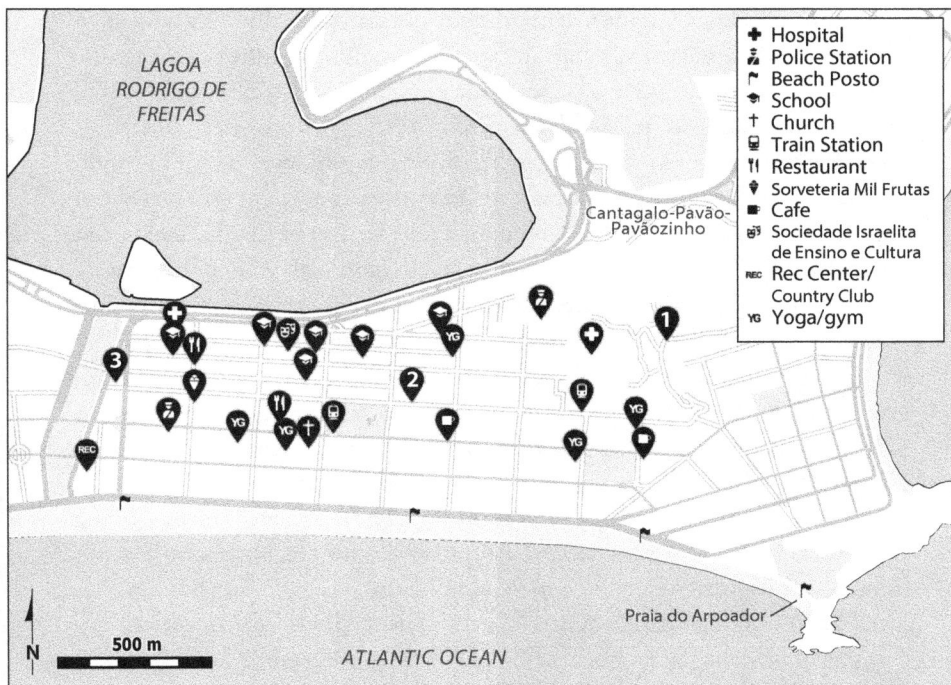

Legend:

- ✚ Hospital
- 🚓 Police Station
- ⚐ Beach Posto
- ⚑ School
- † Church
- 🚆 Train Station
- 🍴 Restaurant
- 🍦 Sorveteria Mil Frutas
- ■ Cafe
- 🕎 Sociedade Israelita de Ensino e Cultura
- REC Rec Center/ Country Club
- YG Yoga/gym

LAGOA RODRIGO DE FREITAS

Cantagalo-Pavão-Pavãozinho

Praia do Arpoador

500 m

N

ATLANTIC OCEAN

1. Solar Meninos de Luz   2. Colégio Notre Dame   3. Colégio Santo Agostinho

MAP 1.1 Ipanema, Brazil. Map created by Tiffany Medina. Map data © Open Street Map contributors

equivalency between feelings and morality in these natural landscapes and orientations; by gesturing outward toward Ipanema's topography, upper-class parents also pointed inward toward the related quality of an interior terrain. This landscape of selfhood allowed for a space that could be imagined, engaged, and traversed as terrain of transformation and possible improvement, as domain of experiential citizenship and alternative forms of sovereignty.

A final important characteristic of child-centered nodules of urbanism was the deliberately ambiguous perspective on interpersonal hierarchy and sociability. This was a critical attribute of the spatialized whiteness and privilege produced in child-centered nodules of urbanism, as class and racial differences were even more densely entangled in webs of affect, suspicion, and care. These entanglements rendered inequality in fact moral and legitimate, contributed to an inherently flexible perspective on the law, and valued intangibles like adaptability or ease. These entanglements were built on Ipanema's structure of feelings and the neighborhood's history of trend-setting bohemian lifestyles and vanguard thinking. Since the 1980s, this structure of feelings has also been rooted in notions of sophistication and elegance, at times mixed with a valorization of *informalidade* (informality; cf. Rodriguez Valle 2005, 46). Rather than interpreting this self-fashioning technique in terms of individual psychology, this "Ipanema feel" drew from the neighborhood's social history and cultural mythology. Dominant perspectives of Rio de Janeiro, and particularly its Zona Sul neighborhoods, as the emotional center of Brazil were enacted through constant references to local forms of *cordialidade* and informalidade that were seen as inherent to being Brazilian.[25]

Being an Ipanema resident came to be described as a set of cultivated cultural, social, and affective practices that required trekking a fine line between hierarchy and informality, democracy and elitism, heterogeneity and exclusivity, self-discipline and *despojamento* ([being] laid back).[26] Ipanema has served as stage for a classic Leftist elite tension: a clear insistence on preserving Ipanema's status as a *bairro nobre* (traditional elite neighborhood), and a simultaneous critique of the eliticization of the old *pés-sujos* (hole-in-the-wall bars) into high-end commercial development (the *enobrecimento de seus espaços*, or upscaling of its spaces).[27] The despojado, or down-to-earth, informal quality, for one, presumably challenged straightforward definitions of "elite," as Eloisa Leme Palmeira, an Ipanema resident, highlighted:

> You really can't pin down what constitutes an elite here. It is very complex. [Bebel, a friend she wants me to meet] goes to Paris for a summer to take classes with the best chefs. She has three nannies, one per child. All she does is train for marathons or hang out with her friends. But she rents her apartment! She's not an owner. Is Bebel more elite than my mother, who is the actual owner of several apartments and rents to her? It depends on the criteria, and here in Rio, and in Ipanema more specifically, there are so many criteria, and even those criteria change. The markers are not evident, because you don't wear them, even if you carry them in some other way.

"Ipanema families have an affinity, despojamento, there is a joy in simplicity, because they enjoy nature and living outside, in public, walking through the neighborhood, beyond household walls," explained Silvana Villela Mattos. "We are not consumption-driven and do not live in their gated condominiums. We don't care about trips to Disney, brand clothes, electronic gadgets. In Ipanema, families recognize how much waste we generate and what that does to our planet. Here you have a beauty that is more natural, maybe even inspired by the Zona Sul geography itself, right?"

As Silvana and I knotted our *pareios* (sarongs) to the back of our reclining lounge chairs on a stunning weekday afternoon, Beto, a Black Brazilian beach vendor in his late forties, spontaneously set up a large beach umbrella for us. "Obrigada, meu querido" (Thanks, my love), Silvana thanked Beto with a tone of full-bodied sweetness that I came to identify, over time, as a cultivated cordiality characteristic of public elite interactions with subordinates. This elite affect, while inseparable from a sense of entitlement that characterized upper-class everyday sociability, particularly manifested toward those subordinate to oneself, effectively sustained (and was supported by) the racialized class hierarchy entrenched in Ipanema's social landscape. Even when it is easy to find counter-evidence for racial democracy in Brazil, and most people are quick to disavow the idea when pressed, the beach is one context where the ideals of racial tolerance and Brazilian cordiality live on in upper-class imaginaries. As James Freeman (2008) notes, "It is not that people cannot see through the myth of the democratic beach. Rather, they choose not to see through it because it supports their interests" (534). Workers that served Ipanema elites, including some of the nannies I interviewed, tended to agree that "wealthy people are sometimes the most humble people, more humble than favelados," as I overheard a beach barraca worker stating.

The physiological and emotional effects of these interactions—the tangible evidence of social difference and white supremacy, as displayed in Silvana's relationship with Beto and the multiple Black bodies at the service of a white elite—appeared as consequences of individuals deliberately trying to complicate, through enduring affective repertoires, place relations. The despojado quality that Silvana highlighted in her interaction with Beto alluded to the broader structure of feeling on which this cultivated informality was enacted, nurtured, and reproduced, and which also required specific feeling rules (Hochschild 1979, 1983, 2016).

These characteristics of child-centered nodules of urbanism force us to view parenting in terms of governance and sovereignty, and to extend our understanding of what parenting cultures really "do" to urbanism, beyond the psychological and idiosyncratic angle that has dominated such discussions. Child-centered urban spaces—and the actions, anxieties, and ideologies they instigate in adults—must be examined in light of the political economy of city and nation, and the ways in which racial, class, and residential privilege acquires materiality in everyday affective relation. While race is traditionally thought about in terms of people, ultimately and historically, the politics of race become comprehensible only when considered in territorial terms. Thus, race is always, more or less explicitly, the racialization of space and the naturalization of segregation; "race order[s] space, social space, from the common to the private" (Lund 2012, 75; cf. Lefebvre 1991). The parenting performed in child-centered nodules of urbanism, like the beachfront playgrounds in Ipanema, transformed urban space, not only physically, but also socially, affectively, and ideologically. These nodules became, more or less explicitly, sites of morally legitimate white privilege, where everyday forms of sovereignty and austerity were translated from the level of national discourse to that of neighborhood routines. A critical question becomes, How do parenting empires transform, under a language and moral legitimacy of protecting (white) neighborhood children, the way in which nonwhite, nonwealthy bodies navigated Ipanema?

Perhaps nowhere were discussions of neighborhood governance and civic duty more salient than in concerns over public transit. In the mid-1980s, bus routes connecting Zona Norte and Zona Sul began operating on weekends, thus enabling Zona Norte and Zona Oeste residents to view Ipanema not only as their place of work, but also as a possible space of beachside leisure. Upper-class Ipanema residents had initially viewed the ease in bus transportation across city zones as a way to get more "cheap" labor. Once the bus routes operated on weekends, however, Zona Sul residents claimed that the (young, dark, usually male) individuals who arrived by bus from the North and West zones of the city to enjoy the beach were "nubes suburbanas [poor area clouds] under the Ipanema sun." They were "not used to the customs of the neighborhood." Upper-class Ipanema residents felt that "[these individuals] are invading our space" and despised that "they come in big groups, always yelling. . . . They are creating a scene of vandalism and terror." Perhaps the government could "make an artificial lake for them over there in the suburbs [poor area]" (J. F. Santos cited in Rodríguez Valle 2005, 112). Since the mid-1980s, these bus routes have been suspended, reinstated, and redirected, on and off, including during the time of my fieldwork in Ipanema, after the arrastão described above.

Likewise, the opening of two metro stations in Ipanema, the construction of elevators leading to an observation deck in the Ipanema favela of Cantagalo, and the overall democratization of mass transport were sources of concern for the Ipanema parents I met, most of whom expressed their fears in terms of neighborhood aesthetics, sense of security, and parenting values. Since September 2009, the Ipanema Residents' Association, to which several of the parents in my study belonged, had been periodically meeting with the State Secretariat of Transportation and engineers from Odebrecht, the company charged with building the metro stations. The infrastructural project consisted of two towers interconnected through a walkway and accessible by free elevators, which would also facilitate access for Cantagalo residents traveling between hillside poor areas (*morros*) and wealthier sections closer to the beach and the lagoa (*asfalto*). One of the towers would have an observation deck, a potential tourist attraction.[28] "This is putting a collar of pearls on a sty" (É colocar um colar de pérolas num chiqueiro), commented one of the attendees at one of the meetings, in relation to Cantagalo. Another Ipanema resident remarked, "We are bringing into one of the most well-regarded neighborhoods of this city a population that, not to say it is an undesirable population, but it is a population that would be better suited for an area where there is more space, like Barra da Tijuca" (Huguenin 2011, 109; cf. A. C. Gomes and del Rio 1998; Ribeiro 1998). Involvement in public transit decisions, undertaken through Ipanema parents' participation in monthly meetings with the municipal police at a private Catholic school, was an example of how governmentality, family life and parenting, and white elite claims to space and neighborhood sovereignty frequently mediated discursive and pragmatic relationships across class, race, and region of residence.

At some level, parents who participated in child-centered nodules of urbanism were somewhat aware of the long and intricate relationship between Rio's asfalto (wealthy areas at the foot of the hill) and its morros, favelas, or comunidades. Some, including many whose voices appear in this ethnography, were also aware of how such morro/asfalto relations were predicated on abysmal class inequalities, and even racial and regional segregation. Many Ipanema parents understood that these spaces were the residence of some of their domestic workers and babás, as well as the symbolic and pedagogical spaces they used to socialize their children into anticonsumption "moral values," develop social commitment, and negotiate a child's first encounters with philanthropy, lessons in "diversity," and social activism. Nevertheless, these ideologically packed spatial configurations, and the pedagogical attributes parents projected onto them, ultimately acted on behalf of the interests of capital, white supremacy, and neoliberalism. They effectively generated images of emboldened Black and poor residents and gave spectacular power to fears about crime, drugs, and bad parenting. Poverty in Ipanema was so ubiquitous, and so much a part of everyday routines and landscape (and of touristic postcards), that for many upperclass residents, it was almost invisible in its hypervisibility.

By the second decade of the 2000s, Ipanema upper-class residents framed the Projeto de Segurança de Ipanema (PSI, Ipanema Security Project) under the slogan "Cidadãos unidos contra o crime e a desordem urbana" (Citizens united against crime and urban disorder).[29] These residents' goal was to "inculcate civility onto those at the margins of society (namely, favela and subúrbio residents)" (da Cunha 2012, 215). The PSI established coercive action against behavior that did not comply with upper-class patterns of civility—from teaching vendors how to handle their own barracas to viewing the homeless as intrinsically dangerous. The group successfully advocated for increasing surveillance cameras from 60 to 350 in 2009 because many Ipanema residents believed that "criminality is related to disorder [and] disorder leads to the favelaization of spaces" (da Cunha 2012, 218). As Cristina Vital da Cunha (2012) argues, when order is provided as antidote against urban violence, favelas and *suburbanos* become the main focus of the upper class's civilizing mission. Critical here is also that public agencies treated Ipanema in an obviously preferential way, and oftentimes, Ipanema residents viewed these public agencies as their own subordinates.

Any PSI effort to be "mindful" of members of Zona Norte subúrbios and Zona Sul favelas was excessively performative and often superimposed a belief that empathy in Brazil erased prejudice (cf. Cardoso de Oliveira 2002). In meetings between Ipanema residents and the municipal police over the time of my fieldwork, designated higher-ranked police officers usually presented elaborate PowerPoint diagrams or detailed street-level maps, pinpointing the number and sites of robberies that had occurred since the prior meeting. These diagrams invariably centered on streets where poorer communities came in contact with wealthier areas, such as the Complexo de Alemão, near the Ipanema/Leblon border, and Cantagalo, near the Ipanema/Copacabana border. A 2015 congressional vote to reduce the age of criminal responsibility received additional levels of attention in Rio de Janeiro, partly because of the high-profile murder, attributed to a minor, of Jaime Gold, a prominent Ipanema physician.[30]

When an explicitly exclusionary discourse of dark, poor youth and crime began to lose moral currency and became pedagogically ineffective in the socialization of white elite children, the focus shifted to notions of order and civility. Whether referred to as "beach rats" (*ratos de praia*), brats (*moleques*), thieves (*bandidos*), or gangs (*gangues*), the young people blamed for neighborhood violence, overwhelmingly dark and poor, became the quintessential outsiders, not only to Ipanema beach sociability, but particularly to child-centered nodules on the beach. That seventeen of the twenty-one people arrested for "terrorizing" or "invading" the beach were underage and would not be as severely punished as older assailants was viewed as a reason that it was so difficult to address neighborhood violence. In social media and newspaper interviews, Ipanema parents and residents demanded lengthier punishment, more police presence and multiagency intervention, more power and authority to the police, and greater surveillance and inspection of buses coming from Zona Norte and Zona Oeste into the Zona Sul beach areas. They advocated for greater civic involvement of Zona Sul residents of Ipanema, Copacabana, and Leblon. In response to an IpaBebê Facebook post, Roberto Motta remarked, "Today I heard an explanation that makes sense: everything got worse after the PW-PT manifestations, when the marginalized [*os marginais*] saw that it was possible to challenge the police and win."[31]

Conclusion

Ipanema is arguably one of the most widely represented neighborhoods in the world, in one of the most stereotyped cities and countries in the world. From the beginning of my research, one of my greatest challenges as a social scientist was to peel off the layers of commodified cultural images of beach democracy and sensual bodies, while also understanding their purpose and value. The emphasis on feelings rather than thoughts in Raymond Williams's structures of feeling (1977) signals that what is at stake may not have been fully articulated, or that it applies to something that can only be regarded as a trajectory, rather than a terminal point. Thus, as a generation, individuals in Ipanema shared a common set of perceptions, affects, and values that they perceived as more clearly articulated in the artistic forms and conventions of the 1960s and 1970s. How do we distinguish between memories that are filtered and organized through a plethora of global popular images and one's own sense of belonging (or not) in the area? Is it even necessary to understand these distinctions? Are they even actual distinctions? Ultimately, child-centered nodules of urbanism in Ipanema, which gained visibility at the start of this century, were plagued by racial and class ambiguities, which had concrete material repercussions and altered or challenged structures of feeling.

Verônica, Fernando, Silvana, Gabriela, Beatriz, and the other Ipanema parents most actively involved in the development of child-centered nodules of urbanism in my ethnography were also involved in the governance bodies that regulated such nodules. For these parents, the beach was perhaps the main stage on which racial and class differentiation—between Zona Norte and Zona Sul, morro and asfalto, bairros praianos and subúrbios—were showcased, downplayed, manipulated, and engaged.[32] In the absence of conventional markers of wealth, like jewelry, clothing, or last names, the invisible yet palpable sense of ease, entitlement, and comfort became even more eminent for anthropological analysis. "We don't care to know each other's last names," Verônica insisted and, with evident pride, added that in Rio's Zona Sul people often used nicknames to refer to others.

Parenting empires operated in this upper-class Brazilian neighborhood by highlighting the conflict between upper-class parents' aspirational selves and the investment in maintaining residential control. Many of these Ipanema parents vacillated between seeking increased police surveillance and gaining understanding of poverty through scientific and psychological discussions of child development. An example of this took place at a June 2014 meeting of Ipanema residents and the municipal police, in which many IpaBebê parents participated. The following public discussion took place:

IPANEMA RESIDENT, FATHER OF TWO PRETEENAGERS: We need to talk about the homeless [*moradores da rua*] that we see all over the place. I'm not sure if what they're doing is legal or illegal, or if something can be done about removing them. Because they are not going to leave the area on their own. They have it too good here. They set up their spot in a corner and smoke pot. Smoking pot is not legal here. What else of what they're doing is not legal? Because, let's admit it, we're afraid of them. The other day I was walking by with my kids and a man was screaming "Estou com fome! Estou com fome!" [I'm hungry! I'm hungry!] My kids got scared. We saw him again on our way back, and he and his kids were there happily eating a cake. They like to be near the restaurants, to get food from them. Life is too good for them here!

SILVANA, IPABEBÊ PARENT: It is our role also to explain to our children about homelessness, and the consequences of poverty. We have brought many psychologists and child development experts to community forums to help us find the vocabulary to do that. We want our children to be able to understand the neighborhood in which they live, not to live in a bubble. This is not Barra. This is Ipanema.

In these child-centered nodules, categories of delinquency become increasingly fluid, as "moradores de comunidade," "homeless," and "potential thief" seemed combined in the same dark-skin (and often young and male) bodies. While some of the postures the Ipanema parents took when it came to issues of public transportation and beach crime were consistent with how most upper-class residents of the neighborhood viewed Black and poor youth, these specific activist parents adopted a more politically ambiguous position. "What is the solution? How do we fix this tremendous inequality we face?" asked Silvana, who continued to wrestle with this issue until she posted an article on "How Can White People Have Conversations about Race?" on her Facebook page. Perhaps this was a contemporary formulation of Antônio Carlos Jobim claim that "Brazil will not be happy until everyone can live in Ipanema."

3

Parenting El Condado

Social History and Immaterial Materiality in San Juan

When the nannies walked down the quiet beach path which bordered the Almanares Lagoon, they insisted they would hear strange moans coming from the nearby swamp that reminded them, they said, of things dying or being born.—Rosario Ferré, *The House in the Lagoon*

Alejandra Rodríguez Emma, a clinical psychologist by training and a stay-at-home parent, couldn't believe her good fortune. Her husband, Enrique Alemañi, and their two young children would be moving into one of the few available four-bedroom houses with backyard in El Condado. Until then, the family had lived in a penthouse apartment in a luxurious high-rise overlooking El Condado Lagoon, the Almanares in Rosario Ferré's *The House in the Lagoon*. Even though Alejandra never mentioned hearing the screams that the nannies in Rosario Ferré's novel associated with "things dying or being born," she did seem almost as fearful of the new neighbors moving into the other, equally luxurious buildings by the lagoon. Thankfully, she would soon be leaving WesCo—the name real estate developers had chosen for the West Condado area—and would be moving about two miles east, closer to where El Condado met the previously shady Calle Loíza area. El Condado is framed by the Atlantic Ocean to the north, the El Condado Lagoon to the southwest, and the colonial area of Old San Juan to the west; farther south, at the other side of the lagoon, is Miramar, the other traditional elite urban neighborhood in San Juan, Puerto Rico.

"Have you seen *The Big Short*?" Alejandra asked. I replied that I had. "Well, the leading character is based on Paulson, the American billionaire who is inciting his billionaire friends to settle in that (western) side of the neighborhood. They are the Law 20/22 people, and they want to displace us. It's like a second colonization. They have that attitude." Under the Act to Promote the Relocation of Investors to Puerto Rico, billionaire foreigners who move to Puerto Rico are subject only to taxes levied by the island, like sales tax and license fees. Even property tax has a 90 percent exception under the law. John Paulson, who became a billionaire by shorting the US housing market ahead of the financial collapse in 2007 and 2008, has funneled an estimated $1.5 billion into Puerto Rican real estate investments, snapping up ritzy hotels on the island, like the Condado Vanderbilt. At an investment summit in 2014, he referred to the island as the "next Singapore."

As Alejandra opened the front gate to show me the grounds of her new Spanish-tiled two-story house, she sighed: "Paulson wants to make that whole WesCo area super high end, but that's not something that is attractive to us. We like this new area so much better. You have reasonable stores, nice restaurants, and near the Calle Loíza which is super cool now. It has lots of new businesses owned by young Puerto Ricans. Nothing like what it used to be, right?"

Despite Puerto Rico's fiscal crisis and the lack of evidence supporting the effectiveness of subsidies to promote economic growth, the two dominant political parties in power over the last few decades had continued granting tax exemptions, providing wage subsidies, and drafting legislation to attract US billionaires. Over the time of my fieldwork, Laws 20 and 22 of 2012 (the Millionaires' Laws) attracted hundreds of well-off Americans to this fiscal paradise. These indiscriminate tax exemptions have made Puerto Rico "a free-for-all fiscal paradise, eroding the tax ethics and tax base system" (Quiñones-Pérez and Seda-Irizarry 2016, 95).[1] The influx of US billionaires came as 10 percent of Puerto Rico's population had abandoned the island in 2015 for economic reasons.[2] The arrival of US billionaires attracted by Laws 20 and 22 predictably generated resentment among Puerto Ricans who had lived through several tax hikes, including an increase in sales taxes from 7 to 11.5 percent in 2015, and spiking water and electricity rates (Strasser 2015). While the upper-class parents in my study were not directly affected by this law or its economic consequences, besides the unfairness of footing the taxes associated with public services that these tax-exempted billionaires also used, the "Law 20/22 people" were particular kinds of US colonial tropes.

Hedge fund billionaire John Paulson, famous for making a $4 billion profit on the collapse of the US subprime mortgage market, pitched Puerto Rico as a new tax haven with "the potential to become the Singapore of the Caribbean" at an investment conference in Condado in 2016. He had been scooping real estate in Puerto Rico and encouraging his friends by claiming that the island would be "the next Miami" (Long 2016). Paulson said, "Puerto Rico is America. I love the Caribbean and other parts of South America, but what makes Puerto Rico unique is that you get the climate of being so far south and you get all the legal protections of the United States" (Neate 2016). As Paulson gave the pep talk to his friends to profit from "bargains" in Puerto Rico, protesters outside the Condado Convention Center said they blamed outside investors for the country's precarious debt and didn't think it was fair to "invite rich people to the country and pay no tax when local people have to pay taxes while enduring declining public services in order to try to repay the island's debt" (Neate 2016). A New York–raised Puerto Rican, Margaret Peña, is one of few locals who actually got any benefit from the arrival of these US billionaires: she opened Sotheby's real estate office to drive new arrivals through the sector in El Condado that in recent years had been most associated with the moguls. "This is WesCo—West Condado," she commented, explaining that she had decided to give neighborhoods catchy names akin to SoHo and Tribeca. The message from any of the individuals involved in "selling" Puerto Rico to the megawealthy is similar: "Puerto Rico isn't just about low taxes. . . . It has luxury apartment buildings, over-the-top resorts like Dorado Beach, and a handful of private international schools that send their graduates to Ivy League colleges" (Burton 2014).

Laws 20/22 people, most of whom settled either in a Ritz-Carlton reserve gated area in the town of Dorado, about thirty miles west of San Juan, or in the western side of El Condado, were ubiquitous in conversations among El Condado and Miramar residents during the time of my fieldwork. As if any further evidence of these billionaires' colonial intentions were needed, Alejandra remarked, "Can you believe that when they did not like the new private school created for them in Dorado, they wanted to hire a helicopter to bring their children to St. John's [School in Condado]? They wanted the helicopter to land on the heliport on top of the Presbyterian Hospital!" Explicit displays of wealth, superficial materialism, and the obvious pursuit of social segregation attributed to the "Laws 20/22 people" challenged how domestic elites in El Condado (as in Ipanema) constructed symbolic and moral parameters and an interiority as *personas sencillas* (down-to-earth people), the Puerto Rican equivalent of being *despojada/o* and sharing social *afinidades* in Brazil (chapter 4).

The parents I interviewed, who were residents of El Condado or Miramar, or whose children attended one of the two most elite private schools in these neighborhoods, were divided about various strategies intended to slow down the island's economic collapse. For the most part, however, they shared hopelessness about Laws 20/22 being a good strategy to solve the country's crisis. They also deployed a language of "being fortunate" about living in El Condado or Miramar more generally and associated these residential affiliations with their social consciousness, liberal leaning, and national pride, specifically grounded in a moral way of being elite and in luck and "being blessed."

In this chapter, I trace practices of parenting through the social history of El Condado and the adjacent upper-class urban neighborhood of Miramar. An argument here is that all affluent urbanism is, necessarily, child centered, as children have acquired a symbolic capital that is often translated into social capital for the parents, and child rearing has become almost inseparable from elite lifestyles, the cultivation of adult friendships, and the "feel" of a place. As in Ipanema (chapter 2), specific historical moments and forms of urbanism changed El Condado spatially, economically, and socially, from an area associated with nonnormative lifestyles (most notably, the LGBTQ community and extramarital making out on the veranda of the Dos Hermanos Bridge, popularly known as "la varandilla") in the 1960s and 1970s to a heteronormative, family-friendly neighborhood. Moreover, just as Barra da Tijuca and poor adjacent comunidades appeared as constitutive outsiders to Ipanema, Guaynabo and sections of Santurce served a similar symbolic function for El Condado parents.

A Brief History of Puerto Rico

In August 2016, as Dilma Rousseff was being impeached in Brazil, the US Congress released the names of seven individuals who would constitute a US-imposed Fiscal Control Board to oversee the restructuring of Puerto Rico's $72 billion debt. This number itself seemed almost arbitrary, and many sectors of Puerto Rico's civil society claimed that significant portions of the debt were illegal and needed to be audited; however, over the time of my fieldwork, two different Puerto Rican governors had objected to the debt being audited. Instead, the fiscal board demanded that the newly elected pro-statehood governor, Ricardo Rosselló, who also happened to be the son of one of the governors responsible for indebting the country, implement austerity policies and find a way to pay bondholders. Esteemed economists, including Nobel Prize recipient Joseph Stiglitz, and international bodies, like the UN, considered the austerity plan not only ineffective but bordering on a human rights violation (Newkirk 2016).

Puerto Rico's government had adopted austerity measures; increased the tax burden on consumption; fired or lost through attrition thousands of government employees, with reduced fringe benefits for those remaining; and implemented big privatization projects and market liberalization policies since at least 2006 (Quiñones-Pérez and Seda-Irizarry 2016). These economic and political crises reached draconian levels, however, after the US Congress imposed the fiscal board's oversight on the island.

Puerto Rico's fiscal crisis of 2006 was the dramatic end of an era that had begun in the 1950s, with the island's rapid industrialization and political reorganization as a US commonwealth. In 1930, three decades after colonial control of the island had shifted from Spain to the United States, and in light of a troubled sugar industry and Roosevelt's New Deal policies, Puerto Rico underwent a state-led economic reconstruction project, which many hoped would prepare the island for independence by creating a more balanced, diversified economy. By the late 1940s, however, both the notion of political independence and that of self-sustaining economic development had been abandoned; instead, the main political elite at the time, under the pro-commonwealth and populist leader Luis Muñoz Marín, adopted a program known as Operation Bootstrap, which offered tax and other incentives to US corporations, including waiving US minimum-wage legislation, unrestricted access to the US market for products manufactured in Puerto Rico, and exemption from federal and insular taxes.

Between 1950 and 1970, per capita income increased considerably, and most Puerto Ricans experienced notable improvement in their standards of living.[3] Even at the peak of Puerto Rico's economic growth, however, the official unemployment rate never fell below 10 percent. The growth of a middle class was in fact propelled by the mass outmigration of 20 percent of the island's population, overwhelmingly darker skin and hailing from the poorest sectors, to US barrios. In Puerto Rico, industrialization was coupled with the dismantling of agriculture, which led to a great dependence on food imports. Economic expansion remained linked to the preferences and moods of US investors, who controlled a growing portion of the island's productive assets (Bernabe 2007).

This prosperity was often presented in contradistinction to the "lesser" livelihood of neighboring Caribbean islands and Latin American countries (particularly Cuba during the Cold War era). Consumerism was, in effect, what modernity became for Puerto Ricans. Operation Bootstrap was a neoliberal endeavor from its inception. By the 1970s, the rapid industrialization formula behind "the Puerto Rican miracle" had lost steam. Once touted as a US-led model of economic development, by the second decade of the twenty-first century, Puerto Rico was clearly embroiled in a struggle for survival. To stay afloat, Puerto Rico sought new federal tax exemptions for US firms, obtaining additional transfers in federal funds, increasing government employment, and issuing public debt in ever-larger amounts. Puerto Rico issued bonds to cover budget shortfalls, and investors snapped them up because the bonds were exempt from federal, state, and local taxes in all fifty states of the United States. In the mid-1990s, the tax incentive to US corporations to settle on the island was halted, as Congress removed Section 936 of the IRS tax code.[4]

When Congress ended hefty tax breaks for US manufacturers and pharmaceuticals, US firms shut down their operations on the island. Puerto Rico doubled its debt over ten years, as Wall Street firms made nearly $1 billion off fees. Instead of changing the model in place since 1947, a political elite preserved it, and more aggressive subsidies were offered in the form of tax breaks, low real wages, cheap infrastructure, and environmental laxity. In 2010, 45 percent of Puerto Ricans on the island lived under the federal poverty line. Whereas apologists for US colonialism often refer to the several billions in US welfare funds spent in Puerto Rico, the very fact that billions are needed to avert misery is an indication of the limits of the colonial economy resulting from more than a century of US rule (cf. Bernabe 2007; Curet Cuevas 2003).

In addition to this uncertain economic crisis, there was an erosion of support for Puerto Rico's political arrangement with the United States, known as the Estado Libre Asociado de Puerto Rico (ELA), and a growing disenchantment with the two major rival political parties on the island, the Popular Democratic Party (PPD), or pro-commonwealth party, and the New Progressive Party (PNP), or pro-statehood party. Under the leadership of Governor Pedro Rosselló Sr. (1993–2000), an administration plagued by a string of unprecedented corruption scandals, the PNP embraced a neoliberal agenda centered on privatizing Puerto Rico's large public sector.

According to elite sectors, Puerto Rico's economic crisis resulted from the erosion of competitiveness and "incentives to work" as a result of public sector overexpansion, overregulation (zoning, environmental permits), "overgenerous" welfare and public service provisions, the "inflexible" work rules imposed by unions, and other obstacles to "entrepreneurial initiative" (Collins, Bosworth, and Soto-Class 2006). As James Alm (2006) notes, Puerto Rico's welfare and public service provisions, inferior to the US equivalents, can hardly be described as overly generous. Promarket recipes are rather a means of leveraging the cost of the crisis of a market and colonial economy onto the shoulders of the unemployed or wage-earning majority (cf. Bernabe 2007).

As in Brazil, in 2014 Puerto Rico's debt was degraded to junk status. The island was effectively shut out of the financial market.[5] Puerto Rico's economy had been contracting for almost a decade: The island's GNP declined by an aggregate of 13 percent between 2006 and 2014, gross fixed domestic investment decreased 24.5 percent, and bank assets plummeted by 41.8 percent. More than one in five jobs was lost, as unemployment stood at 12.5 percent in November 2015, while labor force participation was a dismally low 40.4 percent.[6] Growing signs of resistance had also emerged in community, environmental, labor, and urban development initiatives; they all embodied the struggle of people to more directly control their lives, from their work conditions, the quality of the environment, and the way communities are policed to how the state budget is distributed, as well as reconnecting with the land and agriculture and initiating progressive urban development and artistic projects.

Unlike US states, whose sovereignty does not originate from the federal government but from their existence prior to admission to the Union, Puerto Rico's ultimate sovereignty has been ruled by the Supreme Court as originating with Congress, not the territory.[7] Although most Puerto Ricans were not surprised to hear that the island lacked any real sense of sovereignty, discussions of what this meant gained center stage in popular discourse during the time of my fieldwork. A looming question had to do with the tools Puerto Rico had to restructure its mounting debt and explore the legal limits of its authority. Puerto Ricans vacillated between being stunned and unsurprised by the 2015 US Supreme Court's confirmation that Puerto Rico, while having been removed from the UN Decolonization Committee and presumed to have certain autonomy as a result of its 1952 "Free Associated State" constitution, was irrefutably a US colony. Upper-class El Condado families expressed shock and betrayal at realizing the island's tremendous indebtedness—nearly 100 percent of its total annual economic output and an estimated $30 billion shortfall in its pension. Many of them were intrigued by the very legality of the debt. After the 2015 elections, the incoming pro-statehood governor, Ricardo Rosselló, made it clear that its fiscal priority was to pay bondholders, even if that meant life-threatening cuts in services, including public servant pensions. Ultimately, though, most of the El Condado and Miramar residents I met over the time of my fieldwork recognized that the local government had become inconsequential, as it was clear that the US Congress had the last word.

As Puerto Rico's government became unable to meet revenue targets and struggled to make debt service payments, pay suppliers, and maintain basic services, the US Congress continued to press for further austerity and the Fiscal Control Board became what some consider a "homemade IMF" for Puerto Rico (Gottiniaux 2016).[8] The Fiscal Control Board granted the United States wide oversight powers over public pensions, public corporations, and Puerto Rico's budgets, eliminating any semblance of national sovereignty on the island.

During the time of my fieldwork in Puerto Rico and Brazil, there was a looming sense of betrayal and profound distrust of politicians. In Puerto Rico, politicians were responsible for a level of corruption that cost almost $900 million of public funds per year, according to FBI figures (Quiñones-Pérez and Seda-Irizarry 2016, 96). Although local governors of the two leading political parties were also responsible for the debt, given their irresponsible borrowing at a time when Puerto Rico's economy was virtually stagnant, hedge funds played an equally significant role in the debt. While the cost of the austerity policy adjustments is shared by workers, poor people, and small businesses, the "share of the pie going to the top of our society and external partners increases with the crisis and the adjustments vainly imposed to appease global financial capital and local intermediaries' thirst for more" (Quiñones-Pérez and Seda-Irizarry 2016, 92).[9]

The contemporary neoliberal discourse adopted by ruling elites in Puerto Rico, including the El Condado parents I met, tended to culturalize these political economic and colonial conditions in terms of "a tendency to live beyond our means," "the need for all sectors of society to sacrifice," and the "need to keep costs of doing business low to maintain competitiveness."

El Condado and Miramar, Puerto Rico's Vecindarios Aristocráticos

Until the late 1890s, El Condado and Miramar had been considered weekend or summer destinations for wealthy San Juan families, who commissioned large residences from prominent local, European, and North American architects. During Puerto Rico's transition from Spanish to US colonial regimes, the San Juan areas of Miramar and El Condado experienced rapid development and urbanization.[10] In 1897, a new trolley line, water links, and public communication systems united the walled islet of San Juan (now the colonial area of Old San Juan) with a series of towns in the rest of the island. These venues fostered the flight of the wealthy and upper classes to new nearby areas, principally Miramar and El Condado.

Already by 1901, an American medical missionary, Grace Atkins, had established the Presbyterian Community Hospital on Ashford Avenue, El Condado's main thoroughfare. A few decades later, the American Medical Association approved three residency programs in the hospital. By the mid-1940s, the operation of the hospital was transferred from the Presbyterian church, with mostly American church personnel, to a board of trustees composed of Puerto Ricans, including several businessmen and physicians who lived in El Condado. At the time of my research, El Condado parents emphasized how El Presbiteriano was the first hospital to allow family members to participate

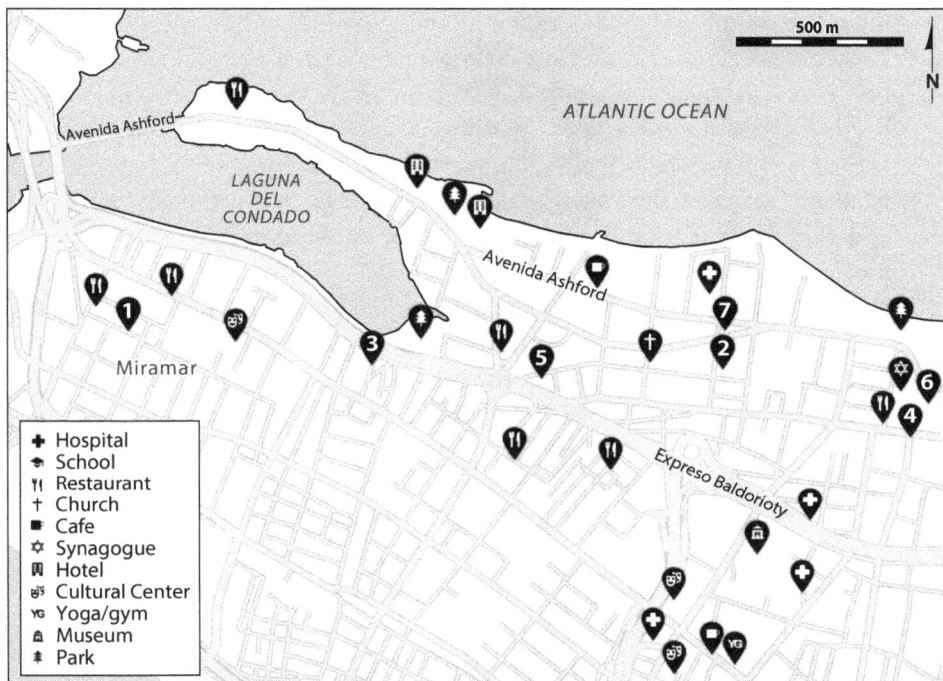

Legend:

- ✚ Hospital
- ⬥ School
- 🍴 Restaurant
- † Church
- ■ Cafe
- ✿ Synagogue
- 🏨 Hotel
- ᵃᵍ Cultural Center
- ᴿᴳ Yoga/gym
- 🏛 Museum
- 🌲 Park

1. Academia Perpetuo Socorro
2. Robinson School
3. Conservatorio de Música de Puerto Rico
4. Academia San Jorge

5. Escuela Madame Luchetti
6. Escuela Dr. Pedro Goyco
7. Saint John's School

MAP 1.2 El Condado and Miramar, Puerto Rico. Map created by Tiffany Medina. Map data © Open Street Map contributors

in births; in the minds of many, this was evidence of how El Condado and Miramar, the main areas serviced by the hospital, were decidedly "family friendly." As one of the fathers I met highlighted, "This was the first hospital in Puerto Rico to receive the certificate of intent to the principles of the global Baby-Friendly Hospital Initiative from UNICEF and the WHO."

Prominent local and foreign families settled in Miramar and El Condado between the 1920s and 1950s, when these areas underwent the most intense period of deliberate, regulated urban planning in their history. The change of colonial governance, from Spain to the United States, brought about commercial and even religious changes to the Miramar and El Condado area. In Miramar, for instance, the first Presbyterian church, along with the Union Club, whose membership was mostly North American, and more bungalow-style houses were built. This contributed to the idea that Miramar, like El Condado, was a North American neighborhood with just a select number of elite Puerto Rican families. Two of the three synagogues in Puerto Rico were also constructed in the first half of the 1900s, one in El Condado and another in Miramar; this presence of Jewish populations of various nationalities was important in how the families I met traced their own Cuban, Spanish, and Latin American ancestry, as well as fostering white privilege as an inherently family-focused parenting project (see chapter 6).

The Behn brothers—socialite sons of a Danish father and a French mother who had originally settled in the Virgin Islands—had inherited a parcel of land from their stepfather, don Mateo Luchetti, and developed the residential park area to resemble an American streetcar suburb. El Condado Residential Park attracted affluent and politically influential Puerto Rican families and eventually wealthy families from the United States, who built their mansions on the lots they bought. The Behn Bridge (El Puente Dos Hermanos) access, a rainwater drainage system, wetland infill, three acres of parkland, and the construction of three boulevards were listed as some of the amenities of living in this area. In fact, an a priori for upscale residential development was to have direct access to the San Juan islet, where the bourgeois families conducted their business. The brothers Behn also saw the growth potential of the telephone in 1917, and through their phone company, they began to buy and install telephones throughout Cuba and Puerto Rico; in El Condado, commercial telephone lines relied on the Dos Hermanos Bridge because the principal military communications headquarters resided in San Juan.[11] Through their vision of El Condado, the Behn brothers established themselves as part of Puerto Rico's social elite. Even back in 1910, the only areas of Santurce that lacked any working-class presence were El Condado and Miramar, where most residents were businessmen or public officers.

The New York and Porto Rico Line, Bull Insular Line, and Red D Line maintained passenger and freight service to transport sugar between the Atlantic ports of the United States and Puerto Rico. Passenger ships became more specialized, and voyages became more frequent, comfortable, and elegant, to meet the expectations of a growing number of wealthy tourists. These voyages showcased Puerto Rico as a tourist destination, since the ships would land very close to luxurious El Condado hotels. Perhaps the most prominent of these hotels, still considered a historical landmark in the neighborhood, is the Condado Vanderbilt Hotel. In the 1920s and 1930s, the Condado Vanderbilt led to the development of early high-end commercial, residential, and hotel industries in Puerto Rico (see also Aponte-Parés 2019). The Condado Vanderbilt contributed to marketing the island's coastline as an exotic yet comfortable vacation destination

The hotel's inauguration took place on October 16, 1919, with an extravagant party that reunited many distinguished people from Puerto Rico's high society. This elite society's theatrical behavior influenced the design of public buildings as places where people could gather and "be seen," providing and firmly instilling into future area populations the scenic variety demanded for society's stage for debutante balls, weddings, and anniversary celebrations. Since its inception, then, El Condado was turned into a timeless, alluring, "both traditional and modern" site that met "the best standards of America," in contradistinction to the extreme poverty afflicting the rest of the island. The hotel brought "honor to the culture and progress of the country" and "people would take pleasure in the Hotel's splendor and refinements that were so agreeable as to elevate human existence" ("Grand Condado Vanderbilt" 2009).

Until the opening of the Condado Vanderbilt, local social clubs did not include beach facilities for swimming; as in Rio's Zona Sul, the beach was not yet associated with leisure and recreation. Once beach swimming was associated with luxury hotels, other prominent society clubs that catered to a select clientele of Puerto Rican society of the time, like El Casino de Puerto Rico, also organized activities around beach swimming. These new ideas of leisure in the local culture transformed how people socialized, as the setting of luxury and leisure transferred from the city to the coastline. In fact, to satisfy these and other new recreational needs, El Escambrón Beach Club complex was created for a local Puerto Rican elite. The new social practice and new thinking about leisure space brought about by the concept of "the grand hotel" became important in helping develop other areas in the city of San Juan. A US-controlled territory where drinking alcohol was illegal, Puerto Rico became by contrast a more reputable tourist destination, "better suited for the family-oriented vacation."[12] The grand hotel typology in Puerto Rico, with El Condado area as the main hub, projected a respectable veneer and family-friendly atmosphere, which was considered a radical departure from the dubious repute of swanky hotels that "catered to adult vice" in Havana and Mexico City (National Register of Historic Places Registration Form, US Department of the Interior, National Park Service, OMB no. 1024 0018, p. 121; see also Morawski 2014). Despite Miramar and El Condado's parallel and intersecting histories and lifestyles, the two have diverged: Miramar residents have pushed back against most attempts to open hotels in the neighborhood, whereas El Condado has developed its cosmopolitan flair through a national hotel industry.

Save for a few decades in the 1960s and 1970s, the neighborhoods of Miramar and El Condado were associated with normative, elite white Puerto Rican and foreign families. A critical factor contributing to this family-friendly perspective of the neighborhoods, particularly Miramar, was the early expansion and development of elite private schools in the area. St. John's School and the Academia del Perpetuo Socorro, the schools from which I drew most of the parents in my Puerto Rico sample, played considerable roles in luring upper-class parents and children to the areas of El Condado and Miramar. In El Condado, St. John's School was established by the Episcopal Church in 1917, and in Miramar, the Academia del Perpetuo Socorro was founded by the fathers and sisters of Notre Dame in 1921. In the early 1900s, the Order of Passionist Priests founded the Nuestra Señora del Perpetuo Socorro church and, in 1921, began an educational program that would eventually become the Academia del Perpetuo Socorro (APS), a private Catholic school popularly referred to as Perpetuo in local vernacular. In 1931, a convent for the sisters of Notre Dame was initiated, and in 1957, a high school was added. By 2010, the Organización de Ex Alumnos APS was created, acquiring its own office, meeting room, and equipment on the same street where Perpetuo is located. These schools—along with a handful of others outside the San Juan area—played critical roles not only in educating the children of the elite, but also in generating enduring social capital among its alumni, parents, and neighborhoods more broadly (chapter 5).

Not long after St. John and Perpetuo were founded, the 1940 census indicated a considerable increase in the Puerto Rican population of Miramar and El Condado (in relation to foreign, Spanish, or North American born); by 1950, neighborhood residents were upper-class Puerto Rican, mostly members of the sugar industry, the academic world, or service professions. These families exerted considerable economic and social power in the country, and they demanded residential spaces that adequately represented their class position and aspirations.

By the 1970s and 1980s, single-family wooden mansions in Miramar had been replaced by apartment buildings and modern residences. Most of the Miramar parents I met came of age during that era and recalled specific buildings—Caribbean Towers, the Palma Real, and the Hotel Clarion—as evidence of neighborhood transformations. While this era in Puerto Rico was characterized by a population movement away from urban areas into the suburbs, particularly the upscale areas of Guaynabo, both Miramar and El Condado endured and retained their respective populations pretty much intact. Puerto Rican Supreme Court justices, university presidents, and prominent politicians had lived in large old Miramar mansions since the neighborhood's beginnings, just as businessmen and entrepreneurs had settled in El Condado. These areas were considered stable and residential, where families lived in the same home for four or more generations. While El Condado continued to be viewed as a touristic and cosmopolitan area, Miramar became noted for its historical preservation and conservation efforts—including various connections with institutions like the Instituto de Cultura Puertorriqueña.

In the 1960s, El Condado and Miramar, along with Old San Juan, Hato Rey, and Santurce, became significant spatial centers of an increasingly visible gay urban community, organized around political resistance, an annual Gay Pride march, and protests against the criminalization of consensual sodomy in the Penal Code of 1974 (Laureano 2016).[13] In El Condado, the high density of gay bars dates back to the 1950s, when the heart of the gay community was the Calle Vendig, a relatively short street that ended at the beachfront on one side and Ashford Avenue on the other. From the 1970s through 2010, the Atlantic Beach hostel on that street displayed a large rainbow flag in the front; the Calle Vendig was also considered a male gay sex work area (Laureano 2016, 156). The annual Pride march in Puerto Rico was first held the summer of 1991, when about one hundred people marched from Luis Muñoz Rivera Park, near the entrance to Old San Juan, to Liberty Park in El Condado. The march was headed by Cristina Hayworth, a veteran of the 1969 Stonewall riot in New York. As Javier Laureano notes in *San Juan Gay*, "In the case of the LGBT Pride Parade in Puerto Rico, the event constitutes an act of visibility and the appropriation of one of the main urban arteries of the San Juan elite, which includes in its urban configuration an important homoerotic element" (2016, 219).

When I asked parents what attribute of their neighborhood they most liked, every single interlocutor remarked on its pedestrian nature. "Where else can you walk and not have to depend on a car? Where else can you use a stroller or walk your children to the park or to school?" remarked Alejandra. El Condado and Miramar were perhaps among the few sectors that had "pedestrian appeal in the San Juan metropolitan area, resulting from [their] privileged location between the sea and the lagoon," as Alejandra stated, echoing other parents. Through the 1960s and 1970s, walking in El Condado and Miramar was associated with cruising, or *el ligue* (checking someone out) in gay vernacular. The anonymous act of walking around the city is nurtured by "el ligue público" (Laureano 2016, 125), a social gaze that sets in practice the protocols of embodied gestures learned within the city, as well as in spaces that predated the consolidation of gay community in El Condado. In fact, the construction of a gay urban identity in Puerto Rico is nurtured by the anonymous urban practices of walking through the city, going to bars, discos, and saunas (Laureano

FIGURE 3.1. Water activities for children and families in El Condado Lagoon. Photo by the author.

2016, 125). Thus, the seemingly simple act of "being able to walk" had been resignified—gone from being associated with "gay cruising" and sex workers in the 1980s to pushing strollers now—through contemporary parenting cultures and heteronormative family practice. Curiously, these were acts of walking that created parallel, not intersecting, cartographies, which activated notions of progressiveness without requiring an engagement with LGBTQ populations.

Another critical aspect of the progressive and cosmopolitan feel of El Condado had to do with an increased interest in the urban outdoors and concern with environmental hazards. In 2004, the strip that bordered the eastern side of the Condado Lagoon became a source of renewed attention. Puerto Rico's National Park Company offered to invest several millions to meet the demands of people who "use these areas to relax and exercise, specially the local residents" (Millán Pabón 2004). A police station, a pier, and a storage area for kayaks would be installed. Members of the Asociación de Residentes y Comerciantes del Condado (ARCC) were overjoyed, as they had been allegedly seeking this form of renovation and surveillance of the lagoon park area since 1968.[14]

Already in 1968, a government plan titled *Environmental Development of the Condado Lagoon* (*Mejoramiento ambiental de la Laguna del Condado*) was drafted in response to how the economic, physical, and social transformation of Puerto Rico over the previous decade had negatively affected El Condado Lagoon and family life in its surrounding neighborhoods of El Condado and Miramar. The document emphasized the importance of preserving the "character" of the neighborhoods adjacent to the lagoon: "The

78 Chapter Three

barrios adjacent to the Lagoon have their own identity. The Lagoon's open space is the spot where residents of these barrios project their gaze, their steps in search of beauty, recreation, relaxation, and conviviality. The type of transit from and toward the Lagoon, as well as between the barrios, is tremendously important for taking advantage of the possibilities for neighborhood conviviality" (Amador 1968, 41).

While El Condado families viewed quality of life and cosmopolitan feel in terms of the lagoon and its urban gay community, in Miramar there was a growing focus on architectural and neighborhood preservation. Over several meetings in 2004 and the early months of 2005, residents decided to challenge "continuous attacks against the residential and historic character of the neighborhood," and they successfully lobbied for the Ley 3 de Zona Histórica de Miramar, the March 2005 passage of which established the area as a historic zone.[15] They also endorsed the creation of recreational parks, becoming the permanent location for the Conservatorio de Música de Puerto Rico and turning some streets into pedestrian-only zones. A Christmas Day breakfast, the Miramar Vive festival, the promotion of a food truck sector, and lectures and walking tours of the community were set in place.

On the morning of Saturday, May 31, 2014, the Asociación de Residentes de Miramar, particularly its Comité Zona Histórica, initiated a series of lectures and walking tours of the neighborhood. The first one, "Miramar: Sus Orígenes," highlighted Miramar in the nineteenth century in relation to the architectural elegance of the neighborhood in the Spanish colonial period. With a certain nostalgia for the times when the leading commercial avenue in the neighborhood, the Avenida Ponce de León, was called Camino Real (Royal Walk), a question raised for discussion was, "What are we willing to lose in this process called progress?"[16] Lectures and walking tours became staples of Miramar, after the initial lecture and walk drew close to one hundred attendees. Issues of conservation and historic preservation were prominent in Miramar and viewed as critical to Puerto Rico's architecture and political and intellectual history.

Miramar and El Condado turned toward the protection and creation of public spaces during the first decade of the 2000s, even though the strategies for doing this varied—a focus on natural resources with parenting appeal in El Condado and on historical preservation anchored in the neighborhood private school in Miramar. The most ubiquitous example of this in El Condado was El Parque de La Ventana al Mar, a green area bounded by the Atlantic Ocean to the north and Ashford Avenue to the south, surrounded by high-end boutiques, jewelry stores, cafés, and family-friendly establishments, like a Ben & Jerry's ice cream parlor.

In "Mapping Childhood in Amsterdam: The Spatial and Social Construction of Children's Domains in the City," Lia Karsten argues that "concerns about safety, stress on personal achievement, and changing ideas about motherhood are strongly reflected in the way the childhood city is and will be spatially arranged" (2002, 232). The spatial transformation of the city is a complex reflection of changing discourses and practices around childhood.[17] Areas of bookstores exclusively reserved for children, children's theater and artistic programs, food establishments catering to them, along with specialty classes and enrichment programs have proliferated to satisfy an increasing pressure that parents face for their children's personal achievements. These measures are inherently punitive to whoever is rendered an outsider to these norms, and who are sometimes considered the ones responsible for the area's social ills; hence, while some children are constructed as producing desirable urban livelihoods, others are considered the cause of livability problems. Rather than focusing specifically on increasing the numbers of families with children, these processes subscribe to what van den Berg calls "genderfication" (2013): specific norms about raising children, gender equality, dual income, and nuclear families became strategies for "upgrading" the city.[18] While some areas bordering El Condado and Miramar were undergoing somewhat traditional forms of gentrification, as Calle Loíza near El Condado and Calle Cerra in Miramar show, these neighborhoods, as a whole, had always been designed and developed for upper-class families. What happened in El Condado and Miramar at the time of my research was a reinvention of what it meant to be part of a national elite in accordance with dominant global perspectives based not so much on marriage or family but specifically on parenting. This may perhaps be more striking in El Condado, an area that has been considered more open to nonnormative lifestyles, including the consolidation of Puerto Rico's urban gay community in the 1970s (Laureano 2016), but it was also the case in Miramar. To achieve these goals, Miramar and El Condado adopted comparable, but distinct, strategies: El Condado assumed an ecological and tourist-industry approach to quality of life, whereas Miramar focused on conservation and preservation and sought status as a historic zone.[19]

As in Ipanema, where symbolic parental borders were highlighted in terms of Zona Sul's "constitutive outsiders"—Barra da Tijuca and the nearby comunidades, particularly Cantagalo—El Condado and Miramar were imagined as radically different from the affluent suburbs of Guaynabo, the gated resort-style living of Dorado, and the adjacent areas of Santurce (Calle Loíza in El Condado and Calle Cerra in Miramar). These areas were not only constitutive outsiders to El Condado and Miramar but also distinct moral spaces against which El Condado and Miramar parents evaluated their own parental and personal growth aspirations. In these comparisons, inequality was morally appraised, so that some forms of "inequality" were viewed as more immoral than others.

GUAYNABO, DORADO, AND THE LAWS 20/22 PEOPLE

Guaynabo figures prominently in popular discussions, analyses, and even satire about class inequality in Puerto Rico; since the 1970s, various upscale suburbs located in the municipality of Guaynabo have become spatial symbols of wealth not unlike those in upscale US suburbs. In 1987, Law 21 allowed for the legal gating of existing Guaynabo neighborhoods; ever since, gated communities have increased in the area. During the mid-twentieth century, to meet the needs of Puerto Rico's growing middle class, urban sprawl emerged as a result of the construction of *urbanizaciones* (subdivisions) and *residenciales públicos* (public housing; Safa 1974; Suárez Carrasquillo 2011). It was during this time that Guaynabo saw a significant emergence of urbanizaciones as a result of its proximity to San Juan.

Manolo Lastra, a single father of two, prominent economist, and resident of El Condado once commented that the term *guaynabito* (for Guaynabo) had come to replace *comemierda* (snob) or even *blanquito* in folk critiques of inequality and the white elite in Puerto Rico, particularly in the San Juan area. He noted, "People don't want to be called that, so the new thing is that you hear people who live in Guaynabo or who are from Guaynabo say things like 'I'm from Guaynabo, but I'm not a guaynabito.' Sure, because now guaynabito means comemierda, right? So they want to create those distinctions. And I tell them, 'Guess what? You are a guaynabito, just like I am a guaynabito. Get over it!'"

In "Gated Communities and City Marketing: Recent Trends in Guaynabo, Puerto Rico" (2011), Carlos Suárez Carrasquillo argues that capitalizing on the increased fear of crime and increased interest in prestigious living, the municipality of Guaynabo began a city marketing campaign that resulted in an Americanized, gentrified, and gated Guaynabo, ultimately transforming Guaynabo into Guaynabo City.[20]

For parents in El Condado and Miramar, Guaynabo—and more recently Dorado, an area where foreign billionaires settled on a Ritz-Carlton reserve—symbolized how explicit displays of wealth and unbridled materialism lacked moral grounding; in these parents' views, Guaynabo wealth, like the wealth of WesCo and Dorado foreign billionaires, was built on hyperconsumption and on a rejection of the diversity and "exposure" that urbanism facilitated.[21]

Such perspectives were often reflected in everyday comments:

TERESITA SANTAELLA (PASTRY CHEF, LATE FORTIES, ONE
CHILD WHO MOVED FROM PERPETUO TO ST. JOHN): Grow-
ing up, my parents had the yacht, the villa in Palmas [del Mar Resort],
all the creature comforts. But that wasn't what was important. I never
compare myself to others, the way people in Dorado or Guaynabo do.
In Guaynabo, people have too much space in their minds to obsess
over material things. My brother and sister-in-law didn't last two years
living in Guaynabo! Depression, marital crisis, an unhealthy seden-
tary lifestyle. They went through it all, until they moved to El Condado again. They put their children in Baldwin or Parkville, schools
I had never even heard about, mind you, but they put them there
because, for them, St. John's and Robinson are *"escuelas de Americanos, de judíos"* [American schools, Jewish schools]. But that's precisely
what I like about these schools, the diversity! Because what exposure
are your kids going to have when everyone else in the school is Puerto
Rican?

MARIBEL SEIJO (MBA, STAY-AT-HOME MIRAMAR RESIDENT,
LATE FORTIES, CHILDREN AT PERPETUO): Miramar is more old
money, El Condado is more foreign and new money, and Guaynabo
is more local new money. Dorado is wealthy hillbilly gringos from
Bible-thumping states. That's really how I view these areas.

MARÍA EUGENIA TIRADO (PUBLIC RELATIONS, NOW STAY-AT-
HOME MOM, LATE FORTIES, TWO CHILDREN AT PERPETUO):
Guaynabo or Dorado is like living in a little glass house. Everyone is
meddling into what you're doing. Miramar is more like El Condado,
even more mixed, because you also have a middle class, not just very
wealthy. When I had my older son, we were living in El Condado,
but came here [to Miramar] to go trick-or-treating on Halloween. We
began walking around Miramar and the houses had lemonade stands,
cookies. It was like when people talk about living in a small town on
the island. Since my family is Cuban, I never had that thing about 'Ah,
in [the small town of] Arroyo everyone leaves their doors opened!'
When I got to Miramar, I felt that warmth.

These immaterial qualities—of inner direction, cosmopolitan exposure yet
small-town manners—produced a narrative that aimed to reduce material
wealth to the immaterial, moral qualities that parents associated with the kind

of children they wanted to raise, the kind of people they appeared to be, and how they expected the neighborhood to contribute to such sociability.

Henri Lefebvre (1991) masterfully argues that territory is a sociocultural entity that embodies our selves and the power to reside, as well as a political entity that determines the boundaries of a "we," state and nation. These parents also noted how the pattern of wealthy living had been altered as a result of the economic crisis Puerto Rico was undergoing, and these forms of immoral inequality were embodied in the figure of the Laws 20/22 people, but also in national elites who self-segregated behind Guaynabo gates. These sectors presumably lacked capital beyond the evident financial wealth; precisely that monochromatic aspect of wealth, ironically, lowered their status in the eyes of even the wealthiest Miramar and El Condado parents I met.

Common among these parents was also something that resonated with the Ipanema residents I met: an emphasis on producing a moral economy of privilege that constructed the material as actually "immaterial," in which values trumped a material world that was, perhaps ironically, tacitly associated with the nouveau riche, the foreign rich, and the local poor alike.

CALLE LOÍZA AND SANTURCE ES LEY: RACIALIZATION, GENTRIFICATION, AND ENTREPRENEURSHIP

The upper-class parents in my sample demonstrated their urban cosmopolitanism by attending street festivals and cultural events, and occasionally connecting with areas otherwise considered peripheral to El Condado and Miramar lifestyles, including Santurce and the Calle Loíza commercial sector.

Many of the parents were aware of how their attitudes toward these areas were different from how they had been socialized to see them in their childhood and adolescent years. Like many other parents, Carlos Varela remarked, "When we were growing up, we would roll up our windows going through La Loiza [Loiza Street]. Now we walk to Bebo's [Dominican restaurant]." Most upper-class parents, like María Eugenia Tirado, had grown up viewing Calle Loíza, near El Condado, and Calle Cerra, near Miramar, as dangerous "drive-through" places, frequently associated with stigmatized Dominican immigrants and the dark-skin Puerto Rican poor. Partly as a result of the financial crisis in Puerto Rico, however, these areas became sites of entrepreneurial initiatives, including a return to farming; fusion cuisine; urban gardens; the sale of local artisanal coffee brands; and, in the urban context, artistic and urban renewal projects in the area of Santurce.

In 2009, a small group of gallery owners gathered near Calle Cerra in Miramar to paint a mural on one of Santurce's ramshackle buildings. What began as an arts-driven neighborhood event grew into an international arts fair. The Santurce es Ley festival—an event that includes open studios, music, experimental media, bright murals, and art installations throughout the neighborhood—was considered, at the time of my research, emblematic of the transformation of a neighborhood through artwork and positive community interaction. The August 2014 issue of *Miramar Siempre!* hinted at a different attitude toward those previously stigmatized areas. Under the title "Festival Cultural-Urbano Santurce es Ley," the Asociación de Residentes de Miramar publication dedicated a section to highlight Santurce es Ley—"the first cultural festival organized by artists, independent galleries and the community to activate the Santurce art circuit"—as an event situated in the Miramar neighborhood and belonging to Miramar residents.[22] Although most artists involved in Santurce es Ley were not Miramar residents, nor did they consider the Calle Cerra as socially similar to Miramar, the Asociación de Residentes de Miramar still tended to claim the "revitalization" efforts of these muralists and artists as a Miramar-led initiative.

What Santurce es Ley was to Miramar, the Calle Loíza was to El Condado. Since at least the 1980s, Calle Loíza had consisted of immigrant businesses—mostly Dominican, but also a few Spaniard owners from the poor rural areas of Asturia and Galicia—and some fast food chain restaurants. The streets perpendicular to this main commercial thoroughfare constituted a working-class Puerto Rican and Dominican barrio, largely ignored and marginalized, with an understudied history of Black urban Puerto Rican life. Since the early 2000s, new restaurants with an "urban chic" style, and even a stylized food truck, opened and were frequented by young upper- and upper-middle-class Puerto Rican residents of neighboring El Condado, Ocean Park, Miramar, and elsewhere. Increasingly, during the 2012 through 2017 fieldwork period, these streets made their way into the neighborhoods in which they were located; they were no longer excluded from Miramar's and El Condado's physical and social mapping or its residents' quotidian routines. Quite the contrary. These areas provided a particular hipness to nearby elite areas and enabled a specific form of self-fashioning to which Puerto Rican parents in El Condado and Miramar aspired, a sort of street credit for people who had grown up with a sense of fear and overprotectiveness—which a mother referred to as "insularism"—that they claimed they didn't want for their own children.

Many of the Miramar and El Condado parents I interviewed considered grassroots projects in Calle Loíza and Calle Cerra as evidence that "we don't have to be government dependent, or have that welfare mentality," as Manolo Lastra remarked. These parents also took great pride in their own ability to move through spaces of difference—which appeared coded for class and even more so for race—with ease. They remarked on this "ease"—and the cosmopolitanism, progressive thinking, and openness attributed to it—as being radically different from the discomfort with diversity they projected onto parents who were raising their children in the affluent "bubbles" of Guaynabo, a more traditional American suburb type of life, or the foreign billionaires.

As I got to meet parent activists involved in Calle Loíza urban development projects, it was evident that they were aware of the meaning their area of the neighborhood had for the more affluent populations of El Condado and Miramar. Marina Arabía, one of the leading activists in projects that aimed to rescue abandoned buildings by rehabilitating them in environmentally conscious ways and putting them to community use, expressed concern that the area's proximity to El Condado would force prices up and squeeze the traditionally working-class and immigrant Calle Loíza residents out. These Calle Loíza and Santurce activists acknowledged how their own investment in developing the area could backfire. Marina explained, "They [El Condado residents] bring their attitude. They want to park their gigantic SUVs in whichever way they want. . . . That's the dilemma here. Are we ourselves contributing? Because we want the area to improve, but we also want the people who have always lived here to benefit from that improvement."

Notwithstanding the artistic, commercial, and even ideological value that El Condado and Miramar upper-class residents often projected onto the revitalization of the Calle Loíza and Calle Cerra, they still justified various measures of controlling access and increasing surveillance in their own wealthier areas by drawing on discourses of insecurity and concerns about crime.

On a breezy Sunday afternoon in 2014, my four-year-old son slowly rode his bike to the Ventana al Mar Park, a tacit divider between WesCo and the rest of El Condado, as I followed him on foot. Spiderman helmet on and training-wheeled bike ready, we approached the park, where we would meet Manolo Lastra and his children at the Ben & Jerry's for ice cream. As Sebastián and I approached the park, a young, dark-skin security guard approached us, almost timidly, to let us know that "bikes are not allowed in the park." My face must have shown disbelief, because the guard tilted his head and made a facial gesture almost shrugging and agreeing with what I was thinking: How could it be that one of the few green areas with cemented lanes in the neighborhood could forbid kiddie bikes? I felt bad for the security guard, who looked obviously uncomfortable at trying to justify something he viewed as ridiculous. Hesitantly, he told me, "They don't want to have an accident of people bumping into bikes. . . . You know, the tourists and all the new people moving in." I reassured him that there was no problem, we would not ride the bike, and asked him if we could at least take the bike with us to the ice cream place, a few steps into the park, so as not to leave the bike in the middle of the sidewalk. He hesitantly agreed, and Sebastián dismounted and walked the bike toward the Ben & Jerry's. When I expressed my surprise to Manolo, he was sympathetic but adamant that the no-bike policy was "unfortunately, a necessity." He explained, "This rule was really not directed to forbid young kids from riding their bikes, but unfortunately, that's the byproduct of it. Here in El Condado we're having an issue with young men from Lloréns [public housing complex; *los muchachitos de Lloréns*] riding bikes, very aggressively and recklessly. They rob, grab cell phones, and when you're with your kids, that makes you very vulnerable. As parents, we had to get involved in that." A group of "concerned parents" had designated another area for bikes, which was almost impossible to find unless you had a Google drop point given to you for biking.

Perspectives on insecurity among El Condado parents, as in Ipanema, were simultaneously spatially circumscribed and impossibly diffused, at once very specific and intractably generalized. On the one hand, insecurity was invariably associated with dark bodies, more frequently with young males, that at times "spilled over" from racialized and criminalized areas—and racialized and racializing spaces, like the Lloréns Torres housing project, a quintessential symbol of "degeneration" in Puerto Rican elite discourse. As expected, such areas, both in Ipanema and in El Condado, were physically close, even adjacent, to otherwise "good neighborhoods," but the residents of these places were socially distant and considered out of place whenever they stepped out of the spaces that defined them, in the eyes of the upper class (Roth-Gordon 2017).

As Inderpal Grewal notes in her examination of security moms, after decades of neoliberal state retrenchment and economic policies benefiting the very wealthy, and emergent moral panics, fears of terrorists, discourses of child predators, and precarious employment, security and fear have become the prevailing structures of feeling in US families (Grewal 2017). Likewise, analyses of Latin American discourse on parenting suggests that "fear," "anguish," or even "panic" are common descriptions used by parents to transmit the emotions that raising children generates (Gómez Espino 2012, 46). These fears are partly rooted in relationships to space, in terms of neighborhood safety, playing on the streets, being abducted, living next to a sex offender, entering neighbors' living areas, and so forth. As I argue in the next section, these fears also provided distinct moral cartographies through which El Condado and Miramar parents assessed their values and evaluated their parenting goals and aspirations.

FIGURE 3.2. Religious pamphlets on how to "Find Family Happiness" placed on shelves in Parque del Indio, one of the main El Condado beachside playgrounds and parks. Photo: Jeanette Zaragoza De León

Curiously, though, conversations about street violence, or the perception of violence, seemed to provide a language for describing more general fears related to child rearing, ranging from pedophilic priests to underage alcohol consumption. This became salient in a conversation I had with Laura Gómez Ayala, a parent blogger, and her husband, Javier Piovanetti, an architect and a developer.

Arriving at Laura and Javier's beachfront apartment in El Condado always felt like stepping into a Martha Stewart magazine. It was not only the freshly ground artisanal coffee from La Hacienda, or the finger sandwiches and *quesitos* (cream-cheese-filled pastries) from Kasalta; it wasn't even the impeccable, sanitized ("I became a germophobe when my son was born") surfaces of tables and counters, or the barely audible jazz against the tenuous sound of the waves through the balcony. It was that Laura thrived in creating atmospheres, an ambience that I came to recognize as the subtle control of space—in all its sensual dimensions. Talking about violence, when so much creative attention had gone to surrounding oneself with comfort, felt peculiar. Yet it was precisely the topic of violence that dominated conversations between Laura and Javier, Laura and her nanny, Laura and her yoga instructor, and Laura and me over the time of my fieldwork:

> They can drive by in a car and kidnap you. Take you to the ATM to get five hundred dollars one day, and keep you until the other day to take another five hundred dollars. Lloréns Torres [housing project], you know, that's a huge site of social infestation. So on weekends, you have gangs of twenty, thirty kids roaming around here on their bikes. Some other parents and I made red diamond signs that say "Ojo al Pillo" [Watch out for the Thief] to alert others that an area is a hotbed of thieves. You probably have seen them. This is a reality we have as parents. Child sex trafficking, sexual abuse, even priests are raping kids, young people caught up in drugs, alcoholism, video games. Violence has unfolded on a global scale. So yes, you have some changes in Calle Loíza, but those changes attract a lot of different kinds of crowds.

I spoke at length with Laura and other El Condado parents about issues of safety, but what is worth highlighting here is how El Condado's three main parks (and later on a park by the lagoon) performed functions similar to Ipanema's beachside playgrounds. They were spaces where some poor and dark bodies were allowed, if they were accompanying a white baby or child, while others—particularly of young dark men—were policed. The difference between these upper-class El Condado and Ipanema parents' perspectives and the perspectives of residents of gated communities was that El Condado and Ipanema parents did experience frequent dissonance between their motivation to live in urban neighborhoods where diversity, technically, could be possible, and their persistent need to regulate and restrict areas of those neighborhoods.

Many of the parents I met in El Condado and Miramar seemed to seek child-centered nodules of urbanism that provided what Giddens (1991) and Saunders (1985) call "ontological security," the sense of feeling at ease or at home in a world that can appear externally threatening. This resonated with the Ipanema residents, who viewed certain unexpected interruptions in their routine—for instance, hearing a passerby speaking a language other than Portuguese—as a positive spatial self-reference and evidence of living in a space that was cosmopolitan and global. While some kinds of experiences were valued over a mundane routine, however, others distorted elite parents' sense of territorial control and personal agency, threatening their class, racial, and residential privilege.

A language of corruption provided the template on which El Condado and Ipanema residents justified their own community vigilante practices of exclusion and surveillance. In October 2018, for instance, El Condado residents escalated their surveillance efforts by hiring private security companies, installing more surveillance cameras, establishing radio communication across area hotels (paid by the Puerto Rican Tourism Company), and setting up security networks that would send security alerts across El Condado condominiums. In a conference held at Parque del Indio, one of El Condado's most popular playgrounds, Puerto Rico's governor responded to area residents' demand for "immediate action by the authorities" (Figueroa 2018) by doubling police presence and investing federal funds into the area's infrastructure and illumination. This commitment of public resources occurred at a time when tens of thousands of Puerto Ricans still lived under FEMA's blue tarps, major intersections lacked working traffic lights, and electricity across the island was erratic at best. A language of corruption shaped how El Condado residents positioned themselves as bastions of moral qualities (e.g., self-reliance) in the face of government inadequacy and national crisis. As the spokesperson for the ARCC stated, "We are not politicians. We do not have an agenda. We will assign an El Condado community leader to each government agency, to hold them accountable on what they have promised today. But if the government is not actively resolving the issue of crime over the next two weeks, we are prepared to take this into our own hands. We're already considering proposals from fourteen private security agencies, many consisting of retired police officers or police officers working in their spare time. We want them to be armed, and to know our community well."

While affluent suburban neighborhoods and gated communities were constitutive outsiders that embodied an amoral materiality, the gentrifying area adjacent to El Condado and Miramar—particularly Calle Loíza's urban entrepreneurship and Calle Cerra's artistic initiatives—contributed to a discourse of Puerto Rican nationalist "self-sufficiency" and "creativity" that directly challenged perspectives of Puerto Ricans as dependent on *el mantengo* (welfare). El mantengo has a long genealogy in Puerto Rico, which could be traced back to US policy and social scientific notions of the "culture of poverty" (Lewis 1966). The view that Puerto Ricans—the poor and dark, both on the island and in US inner cities—are "lazy" and lack initiative or an entrepreneurial spirit associated with European and even other Latin American migrant groups has constituted the core of Puerto Rican racialization on the island and in the United States alike (Briggs 2002). The projects in Calle Loíza and Calle Cerra were important to how El Condado and Miramar residents perceived themselves, their neighborhoods, and even Puerto Rican society and the national fiscal crisis more broadly.

As Grewal noticed in the United States, the project of state security "sutured parental concerns about family security to government concerns about state security, incorporating parents—and mothers in particular—into the security state" (2017, 123). Everyday practices of parenting and sovereignty in wealthy Latin American and Caribbean neighborhoods further contributed to a focus on securing the family from multiple social, economic, racial, and regional threats. Securing the family naturalizes state-sanctioned security as intrinsic to normative perspectives on family, whiteness, and parenting in elite neighborhoods.

Mapping Affluence and Parenting Ethnographic Sites

After Alejandra Rodríguez Emma showed me her new house, we drove to Kasalta, a popular bakery just outside Calle Loíza's official Calle Taft dividing line. We were going to meet a couple whose child attended St. John's School and who had been friends of Enrique Alemañi, Alejandra's husband, since their high school years at St. John's.

Kasalta could be considered a "child-centered nodule of urbanism" (chapter 1).[23] During the time of my fieldwork, Kasalta was where St. John's School parents would meet after drop-off or before pick-up, where school parent committees convened, and where El Condado parents would get together to share information and anxieties, as well as to plan various events on a more or less consistent basis. The Spanish-founded bakery, with its predominantly Afro-Dominican workforce and Cuban management, was frequently crowded with streams of people ordering to go, along with others engaging in lengthy *tertulias* (salons) at the long tables with gyrating stools. Kasalta acquired almost-landmark status when Puerto Rico's former governor Alejandro García Padilla chose the spot to have lunch with President Obama during his visit to the island; the lunch led to the placement of a plaque on the very table where they sat to commemorate the occasion and even a sandwich named after the popular US president. Like Café Paz e Amor in Ipanema, Kasalta was viewed as a place "where all social classes mix," as Alejandra and other parents claimed. While Ipanema's Café Paz e Amor had two differently priced menus—one for the Ipanema elite, and the other for the taxi drivers who stopped there for lunch—Kasalta had just one menu, where a medianoche and a caldo gallego could cost twenty dollars, hardly accessible to all the social classes presumed to "mix" there.

Whenever I did not meet with parents at their homes, offices, school activities, or special family events, the default meeting place was either Kasalta or a handful of other smaller cafés. In fact, after a while, whenever I wanted relative privacy to write up fieldnotes, I would avoid Kasalta because it was almost a given that I would run into one or several of the parents in my sample. Opportunities for casual interactions afforded through such local features as Kasalta contributed to perceptions of inclusion and a sense of community among the El Condado parents in my ethnography. Forms of upper-class white elite sociability became practiced, naturalized, and reproduced in spaces like Kasalta, where the servers, managers, and patrons reflected social and racial hierarchies that the parents in my sample seldom questioned. In Kasalta, upper-class parents felt secure in their progressive whiteness.

When Alejandra and I arrived at Kasalta that morning, Raquel Cohen and Carlos Varela were finishing up a meeting with other St. John's parents, who also belonged to a school committee. These parents had almost wrapped up the meeting and were heading out to run various errands. They were off to Plaza Las Americas shopping mall to get sandals and heading home to finish packing for a skiing trip to Vermont.

MOTHER #1: I just worry about fractures, though the kids wear helmets. I see so many fractures at the hospital [where she is a physician] that I feel panic. I remember during my high school years, a friend of mine who was a senior in San Ignacio [elite boys' school] had a severe fracture from skiing. What I like is the little towns surrounding skiing areas.[24]

FATHER: It was in Vermont that I first got to see that type of snow that Robert Frost describes in his poems. Because those poems have no meaning here in Puerto Rico, but when we saw the Vermont snow, we bought a sled and went down the hills of the cabin where we were staying. And, while we were going down the hill, the kids and I would say "Robert, Robert!" invoking Robert Frost's spirit.

MOTHER #2: Yes, those little New England towns are stunning. And the houses remind you of another era. They have the chimneys and breakfast nooks that are so charming. The ones in Austria are beautiful too. Actually, the von Trapp grandchildren or great-grandchildren have a hotel there.

FATHER: Boricuas in the snow! [laughter]

I transcribed this conversation because it was emblematic of the seemingly casual exchanges that characterized child-centered nodules of urbanism. In

FIGURE 3.3. Weekday morning in Kasalta Bakery, one of the sites I identify as a "child-centered urban nodule," where parenting sociabilities are cultivated and information circulated. Photo by Thomas Abraham

principle, the exchange was unremarkable; a group of volunteer parents were engaging in small talk after finishing a school committee meeting. Yet, I did feel that among El Condado and Ipanema elites, for whom coming across as personas sencillas or despojadas carried considerable social capital, learning the right level of self and family disclosure could make or break social networks; nobody wanted to be considered comemierda or *arrumada* (snobbish). Yet much was conveyed in seemingly casual exchange, as one learns about a mother's professional identity as a physician, a father's sensibility to poetry conferred by a liberal arts education, and an overall global outlook deployed through a distinctly Caribbean elite's gaze of Norman Rockwell's New England and von Trapp's Austria. Mentioning skiing in New England and Austria may perhaps come across as snobbish, given the association in the Caribbean between skiing and elite status. However, this exchange was tempered by passing comments about a delightful experience at a hole-in-the-wall eatery (*friquitín*) in the mountain town of Guavate and a favorite food hut in the coastal town of Fajardo. In these numerous references to US and European towns, places, and restaurants, there was still an inscription of Puerto Ricanness, rather than an unproblematic cosmopolitan aspiration. "Boricuas in the snow" indeed.

Raquel, Carlos, Alejandra, and I stayed a while longer after the other parents left Kasalta. Raquel and Carlos were the parents of an elementary school student at St. John's and lived in El Condado, a few blocks down from Raquel's Jewish parents. With several Ivy League degrees between them, in fields related to philanthropy, law, and business, Raquel and Carlos had launched various educational consulting projects, backed up by Raquel's hefty trust fund. They also automatically assumed the role of consultants to my research project and gave frequent feedback about how to put together a representative sample of parents and where to go to "do observations." On this day in Kasalta, Carlos reached out for his ebony Montblanc and drew a map on a paper napkin to show me how to study parenting in El Condado.

He first identified the three area private schools. "In El Condado, you have St .John's, Robinson is more for special ed situations, and Perpetuo in Miramar," he noted as he drew squares representing each school. As he drew squares and connected lines among the spaces he was describing, Carlos noted, "Most of the activities really happen around the schools. Sometimes, also around soccer—you have Parque Barbosa in Ocean Park. There you have a few kids from St. John's, but also from Lloréns [colloquial name for Lloréns Torres, the nearby housing project] and other so-so private schools, like La Piedad and San Jorge; the soccer group near Parque Central is all top school membership." Carlos continued to draw and remarked, "There are some kid things happening in Guaynabo. I had never in my life gone to Guaynabo as often as I do now that I have a kid, for birthday parties and kid play areas." He also wrote "VSJ" (for Viejo San Juan) to the right of the rectangle that demarcated El Condado on the west and wrote "OP" (for Ocean Park) to the east. "You have the lagoon, where families go kayaking or jogging. And the coast here, but this area doesn't have the best beach. You see a lot of kids, on weekends, by the Ventana area. It has the Ben & Jerry right there, the shallow-water beach, or the park in front of Stella Maris [Church] or the Parque del Indio." He concluded, "And then, you have Kasalta right here. If you want to know what's going on, about parenting and about anything, politics, not just school stuff, this is where you come." He drew an X—a form of "You are here"—and, satisfied with his map, he handed me the napkin.

Raquel and Alejandra agreed with Carlos's graphic display of parenting in El Condado, but Raquel reminded everyone, "Well, you have to remember that you also have Calle Loíza right here in the back. That area now has lots of nice small businesses. It was not like it used to be, when you had to raise your win-

Parenting El Condado 93

dows when you were in that area." Alejandra agreed: "In fact, I met up with some of the classroom moms from Perpetuo in a Mexican place that was excellent, authentic Mexican food, not like those pseudo-Mexican joints that are all nachos and cheese." Carlos added, "Yes, the same is happening around Calle Cerra, with the murals, the Departamento de la Comida [healthy food place], Santurce es Ley."

At the end of our get together, Carlos texted me some contact information for El Condado parents whom he thought I should meet, and I noticed that I already had several of those names on a list that another mom had given me. "That is the thing about this Condado area," Carlos remarked. "If Puerto Rico is a handkerchief, El Condado is a Kleenex. Everybody knows each other!"

The scales that become relevant in the process of tracing the politics of parenting in affluent neighborhoods cannot really be understood in terms of concentric circles, where the nation, the city, the neighborhood, and spaces within the neighborhood exist in descending importance. Rather, these spaces expanded and contracted, sometimes in unexpected ways, when it came to parenting and child-centered nodules of urbanism. While these spaces, with the urbanistic, historical, social particularities and structures of feeling, had specific physical referents, none of them was circumscribed to the material; these were spaces of practice and training, in which sociabilities, personhood, and cultivations of self and interiorities were experimented with, challenged, and reinforced, as I discuss in the next chapter.

4

Whiteness from Within

I've been on an inward journey for a while. . . . Halfway through this process, I met Katia Coutinho, a life coach by training. What began as professional coaching became a much deeper process of self-understanding. Katia helped me establish goals based on what I knew about myself, to get to know my values, the beliefs that were limiting me, how I was sabotaging myself and, ultimately, my life's purpose. I wanted to give [my son] a better world, I needed to begin from the inside out.—Luciana Ribeiro Oliva, lawyer, Ipanema resident

In India, I experienced a spiritual awakening, a sense of clarity about how fatherhood was also about personal growth. I realized that I was not only ready for it, but craving it. Going to India, experiencing the Mani Mahesh Yatra in the Himalayas, was life altering. It wasn't just a touristic, you know, vacation. I began to move away from religion and toward spirituality, a profound desire for simplicity, a more austere life. As soon as I returned from India, I told Evelyn "Let's start trying [to conceive]." From the moment the belly started growing, I began to read, became more concerned with security, safety, and also economic security, saving, being very fiscally responsible.—Omar Tartak, educational consultant, El Condado resident

In addition to working one-on-one with life coach Katia Coutinho, Luciana Ribeiro Oliva had become a member of a transnational group of Brazilian women, living in Lisbon, London, São Paulo, and Rio. A lawyer mother of two and Ipanema resident, Luciana connected virtually with this other transnational network of Brazilian women a few times a month to discuss their personal, professional, and civic goals and be accountable to one another. "We are citizens of the world, and tomorrow we could be in any other place, but we'll still stay in contact! We'll continue to be grateful for the opportunity to grow and evolve," Katia mentioned once, in a conversation we were having through WhatsApp. As Luciana explained once over coffee in her Ipanema apartment, "We wanted to identify a life purpose and gain greater insight and depth, self-knowledge, because it is quite difficult to go against the great tendency, particularly among Brazilians, toward materialism, consumerism, and being superficial."

Medium height, stocky, and in his mid-forties, Omar Tartak was an executive in the field of educational consulting in Puerto Rico, and he was frequently considered one of the most involved, "hands-on" parents in his social network of other El Condado parents. Given his personal interest in all things parenting, I was surprised to hear about Omar's hesitation to have children, which had almost cost him his relationship with Evelyn, his wife. "I just didn't want to have kids, because I knew that having children would alter the possibility to be socially involved, to be a global citizen," Omar explained. A few years into the marriage, Evelyn and Omar faced an impasse about having children. They went to a couples counselor who, according to Omar, told him: "Omar, you are always telling us about your amazing experiences of global service [having volunteered and worked in various cities of Asia, South America, and the United States], and your interest in leaving a mark in the world. Wouldn't you want to give that experience to a child?" The therapist's remarks, as well as devouring an impressive number of popular psychology and Eastern spirituality books, made a dent in Omar's hesitation. As anthropologist Edgar Rivera Colón remarked in relation to US elites, there is a paradoxical, performative contradiction in that individuals go outside the Western sense of self—their dominant quotidian ethnophilosophy—to go profoundly inside. To put a Lacanian neologism to a very different purpose, Rivera Colón highlights "extimacy," the ecstatic externality of intimacy, as central to how these elites' yogic disciplines become empirical evidence of what could be described as intimate and interior (personal conversation, February 9, 2019; cf. Lacan 1997). It wasn't until the "spiritual awakening" Omar experienced in India that he decided to make the leap into parenthood.

Among middle and upper classes throughout the world, Luciana's and Omar's remarks would be fairly ordinary. Concepts like "self-knowledge," "spiritual growth," "emotional intelligence," and "self-esteem" have entered popular culture, as they loosen from their sociological and scientific moorings to become entrepreneurial objects of educators, parenting experts, pop psychology, and life coaches, like Katia Coutinho. At a time when Eastern philosophy is intertwined with the fitness routines of yoga and meditation in gyms around the world, we have come to view these products of self-fashioning as conceptual resources for entire cultures (Callero 2003; Hewitt 1998). In an everyday experience of neoliberalism, the individual, the couple, parenting, and the family are believed to require deliberate kinds of nurturing and engagement, including services in the marketplace and service workers who free up both time and emotional energy for parents to invest in themselves. "Self-knowledge"—and other iterations suggesting inner searching, like "life's purpose" or "personal growth"—have become projects intrinsic to skill development in an era when "emotional intelligence" is a requirement in job descriptions. Self-knowledge, in Luciana's usage, was a named emotion or mood that had been elaborated with diverse cultural meanings and aspirational qualities, in terms of not only Luciana's life but also her parenting practices and civic engagement in Ipanema and beyond. As in Omar Tartak's case, members of Ipanema and El Condado upper classes frequently situated the self in cultural and historical origins that deployed Orientalist interpretive lenses.[1]

The influence of popular psychology—a term I use loosely in reference to media-circulated psychological language and practices that are promoted partly by multimillion-dollar global industries—has a long, well-documented genealogy in the United States. In Latin America, however, popular psychology has not been a subject of adequate academic inquiry.[2] In the cases of Brazil and Puerto Rico, ethnographic examinations of personhood, the self, and inner worlds have focused, for the most part, on the study of traditional European religions and beliefs (like Catholicism and evangelical churches, as well as Judaism, Islam, and Kandercismo or espiritismo); the ubiquity of African belief systems (like Umbanda, or Candomblé, in Brazil, and Santería in Puerto Rico); the role of "community psychology" in grassroots initiatives for and by the poor (e.g., liberation psychology, liberation pedagogy); and historical examinations of South American psychoanalytic traditions or Caribbean-focused psychological pathology rooted in culture of poverty perspectives.[3] In the late 1970s in Puerto Rico and about a decade later in Brazil, the period when most of my interlocutors were coming of age, there was a remarkable increase in media documentation of New Age trends, including the sales of esoteric books and a network of shops, seminars, therapeutic clinics, and even consulting groups (Rocha 2006). These white, intellectualized upper-middle classes viewed the benefits of trends in meditation, Buddhism, yoga, and other combinations of practices they associated with an exotic "Orient" as indispensable for cultivating inner peace, tranquility, and balance in urban and political environments they associated with violence, corruption, and instability.

Like their European and American counterparts, the Latin American upper classes at the center of *Parenting Empires* were invested in a cultivation of "inner selves" that required self-help manuals, life coaches, personal trainers, spiritual tourism, psychological and religious counselors and others, and that connected them, at least in theory, to other cosmopolitan populations around the globe.[4] More precisely, though, the Ipanema and El Condado upper classes viewed inner-self cultivation in terms of the search for an ethics and wisdom of privilege. They struggled to view their wealth and racial privilege in terms of localized leadership in a national context, which they considered inherently corrupt. This interiority focus represented a moral approach to one's person-hood and an ethical way of existing as a privileged wealthy person. Such self-orientations were invested with claims to one's ability (and even responsibility) to heal social inequality and environmental pollution, as well as handling com-petitiveness and anxiety around the socialization of children.

Viewing these trends as Euro-American impositions would not accurately describe how the parents I met in Puerto Rico and Brazil cultivated inner worlds and fashioned the self, or how interiority currency became an impor-tant form of class and racial positionality in the field of parenting. Rather, I develop "interiority currency" in this chapter as an analytic term through which to consider the possibility that some of my interlocutors in fact har-bored a sincere belief in their own capacity for personal and even spiritual development, and that this belief was related to a general distrust of national governments. To this goal, I highlight the use of "currency," instead of Pierre Bourdieu's classic conception of "capital" in my analysis. Rather than reiterat-ing Bourdieu's assumption that social action is always already oriented toward accumulating capital or advantages of different forms, I focus on how an inner-world orientation was irrevocably connected to evolving relations to class and racial inequalities and forms of positioning oneself vis-à-vis perspectives on austerity and corruption.

A range of therapists, including couples counseling; psychotherapy; home-opathy; personal exercise training; and spiritual guidance, along with mind/body integrative services (e.g., yoga and Buddhist meditation) were just a sam-pling of how Ipanema and El Condado upper-class parents cultivated forms of psychological cosmopolitanism, not just the bodily aesthetics for which in-dividuals "in the tropics" have been stereotyped. These forms of psychological cosmopolitanism were often amorphous references to body care, therapeutic self-awareness, Oriental(ist) spirituality, global outlook, contentment, life bal-ance, and even a liberal social learning (largely unrelated to electoral politics).[5] Rather than evaluating projects or entrepreneurial initiatives involving popular psychology or wellness industries, my intention here is to examine individuals' cultivation of their inner worlds and the social and material conditions that those personal journeys in fact produce in the Global South. While surely having children is not a precondition for such personal journeys—and it could be a deterrent if one did not have disposable time and income—Ipanema and El Condado interlocutors expressed that these journeys were core aspects of their parenting; in fact, this cultivation of interiority currency was, as many noted, what rendered them different from other equally wealthy individuals in their own countries. Central to processes of parenting empires, these projects produced a unique kind of enlightened subject, which, as I demonstrate in this chapter, was white and wealthy, and which reproduced Latin American and Caribbean forms of whiteness.[6]

In the first section of the chapter, I demonstrate how a common elite tendency to psychologize the social (and to sociologize the psychological) manifested as a search for afinidade in Ipanema and for becoming personas sencillas in El Condado. In the second section, I examine how Ipanema and El Condado upper classes shifted the sociological field from the material to the metaphysical, altered local moral economies, and granted legitimacy to increasingly widening racial and class inequalities. In this chapter, I show how these transformations happen in several ways, including by attributing certain therapeutic and healing qualities to a natural (whitened) landscape; deploying Orientalist narratives and genealogies; presenting an evolved masculinity as evidence of gender equality; and situating capitalist accumulation in a language of "miracles" and "manifesting." I conclude with a discussion of how an abject language of material superficiality is ultimately a way of rendering racialized and classed others as less complex, evolved, and self-aware, while sustaining racial and class privilege in the moving-target terrain of the metaphysical.

Elite Interiorities: Privileged Selves, Afinidade, and Personas Sencillas

The salience of psychological language and the overall confessional quality of conversations among parents in Ipanema and El Condado was undeniable. A question about one's program of study in college would lead to a dissertation on self-actualization, trauma in one's family of origin, strategies to deal with the body's biochemistry, and verbatim scripts of sessions with one's psychoanalyst. Initially, I assumed that perhaps interlocutors sensed a similarity between clinical therapy and ethnographic interviewing, or that, in Ipanema at least, this was a spillover of a South American psychoanalytical tradition. The tone, themes, and flow of the conversations, however, remained consistent in contexts that did not involve direct one-on-one interviewing; more significantly, there was a continuous aspiration toward depth and complexity that at times provided structures of control and ease in social interactions.

Luciana Ribeiro Oliva, an Ipanema resident in her forties, had occupied various governmental and corporate positions in the field of law. A tall, elegant white Brazilian woman, Luciana was married to Marcelo Safra Caldeira, a prominent Ipanema physician, and the couple had three children. Luciana's wit and cynical humor were tempered by her sense of agency, optimism, and curiosity about a range of topics, particularly in the fields of psychology and education.

On one of the brisk morning walks she and I would frequently take together on the beachfront sidewalk alongside Avenida Vieira Souto, Luciana recalled, "In the middle of my [postpartum] depression, I felt a very strong intuition, an internal voice urging me to 'Go and walk, go and move.'" Luciana had begun taking these daily walks after the birth of her first child, almost two decades prior. As our sneakers stepped on the gray and white stone of the *calçada,* a trademark of Zona Sul neighborhoods, Luciana described the routine with reverence: "This is my pilgrimage, my Santiago de Compostela. I bring a mental drawer, open it, and begin to take things out. I try to make my load lighter. . . . Early on, I realized how walking to Posto 12 and back, sitting under the sun rays and drinking agua de coco would, little by little, make me feel lighter, from the inside out." Sometimes, Luciana would complement her morning walks with Ayurveda treatments, restorative yoga, or Buddhist meditation. Like a few other parents I met in Ipanema, Luciana also followed the espirita teachings of Allen Kardec (Kardecismo) and its various Brazilian versions, like that of Chico Xavier.[7] As part of her "postpartum healing," she participated in various informal parenting groups, which eventually led to IpaBebê (chapter 2).

When I would ask Luciana what she felt she had in common with her parent-friends, she would not think twice: "We have an afinidade, a desire to raise children who are compassionate, who care for the environment, kids who are emotionally and socially intelligent, and feel connected to the world, not to the iPad or the TV. We reject those forms of consumption, brands, and how those disintegrate the social fabric." Over the years of talking with upper-class Ipanema parents, I had become aware of the general resistance to bring conversations to the realm of the social, in favor of more philosophical or abstract discussions, so I would often press on. "What else do you think you may have in common, in terms of your background?" I asked. And the predictable resistance became embedded in the response: "To us, background doesn't matter. Where you live doesn't matter. We never ask about a person's background [*a gente nunca perguntou qual era a origem*]. Our kids [*os garotos*] would hang out together at the beach, and it was really people from Cantagalo [Ipanema favela] together with people from Vieira Souto [most affluent Ipanema area]. We shared the same language [*a linguagem é a mesma*], that afinidade."

Afinidade was a curious concept, because it operated to enable, at least in theory, the possibility that one could share interests with a socially diverse group of people, who might not, in fact, be white or upper class; however unlikely that possibility was, it was enabled by the assumption of democratic public spaces in the neighborhood, particularly the beach. Rather than claiming sameness, afinidade was conceived as an emotional and affective disposition toward the same values, including the value of "diversity," which in fact benefited the construction and strengthening of white privilege.

On another occasion, this time surrounded by floor-to-ceiling statues and artwork by renowned Brazilian artists, and overlooking the imposing Zona Sul beachfront from her large terrace, Luciana recalled her own experience of becoming a mother. Motherhood marked the first time she noticed the strength of that afinidade. "Not everyone who becomes a parent has the same resources, and I don't mean material resources, I mean internal," she mentioned in relation to a conversation about Matilde, the daughter of Angelina, one of Luciana's *empregadas* (domestic workers), who was pregnant by an abusive man. She continued:

> You know what a friend of mine who is a psychoanalyst told me when I was first pregnant? [She said] "One becomes a mother before even getting pregnant." Part of that is doing all the internal work to extrapolate yourself from relationships that are abusive. And once the child is born, this continues when you seek new relationships among people who share these perspectives [*pessoas de mentalidade semelhante*], who view child rearing as an intimate process of becoming a citizen of your community, not of trying to get your child to love you by buying him stuff. Do you know what Angelina's first reaction was when she knew Matilde was having a boy? What kinds of toys he would like! This is someone who, in a few years, will be spending her full salary to get a Nintendo. Even my wealthy friends, who could easily afford ten Nintendos, would not think that way.

When intimate relations unfolded in deeply sociologically unequal national contexts, as in Brazil and Puerto Rico, many upper-class parents deployed psychological or therapeutic interpretive languages to assess affinity. On one side of this affinity assessment are Matilde and Angelina, whose forms of mothering were suspect because of their unwillingness to "do the work" to end an abusive relationship and for embracing a frivolous, consumption-driven attitude. On the other side of this assessment are Luciana and those with whom she has a parental affinity. These were individuals who had stable relationships; did considerable "inner work" prior to conception, during pregnancy, and after birth; and who rejected conspicuous consumption in favor of viewing child rearing as an intimate process of raising citizen-subjects. While relationships between domestic workers and parents are the topic of chapter 7, it is important to highlight that perspectives on afinidade and the anticonsumption assumptions behind them (regardless of actual rejection of consumption in practice) reframed subordinate-superordinate class and racial dynamics, and coded these dynamics as the outcome of who is perceived to do "inner work" and who is not.

The focus on "common values" and "like-mindedness" was sedimented on a process of pursuing a labored form of wellness. When I raised the issue of her postpartum depression, and the way in which, regardless of how much preparation goes into parenting, challenges do arise, Luciana once again suggested that any challenge could be resolved through "non-material" inner work. In fact, material privilege could even contribute to one's inability to attain well-being, she insisted:

> Right after the birth of my first child, a friend of mine who does corporal readings noticed that I wasn't doing well. She wanted to help me, but I was too trapped [*muito presa*]. My friend tried to talk to me, to get me out of the apartment [crying]. She would tell me, "You're too young to look as old as you do, to be trapped by these four walls." That's when I met a Japanese doctor, of Japanese descent, who began taking care of me. I began doing shiatsu, acupuncture, meditation. My body had somatized [*somatizou*] all the unhappiness I was feeling, the heaviness. [What did you find most difficult about that time?] I had an existentialist crisis as a woman, as a human being. My child brought happiness to everyone, but I couldn't fully feel that happiness. I remember once my husband told me, "I just wanted to respect your detachment, your distance." But truthfully, what I wanted was not detachment. I wanted him to understand my internal turmoil.

Luciana's luxurious magazine-featured apartment was presented as a prison cell from which her more *atenada* (enlightened) friend had to rescue her. The intermingling of alternative medicine, therapeutic culture, and Orientalist perspectives on interiority, evident in Luciana's narrative, was so pervasive that it was often difficult to disentangle the methods, practitioners, dogmas, and rituals.

These practices and their associated affective dimensions, however, were also tied to a neoliberal cultural economy of flexibility and a changing social order; as Carla Freeman rightfully notices, "They reflect a new ethos of living, working, partnering, parenting, and self-definition that for many also bear unmistakable spiritual elements" (2014, 201, 203).

In El Condado, most parents also sought "affinity" in their relationships with other parents, but this was not as ubiquitous in their articulations of inner quests. Rather, virtually every single El Condado interlocutor highlighted one common quality they strove for: the imperative to be, and be surrounded by, personas sencillas (down-to-earth people). Persona sencilla was an invocation of someone who, despite having the wealth and material resources to justify pretentiousness, was unassuming, modest, and colloquial (e.g., a lack of affectation, using popular language and phrases that were below the linguistic level they had access to). Interestingly, as I show in chapter 7, nannies and domestic workers also associated persona sencillas with good employers and with great wealth. To be a persona sencilla, a tacit aspirational quality, one had to first be known to belong to the upper classes, because being a persona sencilla needed to be clearly a choice, not a lack of options due to material constraints. Persona sencilla was different from *persona humilde*, the latter usually used in reference to being humble due to unfavorable economic circumstances. Each carried, almost by definition, different moral currency; being a persona humilde is a class and status attribute, whereas being a persona sencilla was an active way of being available to individuals who had the choice of being pompous but chose instead to be self-contained or demure. Personas sencilla thus carried a level of interiority currency that the (working-class, dark-skin) personas humildes did not have access to.

During my first visit with Liliana González Padín, an El Condado parent whom most others considered a persona sencilla, I was more clearly able to pinpoint what it was about the upper-class parents, in both Ipanema and El Condado, that made interactions so affectively peculiar and the spaces they occupied so harmonious and ambience-conscious. Liliana had completed several graduate degrees in fine arts, photography, and interior design before having two children with her husband, Raúl Bustillo, a physician in private practice with his father and brother.

I was dealing with mild anxiety over parking my rental car and not knowing if parking in the cul-de-sac near Liliana's weekend home in Dorado was legal. As I was debating the parking situation with myself, Liliana opened her heavy, rustic entrance door. Wearing loose white linen pants, a flowy lavender tunica, and strappy leather sandals, she joyfully greeted me: "Welcome,

welcome." She exuded a calmness and comfort in her own skin that I had come to expect from upper-class women and most men. "Maybe we can sit in the terrace. It's breezier there," she jovially suggested as we headed through the large living room to an outdoor terrace that led to a beautifully land-scaped patio. "Is it okay if I leave the car parked there? I'm just noticing that the security guard has come around the cul-de-sac twice, and I'm not sure if maybe I didn't park in a good spot . . . or?" I explained, concerned that the guards would think my silver Kia rental was a stolen car, tow it, and leave me stranded in Dorado Beach. "That is not a problem at all," she steadily assured me, putting me at complete ease, confident that my car would be there when I came out, and even if it weren't there, it would still not be a problem. She gave clear, mild-mannered directions to whom I imagine was the cleaning lady in the kitchen, as we sat on plush terrace furniture. The term *cuidarse* (to take care of oneself), which appeared in a range of Puerto Rican registries, from fitness, food quality, medical care, and general personal upkeep to a he-gemonic integration with one's surroundings and sense of well-being, applied to Liliana perfectly.

Liliana conveyed, almost embodied, the El Condado definition of persona sencilla, a down-to-earthness, at least if the Earth were full of calmness and zen. Her warmth and containment, while ubiquitous, could not be attributed to any one isolated trait or unique aspect of her temperament; in fact, describing her is helpful in conveying what I found to be a cultivated spiritual demeanor, confident diplomacy, and emotive disposition that constituted a certain form of elite affect.[8]

A question that my colleague Ulla Berg and I asked in our article on racial-ized affect (2015) was, How much psychologizing, how much extrapolation from the individual could we impose on a group, as we aim to examine the po-litical economic context? This has been a difficult question for anthropologists interested in examining affect empirically, as the fear of generalizing and the limitations of translating intangibles onto ethnographic writing always linger. With this concern in mind, I still couldn't help casting an impression of the collective when a certain "epiphany" emerged from moments of self-conscious interaction with both Ipanema and El Condado elites.

Like Liliana, most upper-class parents came across as fully comfortable in their own skin, diplomatic in their opinions, but without sounding wishy-washy; they clearly had a well-thought-out opinion but made sure you under-stood that they were open to other interpretations and valued all opinions equally, at least as long as those opinions came from someone they esteem at some level. Perhaps what highlighted this wealthy down-to-earthness in personas sencillas like Liliana was the physical context in which it was executed. Personas sencillas generally expressed their down-to-earthness in contexts of affluence and in relationships with inanimate objects and curated spaces—"spectacular yet tasteful" wedding rings, home décor, well-chosen paintings, sculptures, and photographs, the ability to wear not only high couture but, more importantly, casual clothing as couture, to name a few. These parents were perfect hosts, immediately calming and dictating the affective emotive energy and tone of the interaction without missing a cue or coming across as manipulative or overbearing. Formations of an interiority currency and images of personas sencillas as the social manifestation of that affect were instrumental to how class and racial privilege acquired legitimacy in a political moment when sovereignty and austerity viewed wealth and political influence with suspicion. Attunement to ambience and an embodied ease were foundational to this elite affect and the psychological cosmopolitanism to which Ipanema and El Condado upper classes aspired. As Talal Asad (2009) shows, one of the central elements of contemporary spirituality is the gradual incorporation of values such as happiness, well-being, and personal growth, and the demotion of the spiritual role of suffering. It was really hard, even for a hyperattuned social scientist, to identify any old-school snob.

In "Interior Horizon: An Ethical Space of Selfhood in South India," Anand Pandian notes, "Such reflection depended upon an imagination of one's own heart and mind as a landscape of moral choice, as an interior space that could be occupied and navigated in the same way that one might pick one's way through a rural landscape of many paths" (2010, 65). A strong desire for a newly imagined intimacy, self-understanding, and new ways of feeling and expressing emotion figured throughout my interlocutors' testimonies, frequently trumping their own sociological insights and observations. At times this dictated how local boundaries and forms of inclusion operated, as noticed by Beatriz Pissollo Itamar, a photojournalist from São Paulo who had lived in Rio de Janeiro for more than a decade and was the single mother of a son.

For many other Ipanema parents, Beatriz came across as "too negative" and "prone to worry"; they attributed Beatriz's "glass half-empty" perspective to being from somber, conservative São Paulo. While Beatriz was not necessarily an outcast, she knew that other Ipanema parents had difficulty reading her: "Have you heard that saying about the Corcovado having opened, welcoming arms, but never closing them to embrace you? That's the carioca way. Here people tell you 'Go to the beach, have an agua de coco and let the problems dissolve!' They can't deal with somebody else's dark spaces." When I mentioned the almost excessive willingness, even eagerness, of each person I knew in Ipanema to explicitly, in detail, lay out the machinations of their psychological self, including dark spaces, Beatriz clarified: "Oh yes, definitely, people here psychoanalyze themselves and each other ad nauseam. They really put themselves out there [*se expõe muito*]. They describe their therapy sessions almost minute by minute. This gives you a false sense of closeness. You can tell this is not a form of intimacy because they do the same psychoanalysis of politicians, and the condition of the country. What does that even mean?" I tried to push a bit to see how she wrapped her thinking around the simultaneously superficial forms of intimacy and the great psychological awareness that individuals seemed to have about one another's histories. She then noted, "There is an Ipanema 'No,' which means that people see each other in the beach or run into one another and are like 'Yes, yes, we need to meet! We'll have a coffee! We'll go here and there. Beijo, beijo, querida!' But they know, and you should too, that that will never happen. It is a way of saying no without compromising carioca politeness, avoiding confrontation."[9]

Janelle Taylor (2005) proposes the notion of "surfacing the body interior" as a frame to facilitate ethnographic explorations into bodies, their interiors, and their surfaces as contingent configurations made and unmade through practices that are at once social, material, and representational. The term "surfacing" can mean giving something a surface (as in surfacing the road), but it can also mean coming to the surface or bringing something to the surface. Embracing all these meanings, surfacing the body interior points toward the range of practices and processes that materialize bodily surfaces as significant sites within broader orders as well as that which lies hidden beneath them. A focus on surfacing the body interior may help us situate bodies in relation to broader orders without presuming artificially to fix their parameters in advance, if we take it as a means to explore the materializing practices out of which bodies, publics, sciences, and economies are precipitated. I now examine the social value of the "intimate superficiality" Beatriz described, and how notions of Ipanema's afinidade and El Condado's personas sencillas contributed to the production of a social context that was heavily psychologized, an important characteristic of how racialized affect acquired materiality among white Latin American elites. These inner-world aesthetics in fact created an ambience, a rhythm, and a tone in social encounters that I came to view as critical to the production of Latin American and Caribbean whiteness, everyday forms of sovereignty, and the configuration of a moral economy of austerity in the image of personas sencillas in El Condado and evaluations of afinidade in Ipanema. Interiority currencies positioned neighborhood social, racial, and ethical registers on metaphysical planes that were in alignment with national calls for austerity and self-regulation.

The Psychologizing of the Social

Parenting has become a genealogy of personhood, the production of a kind of social self to be learned and monitored, as well as an affective lens through which to read and filter broader political economic conditions and urban expectations and imaginaries. In a context of economic crisis and austerity politics, anxiety was often evident in parenting narratives of future goals and aspirations. These anxieties, however, were also indicative of how privilege in Ipanema and El Condado was recast; the interlocutors in this ethnography had managed a sincere balance between striving to embody privilege in an ethical or a moral way, while still assessing tilting points in social and racial hierarchies that could affect them and their children. This was done in a perhaps counterintuitive way, considering the long associations between modernity, consumption, and status in Latin America (O'Dougherty 2002). Ipanema and El Condado elites aimed to morally qualify their wealth in terms of their "hard work," not in the labor market but as measured by their interiority currency. Such interiority currency was uncoupled from forms of material wealth, even though it was clear that material wealth largely enabled it in the first place. I consider three ways in which interiority currency and valorization of affinity, down-to-earthness, and metaphysical aspirations acquired specific social, economic, and racial currency in Ipanema and El Condado: (1) the development of personal "depth," usually through Orientalist spiritual appropriations; (2) the crafting of new masculinities and perspectives on gender equality; (3) and a recasting of corporate and capitalist projects as "miracles."

LATIN AMERICAN ORIENTALISM

My husband—or rather, the mere mention of my husband's national background—attracted a lot of attention. Questions and conversations that led to the revelation that he had been born and raised in India attracted such attention in Brazil and Puerto Rico. A weekend in mid-August 2013, at a Father's Day event at the Ipanema crèche our son, then three years old, was attending, my husband, Tom, met Hugo de Carvalho Ribeiro, the father of a girl in Sebastián's group. When Hugo realized Tom was from India, he immediately responded in British-accented English: "I thought you were Brazilian! Brazilians and Indians, we have a great affinity; we have a lot in common." He enthusiastically went on to explain that he had many Indian friends from his days working in London, as well as his attachment to "Indian culture" and Buddhism.

Semán and Viotti (2015) argue that while Orientalism in Latin America can be traced to the European elites of the nineteenth century, current New Age spirituality is a product of social transformations that integrate a language of energy, positive philosophy, vegetarianism, and personal growth. Common among a liberal intellectual elite at the turn of the twentieth century, early Latin American Orientalism was fostered, among other things, by the Spanish translation of *The One Thousand and One Nights* (*Las mil y una noches*), Omar Khayyam's *Rubaiyat*, and Rabindranath Tagore's visit to South America. Since its inception, Orientalist perspectives created common spaces for Latin American intellectual elites and European immigrants, producing an early foundation to a whiteness that was generated "from the inside," in a spiritual sense. More significant to my discussion in this chapter, however, is that, despite the Asian origins of these practices, Latin American elites viewed them as ways to accomplish personal interiority projects that would, ideally, put them in closer contact with secular European and North American worlds and distance them from peer economic elites.

Remarks about "Indian culture," vegetarian Indian food, Buddhism, meditation, "a love for Eastern philosophy," commonalities between Brazilians and Indians, histories of Middle Eastern and Asian spiritual influences, life-altering visits to ashrams, and other personal epiphanies were prolific, in both El Condado and Ipanema. In addition to explaining a departure from a constraining Catholicism (or Judaism) to deeper forms of Eastern spirituality, these Orientalist attachments also conveyed a general uncertainty about institutions and a lack of faith in secular alternatives—including politics, consumption, government. Such profound mistrust of institutions, heightened over the time of my fieldwork, certainly paved the way for experimentation with new beliefs and practices. I came to understand these tendencies and interests in terms of a longer lineage, however, which ultimately produced a form of interiority currency that, precisely because of its Orientalist orientation, sustained white supremacist values from the deepest possible space of the self. One could interpret these inner-world orientations as part of the highly individualistic "seeker" culture and "self spirituality" of postmodern Western Europe and North America; after all, the aspiration to modernity, with its plurality of religions, constitution of a marketplace, and privatization of choice, fosters these religious fields. Yet, these pursuits of the esoteric, an attachment to social-emotional learning, and Orientalist inclination among the Ipanema and El Condado elites very much weaved the self as a social and political agent in ways that were not inconsistent with traditional communitarian religions in Latin America. More significantly, such cultivation of interiority currency ultimately sustained (and even exacerbated) class and race hierarchies.

While there was certainly an element of enchantment with the exotic in remarks like those uttered by Hugo de Carvalho Ribeiro, the father at the Ipanema crèche, I also noticed that this Orientalist fascination ultimately contributed to what I came to see as a dissolution of the social through parenting. Remarks about my son's looks were common, in both Puerto Rico and Brazil; however, while explicit comments about his dark eyes, thick dark hair, and tanned skin were common in both countries, the Indian side of this mix, and never the Puerto Rican side, ultimately mattered. When I would ask Brazilians to expand on their claim that Brazilians and Indians were very similar, the answers varied from a shared "attraction to the spiritual and mystical" to being sensual or sexually open (references to the Kama Sutra and tantric practices were offered as evidence). And, while I heard similar comments from Brazilians in the United States about how some Puerto Ricans, me included, could pass for Brazilian (Ramos-Zayas 2012), not once did I hear any Ipanema resident declare a similarity of any kind between Brazilians and Puerto Ricans, or Brazilians and any other Latin American or Caribbean nationality for that matter. When Ipanema or El Condado interlocutors learned that my husband had grown up Catholic, not Hindu or Buddhist, and that his interest in practicing yoga began after reading a *New York Times* article about the health benefits of the practice, they were puzzled and, quite frankly, disappointed.

In *Expulsions and Receptions* (2014), Bahia Munem extends Edward Said's framework of Orientalism by analyzing its machinations in Brazil. Assessing the resettlement of Arab populations, particularly Palestinian refugees in São Paulo and Rio Grande do Sul, Munem considers how Brazilians, already globally stereotyped as hypersexual, sensual, and affectively light, construct Palestinians in Brazil through a "neo-Orientalist g(l)aze." This formulation takes into consideration the racialized and exoticized constructions of Brazilians to examine how these essentialist ideas are in turn reconfigured to Orientalize (Arab or Middle Eastern) others, as evidenced, for instance, in popular Brazilian telenovelas like *O Clone* and *Camino das Indias*. This neo-Orientalist g(l) aze, I argue, was critical in how the crafting of an interiority currency and the valorization of affinity, simplicity, and all things metaphysical acquired specific social, economic, and racial currency among Latin American elites.

Just like Omar Tartak, the Puerto Rican father in this chapter's epigraphs, explained how a trip to India had finally convinced him to become a father, many other parents also framed parental aspirations in terms of life-altering moments or epiphanies related to Eastern philosophies, experiences, or practices. When I asked Raquel Cohen, who was raised Catholic and Jewish in a wealthy and influential El Condado family, what it was about her connection to India that had been so life altering, she explained: "In India, I realized that poverty does not have to be about marginality. In Puerto Rico, poverty comes along with certain pathologies, drug addiction, dependence on welfare, violence. In India, even the poorest people, people way poorer than those here, create magnificent temples, wear colorful saris, and experience a deep joy in children.... In India, I began to see parenting as a way to assume more fully a global imperative, a universal connection. Because when you become a parent, you don't just see trash, you see a planet going to waste." Genealogies of interiority in Raquel's statement promise to reveal the kinds of exteriority-embodied acts, social and pedagogic relations with others, and inhabited environments that might be folded into the selfhood at stake. They highlight the making of a space of interiority through moral dissension and ethical struggle with oneself, as individuals come to populate themselves with the feelings of others.

Anand Pandian (2010) notes how selfhood in the West has long been imagined to concern an interior space of personal discovery, attention, and struggle. Pandian argues that certain forces are especially significant in the making of such interior relations with oneself. Against this image, many anthropologists have stressed the social, exterior, and impersonal dimensions of selfhood elsewhere, casting the idiosyncrasy of modern Western selfhood as almost a truism (C. Taylor 1989, 111). The image of a fold, its interior depths formed by the turning of a surface against itself, may provide the clearest means of grasping the openness of this "interior horizon." "Interiorization" here may have also involved "a new way of being-in-the-world," of becoming aware of oneself as a part of cosmic nature (Hadot 1995, 211). These Orientalist perspectives in the context of parenting practices in the Global South are critical, yet understudied, mechanisms of whiteness in Latin America, so that whiteness is constructed as a type of children's crusade ("it is for the well-being of the children"), in which privilege and segregation are veiled by the parents' "selfless-selfish" concern with the well-being of their offspring.

My conversations with Ipanema and El Condado parents were simultaneously hyperembodied and metaphysical. Spending time with individuals like Omar Tartak, Liliana González Padín, and Raquel Cohen in El Condado, or Luciana Ribeiro Oliva in Ipanema always left me feeling that I had just engaged in conversations that were about the physical minutiae of the body and illness (the various incisions left from a cosmetic procedure, for instance), on the one hand, and about the most esoteric understandings of the universal self, on the other.

This disembodied hyperembodiment existed alongside an almost metaphysical field that fostered a view of oneself as socially unencumbered, without an identifiable or reducible social identity. Whenever I would ask about social difference, about whether a parent from a poorer area might disagree or view something in a different light, Verônica Igel Botelho, like most other Ipanemenses, would shift to a metaphysical discussion of humanity, beauty, and universality, as basis for her own identity, growth, and acquired emotional intelligence: "We are all connected." She added, "I began learning that through [a guru she had met]. Once you realize that we're all connected, then you let go of fear, of anxiety, of jealousy." Verônica would point to the physical body for evidence of various mental states, purifying needs, aesthetic appraisal, and pleasure. She acknowledged the centrality of body awareness in developing caring contexts in unorthodox family situations, in what appeared to be a complicated dance of dealing with one's jealousies and sense of betrayal precisely by erasing someone else's sociological condition—"no matter how rich or how poor or what color"—and adopting a metaphysical awareness to reach a higher moral ground.

César Schumer, a prominent Brazilian lawyer and the father of two adult daughters and a school-age son, was married to Silvana Villela Mattos, a mother I met through the beachfront playgrounds. When I asked him about his relationship with other Ipanema families, his answer developed from a commentary on his own spiritual journey to a perspective on social welfare that was common among Ipanema residents:

> My family is Jewish. But to me, the biggest change in my life was the time I spent at the ashram [in India]. It is still the base of the work I do, how I try to reframe how I engage with my surroundings. And, quite frankly, if we did more of this here in Brazil, we could get to solve issues in a way that no number of Bolsas [social welfare programs] will ever solve. A friend of mine told me something I found very interesting. Maybe you being an anthropologist have read [about this]. In the favelas and the poorest regions of the country, it is very common for women to have one pregnancy after another, because they are treated better when they are pregnant. When the pregnancy is over, they return to the real world, [and] the spiritual, emotional emptiness comes back.

Upper-class Ipanema and El Condado parents framed inner quests as labor, to understand makeover fantasies and personal transformations that, in turn, became a dominant political discourse of social transformations. Not unlike other white urban elites, Ipanema and El Condado interlocutors professed a rejection of individualist principles, hierarchical structures, body/spirit or nature/culture dualities; in fact, these elites viewed social transformations as an almost exclusive project of personal growth and working on one's interiority.

In place of traditional testimonials of religious conversion, these transformations were oftentimes operationalized through an array of modalities (including a new masculinity, postpartum changes, and other before/after narratives) and added to an arsenal that enhanced interiority currency. The relationship of self-help culture to religion in Ipanema and El Condado was not necessarily a means of "shrinking God" for a secularized world (McGee 2012, 687; Simonds 1992); rather, it was a way of seeking otherworldly aspirations and inspirations that were more cosmopolitan and marked white elites as complex and "deep," as opposed to the "simple" and stereotypically predictable darker lower classes. In the case César alluded to, women in the poorest regions of the country were so incapable of accessing their inner worlds and asserting their value in metaphysical terms that their only strategy was to become dependent on the government and seek community praise through pregnancy. His statement corresponds to a general misrecognition of issues of social arrangements and self-reflection capabilities and investments as individual traits that must presumably be resolved for social equality to be achieved.

NEW MASCULINITIES THROUGH
AFFLUENT PARENTING

Most Ipanema and El Condado residents, men and women alike, remarked on how "hands on," "involved" (and "evolved") fathers were in their neighborhoods.[10] Carlos Varela, in El Condado, and Fernando Coutinho Leite, in Ipanema, were probably who most interlocutors had in mind when producing these imaginaries of a "new masculinity."

While having an early breakfast at Kasalta, the bakery where Carlos often met with other father friends from his son's school, he mentioned that most of his male friends, many of whom he had known since elementary school or had met while studying in the United States, were "first and foremost dedicated to being dads." He explained, "We reject that image of the distant father, a product of machismo, in past generations but also in ours. We realize that our levels of anxiety are very high, largely because of what our country is going through. It is very easy to fall prey of that anxiety, anxiety over safety, financial security, is your child is going to have a learning issue or something else. My friends and I care about those things. We support one another. We try not to get neurotic about the everyday, because it is very easy to go that route."

The making of the new father through claims to possible neuroses and anxiety, in contradistinction to the "rational" and stern fathers of the past, was particularly prominent in El Condado, where, at the time of my fieldwork, parents worried about the country's economic and political situation. These fathers worried, sometimes incessantly, about their children's life outcomes, about addiction and bad influences, about possible learning and behavioral issues, about crime and street violence. Conceptions of adequate parenting were important ways in which new kinds of people—and a new masculinity— were made through a medicalized language deployed in the domestic and public spheres, not only the private clinical encounter. Like mothers but perhaps even more explicitly, fathers liked to reflect on their parenting practices; they traced the developmental milestones of their children and engaged in conversation about topics related to fatherhood and masculinity.

In El Condado parents evaluated this "new father" role in terms of emotional competence, a man's ability to read and narrate their children's inner worlds, and, as some of these men claimed, to do this even better than their spouses. Ultimately, a new patriarchy was allowed precisely by the unusualness or uniqueness attributed to men who, unlike dominant patriarchal models, not only were able to discover complexity in their children and themselves but did this even better than the mothers. A conversation with Omar Tartak and his friend Manolo Lastra, a divorced father of two who belonged to a well-connected Puerto Rican political family, was instructive about how this new father role was forged as superior to traditional masculinities, but also as superior to contemporary motherhood:

OMAR TARTAK: We are *nenes-nenas* [girly-boys]. If you think of our fathers' generation, that generation who grew up in the 1960s and 1970s, what was their way of bonding? Getting drunk, playing golf. Conversations were about sports or work or politics. That's very different from our conversations now. Our Saturday morning get-togethers are in playgrounds, at Kasalta, or at the soccer game. We talk about our kids, our concerns.

MANOLO LASTRA: My ex-wife would lose patience with the girls, forcing them into the shower, screaming at them in the car. Even though I loved her, I realized this situation was not healthy for my daughters. When we separated, the first thing I did was get full custody, at least until she received treatment for anger management, which she is now doing.

Although an inclination of feminist scholarship is to associate parent with mother, in this ethnography, the data early on led me to disentangle that association; parenting empires were possible largely because of the increasing disassociation between "parenting" and "mothering," and the masculinization of the parent-subject. The "new father" provided both a revisionist narrative about patriarchy and assigned modernity and cosmopolitanism to child-centered nodules of urbanism. Public expressions of fatherhood, significantly more so than motherhood, inscribed classed and racial hierarchies through a tacit understanding that these much-praised white and affluent fathers were, in fact, remedying what other, nonwhite and poor, but also older-generation fathers had created: a cadre of men who were irresponsible, hands off, and emotionally or physically absent from their children's lives.

In Ipanema, Fernando Coutinho Leite, an architect in his late forties, has an unassuming presence and spectacled intellectual air about him. He and Gabriela Braga Vellozo, his wife of almost twenty years, were parents to Isadora, who was about ten years old when I met her in 2013. On one of the many occasions I was invited to their home, and after showing me Isadora's art projects and written Mandarin assignments, Fernando remarked, "I always wanted to have a family. We were married for ten years before having kids. At that point, Gabriela was reaching what one would think of as a biological limit to have children and—" Gabriela interjected, "Even at that time, I was almost thirty-four, I still wasn't very moved by the idea of becoming a mother. It was really Fernando who had that instinct." Both Gabriela and Fernando considered Fernando the most involved parent, but also the most anxious one.

> FERNANDO: I just notice everything that goes on with Isadora. I first noticed her social anxiety when it came to relationships with her peers, for instance. She goes to therapy once a week, and sometimes all three of us go together. For me, even the smallest little thing leaves me obsessed the rest of the day. I can't stop thinking about it. Right now, I am anxious about her anxiety! [laughed]

> GABRIELA: Please, what can you do about that, Fernando? You can't take on Isadora's anxiety, Brazil's anxiety, and the anxiety of the whole world on your shoulders! [laughed]

Although most parents in Ipanema and El Condado were invested in being able to translate their own children's inner worlds, this seemed especially critical for fathers. Forms of embodiment by proxy (Merleau-Ponty 2004; Rouse 2004), these radical translations of children's inner worlds blurred the boundaries between parent and child in an effort to make intelligible to the world each other's values and identities. The perception and reality of a national crisis contributed to eviscerating and reformulating these forms of emotional sociability and self-concept, as well as the role of the new father. This is not to suggest that the "new father" is a historically unique or more progressive gendered form, but rather that the active, performative abjection of a toxic masculinity—attributed more explicitly to past generations—becomes an elite and white sociability in parenting empires. This new father, and the social capital this collective subjectivity enables, requires the cultivation of recognizable and demonstrable interiority currency.

"Nowadays, parents who possess greater cultural capital also understand the importance of being with their children, to dedicate time to their children," Gabriela noted. And Fernando added, "It is important not to be that distant, formal, stern, or altogether absent father. Here in Ipanema, because you have a higher cultural level and knowledge of the world, fathers already have this understanding of the need to be present. In the past, a father's relationship with the kids was tightly intertwined with the marriage. That has changed."

Fernando was convinced of his daughter's complexity, and he believed that this complexity justified his own parental anxieties and required him to cultivate his own inner world: "Because of her complexity, I am forced to reflect on each decision I make. When there is no time to reflect in preparation for something, then I reflect on it after. Isadora can be challenging. She is not a simple child [*criança simple*]."[11] Fernando's remark about Isadora, while presented as a concern, had a back-handed element of pride: "When Isadora was only three, she said: 'Dad, you are the lion. Mom, you are the lioness.' And I asked her: 'And you, Isadora, who are you?' Thinking, of course, that she would say 'I'm the cub,' right? She responded: 'I am the owner of the zoo.' She has the need to be in charge, to make decisions, to make her presence be felt." While a comment like this might at first glance suggest a concern about a child's behavior, I came to identify a fairly consistent pattern among upper-class Ipanema and El Condado parents: there was a tendency, a tacit desire, to view girls as challenging, stubborn, and strong willed, and to view boys as good natured, easy going, and mellow. A boy who was mellow would presumably grow up to become a man who possessed the emotional intelligence and sensitivity associated with new forms of masculinity, which were associated with socially "progressive" spaces, but also with white upper-class spaces, like Ipanema and El Condado. Likewise, a strong-willed girl would have greater success in the professional realm and depart from traditional gendered forms of domesticity.

ENTREPRENEURIAL MIRACLES

For elites and the individuals they considered personas sencillas, in El Condado, and with whom they shared an afinidade, in Ipanema, the language around the value of the immaterial—of Orientalist sensibilities and new masculinities—in fact extended to the context of entrepreneurship. Rather than its common association with financial wealth or a corporate persona, entrepreneurship in El Condado and Ipanema deployed a language of personal epiphany and miracles. The professional success narratives of Camila Sandoval and Raquel Cohen in El Condado, and of Silvana Villela Mattos in Ipanema came across almost as a literary genre with its own narrative arc; rather than describing a capitalist venture, these narratives elicited the language of serendipity, miracles, and manifesting one's desires. In fact, this language of "manifesting," as an ability or intuition that resulted after dedicated self-awareness and mastering a combination of psychological and spiritual logics, was also emblematic of how interiority currency operated on behalf of economic productivity and a moral economy of wealth.

When I met Camila in El Condado the summer of 2014, she was a recently divorced empty-nester in her midfifties whose daughter had just left to attend a prestigious liberal arts college in the United States. Camila's two self-reported passions were filmmaking and chocolate. When the travel demands of movie production became incompatible with her daughter's schedule, Camila redirected her energy into her other passion—chocolate. As her story goes, in a trip to Paris with a friend when she was in her twenties, Camila exited the Musée d'Orsay, walking along the Seine and heading to the Saint Germain neighborhood, when she "looked through the glass window of a dimly lit boutique." A man wearing a tuxedo and silk gloves was handling something gently. "Surely a jewelry store," Camila thought. But then she realized that what the man was so sensually accommodating behind the glass counter were chocolates. Describing the experience as part of "a trance," Camila entered the chocolate boutique and ate one and then another and then another piece of expensive chocolate, until she had "fallen in love" with Le Bombom Chocolaterie. From then on, whenever she would go to Paris over the next twenty years, she would bring Le Bombom chocolates as souvenirs. One evening, shortly after being forced to quit her filmmaking career, Camila reflected on her passions in life and remembered the French chocolates. On impulse, she hand wrote a three-page letter to the chocolatier and owner of Le Bombom, describing her visceral experience with his chocolates. She had a business proposition for him: she wanted to open a Le Bombom Chocolaterie in El Condado. At the time, there were few franchises outside Paris. A few weeks later, she heard the buzz of her fax machine, and she "just knew": "That's from Monsieur Georges from Le Bombom," she told her then husband. Sure enough, the owner had written back and was willing to meet with her to discuss a business plan. A week later, Camila traveled to Paris, filled out the paperwork, and became part of an international group of chocolatiers. A dimly lit room where chocolates were enclosed behind glass and the word "degouter" was used liberally, Le Bombom would soon become a primary space of upper-class socializing in the neighborhood.

Nearly twenty years later, I was interviewing Camila at her upscale chocolate boutique in El Condado and going through a visceral experience like the one she probably had in Paris decades earlier. During the interview, Camila's assistant, a tall and distinguished Argentine man who looked to me like Batman's butler Alfred, brought a small intricate silver tray with two chocolates—one made of roasted walnut and the other with Puerto Rican rum, an "adaptation to the Puerto Rican palate," as Camila explained. "You're going to eat first the one with walnut, in two bites, tasting it with the middle of your tongue before biting into it," Camila instructed. I had never eaten chocolate with as much intentionality (or as self-consciously). After we had begun our first formal interview, I reached out for the second chocolate, when Camila stopped me: "That one you will put in your mouth, but don't bite on it. You have to wait for it to open up and . . . melt . . . there." I was unable to enjoy these chocolates as much as I felt I should, but I did feel a sort of Bourdieuian moment: I sensed that there was some knowledge I was supposed to have, but also that I couldn't taste what I was supposed to taste. I couldn't get all my senses attuned to the experience.[12] Camila proceeded to describe her entrepreneurship as the culmination of something that was simply "meant to be."

Raquel Cohen, another El Condado resident from a prominent Puerto Rican banking family, had been involved in her family's philanthropic foundation for many years. Carlos Varela, the father who drew an El Condado parenting map on a napkin at Kasalta, was Raquel's husband. After toying with various unsuccessful corporate initiatives, and after the birth of their son, the couple realized that they needed to find "ways to improve the lives of poor families on the island." They traveled to Berlin, Buenos Aires, Madrid, and various US cities to get ideas that they could adapt to Puerto Rico. Emulating the open floor plans of Silicon Valley workspaces, they decided to establish a think tank in one of the rapidly gentrifying areas of Santurce and draft a mission statement: "We are parents and professionals in diverse fields. We take the wellbeing of children on our Island seriously. We hope this forum allows us to collect information, channel issues, develop initiatives and allies that improve the life of our families and create a community focused on providing resources and needed love to each child in Puerto Rico for a healthy development."

In addition to explaining the origins of their consulting firm as a "miracle" or "destiny," Carlos and Raquel also understood it as a personal calling. They explained that, while they could have stayed in the United States after graduating from their respective Ivy League programs, they had instead decided to put what they had learned "to benefit Puerto Rico." I asked Raquel what they had learned, and she responded, "That what we need as a people is a belief in the power of our minds, our intentions. We have been led to belief we can't accomplish things on our own, without government interventions of various kinds. We view this crisis as an opportunity to force ourselves to change those mindsets."

Carla Freeman (2014) notes that, while once entrepreneurship was a mechanism of survival for the poor, it has now become both a mandate and an impetus for an alternative form of middle-class respectability. An especially fascinating feature of the upward mobility of these long-standing traditions, which Freeman notes in the case of Barbados, is that the linchpin of these flexible, resourceful practices is found in "the growing significance of affect as a site of labor and exchange, whether intimate, inward looking, or public and market based. The questions—who am I in the world? How do I wish to live and feel?—were being articulated in new ways that were intertwined with a general entrepreneurial ethic and neoliberal spirit" (5). The simultaneously entrepreneurial and therapeutic dimensions of such endeavors was also unmistakable in the cases of Raquel and Camila, as well as other Ipanema and El Condado upper-class parents. Regardless of the specifics of the respective ventures, the focus of the business was always described in terms of nonmaterial (immaterial?) attributes: self-fulfillment, destiny, a life path, a spiritual mission, a continuous search for (an often elusive) passion. This was particularly remarkable given the context of national economic uncertainty in both Brazil and Puerto Rico.

Toward the end of my fieldwork in Ipanema, Silvana Villela Mattos, one of the parents I met through a beach playground, had developed a not-for-profit group whose main goal was to stop commercial advertisement directed at children, and to urge families to reject the pressure of introducing name brands to their children. "We provide support for parents who want to fight against the pressures that turn children and young adults into consumers," Silvana explained. "There is a consumption logic (*lógica consumista*) that has an impact on children's physical, cognitive, and emotional development. Childhood obesity, alcohol and smoking, the sexualization of children are all related to this. Children in the comunidades come to see the shopping [mall] as their main source of entertainment. I find that so disturbing!"

While some US-inspired "commercial-free childhood" campaigns had made it to Brazil in the late 1990s, including a forum in São Paulo in the early 2000s, they had acquired greater tracking in Silvana's life since her "sabbatical year," as she called the year she dedicated almost exclusively to finding her true calling. She highlighted a key moment as her epiphany: "I went to a lecture on childhood obesity, and that was the final life-changing moment for me. That's when I really became committed to understanding these passions holistically. How consumption, environment, parenting, and even Eastern philosophy, which my husband and I had practiced over the years, were related. After the lecture, I told [the lecturer, who was also an Ipanema parent]: 'Carla, this is it, this is my calling!' And she said: 'I wholeheartedly support you.' It was miraculous."

During that sabbatical year, Silvana organized discussions at the largest neighborhood bookstore and hosted parenting groups in her home around the topic of child obesity. Along with a group of other Ipanema parents, Silvana celebrated days of "play, not consumption" and denounced how childhood consumption was a threat to sustainability and the environment.[13]

Entrepreneurial stories of miracles and new father images were approaches to class and race produced at the intersections of the economic and the affective, the material and the subjective. I want to take this perspective a step further, however, to highlight the reason that class "worked" for the Latin American and Caribbean upper classes when it was asserted as "im/material"—that is, when class was approached as, literally, not mattering or lacking relevance in the face of what really mattered: the metaphysical, emotive, and spiritual projects enabled by liberalism. Disentangling the significance of a presumed im/materiality of class, strongly associated with becoming and being a parent, enables us to see how inner-world aesthetics might shed light on how whiteness, an elusive racial formation, is produced and articulated in Latin America and the Caribbean. This whiteness operated as a tendency to psychologize the social and render inner worlds, at the expense of material conditions, more legitimate sources of agency. That everyone either had equal access to these inner worlds, or at least should display the same interest in their cultivation, gained great currency in a national climate characterized by harsh austerity measures and crises of sovereignty.

Parenting empires allowed individuals to fashion for themselves a space of reflexive interiority. Interiority currency included the plural teachings, cues, and reminders of others (including prolific pedagogies of parenting and scientific expertise) beyond the boundaries of an individual selfhood.

Conclusion: Interiority Currency, Austerity, and Whiteness

The world of upper-class interiority in Ipanema and El Condado, unlike the inner worlds fostered in the prosperity gospels of the working classes in Brazil and Puerto Rico, for instance, was contingent on austerity of a particular kind: austerity became a form of subjectivity, which only the wealthy could in fact embody and claim, because a precondition for such austerity was, precisely, wealth. While Brazilian and Puerto Rican lower classes have moved from Catholicism to Pentecostalism and other evangelical religions in search of immediate material results in the last few decades, the upper classes, who have financial security and can wait on the benefits of meditation and self-cultivation, have increasingly accumulated interiority currency that allow them to find satisfaction in "the path," intention, and effort itself.[14] The process of accumulating interiority currency—and its perceived lack of dogmatism and hierarchy, respect for nature, and general belief in science (or at least not a dependency on faith)—emerges as a new method to deal with violence, fear, and corruption, placing the responsibility for peaceful relationships and overall quality of life on individuals. Compassion, in all its true genuineness, becomes a way of life.

In this pursuit of interiority capital, one had to demonstrate that self-control or abstention from conspicuous consumption was in fact *a choice*, not the outcome of material scarcity but quite the contrary: an abundance of material resources that one chooses not to demonstrate, at least not explicitly or through conventional consumption markers, in the public realm. If progressive attitudes were associated with these austerity subjectivities of the upper- and upper-middle classes in Ipanema and El Condado, then the working classes were tacitly or implicitly perceived as retrogressive and shallow. Contemporary forms of self-awareness did little to undo this; rather, such pressure toward self-awareness in fact pushed back or more into hiding what otherwise could have been real conversations about race, class, and inequality.

Bruna Alves Teixeira, one of a handful of Ipanema residents whose wealth was the reflection of remarkable social mobility through education, social welfare initiatives, and marriage, demonstrated that the wealthy often projected a lack of internal depth onto the poor. Part of Bruna's socialization into Ipanema's wealth involved transforming explicit expressions of disgust toward dark, poor bodies into a more coded, neoliberal racial language akin to US multiculturalism. I trace this transformation through an examination of "disgust" in Bruna's birthing story. I am not focusing here on intentionality, how individuals might assume their inner-world cultivation might turn out, but on the outcome of their practices, whether intentional or not, and what elites perpetuate as they turn to the self.

Of the negative effects, contempt is an immensely powerful indicator of the interface between the personal and the social; like the disgust it sometimes carries, contempt feels personal and visceral and invokes collective sentiments, as individuals sharing similar social backgrounds may share their relationship to the object of contempt. Bruna described the day when her doctor told her that she needed to have an emergency C-section, and that the procedure would have to take place at the public municipal hospital, instead of at the private hospital Bruna had expected:

> We arrived at the Perinatal [municipal hospital], and there was a group of blacks that had a super strong odor [*um grupo de negros que tinha um cheiro super forte, super*]. And pregnant women, we have that power of smell. I turned to my husband. "Mauricio, I don't want to have my son here." I began to cry right there, in the Maternity Ward. . . . When the doctor arrived, she saw me crying, hysterically, my robe wet from all the tears. "What happen?" "I don't want to have my son here." "Where do you want to have your son?" "In the Casa de São Jose [private hospital]" "Why?" "I don't know. I don't want to have my son here." She was very, very mad at me, and she told me afterward. She moved the whole birthing team to the São Jose, and it looked like a funeral, not a birth. At the moment I couldn't articulate a reason, the odor, the noise. . . . In retrospect, I know that it was that I wanted a nice, beautiful, nice-smelling world for my son to be born into.

Bruna's visceral narrative was exceptional in relation to those I heard from other Ipanema and El Condado upper-class parents, whose antiblackness was much more coded. Disgust hinges on proximity (Skeggs 2004); when spatial or legal boundaries between racial or social groups are challenged, social hierarchy finds other ways of expression, including odor.[15] Class and race were rarely as explicitly invoked in expressions of disgust as in Bruna's case. This was not only a classed relation to the aesthetic—akin to Bourdieu's "taste"—but a morally sanctioned (and moralistic) endorsement of whiteness through parenting. Implied in Bruna's statement was a recognition of (and horror at) the possibility that she—or, more precisely, the child she was about to give birth to—could be like all those dark bodies who smelled.

It was Bruna's explicit allusion to blackness that most stood out in contrast to Ipanema and El Condado parents; whereas other parents, when pressed, handled race with white gloves and neoliberal narratives of diversity and inclusion, Bruna wanted to get into the messiness of racism in ways that were as offensive as they were genuine and unfiltered. Ironically, Bruna's lack of an inner world that could be considered refined by Ipanema parenting standards in fact produced a rare racial sincerity. Bruna was unique in her unfiltered expressions of racism, so the choice to use this vignette to introduce this section needs to be explained, in terms of what I noticed as an important, if tacit, objective of whiteness in Latin America: elites in El Condado and Ipanema, including Bruna's Brazilian doctor, would be appalled by her explicit reference to Black bodies in terms of *cheiro* (foul odor), or at all. Ironically, Bruna was probably the only interviewee, in Puerto Rico or in Brazil, who engaged with race affectively, who viewed racism as something she could not ignore. She was deeply self-reflective about her own racism, to the point of accepting and even seeking personal discomfort. Bruna seemed to appreciate our formal interviews and casual conversations as opportunities to work through something that was tremendously conflictive for her, and which she sensed affected how she parented her son.

One of the several times I tape recorded an interview with Bruna, I posed a general question about the aspirations she had for her son. If anything, this was a sort of "feel good" question for parents; they could show off various positive qualities they admired, including "having a job they feel passionate about," "being a good human being," "getting to know the world and travel," or some variation of those. By contrast, Bruna's response was

> Listen, Ana, I am very racist. And I suffer a lot as a consequence. I don't want my child to go through this. My father didn't like blacks. Beautiful black women, yes [*neguinhas gostosas, sim, né*]. It is very hard for me to get rid of that upbringing. I see a black guy [*um neguinho*] in the street, and I'm already [makes gesture of pulling away, holding on to a purse]. It is fear. It is prejudice. It is acting like a crazy person [*uma coisa de louco*]. How can I get to like something I've been taught to dislike? [in tears]. I am telling you all this, because you're not judging me, even though I've verbalized it already. Once I acknowledge that I am prejudiced, how do I change it? I don't want to change it. Because I don't want to admit it to anyone else. I simply want to keep that hidden inside. I don't want my son to be this way, to have this inside.

Given how fluent some elite liberal parents in Ipanema were, Bruna felt alone in her anti-Black racism and the rawness of her feelings. This aloneness, guilt, and hidden racist feelings effectively led Bruna to locate racism on the realm of the "self," away from collective institutions and structures.

About a year after our first meeting, Bruna, who had described herself as "morena," stated that she was "the granddaughter of blacks."[16] Sensing my confusion, she explained: "My grandfather was black, and my grandmother was of Korean descent." It was initially hard to tell whether Bruna was evoking some modified version of the racial democracy mythology, by which most interviewees considered themselves "mixed." Bruna has straight black hair and a permanent *bronceado* (tanned body) common to most parents I met. In the United States or Europe, Bruna might have been considered Italian or Greek. Her racial self-perception conformed to what Patricia de Santana Pinho (2009) calls, in a different context, "white but not quite"

Bruna had achieved remarkable upward mobility, hailing from a precarious working-class background and marrying into a wealthy Ipanema family (chapter 6); perhaps she did not fear the messiness of race partly because of her own displacement and emplacement. She was one of the few Ipanema residents who was able to explore her own anti-Black racism in a way that was actually about substance rather than form; for her, it was not simply a cosmopolitan strategy, liberal self-fashioning, or learning a socially acceptable vocabulary, at least initially. For Bruna, Ipanema was violent, and her own whiteness was unstable and deeply challenged in social interactions with parents with greater degrees of social and cultural capital in Ipanema.

My conversations with Bruna got much deeper in some ways, but between 2015 and 2016, a racial sincerity had been lost; she was handling racial messiness with the same domesticated white gloves of other upper-class Brazilian and Puerto Rican parents: a new, more modulated perspective on race, akin to the one common to parenting empires, took over. Like other Brazilian parents in Ipanema, she became focused on teaching "racial fluency" to her child, which could and often did exist independent of antiracist practice, and which became central to Bruna's child-rearing and educational concerns.[17] At the urging of her boss at Petrobras, Bruna had hired a life coach, and she showed me a meme she had downloaded from her life coach's Facebook page: "Crisis? We heard about it, but decided not to participate. Thanks!"

I asked her why she thought her life coach had posted that meme. "Because I was so overwhelmed with my own prejudices, like I spoke to you about. But that is not going to change, just like the situation in the country is not going to change. All you can do is select where you put your energy, what you choose to focus on. I want to focus on growing as a human being and better understanding

FIGURE 4.1.
Motivational meme circulated by Brazilian life coach on Facebook. Translation: Crisis? We heard about it, but decided not to participate. Thanks!

my own internal schemas, what is preventing me from achieving all my goals. That's the lesson I want to pass on to my son." A neoliberal emphasis on self-improvement eclipsed any grammar of exploitation with the use of a language of individual psychology, such that specific elements cast as horrific or repulsive came to be associated with populations that were similarly understood, but the language used to address issues of racial disgust and contempt shifted.[18]

Individuals not only diagnosed themselves, their children, and others with whom they came into contact, but also discussed the symptoms gripping their neighborhood, their city, and their country: emotional numbness, depression, anxiety, aggressiveness, disengagement, neurosis, impatience. There were certainly instances when the therapeutic impulses were halted and diagnoses challenged, and by no means did every single Ipanema or El Condado parent subscribe to this interiority cultivation, or to the same degree; however, most of the parents I met in these neighborhoods considered these forms of inner-world cultivation as part of a progressive interiority that characterized liberalism, austerity, and moral regulation.

In elite, progressive Latin American neighborhoods increasingly powered by self-actualization projects, morally justified through parental aspirations, the idea that happiness should be engineered from the inside out rather than the outside in took on the status of a default truism akin to those in the Global North. Bruna came to accept the way her life coach framed happiness, as a journey of self-discovery rather than the natural byproduct of engaging with the world, particularly the world of Brazil in crisis. This is a way of being happy that stressed emotional independence rather than the interdependence necessary to examine enduring white supremacy perspectives and social justice, as the focus becomes on searching for meaningful contentment through the exploration of the self, a deep dive into our innermost souls and the intricacies and tripwires of our own personalities. Drawing on a newly found interest in self-cultivation, rather than her original goal to explore racial justice, Bruna, like other parents in Ipanema and El Condado, adopted a form of sovereign parenting premised on inner qualities and austerity subjectivities. Like the territorial claims exerted through child-centered nodules of urbanism, the accumulation of interiority currency was a deliberate project to prepare children for neoliberal cosmopolitanism and the progressive reproduction of white privilege in the Americas, as discussed in chapter 5.

5

Schooling Whiteness

Adult Friendships, Social Ease, and the Privilege of Choosing Race

She discovered with great delight that one does not love one's children just because they are one's children but because of the friendships formed while raising them.—Gabriel García Márquez, *Love in the Time of Cholera*

Michelle Forastieri, Maru Ramírez de Arellano, Mónica Amador, and Alejandra Rodríguez Emma were residents of El Condado whose elementary school children attended the Academia del Perpetuo Socorro in the adjacent neighborhood of Miramar, Puerto Rico. On this specific evening, when I drove to Guaynabo to meet up with them, the four women had just finished a volleyball practice at the Caparra Country Club. Save for a few interruptions due to challenging pregnancies, attending elite US college or graduate schools, or being away on vacations, these four women had been playing volleyball together since high school. Their husbands also knew one another from high school or had met through common high school friends.

"Do you know what's the first question Puerto Ricans ask each other when they first meet?" Michelle Forastieri's husband, Guillermo Dávila, asked me when he knew I was interviewing some parents at his children's school. I knew what the answer was, oddly enough, but he still proceeded: "[It is] 'Where did you go to school?' You can run into another Puerto Rican in Miami, Madrid, or China, and that's what they ask you right away . . . to place you [*para ubicarte*]. And you know what the weird thing is? Eventually you find the connection." Maru, Mónica, Michelle, and Alejandra frequently socialized together; they celebrated birthdays, graduations, and anniversaries in one another's houses, and occasionally went with Mónica and her husband, Jaime Carvajal, on their yacht to the island municipality of Culebra, where the couple had built a three-story weekend mansion. Among the eight of them, these husbands and wives represented a handful of elite schools in Puerto Rico; two of these high schools, the Academia del Perpetuo Socorro and St. John's School, are in the Miramar and El Condado neighborhoods, while others—Colegio San Ignacio and the Colegio Puertorriqueño de Niñas—were in upper-middle-class areas of Guaynabo.[1] Every single conversation with El Condado parents about schools—what high school they had attended—invariably plugged the respondent into an entangled web of personal connections (friendships, best friendships, cousins, lovers, exes) with a broader universe of people I had met, heard about, or interviewed.

While Ipanema parents also cared deeply about the schools their children attended, their own adult networks did not primarily consist of friendships lingering from their high school days. In fact, none of the Ipanema parents I met had attended the schools they chose for their children, even if they had grown up in Ipanema in the 1970s and 1980s. Ipanema parents knew one another "from the beach," "from the crèche," "from the academia [gym]," or "from the school [their children attended]"; the neighborhood, in Ipanema, was a dense space of intersecting routines that were not necessarily mediated through elite private schools, most of which were not even located within official Ipanema borders. Following John Scott's analysis of social networks, this meant that Ipanema networks were characterized by "multiplexity"—that is, dependent on how many different capacities individuals knew one another in—whereas El Condado networks were characterized by both multiplexity and "density," how many individuals in a network knew everybody else, and schools carried value across generations.[2]

While friendships and schools intersected differently in El Condado and in Ipanema, in both neighborhoods, schools consolidated and routinized the lives of parents and provided a sense of intimacy and familiarity, cohesion and internal solidarities (cf. Elias 1997). In El Condado, parents' own high school experience still shaped their adult friendships, while in Ipanema, parents viewed their *children's* schools, which oftentimes were not the schools they had themselves attended, as places where they would get to interact and meet possible friends.

Schools are important institutional agents in the formation of national and colonial subjects in the Global South; scholars have compellingly examined the role of curricula, student culture, educational policies, and school leadership in the process of crafting colonial and national subjectivities (e.g., Dávila 2003; cf. Maxwell and Aggleton 2016). When we understand elite parenting as a US imperial formation in the Americas, however, it is imperative to unpack how upper-class parents become ubiquitous in the everyday functioning, pedagogical objectives, and ideological reconfiguration of schooling and its outcomes.

Not unlike middle and upper classes throughout the world, school choice in Ipanema and El Condado indexed political leanings, aspirations, and national and transnational affiliations that illuminated divisions and heterogeneity among elites. School choice mattered not simply because of the instrumental benefits of the particular class positions schools could confer, but because class distinctions were enmeshed with moral distinctions about the relative worth of people, explicitly in terms of class and implicitly in terms of race, and the competing definitions of a good life that could be forged and preserved. Marks of distinction were never static, nor did they remain the exclusive property of an elite; therefore, considerable energy was spent in configuring and reconfiguring cultural and symbolic capital, frequently in perhaps counterintuitive ways (cf. Bourdieu 1977).

Adult friendships figured prominently in how Ipanema and El Condado parents chose schools for their children and related to memories of their own schooling. Schools were practices of recognition within kinship networks that approached specific elite private schools as known, familiar environments and spaces of (re)socialization for children and adults. While most development literature in the field of psychology and popular culture (and lifespan models) has focused on adolescence as the most rapid and active period of identity development, an equally powerful investment in identity—an "adult identity"—takes place in adulthood around ideas of parenting (cf. Grusec 2011). Ultimately, school choice was suggestive of an inherent ambivalence that the Ipanema and El Condado upper-middle class harbored toward inequality, and a relatively new global, if often rhetorical, regard for "diversity" and "inclusion."

Schools enabled a deeply moralizing register that highlighted both individual biography and collective histories. Regardless of the impetus behind school choice, parents in both neighborhoods ultimately viewed schools as a leading site for forging a sovereign moral subject—for valorizing national language and culture, repositioning race outside the realm of political economy and social inequality and into the realm of aesthetics and selective visibility, and fostering a habitus of legitimate privilege in their children.

In the first section of this chapter, I examine how schools serve as eminent spaces of parenting empire and everyday governance. In relation to school choice, discussions of religious versus secular culture, native-language education versus English-dominant instruction, and performances of affluence contributed to forging contemporary versions of noblesse oblige. In the second section, I consider approaches to diversity and inclusion that Ipanema and El Condado parents adopted, with ambivalence, trepidation, and emotional discomfort, to associate their wealth with morality and cosmopolitanism, and to initiate their own children into projects of interiority currency. I focus on strategies parents deployed to introduce their children to socially mixed contexts, and the counterintuitive "social envy" those strategies generated. In the third section of the chapter, I consider how rendering wealth as moral and altruistic intersected with a racial aesthetics and misrecognition, often developed from parents' own school memories. Parents' memories of their own schooling, and the objects that sustained those memories, including yearbooks, in fact solidified white privilege through the insistence on a Latin American whiteness that was based on aesthetics, deliberate racial misrecognition, and global forms of white supremacy.

Parenting Nations: The Ideologies, Languages, and Social Networks of Elite Schooling

There was a small universe of schools that Ipanema and El Condado parents considered suitable for their children. The process of choosing a school was not only anxiety provoking, but also pointed to the heterogeneous dispositions and subjectivities within the upper class, its disagreements and hierarchies, and the different orientations toward sovereignty, values, and the global and the national. For individuals whose wealth was less established, having their child attend one of a handful of private schools in El Condado or Ipanema was often an important step toward belonging. Even among parents who felt quite secure in their social standing, whose schooling was part of a broader intergenerational class project, and who were themselves and their children "legacies" in given elite schools, school choice carried considerable subjective aspects. Parents went beyond rational analyses of college placement, course offerings, and class size, also considering feel of place, sense of familiarity, affinity with the school community, and perceived similarity of values. Families who occupied the same socioeconomic position made very different school choices according to a constellation of values and a series of subjective elements that reflected these parents' largely cultural and idiosyncratic positions.[3]

Sociological literature in the field of elite education has identified a dominant orientation toward global and international citizenship in the mission statements, philosophy, and curricula of US and European elite private schools (e.g., Gaztambide-Fernández 2009; Gaztambide-Fernández and Howard 2012;

Khan 2012a). Such global orientation in European and North American elite schooling is consistent with a perspective on nationalism as the ideological orientation of the conservative white working classes in suburban and rural areas (cf. Hochschild 2016). The approach to elite education was significantly different among upper-class parents in Ipanema and El Condado, however; despite global and multicultural gestures in the curriculum of elite schools in Ipanema and El Condado, upper-class parents in these neighborhoods viewed Puerto Rican and Brazilian cultural nationalism as intrinsic to parenting empires and framed elite private schooling as important sites of anticolonial and anti-imperial critique.

School selection criteria highlighted how nation-state projects were narrated in El Condado and Ipanema as a function of school affiliation. There were three criteria for school selection common to Ipanema and El Condado: moral and pedagogical ideologies (e.g., religious versus secular, progressive versus traditional), language of instruction, and the adult friendships enabled by the school community.

"SPIRITUAL BUT NOT RELIGIOUS": ALTERING RELIGIOUS TROPES IN LATIN AMERICAN ELITE SCHOOL SELECTION

Silvana Villela Mattos constituted part of a cultural and social Ipanema elite whose material wealth was rendered legible through presumably altruistic goals for their children; she wanted her child to be concerned with social justice and an agent of global change, to rely on "his own merits and efforts," and to develop personal and educational strategies to be happy, fulfilled, and successful. Like other Ipanema parents, Silvana talked about her decision not to send her son to the "elitist" Escola Britânica: "Could we have afforded the Escola Britânica? Yes. But we didn't want to raise the kind of child who feels entitled to go skiing three times a year, and talks about the hotel in Aspen and skiing equipment with great familiarity. And, besides, in those trips you are in a hotel, with other Brazilians, you are not connecting with the local surroundings. It is a very provincial cosmopolitanism. Ultimately the question becomes: Who do you want as friends?" Parents were, either intuitively or explicitly, aware that excessive elitism or setting rigid social boundaries around themselves would weaken the forms of symbolic and cultural capital through which they signified their material wealth as moral. Silvana also explained that religion had been an important factor in her decision. Since her husband, César Schumer, is Jewish, they had realized early on that they did not want any of the acceptable Catholic schools near Ipanema. They could have chosen Corcovado, a secular German school, but between César's Jewish identity and Silvana's own Polish background, they considered the German factor a crazy joke. After eliminating those schools, the only one that was acceptable was Escola Parque, which had a constructivist, secular orientation, unlike more traditional elite Catholic schools, like Colégio Santo Agostino in nearby Leblon.

Being critical about the Catholic church and Catholicism in general was considered a sign of cosmopolitanism and expansive worldview, as shown in the following conversation with Liliana González Padín and her husband, Raúl Bustillo, residents of El Condado whose children attended St. John's, a secular private school in El Condado. A common remark among El Condado parents, like Liliana and Raúl, was that Puerto Rico tended to be ethnically homogenous, and that they had come to experience "true diversity" when they had lived or studied in the United States:

LILIANA: We had friends from all over the world, from India, China, other parts of the US. We met Jews, Hindus, Buddhists.

RAÚL: St. John's, being a secular school, draws parents who are more cosmopolitan, more global. You have your typical American ex-pats, but you also have Puerto Rico–born generations of Hindus, Chinese— jewelers, owners of those Chinese restaurants, ice cream places. And you have a huge Jewish community. It is a Puerto Rico that you don't know exists when you attend regular Catholic school. It is the multicultural Puerto Rico, multiethnic. They don't become 100 percent Puerto Rican either, because St. John's doesn't promote that. It is more generic. You don't have a nationality. You also have more of the sophisticated Puerto Ricans, who don't want to deal with nuns.

The choice of secular St. John's School was not only a way of challenging historical associations between Puerto Rican elites and Catholic education, but also a way of reframing one's elite status in a global, cosmopolitan order that was not about relating across ethnic lines, but about existing in circles that were endemically considered exotic in an Orientalist sense (chapter 4).

Regardless of how anticlerical and admiring of Eastern philosophies Brazilian and Puerto Rican elites were, however, a considerable part of the liberal upper-class families I met in Ipanema and El Condado were not opposed to the Catholic Church or Catholicism. In this regard, they tended to be like most Latin American elites everywhere, even the ones most invested in modernizing projects. Like the Argentine elites studied by Victoria

Gessaghi (2010), political elites in Brazil and Puerto Rico never considered it necessary to eliminate the church-state union. Catholicism, and Catholic schools, stressed the contradiction between money and values, and the Catholic focus on gratitude appeared to be a common way in which parents addressed that conflict. Presumably, God or destiny gave some people a lot and gave others nothing, and those who got a lot needed to be grateful and give back in the form of community service or being aware and appreciative (Howard 2013).

Fernando Coutinho Leite and Gabriela Braga Vellozo, an Ipanema couple and parents of a student who attended Santo Agostino, an elite Catholic school near the Ipanema-Leblon border, remarked that, "In Brazil, it is very common to be Left and liberal in terms of politics, but to be more conservative in terms of religion. These are very common contradictions in our society, particularly among the upper classes. They get married in church, baptize their children, but rarely go to mass." Gabriela added, "Santo Agostino has a strong sense of social commitment. They maintain a crèche at Jardim de Allah [poor community] and are always raising money to help the children there. The older students travel to the North of Brazil, where the school also supports poor communities. A student from the school even founded an NGO to construct a school in the Amazonian region. The Catholic school has a Left political leaning and had a strong role during the military dictatorship."

The choice between secular and religious (which always meant Catholic among my interviews in both Ipanema and El Condado) was less about a dogmatic approach to Catholicism or a secularist rejection of religious education than about parental perspectives on a form of Third World Catholicism and ethical-political project; in some ways, this choice solidified Catholicism as a national religion. Through various religious orders, the Catholic Church in Puerto Rico and, to a lesser degree, in Brazil took on the education of the children of upper and middle classes through a network of schools that ranged in levels of prestige; in Puerto Rico and Brazil, only the poorest and lowest working-class families attended public schools.[4] Whether secular or religious, the upper-class educational project aimed to instill in children spiritual values that tacitly configured privilege and inequality in terms of feelings of gratitude. These values further contributed to the cultivation of interiority currency and would, in turn, bestow the parents and children with a level of social responsibility expressed through charity and community involvement. Like other forms of self-cultivation discussed in chapter 4, the enlisting of private educational institutions in the accumulation of interiority currency lays out how parenting empires curated white privilege as something almost mysterious and grounded social inequality on luck and destiny.

DEFETISHIZING ENGLISH: A LATIN AMERICAN ELITE'S ANTI-IMPERIALIST CRITIQUE

While we waited for our falafel sandwiches at a trendy Middle Eastern café near Carlos Varela's Silicon Valley–style office near El Condado, I asked him, the executive director of an educational nonprofit in Puerto Rico, what he felt were the things that, as a father, he would most like to teach his son. I found Carlos's answer a bit unexpected. Almost choking, he stated, "For me the most important thing is that he learns Spanish really well. I want him to feel very proud of being Puerto Rican." I was taken aback not only by his response, but by the evident emotions this raised for him, his slightly unsteady voice and tentativeness as he tried to figure out whether I could see how much the Spanish language and Puerto Ricanness meant to him.

Paula Pelegrino Da Costa, an Ipanema mother of two college students, had worked at Rio de Janeiro's Escola Britânica, an international school considered highly selective but also associated with a Barra da Tijuca new US-oriented elite. Paula's own children had attended Escola Parque, and she also knew several Ipanema families who, after struggling to get their children in international schools, had ended up transferring them to Escola Parque or Santo Agostino, where Portuguese was the main language of instruction. Paula explained: "The main concern of Zona Sul parents is to get their children ready for a type of presence in the global world. But, there is another side to this. I've known many parents who are at first adamant about a foreign-language education, but, once they realize the Portuguese language will suffer, they change their mind. They end up seeking a traditional Brazilian school where Portuguese is the primary language of instruction."

There have been numerous claims about the importance that Latin American elites place on the English language as a leading globalization, cosmopolitan, and social reproduction tool. While parents in El Condado and Ipanema expected their children to learn a second language, with English often being the preferred one, the parents I interviewed were much more concerned about their children learning a "proper" version of their native language, Spanish or Portuguese. In fact, they were often critical of the fetishization of English and were aware of the ways in which English could serve as a global tool of local control.

Suzanne Majhanovich (2013) demonstrates how English as a lingua franca has been tied to particular neoliberal development strategies imposed by the

IMF and the World Bank. Investigating the political effects of global English, Selma Sonntag (2003) detailed how English, as transformed by the contemporary world economy, has reestablished the terms and articulations of power on an international scale. Lionel Wee explores the role of economics in shaping the linguistic value of English through what he calls "linguistic instrumentalism," defined as "a view of language that justifies its existence in a community in terms of its usefulness in achieving specific utilitarian goals, such as access to economic development or social mobility" (2003, 214).[5] Likewise, Ingrid Piller and Jinhyun Cho note, "Neoliberalism, with its imperative to compete, is a covert form of language policy, which imposes English as a natural and neutral medium of academic excellence. In this guise, neoliberal economic restructuring has managed to impose English on ever-more domains of global life while actually dissimulating its operation" (2013, 24).

Among most Ipanema parents, the supremacy of English was associated with a business or economic elite with questionable intellectual dispositions and cultural capital, which were very different from what many Brazilian parents called an *élite intelectualizada* (cf. Windle and Nogueira 2015). The Brazilian elites in Ipanema did not seek to position themselves within a global field of power defined by US hegemony as much as they sought to confirm their power domestically, in everyday ways that focused on expressing forms of sovereignty and civic leadership. The undemocratic nature of access to English, or any second language, in Brazil—the fact that 80 percent of the Brazilian middle class speaks only Portuguese—was reinforced by this elite through the provision of English almost exclusively through extracurricular language courses. Nevertheless, maintaining local sovereignty required an insistence on having children who spoke "proper" Portuguese.[6]

Among Brazilian economic and cultural elites, the prestige of knowing English required not only a communicative knowledge of English words or the ability to produce phrases in the language, but possessing total fluency and a correct accent in speaking; a strong Portuguese-accented English was the object of ridicule. In Brazil, parenting practices have been marked by a heavy investment in English and in international travel to Global North destinations for educational purposes since the 1990s, a time when elite private schools in Brazil were also beginning to establish international partnerships on a large scale. By the middle of the first decade of this century, elite bilingual schools were opening, and exchange and language course programs were consolidating. This was different from the Puerto Rican elite's relationship to English accent and fluency.

In Puerto Rico, US-raised and return Puerto Rican migrants—people who had lived in working-class urban areas of the United States—were also fluent in English, rendering fluency ineffective as a status marker. Ultimately, Ipanema and El Condado cultural elites considered English valuable as long as it was spoken in a standard form of the language and did not interfere with one's ability to speak "proper" Portuguese or Spanish. Thus, while everyone valued English as a secondary language, there was an equal, if not greater, value placed on the national languages as elite symbols. In a few cases, especially among Ipanema parents, the emphasis was as much on learning English as on knowing any other second language beyond Portuguese; several parents had considered German-language schools, for instance, and many others signed up their children for Mandarin or French programs.

The colonial context of neoliberal global English is an enduring structure of power that continues to establish hierarchical difference through linguistic othering.[7] Funie Hsu (2015) argues that, rather than exemplifying a neutral language of international communication, the global domination of English during the contemporary era of neoliberalism continues a colonial pattern of language and power beyond the period of formal colonial administration. The colonial policies of English instruction normalized colonial occupation and the unequal dimensions of imperial power that initiated the global spread of English. The colonial dynamics of language, power, and invisibility persist in the current period, neutralizing the neoliberal global privileging of English as merely a factor of being "in the right place at the right time" (Crystal 1997, 110). Neoliberal practices of global English mystify the fact that for many communities that have historically experienced colonial stratification, no level of English fluency can guarantee an equal footing in a world order that has been, and continues to be, predicated on the hierarchical difference of coloniality (Hsu 2015, 139). English policies in Puerto Rico, for instance, functioned on curricular and broader social levels to justify conquest by invoking the political economic language of salvation as expressed through the Americanization campaign.[8]

Some white upper-class El Condado parents subscribed to perspectives on "proper Spanish" that not only distinguished them from the presumably "improper" Spanish of the lower classes, but also allowed them to challenge a fetishization of English that they associated with financial or corporate elites.

MARU RAMÍREZ DE ARELLANO (RESIDENT OF EL CONDADO):
    Even though St. John's is closer to us, we decided on Perpetuo because we wanted our children to speak Spanish well. At St. John's kids speak English, are practically American. Perpetuo is a more Puerto

Rican school. It is people who value Puerto Rican culture. St. John's has more the tech industry people, financial sector; wealthy but have never held a Puerto Rican history book in their hands.

MARIBEL SEIJO (MBA, MIRAMAR, STAY-AT-HOME MOM): Nowadays, regardless of what school they go to, many children are speaking English among themselves. I don't get that, but it happens at Perpetuo too. And it's not even that the parents speak English at home. I think part of it is that they never watch TV in Spanish, because all that those channels have is telenovelas.

FRANCES GAUTIER (UNIVERSITY PROFESSOR, MIRAMAR): There was a bunch of elementary school girls getting a spa day at the beauty salon today. They were getting the hair, the nails, the makeup, and all of them were speaking English among themselves! And I can't stand that. I had to tell them to speak Spanish. For one, what are these ten year olds doing wearing makeup? But also, that whole issue of speaking English, when Spanish is their first language? Why?

These parents seemed to agree with what Hsu notes: "English did not suddenly appear in various global locales by mere virtue of its perceived superiority as a unifying language, nor did any special attributes of the language inspire a voluntary proliferation across the world. Rather, English was spread through particularly violent processes of colonial domination that maintained a colonial power structure, which privileged western knowledge systems, secured the global division of labor, and established racial, gender, and sexual hierarchies" (2015, 138). The primacy of English in Puerto Rico was reinstituted in the school system with a nod to the current neoliberal global market in 2012, as part of Republican governor Luis Fortuño's Generation Bilingual program. This program reinstituted the primacy of English in the school system with a nod to the current neoliberal global market in a way that paralleled Fortuño's campaign to solicit international corporate investment on the island, because many American multinational firms on the island conduct their operations in English (Barreto 2001, 92).

Among the Puerto Rican upper and upper-middle classes in my ethnography, the English language was a symbol of both status and undesirable (colonial) assimilation to the United States.[9] The upper- and upper-middle-class individuals I interviewed in Puerto Rico felt they had inherited the experience of US racialized Puerto Ricans. A focus on "proper Spanish," for them, was intended to struggle against those racialized US-based images, as Spanish became almost a practice of ethical self-conduct to fashion themselves an interior space of reflexive selfhood. Perhaps more than any other context, schools provided not only institutional spaces of linguistic performance, but also spaces where upper-class anticolonial critiques were forged.

Poking the Bubble: Social Envies, Emotional Discomfort,
and Mixed-Income Experiences

On an evening in June 2017, as we waited for our children's swimming practices to begin, Maribel Seijo restated what she had been telling me over the several years we had known each other: the national swimming academy sponsoring the classes was "diverse," and she had kept her son in the team precisely because she wanted him to be able to relate to "all sorts of people." On this particular evening, I was spending time with Maribel, whose children attended Perpetuo, and with Omar and Carlos, whose children attended St. John's School in El Condado.

While "progressive" parents in global urban centers in the United States and Europe typically seek public schools where their children could come into contact with a "good mix" of people across class and race lines (Byrne 2006), not one single family in El Condado or Ipanema considered public school a viable option for their children.[10] Notwithstanding the unanimous choice of Catholic and secular private schools, Ipanema and El Condado parents insisted that they wanted their children to learn to "be comfortable" among different types of people. Stories of emotional discomfort and awkwardness in socially mixed spaces raised questions for parents about how to help their children "work through" that discomfort.

Predictably, a conundrum these parents, like other upper-middle-class urban parents around the world, faced was how to raise children who not only were conversant about issues of inequality, diversity, and multiculturalism, but could also feel at ease in encounters with "difference," while still maintaining spaces that were exclusive enough to validate their social and racial privilege.

In sociologist Rachel Sherman's (2017b) discussion of entitlement among wealthy New York parents, she identifies a set of practices that parents deployed to demand that children behave appropriately and treat others as equals, that they be kind and not demand special treatment. The New York parents in Sherman's study taught their children to occupy their elite position in an appropriate, nonelitist way by adopting two complementary strategies: a "strategy of constraint," which sets limits on consumption and behavior, and a "strategy of exposure," which exposes children to their advantage relative to others. Versions of these strategies resonated with how Ipanema and El Condado upper classes resolved tensions around being an elite in neighborhoods where drastic inequalities and poverty were endemic to the landscape. In its external manifestation, the interiority currency on which parenting empires were premised required that parents cultivate and reproduce the ability to navigate, with a convincing degree of ease, spaces of racial and class heterogeneity. This was institutionally accomplished, presumably, not only in everyday relations with subordinates (chapter 7), but also by participating in organized activities that contributed to blurring the sharpness of their social advantages. Ipanema and El Condado elites resolved possible tensions between egalitarianism and elitism by inculcating ethical-political ideals not very different from those fostered by Catholic schooling. The Ipanema and El Condado parents I met were careful not to come across as arrogant in their interactions with school personnel; rather, they frequently viewed their role, in somewhat paternalistic ways, as one of "educating the teachers" about who their children were as individuals, psychologically, affectively, and emotionally. These parents were often successful in pushing schools to consider the latest methods, philosophies, and neuropsychological/pedagogical research, and to treat their children in alignment with parenting empire views on emotional depth, anticonsumption, gender expression, cognitive diversity, and global trends, such as multiculturalism.

I witnessed frequent gestures toward what Allison Pugh (2009) terms "symbolic deprivation," the strategy to manage children's consumption, as a function of upper-class parents' own anxieties over the desire to raise good people who treat others well, consume reasonably, and locate themselves appropriately in social space. These strategies were evaluated largely in terms of emotional and social learning outcomes, and on a few occasions, parents described this through the US psychoscientific language of "emotional intelligence" (Mayer, Salovey, and Caruso 2000). Strategies akin to those of "exposure" and "containment," which Sherman describes, were also a means through which Ipanema and El Condado parents aimed to develop agency, confidence, entrepreneurial skills, a sense of ease, emotional well-being, and psychological depth in their children.

In the Latin American and Caribbean contexts of my work, legitimately inhabiting privilege raises the question: Why are elites so invested in being considered "good people" when, in reality, their material well-being and livelihood are not dependent on those marginalized populations to whom they strategically reached out? When did those "below" become the grantors of cosmopolitan or street credit to those "above," particularly in Latin America and the Caribbean, societies where hierarchical arrangements have historically gone unquestioned? Ultimately, a question that the moral dilemmas of the wealthy led to was, Why were these upper-class progressive parents, whose parenting was a powerful tool of sovereignty and surveillance, concerned with mastering the emotional stress and psychological discomfort that social diversity often caused them?

In theory, the Latin American and Caribbean elite parents at the center of this ethnography could have continued to ignore the poor and dark, the marginalized or those "below," and just carry on with life in socially segregated, homogenous circles. Presumably, such homogeneity could continue to bestow the comfort of familiarity and like-mindedness. Upper-class Ipanema and El Condado parents, however, frequently mentioned that being emotionally indulgent or overly protective of their children would limit not only their children's "understanding of the world," but also their own interiority currency. Arguably more than any other role, parenting was characterized by a tension between seeking out "diversity" experiences for children and, perhaps counterintuitively, feeling "social envy" toward certain aspects of working-class lives.

As we waited for our respective children to be done with their swimming sessions, Omar, Carlos, Maribel, and I sat together at one of about six cement tables by the Olympic pool at the University of the Sacred Heart. Omar, Carlos, and Maribel would point out the "kid from Lloréns [housing project] who is an amazing swimmer," or the one from Comerío [small rural town] "whose mother would drive him to San Juan six days a week for swimming practice." Near us, I could identify some parents of the kids in question, which Omar, Carlos, and Maribel considered to be part of "another Puerto Rico." "This is what I told you," Omar reminded me, "many of these parents see sports as the mobility route for their children." I never confirmed how the working-class parents experienced this particular child-centered nodule of urbanism; after all, it is well known that physical distance does not have to correspond to social distance. Over time, I witnessed only minimal interactions, beyond the polite exchanges and discussions about logistics related to the swimming team.

In the exceptional cases in which more intimate relations did develop across class among parents, however, these were frequently conditioned by "social envies" (Hughes 2007). The directionality of these envies, though, might be counterintuitive; they were not on the part of the poorer toward the richer parents, but the other way around. Christina Hughes (2007) contests that envy is a site where concerns over inequalities and exploitation are articulated, so that certain forms of envious feelings can arise, quite legitimately, in response to distributive inequalities. Through the conceptual frame of "social envies," Hughes assumes that the envy has necessarily to manifest in individuals who are "below" in the class structure toward those who are "above." I noticed, however, that in increasingly competitive parenting contexts, there were frequent instances, particularly in El Condado, in which the envious gaze went the other way: from the wealthy to the lower classes.[11]

RICH JEALOUSIES AND SOCIAL ENVY IN
INCOME-MIXED EXPERIENCES

Alejandra Rodríguez Emma, an El Condado resident whose children attended Perpetuo, took great pride in her ability to cultivate friendships, not just having acquaintances, from all social backgrounds and neighborhoods. From such relationships, she had developed her own sociopsychological theories of how the poor's self-presentation clashed with how her wealthier friends interpreted those populations. In reference to the working-class mother of a girl who was in her son's same classroom at Perpetuo, Alejandra highlighted how the mother came across to other parents versus the reality of this woman's life:

> Sometimes the more pretentious people are the ones who have the least reason to be. There is a mom at Perpetuo, Marisela Pabón, whom other parents consider an *arrimá* [social climber] and *comemierda* [snobbish], but I know the background. I know her husband was unemployed for three years and now works at the post office, and that she works at the counter of [a cosmetic store], which is . . . you know. They live in Barrio Obrero. Their entire salaries go to pay Perpetuo's tuition and swimming classes for their daughter. The girl is really smart, responsible, motivated, a ranked swimmer. . . . The other day, I called this woman's house because my son had forgotten the English homework, and I wanted to get it from the girl. The girl was asleep, and the mother tried to read the English homework to me. I couldn't figure out one word she was saying. Who would Harvard want, a kid like my son whose parents went to college and grad school and forgets his homework, or this girl who is in his same school but comes from those other circumstances and had to overcome obstacles?

Notice something here: Alejandra was not making an anti–affirmative action statement akin to those of conservative US populations. She was not suggesting that her son and his working-class classmate deserved the same opportunity for an Ivy League slot. Quite the contrary. To Alejandra, the social envy emerged because it made perfect sense that Harvard would choose the girl over her son. Like other upper-class parents, particularly in El Condado, Alejandra was drawn to other people's rags-to-riches life stories, which she could not reproduce for her own children. When it came to presumably more democratic educational contexts, like college, social envy shaped complicated affective narratives.

The dynamics of status-bridging relationships have broader implications for processes of social segregation and the reproduction (or intensification) of social inequality. When managing these friendships, people try to resolve structural contradictions at the micro, everyday level and, therefore, reach limited solutions. Even if they are aware of such structural and unjust causes of inequalities, it is impossible to resolve these injustices within the context of a friendship, which by definition is based on principles of reciprocity and equality.[12] In contexts of mixed-income friendships and close acquaintances, Ipanema and El Condado parents encountered and handled not only economic inequalities, but also moral dilemmas around deservingness, the lure of overcoming obstacles, and the consequences of having raised sheltered and privileged children. Importantly, the practical management techniques in such mixed-income friendships provided a unique site not only for understanding what the everyday discourses of inequality were, but also what these discourses did. Managing such relationships meant developing skills to understand what would lead to (or prevent) the erosion of these friendships at a micro level, as well as how particular historically situated repertoires of lay understandings of inequality generated practices that deepened segregation between social groups. Social envy among the Ipanema and El Condado wealthy acquired concreteness through perspectives on global competitiveness in the higher education context, particularly the Ivy Leagues, with Harvard as the main proxy. The issue of institutional access, however, was only a side of the social envy picture. All the parents who mentioned Harvard also feared that their respective children lacked drive, resilience, and motivation. They feared that privileged children were deficient in some aspect of "emotional intelligence," which presumably abounded among children who had to struggle and be more independent, mature, and self-sufficient.

Parents viewed community work as formative events that shaped their children's inherited wealth to conform to specific moral requirements, even if, in fact, this "service work" required no contact or minimal contact with "the needy." Parents wanted schools that helped them, in a sense, become a modern type of noblesse oblige, individuals who had a social responsibility and cosmopolitan orientation and whose children developed specific "ethics" and "ethos" about their future role in their communities, nations, and the world. This was how an almost inevitable engagement with race and racialization practices, long avoided, undermined, disregarded, and altogether invalidated by the white Brazilian and Puerto Rican elites, came to acquire nominal and even strategic salience at the intersection of parenting cultures and everyday forms of sovereignty.

AQUÍ NO HAY NADIE FEO (THERE'S NOBODY UGLY HERE): CHOOSING RACE AS ELITE AESTHETIC PROJECT

"¡Dios mío, yo tenía el pelo bien grifo!" (Wow, my hair was really kinky back then!), remarked Maru Ramírez de Arellano, in the same tone one would use to lament a mistake of youth, like dating the wrong guy. *"Sí, esa fue tu etapa de pelo malo"* (Yeah, that was your bad hair stage), joked Mónica Amador, as she continued to flip through the pages of their high school yearbook, from nearly thirty years prior. Most people obviously change, sometimes drastically, from their yearbook pictures to their adult selves; weight changes, period fashion, hairstyle, skin texture, even photo technology all contribute to these changes. Even taking those age-related changes into account, however, a few of the parents I met in El Condado looked not only *radically* different but *racially* different. It was not that they "looked black" back then and "looked white" now. Rather they looked "whiter" now than they had back then. In many contexts in Brazil and Puerto Rico, whiteness was only considered a source of privilege when associated with demonstrable European origins, including last names or narratives of relatives who migrated from Europe to the Americas between the end of the nineteenth century through the twentieth (chapter 6). Nevertheless, the social category of whiteness among Ipanema and El Condado interlocutors was not rooted in these Europe origins alone but also required cultural, social, and aesthetic codes and networks inscribed in class relations (cf. Piza 2000).

These racial looks were frequent topics of conversations, largely filtered through memories of high school life and in relation to life changes and personal aesthetics. Friendships became a mirror of life choices, including racial choices. For the white Latin American elites in this ethnography, friendships forged around schooling effectively produced race as a malleable, almost cosmetic aspect of one's embodiment and affect; for some parents, they had "grown out of" various racial identifiers from their high school years to the present.

Parenting empires in El Condado and Ipanema were framed by a seeming contradiction: not unlike in the United States and Europe, elite parents in Brazil and Puerto Rico realized that they needed to be competent in the liberal language of multiculturalism to prepare their children to assume their privilege responsibly and in accordance with a cosmopolitan, global outlook. From this perspective, Ipanema and El Condado elites were interested and often quite successfully cultivated the ability to engage in "race talk" (Sheriff 2001) in intellectual and even personal terms. They were critical of "racial democracy," even though these perspectives have been historically associated with white elites in Brazil and Puerto Rico (cf. Ramos-Zayas 2012).[13] Overwhelmingly, the individuals I met in Ipanema and El Condado acknowledged anti-Black racism in their respective countries and, when pressed, could provide examples of this. Yet perhaps unlike in the United States or Europe, Ipanema and El Condado elites did not always take their whiteness, or their children's whiteness, for granted. They appeared consistently invested in producing the relational, social, and structural conditions that allowed them to configure their own whiteness as a racial choice and malleable aesthetic. These efforts are validated by the fact that Latin American and Caribbean whiteness has always been rendered invisible, as various tropes of "racial mixture" continue to be the traditional forms of representing racial relations for which the Caribbean and Latin America are globally known (Wade 2004)

"Being white" was not enough; they had to create a range of choices about how to "be white" and what that meant for their racial privilege across various scales, including the neighborhood, the region of the country, the nation, and transnational or global referents. Spontaneous conversations about anti-Black racism were rare among elite white parents, unless elicited in an interview context. There was a tendency in everyday relationships between nonintimate individuals to avoid overtly referencing a person's color, regardless of skin color, but especially if the person was considered black. This corresponded to Robin Sheriff's (2001) findings that silence is a shared cultural convention through which all Brazilians dealt with racism; a form of cultural censorship, silence about racism and color also has different meaning depending on the social position of the individual who produces it: it may express a form of resistance to discrimination or, conversely, a means of preserving social privilege (cf. Morrison 1992). Valeria Ribeiro Corossacz (2015) furthermore argues that silence, as a communicative act, also implies a recognition that the system of color classification is not neutral but rather imbued with racist meanings, the value difference between white and black.

Notwithstanding these perspectives on racial silence, conversations about personal perspectives on the racial aesthetics of self and kinship networks were frequent and common (cf. Godreau 2015) in Ipanema and El Condado. They revealed a great deal about instances in which identities transcended conventional intersectional paradigms to be imagined as either wholly or partially privileged (Bonilla Silva 2013, 2015; Nash 2008; Sovik 2010). Symbols and discourses about race in and out of colonial contexts are resilient to contrary evidence; they strive smugly unchallenged by empirical claims and largely come to depend on "an impression," "a hunch," "a feel." Reassessing what we think we know about empire—its historical specificities, afterlives, durabilities—entails reassessing what counts as evidence of racial belonging and the privilege of racial choice. Imperial effects are intimately bound to whom, where, and what we are asking.

Rather than viewing race as something they identified exclusively in darker others, the upper-class individuals I met in El Condado, and to a lesser degree in Ipanema, were constantly assessing, managing, and discussing degrees of whiteness and blackness in themselves, in their friendship groups, in their extended families, and in relation to their children. This was not a denaturalization of a neutral whiteness, as many critical white studies scholars have noted in the case of whites in the United States. Rather, this was how Latin American white elites articulated racial privilege *as the privilege of racial choice and malleability*, not necessarily a pretense that race did not matter. This was not a version of a "mulatto escape hatch" (Skidmore 1974) or a recrafting of national mythologies of "racial democracy" (cf. Freyre 1933) but a neoliberalization of whiteness consistent with their own neoliberalization of the self; according to this logic, everything about oneself can be "worked on," "improved," or "transformed." Choice and malleability were associated with an active aesthetic and discursive production of phenotypes among whites. This was not exclusively a movement "away from" blackness but a strategic engagement with darkening and the power to decide what they wanted to be considered, racially speaking.

From Maru's adolescence through her midforties, she had undergone a pretty radical transformation, which was evident in photos, including those in her high school yearbook. Although I had not been friends with Maru in her high school days, we frequently saw each other at National Honor Society events in which private and public schools all over Puerto Rico participated. So, in addition to the yearbook photos, I had my own recollections of high school Maru. Those closest to Maru knew that she had gotten a nose job and chin and cheekbone implants, making her face more elongated and narrower, and a breast implant that highlighted some weight loss. This was neither a tight secret nor a source of gossip; it was just part of Maru's life in her postsecondary decades. She had also straightened and highlighted her previously curly dark hair. Maru was not a brown-skinned person aiming for a white aesthetic, but a white person aiming for an even whiter aesthetic. By most Latin American standards, and even some European or North American ones, individuals like Maru would never be considered black or even brown. Nevertheless, they definitely had come closer to a European or US white ideal in their postsecondary years.

In some ways, Maru's racial self-perception and active racial self-fashioning, the way she exerted white privilege through aesthetic projects, could be understood in the broader context of her extended family, including her parents and sisters, whom I got to know well. Over the years, I witnessed how preferences and affective attachments circulated in Maru's extended family. While it would be impossible for me to attribute definite favoritisms to differences in each family member's race or color, I did know that Maru felt her other sisters were the respective favorite daughters of her father and mother. By undergoing cosmetic procedures, Maru in fact looked more similar to her sisters. Maru was not the only, nor even the most dramatic, execution of these racial aesthetics. Among the El Condado elite, she was one of several cases that became important in examining the intersection of gendered expectations of beauty, the recasting of privilege not as whiteness but as racial choice, and the affective aspects of race in general, and of whiteness in particular.

Elizabeth Hordge-Freeman (2015) notes, for Afro-Brazilians in Salvador, the socialization of racial affect that occurs in families. She demonstrates the significant developmental implications of these racial distinctions, noting that "the unequal distribution of affective resources in families leads to differential experiences of support, love, and encouragement, which has a lasting impact on one's life chances. . . . Racial hierarchies in families lead to an unequal distribution of emotional resources and differential family interaction that influence perceptions of support, love, competency, and belonging" (Hordge-Freeman 2015, 131). The structural or material consequences of racial choice for Maru were not equivalent to those of the Afro-Brazilians Hordge-Freeman describes, but the focus on race as the lens through which Maru engaged in perspectives on affective and family belonging were similar. The emotion-laden experiences of racial socialization are crucial not merely because they help us learn about how families make race and participate in racialization, but also because differential treatment leads to unequal access to affective capital. As John Burdick notes in his examination of the relationship between race, color, and family, "it is precisely because of the strength of emotion present in families, of the high expectations within them for love, unconditional acceptance, and affection, . . . that experiences of differential treatment within them create deep psychic wounds" (1998, 43).

Ipanema and El Condado parents tended to circumscribe whiteness to the point of people who "could pass" for American or European, not only in Latin America and the Caribbean, but anywhere in the world. So, while I felt that every single parent I met would be considered white by that locally generated standard, only a handful of parents in Ipanema and none in El Condado felt they would qualify as white. Most of the individuals I met in both Brazil and Puerto Rico were likely to agree on who was a "Black Puerto Rican" or a "Black Brazilian," even if there was also considerable ambivalence about identifying "darkness" in people who were not "obviously Black." Focusing on the plight of Brazilians who are "white but not quite," Patricia de Santana Pinho examines how racial ambiguity is projected onto people's faces, hair, and bodies, thus transforming their whiteness into a mobile intermediary position, which "sometimes moves up and sometimes moves down in the racial stratification of Brazil's pigmentocracy" (2009, 40).

Zaire Dinzey-Flores presents a "dynamic situational model of racial binaries" as a framework to highlight that deploying binaries in everyday social encounters in Puerto Rico is not inconsistent with the idea of the continuum.[14] Dinzey-Flores notes that "inclusion and exclusion is based on the ability of the particular person to position herself or be positioned by others at either side of the binary" (2006, 10). In Dinzey-Flores's compelling analysis, these are "spontaneous binary distinctions with a singular color line"; in this sense, a "panchronic structure of race in Puerto Rico may be continuous, but the synchronic elements are constituted through binaries" (11; cf. Cerón-Anaya 2018). White Puerto Ricans are likely to spend the sum of their "binary" experiences on the nonblack side without difficulty or challenge. In Puerto Rico, whiteness may be constructed from a different vantage point, one where whiteness needs to be asserted, practiced, and reaffirmed in similar ways as the conscious category of Black is in the United States. Maru's life trajectory was characterized by a racial aesthetics of the upper class, the privilege of racial malleability, and a "racialization of class" dynamics (Cerón Anaya 2018). Parents' memories of their own schooling, and the objects that sustained those memories, including yearbooks, in fact solidified white privilege through the insistence on a Latin American whiteness that was based on aesthetics, deliberate racial misrecognition, and a racial understanding legible to individuals of one's class and in relation to global forms of white supremacy.

Maru Ramírez de Arellano was genuinely uncomfortable with the fact that her kid could be the darkest one in his Perpetuo class. Being the "darkest one" in the context of this particular private school meant being the "least white" kid. The fact that it would be highly unlikely that her son would experience discrimination or racism based on his looks perhaps accounted for the fact that her son's looks only triggered discomfort, hardly the genuine concern that parents of black children face. So why the focus on what she views as her son's limited whiteness? Statements like "aquí no hay nadie feo" (there's nobody ugly here), a comment Maru made in reference to her observation that all the families at a Perpetuo event were light skinned, exemplified moments in which "attractiveness" or a perceived alternative aesthetics both sustained and obfuscated elite's perspectives on the nature of race and racism.

Like other Ipanema parents, Vera Ferreira de Oliveira associated blackness with an exoticized, sexually subordinate female beauty that had become mainstream. Alluding to this presumed "post-racial" moment, and deploying a conventional class-trumps-race narrative, Vera remarked, "In Brazil people believe [that] 'the people who live in the *morro* is because they are poor, not because they are Black." And she claimed that being suspicious about dark-skin bodies was "a thing of the past" in Ipanema:

> If you walk down the streets, you see how German [tourists] adore black women. In the past, someone would think "Uff, what does that German guy see in her?" Now I see it as, "Of course!" A German guy never sees that color there [in Germany]. This is exuberant, unique for him. It is a kind of trophy. "Nobody has a woman like mine." . . . Maybe social media also has to do with that change. People can no longer do as they please. If that person is racist, that person will be judged. Once I heard someone say, "Why am I going to give my opinion, if the court of Facebook already decided?"

Unlike other Ipanema parents who explained antiblackness in Brazil by deploying intellectual narratives circumscribed to a national history of slavery, Vera attributed a change in the public language of race to increased social controls (e.g., Facebook) and a generalized concerned with being considered *antiquado* (dated or passé). The remark about the German tourist, as emblematic of a subject from a country most Brazilians considered the antithesis of Brazilian dysfunction, further highlighted the association of Black aesthetics and modernity.

Although in Brazil, aesthetics and esteem questions were often discussed as they related to women, given the way beauty has historically been used to link women's worth to their physical appearance, men also figured centrally to such discussions in Puerto Rico. Explicit discussions about racial aesthetics among the Puerto Rican upper-class parents I met frequently drew from high school memories and experiences.

CARLOS VARELA (EDUCATIONAL NONPROFIT, EL CONDADO RESIDENT): When my wife was a student at St. John's, her best friend was the only scholarship kid in her grade. He could be considered poor, because he lived in Carolina, the father was a town doctor for a religious community. . . . The mother was black. Really, really black, like Big Mamma, Aunt Jemima black. The father is white. My wife's friend is a pretty guy. He does modeling, photo shoots in New York. He is that elegant, urban type.

OMAR TARTAK (PRESIDENT OF FOR-PROFIT EDUCATIONAL INSTITUTION): I had a friend in high school who was *negrito* [diminutive of "Black"], and even he didn't talk about [race]. That guy was . . . and pardon my expression, but I'm talking to you openly [*con confianza*]. . . . He is *un negro lindo* [a cute Black guy]. . . . [What do you mean by that?] He is *perfilado* [suggestive of a narrow nose]. He's more like a dark *trigueño*, you know. He didn't have bad hair. He had good hair [*el pelo no lo tenía mal, el pelo lo tenía bien*]. The [black] people from high school who got ahead were the pretty, approachable, cute ones, you know?

MARIA EUGENIA TIRADO (STAY-AT-HOME WITH MBA, KIDS AT PERPETUO): When we were in high school, to be even a bit tanned [*quemaíto*] was a bad thing. Now it is the opposite. In kindergarten, my son once came home crying. "What happened?" "I want to be darker, like Félix." That's his best friend. My son is so pale that other kids were making fun of him, *pote 'e leche* [milk bottle]. In that way we have progressed in Puerto Rico. . . . [Is Félix Black or is it more that he is moreno?] Félix is dark. In the US, he would be Black. Now the more *quemaíta* [tanned] you are, the prettier you are. To be *jincho* [pale skin] is not considered attractive, either for boys or girls. [Could it be that being tanned is associated with that beach culture or athleticism?] Maybe, but also, now having a butt is considered fashionable. I'm glad for my niece who has a butt, because I lived my high school years covering up my butt.

As noticed in Carlos' and Omar's quotes, there was an assumption that anti-Black racism could be modulated by a Black individual's cultural capital—for instance, being "approachable" and "elegant." Carlos and Omar did not view any contradiction between their own racist remarks (e.g., "good hair/bad hair," "Aunt Jemima") and their insistence that attractive or stylish Black men can avoid racial prejudice. Maria Eugenia, in the last quotation, took this discussion in a slightly different direction. She placed Black, *quemaíto,* and tanned against an undesirable set of attributes she associated with whiteness—*jincho, pote de leche,* and pale skin. In all three quotations, race was located in the assumption that race had a cultural dimension that ultimately determined how a Black individual was treated. These aesthetic and cultural approaches to race, as highlighted in an image of an eliticized Black masculinity, in Puerto Rico, and an exoticized modern femininity, in Brazil, was central to Latin American white supremacy and the rootedness of an idea of race as choice and in relation to interiority projects (chapter 4).

It is significant that whiteness among El Condado upper-class parents was often associated with experiences in school, as well as a "discovery" of racism while attending college or graduate school in the United States. As Omar Tartak noted: "In high school, race or racism were never talked about. Because here in Puerto Rico there's a denial of racism. I only came to hear those discussions in college [in the United States]."

In Puerto Rico, the concept of *estudiar afuera* (study abroad) was entrenched enough in elite parenting culture, US colonial relationship, and popular conversation that there was no need to specify that "abroad" meant the United States.[15] Among the Ipanema upper class, there was not an automatic assumption that the children would go to university abroad; in fact, Ipanema parents raved about the excellence of higher education in Brazil and were not too concerned about their children attending US universities. As an Ipanema mother of graduates of Escola Parque noted, "Families here provide enormous support. They shelter the next generation, activate whatever contacts they have to find good jobs for their children. And for most families, the main contacts are here, in Brazil" (chapter 6). El Condado families viewed going to college or seeking temporary work opportunities in the United States as moments when their children's bubbles would definitively be poked, as they would become "minorities," labeled "Hispanic," or considered "people of color."[16] Estudiar afuera was directly implicated in conversations about race, racial epiphanies, and whiteness among the El Condado elite.

Maribel Seijo, who had attended university in Texas in the 1990s, once told me, "I'm perfectly aware of my white privilege." Yet she promptly added that once, in a bar near campus, the bartender who carded her stated, "We don't accept licenses from Mexico here." This was her way of stating that "despite being white with green eyes," she had been discriminated against. The fact that her Puerto Rico driver's license was assumed to be from Mexico further confirmed that, in the United States, anyone with a Spanish surname would be lumped together.

Like most other El Condado parents, Omar claimed, "It was in college [in the United States] where we began talking more about racism and inequality. That's when I realized that there is racism here [in Puerto Rico]. That it is about race, not just class." Omar situated these discussions in his interactions with Puerto Ricans from working-class urban areas of the United States:

[Upper-class] Puerto Ricans from the island would say, "Well, since we were raised as part of the mainstream, we don't have the chip on the shoulder [*complejo*] [US-born Puerto Ricans] have." We felt they attributed everything to racism and not to the fact that a particular person might have been an asshole. I didn't have a clue about what they had to go through, because my expectation, and that of other [island] Puerto Ricans was that we were an elite leadership class in the making. We were coming back here. But when you see how you are treated, and not only by whites, but even by other Latin Americans, that changes too.

Like other El Condado parents who had gone away to college, Omar had frequent contact with other Latin American elites while living in the United States. They had stories about how these other white Latin American elites would view Puerto Ricans as outliers in the context of Latin America. Puerto Rican Spanish, for instance, had become a ghettoized form of the language in the view of the South American friends many of these individuals had. Puerto Rico's political status as a US colony, limited economic agency in the geopolitical region, and distinctions in how prestige was differently disbursed to the "Caribbean" versus continental "Latin America" also shaped Omar's experience. These elite parents in both Ipanema and El Condado acknowledged racial inequality as long as they could claim for themselves a privileged imaginary of racial malleability.

An element that gets lost in transcription here is that, in this conversation, as well as in numerous others in El Condado, parents expected a certain level of reciprocity and complicity from me in their assessment of their whiteness or their children's whiteness. They wanted various kinds of assurances, but the main ones were in relation to their children's race. Only by engaging in such complicity, allowed by my own whiteness, were these conversations moved away from conventional, scripted narratives to more genuine ones. This was a characteristic of El Condado parents, not very common among Ipanema's elite, whose examples of race and discrimination were often speculative and rooted in hypothetical scenarios, not lived experiences. The fathers I interviewed would in fact "show me," rather than label, their color; like Omar, they would state *"así, como yo"* [like me], pointing to the skin in their forearm, implying that I would agree with their assessment.

When I finally relented to giving Omar the feedback I sensed he wanted, and told him that I did not see him as dark, that he and I were about the same color, he appeared reassured. "I guess we are about the same, right?" he mentioned. I could tell, however, from several references he made to his son's "blondish look" that did not elicit confirmation from me, that he was anxious about how his son's "look" could be racialized. For many parents, this anxiety was reflected in multiple improbable narratives about how some children who are dark now had actually "been blond" as newborns. Also telling was that they viewed themselves as darkened by the fact that they viewed their children as lighter skinned, white, and blond, even though their children, in my view, were almost their exact same color. Interestingly, while in Brazil someone like Omar, whose grandparents had migrated from Palestine to Puerto Rico in the 1940s, would have highlighted this family background in reference to racial self-identification or claims to *moreneidade,* I had to probe to learn more about Omar's family background (chapter 6). The expectations and aspirational aspects of parenting itself exacerbated the instability of these upper-class individuals' own racial self-concept and perceptions; these racial self-perceptions at times provided an intimate lens through which racial ambiguity and malleability became recast in terms of aesthetics.

Conclusion: When Social and School Networks Break Down
and Nothing Happens

A relatively small number of elite schools produced, transformed, and translated, in contradictory and diverse ways, family histories, racial self-fashioning, and social connections. Private schools corroborated the values, behaviors, and customs that either moralized wealth or rendered it suspect. These processes depended on a complicated focus on positioning elite racial privilege in a context of racial options, not necessarily on a belief in racial democracy and its tenets. El Condado and Ipanema upper-class parents recognized that the neoliberal language of diversity and multiculturalism was an increasingly important one to master on a global stage. They knew that they were expected to be conversant about issues of race (*essas questões de raça*), ways unknown to even a generation prior (chapter 6).

Parenting empires cultivated everyday forms of sovereignty as affective entanglements and local sociabilities. As opposed to authoritarian sovereignty, the forms of sovereignty implicated in parenting empires built on the image of a moral, ethical, and compassionate person; they were about fundamentally good intentions. The issue with a focus on intentionality, though, is that it places the evaluation of morality on the impetus, regardless of the outcome. Moral economies of privilege are inherently tied, specifically, to race. They are, more precisely, the very foundation of whiteness, its values, capaciousness, expansiveness. Through parenting, sovereignty and empire acquire institutional hold in schools, as parents exerted substantial influence over how their children were treated and how teachers and staff related to their child, but also over how details about their children's appearance—a combination of manners, looks, and displays of cultural capital—were evaluated by other parents, teachers, and classmates. Adult friendships mediated by the school context were also instrumental in fostering and circulating broader pedagogical and cosmopolitan parenting trends. Focusing on adult friendships, and the role of schools in mediating them, allows an examination of how the moral economy of wealth—with its anticonsumption, antimaterial, conservationist, and minimalist bend—was only available as a project of white supremacy.

In this chapter, I have shown how choosing and cultivating relationships with specific schools, developing adult friendship networks that were extensions of the schooling experience, and viewing elite schools as vehicles to develop intersocial "ease" and learning race talk were fundamental aspects of reaffirming everyday forms of parenting empires. They were emblematic of shifts in Brazilian and Puerto Rican society in terms of the role color played in defining identities, social relations, and cosmopolitan aspirations, owing in part to how public opinion has come to involve extensive and heated debates on racism and the institutional tools tasked with combating it (Steil 2006).[17] Parenting, rather than more traditional tropes like "the family," "the church," or "the citizen," became the dominant modality through which El Condado and Ipanema elites rendered their wealth "moral" and their whiteness "optional" or "malleable." Private schools were an important incubator of adult relationships in Rio de Janeiro and a foundation of class identity and enduring social networks in San Juan; as such, private schools provided institutional grounding to always changing strategies of social reproduction among Latin American and Caribbean elites.

In 2017, Escola Parque parents, like Silvana Villela Mattos, César Schumer, Beatriz Pissollo Itamar, and Bruna Alves Teixeira read in the *Valor Econômico* newspaper that 5 percent of the school had been sold to Bahema Educação, a hedge fund that would be given, over the following three years, the option to buy the remaining 95 percent of the school. Parents approached the Bahema's takeover from an array of perspectives, including, in Silvana's and Bruna's case, a certain optimism about the school's future. After all, Bruna had been anxious that Parque was "the kind of school where teachers thought it was acceptable that five-year-olds were not reading and writing yet"; maybe that would change now. A smaller group of parents, including Beatriz Pissollo Itamar, were appalled. They set up meetings and a WhatsApp group, signed letters opposing the initiative, demanded explanations from the school director, and considered changing schools. "Parque already belonged to Bahema, even before being bought," a parent in the WhatsApp group noted, highlighting the ideological betrayal he felt.[18]

Bahema Educação and Escola Parque were indeed strange bedfellows. Bahema emerged in the 1950s as a company of agricultural machinery and sustained agribusiness activities in Bahia. Its main stockholders were the Afonso Ferreira family, with nearly 58 percent ownership, and the Caixa Econômica Federal (Funcef) workers' pension fund, with 20 percent. In 2016, the holding created an educational group, Bahema Educação, which was interested in investments in elementary school education in Brazil. The day after Bahema announced the purchase of Escola Parque and two other schools, on February 14, 2017, the hedge fund stocks closed with an increase of 23.33 percent, the third highest of the Bovespa and the highest numbers since June 2015. Founded in the midst of the military regime in Brazil, the Escola Parque had an experimental, constructivist teaching philosophy from its inception; values like student autonomy, respect, cooperation, and critical thinking always accompanied official descriptions of the school and were often mentioned by parents as reasons for choosing the school over other traditional elite schools.

Bahema's main stockholder, Guilherme Afonso Ferreira, a collaborator in one of the conservative groups that coordinated Dilma Rousseff's impeachment, remarked that he was in favor of having the state provide universal education, but that the state should not necessarily direct all the schools.[19] In classic liberal fashion, the quality education fundamental for a democratic, stable society would be paid for by the state but could still be executed and designed by private initiative. The Bahema financial group had thus profited from a catastrophic juncture in Brazilian public education—the first victim in the state's draconian austerity measures initiated by the new conservative government in 2016. Many Ipanema parents whose children attended Parque quickly justified the Bahema take over as evidence of how Escola Parque's constructivist curriculum could now be packaged and introduced into private and public schools throughout Brazil, the reason given for Bahema's interest in Parque.

Michelle Forastieri, one of the El Condado mothers who had belonged to the long-standing volleyball group since her high school years, described her divorce from Guillermo Dávila as painful but inevitable. She professed the truism, "These are the times when you know who your friends are, and when I appreciate my siblings, my parents, the fact that my father raised me to be a self-sufficient and independent woman." Other than a discreet shift from "married to Guillermo Dávila" to "single" in the relationship status on her Facebook profile, it was difficult to guess that this marriage had ended.

I met Michelle for lunch in June 2017, and albeit looking slightly thinner, she was just as stylish and energetic. A physician in private practice, Michelle had become a mentor to a premed Brown University student, a young woman who was interning with her for the summer. A white Cuban Puerto Rican, graduate of Michelle's own elite girls' school in Guaynabo, and attending Michelle's parents' own Ivy League alma mater, this young intern was already activating her family's social networks. "She gives me hope of what this generation of Puerto Rican women can do!" Michelle praised the young woman, and then joked that this young woman was her mini-me. It was this consistency that I found remarkable among the individuals who stayed connected to deep high school networks in Puerto Rico, as if in the world there existed no accidents or detours, as if divorces, health concerns, or personal tragedies had no impact for some. In fact, as I wrote the epilogue to this book, Michelle and Guillermo were "seeing each other" again.

Friendships that emerged or were cultivated as a function of schools—whether one's own school or the schools one's children attended—revealed important moments of alliances and fragmentation among Latin American and Caribbean upper classes in Ipanema and El Condado. The forms of relatedness, routines, and ethical ideals built around school choice contributed to giving institutional shape to how elite parents understood their interiority, not only in terms of psychological goals, but as a function of social ease in contexts of inequality; achieving competency in the language of race and moving through the discomfort of socially unequal spaces became a proxy for emotional intelligence. More significantly, as schools collaborated with parenting goals and interests, they also framed neoliberal approaches to education and social difference, including supporting the white privilege of racial choice and malleability and revealing social envies.

Escola Parque was emblematic of how progressive Ipanema parents had come to endorse the corporatization of the private, and possibly public, school system in Brazil under austerity politics, while the relative stability in Michelle's and Guillermo's lives after divorce suggested the endurance of social networks and identities forged through elite schooling in Puerto Rico. The final two chapters of this ethnography focus more explicitly on how parenting empires translated and gave affective currency to national and hemispheric projects—like neoliberal austerity measures and conceiving Latin American and Caribbean governments as uniquely corrupt. Notwithstanding their moral dilemmas around class and racial privilege, Ipanema and El Condado parents harbored pride in their extended family heritage and inherited wealth; their counterintuitive perspectives on wealth and "merit" produced austerity subjectivities in alignment with neoliberal national politics, as discussed in chapter 6.

6

The Extended Family

Intimate Hierarchies and Ancestral Imaginaries

My parents had so much help when I was growing up. We would spend vacations at my grandparents' fazenda in Minas. We had that concept of the extended family, very much part of Brazilian culture. My grandfather was very involved in state politics, so they always had visitors, conversations around the table. Those are experiences my children will not have. . . . My mother is always sending my children expensive presents, and I wonder "Is she trying to make up for not spending more time with them?" I keep telling my mother, "Do not send toys, iPads, games. Do not mistake love for consumption."—Cleide de Moraes, forties, Ipanema native, moved to São Paulo in 2015

I know that Cleide would want me to be there with them, but I cannot imagine doing that. I have my life here in Rio. If she needs me, "Mãe, vem," I get on a plane and go right away. If I can't go, I send Tereza [one of her longtime empregadas]. [Doesn't she have a nanny?] She has three now! One for each kid, and the folguista [weekend nanny]. She thinks that if I come to São Paulo, she'll have another member of the family to be there, supervising, managing the empregadas, with the kids. They don't have a group of families around, like we used to, when she was growing up here in Ipanema.—Otávia Camargo Correa, early eighties, Ipanema resident

Otávia Camargo Correa lived with two empregadas and her younger brother, Moacyr, who was in his seventies, in the penthouse of an exclusive Ipanema high-rise. Through the course of my fieldwork, I would come to visit many apartments as spectacular as Otávia's. Those residences' décor and layout often allowed me to envision aspects of private lives that I never witnessed. I could imagine, for instance, Otávia and Moacyr sipping their morning coffee or admiring the Ipanema sunset in comfortable chairs on their enormous terrace.

I could imagine them, reflectively, overlooking the Zona Sul from the Arpoador beach to the entrance to São Conrado, as the Vidigal favela became the euphemistic colorful scene of Rio postcards. I could also imagine Cleide, Otávia's only daughter, as a teenager in the 1980s, getting ready for beach volleyball games with her friends from the German elite school she had attended. Beyond marking one of my early close encounters with movielike real estate, my visits with Otávia and Cleide shed light into the role of extended families and intergenerational relations in the lives of contemporary Latin American elites. These visits, and those with other grandparents in Ipanema and El Condado, allowed me to witness unmet expectations, resentment, fear of loss, and complicated parent-child-grandparent dynamics. These intimacies highlighted national family contributions, foregrounding privileged ethnic heritage and regional backgrounds, and ultimately sustaining familial claims to the neighborhood, city, and state.

Intergenerational disagreements over child-rearing practices—and the resentment, pain, and misunderstandings these raise—are nothing new. What remains interesting in the cases of Ipanema and El Condado was how the extended family became a central locus from which upper-class parents engaged in a critique of consumption and materialism, and forged austerity subjectivities. Within the extended family, materiality was supposed to become "immaterial"; lineage, contributions to the nation, and ethnic ancestral sagas were dramatized; and accusations against "uninvolved grandparents," "neurotic parents," and "buying love with gifts" forged a moral economy of wealth in the Caribbean and Latin American upper classes.

The extended family has often been deployed as a traditionally Latin American (and sometimes US Latina/ox) cultural trope. The assumption is that, in contradistinction to the nuclear family focus of the United States, Latin Americans view families in collaborative, intergenerational terms that transcend the self-contained nuclear family household. The distinction between nuclear and extended family orientations is, arguably, one of the leading popular stereotypes assigned to "Latin culture" to distinguish it from Anglo cultures.[1] Despite enduring perspectives on the extended family as a Latin American cultural phenomenon (cf. Keefe, Padilla, and Carlos 1979), surprisingly little scholarship in the region has examined the nature of emotional relationships across the conjugal, intergenerational, or filial continuum. Even within the parental bond, most of the emphasis remains fixed on tangible, material forms of support and care, with little discussion of emotional experience, longings, or expression beyond such financial transactions.

Although the extended family was often viewed as a natural social category, it was the product of arduous, emotionally practiced, and calculated everyday interactions. Contemporary parenting cultures and ideologies influence not only the nuclear but also the extended family. The relationships between the parents in my ethnography and their own parents, siblings, in-laws, and relatives were critical to how the extended family forged its traditions, financial and work trajectories, tensions, moral codes, and white privilege.[2] They also provide the spaces and imaginaries through which neoliberal austerity politics of the state acquire everyday resonance under processes of parenting empires.

The extended family functioned as a leading affective vessel through which Ipanema and El Condado parents explored resentment, gratitude, trauma, insecure adulthood, and ambivalence toward life choices, on the one hand, while securing racial and class privilege through connection to family lineages and financial resources, on the other. Upper-class El Condado and Ipanema residents often deployed the concept of the extended family to distinguish between legitimate and illegitimate social practices, and to exert claims on how intimate social relationships invoked a moral repertoire for all kinds of financial exchanges and transfers.

As a series of affective, financial, and symbolic relationships, the extended family gained salience at a time when wealth was becoming increasingly suspect and associated with political corruption and with those responsible for (and who benefited from) the political and financial crises of the nation-states. The extended family often set the parameters for what constituted "moral wealth," or the legitimate forms of obtaining and using money and selectively rejecting materiality.

In this chapter, I look into the lives of extended families, and what they reveal about upper classes' beliefs about justice, fairness, and adult responsibility. I examine these processes in relation to how parenting and empire intersect by focusing on how a moral economy of wealth was forged among elite extended families in Ipanema and El Condado. Moreover, I consider how various forms of inequalities within extended families were interpreted among family members. The second half of the chapter focuses on how extended families intersected with two leading national discourses at the center of the parenting empires framework laid out in this ethnography: the claim to higher political involvement and patriotism of the upper class, and migration sagas of model ethnic groups, namely, Cubans (including Cuban Jews) in Puerto Rico and various Middle Eastern nationalities in Brazil. I demonstrate how these national discourses became endemic to white supremacy and racial inequality in Latin America and the Caribbean, producing a context in which white purity was not valorized, but in which whiteness continued to constitute social value and a form of status whose power was effectively rendered invisible.

Los Abuelos No Son Lo Que Eran Antes *(Grandparents Are Not What They Used to Be): Ambivalent Adulthood and Extended Family Values*

Maru's parents, Violeta and Pepe Ramírez de Arellano, were among the grandparents I met over the course of my fieldwork. Violeta and Pepe had just celebrated their fiftieth wedding anniversary when I formally interviewed them in their spacious Spanish-tiled home in El Condado. This was the same house where they had raised their four children, including Maru. Over the last ten years, their yard had become a child's paradise, with a tree house sitting among lush vegetation, a pool with a slide, and even a zip line, which their seven grandchildren enjoyed. Like some of the other grandmothers I interviewed in Puerto Rico, Violeta had worked, as a social worker, before becoming a stay-at-home mom once her first child was born. In her seventies, Violeta shared, with other grandmothers I met in Ipanema and El Condado, a dedication to her appearance. She had celebrated her sixtieth birthday with a facelift and remained attentive to her makeup and hairstyle, wore fashionable clothes and understated family heirlooms, and had weekly appointments with the same hairstylist and manicurist she'd had for several decades.

Violeta and Pepe, like many members of extended families I met in Puerto Rico, and some of the ones I met in Brazil, had appeared in local society magazines like *Imagen* and *Caras*. They had been profiled in these magazines for their home décor and fashion sense, work achievements and legacies, philanthropic contributions, and how they celebrated holidays and family traditions; these were public images of family cohesion, political influence, and parenting successes. In these magazines, the upper-class family was contextualized in broader genealogies of recognition—for instance, profiling how fathers and sons shared a talent for business or medicine, or how a mother and daughter shared an interest in fashion, interior design, or art collecting. These representations unified the upper class and racialized inequality in a common language of success, talent, and achievement conveyed through a genealogical narrative based on biology, inherited dispositions, and upbringing.

Relationships between the parents and grandparents I met in El Condado tended to be characterized by both mutual resentment and mutual admiration, as well as considerable dependence of the parents on the grandparents for financial and other forms of support. When I asked Violeta if her children's expectations about her as a grandparent corresponded to her own desires for herself as a grandmother, she explained: "Well, I've had to set boundaries. Initially, my daughters expected me to do a lot more childcare than I was willing to. I want to spend time on me, and they have a hard time understanding that. They all have babysitters. They also have very involved husbands. Pepe [her husband, the grandfather] was never involved. So now, sure, he's the greatest grandfather. They think he's a better grandparent than me. But they don't understand that for him, this childcare thing is something new. He didn't spend his life raising four kids." Even among professional mothers in El Condado, traditional gender expectations surfaced, pretty forcefully, in relation to their own mothers; just like they resented their mothers' childcare boundaries, so they praised their fathers' hands-on involvement with the grandchildren. There was also a stronger expectation that the maternal grandmother would be more involved than the paternal one.

The grandmothers I met in Ipanema would rarely, if ever, be expected to care for their grandchildren on their own, without the help of paid domestic workers or nannies (chapter 7). In Puerto Rico, however, parents like Maru Ramírez de Arellano and Mariblanca Giusti had grown up expecting that their own parents—or significantly, their own mothers—would provide on-demand childcare once they had children. When those fantasies were not met, there was considerable friction in the extended family.

MARU: A week before we were about to leave to Vietnam [where she and her husband had planned to go on vacation], my mom tells me "I can't stay with Diego [her son]." We had a big fight. I felt a sharp, physical pain right here [points to her chest]. To me, this was a rejection of my son and our parenting. She may not say it, but I know she feels my sons are savages, undisciplined. I talked to my therapist, and she told me: "Your children are your responsibility, not your mother's. If your mother takes care of them, it is as a favor, not because she has to." I understand that, but all I'm saying is that the rules have changed. My siblings and I were practically raised by our grandparents.... Now grandparents pay for things, for school tuition, computers, the family ski trip to Vail. They would much rather pay for the nanny or after-school activities than babysit their own grandchildren. Grandparents are not what they used to be.

MARIBLANCA: My son had just been diagnosed with attention issues, and my mother takes him to Burger King. I lost it. Here I am trying to make changes in his diet, to see how I can deal with this situation in a healthy, more holistic way, and she takes him out to eat crap. My child had never even set foot in Burger King, even before the diagnosis. I confronted her, and she got upset, telling me that there was nothing else open [this was a few days after Hurricane Maria hit Puerto Rico], and that if I was going to impose on her this way, she'd rather not babysit for me. My own grandparents would have never threatened my mom that way!

From a symbolic, affective, and pragmatic perspective, extended families gained currency through parenting, when individuals became more concerned with social reproduction in relation to broader collective family projects, traditions, expectations, and kinship networks.[3] Extended families required that parents manage expectations about what grandparents ought to be versus the realities of what grandparents were willing to be. These expectations influenced a moral economy of the Latin American extended family in the upper class, particularly when it came to conflictive relationships to materiality and materialism.

When I arrived at Pepe and Violeta's house on a Sunday to have lunch with the whole family, I could tell that there was some tension between Violeta and one of her daughters, Annette. Seemingly out of nowhere, full of irony, Violeta remarked, "I guess now you can't even correct a child's way of talking, because it's bad for their self-esteem. But how will they learn that you don't say 'tigurón' [instead of tiburón] if you don't correct them?" Annette rolled her eyes and stated, "He is going to a speech therapist. Just leave it alone!" To this, Pepe, Annette's dad, interjected as if talking to nobody in particular: "They have therapists for everything nowadays! I didn't learn to say the letter B until I was four and nobody thought of taking me to a therapist." El Condado extended families were invested in ensuring continuity and "proper" children's sociability, including a focus on genealogies, school traditions, navigating exclusive national and international spaces, and speaking properly.[4]

In another conversation with Annette and her husband, Carlos Andrés Pagán, Annette noted that when she and her siblings were young, their father would always tell them that they had no money. He would rarely indulge them. Annette added, "In retrospect, we were obviously not poor, but that strategy, of saying we had no money, worked. Now my parents don't allow us to do the same with our kids. And this is especially my mother who wants to buy their love with gifts, instead of spending time with them." Carlos Andrés added, "I don't want my children to think they can have anything they want, even if we could . . . you know . . . we can afford it. We can't tell them 'we don't have the money for that,' when we obviously do. And if we don't get something for them, the grandparents will. At the grandparents' house, they tell the maid to bring them a plate of food upstairs and stuff like that. We would never allow that."

Possibly like grandparents worldwide, the grandparents I met were often suspicious about their children's parenting practices and the continuous emergence of parenting trends. Moral absolutes endemic to contemporary parenting cultures—from the simple, like what foods to feed children or the quantity and quality of time spent with them, to the more complex, like how to teach motivation and gratefulness—often created tension between parents and grandparents.[5] These tensions between traditional cultural practices that drew extended kin together and newer methods of childcare that drew them apart contributed to how familial connections and disconnections were framed. Family ties were frequently characterized in terms of resentments, anxieties, ambivalence, gratitude, and neuroses. The parents I met worried that the grandparents were not as involved as their own grandparents had been or were not involved in ways that were consistent with the parents' child-centered routines, ideologies, and aspirations. In such instances, members of the extended family were portrayed as a threat to the nuclear family's normality, because they were out of touch with more modern, scientific or expert-guided practices or too focused on conveying closeness through gift giving and consumption.

Cleide, the Ipanema mother quoted in this chapter's epigraphs, recognized these intergenerational variations in child rearing, as she termed her own children's generation the Geração Peito de Frango (Chicken Breast Generation), because "in my parents' generation, the father would sit at the head of the table, and get the best part of the chicken. Now it is the children, not the parents, who get the chicken breast, you see?" As adaptability and resilience become globally identified as crucial skills to academic and career success, elite parents doubt their ability to socialize children in ways that encourage self-motivation and drive when their family privilege rendered things too easy.

There has been a convergence of risk culture and parenting; parents are viewed as both source and solution to a wide variety of social concerns. In El Condado and Ipanema, such risk culture and life challenges—from financial challenges to learning disabilities to divorce—were cushioned by the material, affective, and social forms of capital that extended families could provide at critical points in a parent's life. Many parents talked about how, without the help of their extended families, they would not have been able to follow a path they had set for themselves, such as becoming homeowners, going on expensive vacations, or having their children in private schools. These discussions gained salience in mixed-income couples, where spouses came from different social backgrounds, a feature not too rare among the Ipanema parents I met. The lower-class members of such mixed-income couples were key in the production of narratives of "self-made" versus "inherited" wealth; they were front-row critics about how the older generation, the grandparents, had contributed to raising *adultos infantilizados* (childish adults).

MIXED-INCOME MARRIAGES AND INTIMATE HIERARCHIES OF WORTH AND WORK

While in El Condado most parents were from well-established, even old money families and continued to be endogamous in terms of class and, almost by default, race, that was not always the case in Ipanema, where I encountered several instances of considerable upward mobility among one of the individuals in the married couples. In my sample, this individual was usually the woman.

Paula Rios and I agreed to meet in front of the Ipanema crèche our sons attended. The evening before, Paula had warned me on the phone that she was barely getting reacclimated to her Rio routine, after having spent two months with her three-year-old son in the South of France. Influenced by the South of France reference, I was imagining Paula as a Brazilian *dondoca* or *perua*, a cartoonish popular image of a carioca socialite or lady who lunches, which never really materialized over the period of my fieldwork.[6] Perhaps Paula would be the first, I thought. Sporting stylish gym gear, coiffed shoulder-length black hair, and a Coach bag, Paula greeted me and suggested we walk to the apartment where she lived with her husband, Mauricio Carvalho Cardoso, and their son, Rogelio. The apartment was a bright, sparsely decorated three-bedroom flat on the eighth floor of a small doorman condominium closer to the lagoa area of Ipanema than to the more affluent Avenida Vieira Souto beachfront. I was surprised, first, that Paula would be so quickly persuaded to talk to me, and second, that she would invite me to her home. Although I had already met many parents at the beach playgrounds at the time, I had yet to be invited to any of their houses; in fact, getting invited to someone's house, other than for a special birthday celebration or organized activity, was rare over the early months of fieldwork in Ipanema. In many ways, Paula was an extreme example of upward mobility. Her case alerted me to how class performances, no matter how well executed, need to be examined carefully in elite Latin American neighborhoods.

About halfway through our first recorded interview, when I asked Paula what she thought of Ipanema, she could not contain tears. Unbeknownst to even some of her closest friends, Ipanema was a foreign world for Paula. Her story was about the pain of rural Rio de Janeiro, extreme poverty, and astonishing social mobility through marriage, of feeling both marginal in Ipanema and grateful for the opportunity to live in a neighborhood that still awed her. Still sobbing and apologizing, Paula continued, "Ana, even nine years later, I still can't believe this." She spread her arms as if trying to both show me her stylish home and embrace the surroundings: "Psychologically, I still live with the fear of loss. It was my husband's [extended] family, not my husband, who bought this apartment, right before we got married. He told me he was going to buy it and I said OK. That's all I was able to say, OK, because it was really his family's money."

In Ipanema, real estate was a main material connection between the parents I met and the extended family. Nevertheless, these purchases were reframed not so much in terms of material value but in terms of emotional and psychological support. About half of the Ipanema parents I interviewed were apartment owners, compared to every single parent in El Condado, who frequently owned more than one property, including in the United States or Europe. Of those who were homeowners in the two neighborhoods, more than half had either inherited their apartments from family members—more often their parents—or had received substantial financial assistance from relatives to be able to purchase their place.

Paula and Mauricio had been married for nine years when I first met them in 2012, though they had known each other for well over a decade. At nineteen, during a visit with friends to a hang-gliding area in São Conrado, Paula met Mauricio, an affluent Ipanema native and ten years her senior. Paula recalled telling her friends, "He's rich, I'm poor. I don't think this is going to work." The friends encouraged her to give him a chance, that even if it didn't work out long term, it could be "an experience to gain culture and an opportunity to grow." Paula had many stories of the early days living in Ipanema, including the fact that the only person she had developed a connection with turned out to be a prostitute whom she met while standing in line at Bradesco; that her name was not on the apartment her husband owned; that she felt inadequate, intellectually, emotionally, and physically to fully belong, even in parenting groups.

One late afternoon, after Paula, her young son Rogelio, and I had been drinking coconut and acerola juices at a corner *boteco* on Visconde de Pirajá, Rogelio begged to go to his grandparents' house, just a few buildings down from Paula and Mauricio's building. While Paula helped one of the live-in maids give Rogelio a bath, Paula's mother-in-law, Dona Dirce, invited me to a glass of wine on the terrace. As the conversation unfolded, with an illuminated Corcovado as background, Dona Dirce remarked that Paula had "turned out to be a good mother, after all." She had had some reservations about Paula when Mauricio had first introduced her to the family: "I knew Paula's parents had separated and that she pretty much was raising herself. I just wasn't sure how that profile [*perfil*] would fit with my son's upbringing. He was raised in a household with mother, father, siblings, and with a solid extended family, very typical here in Brazil, right?"

Over the time I knew them, Paula and Dona Dirce experienced on-again, off-again tension, usually depending on whether Paula was holding a job (less tension) or not (more tension). The tension had to do with each woman's expectations and engagement with the world of work. Dona Dirce occasionally worked in her husband's hotel chain. Even though Paula had worked since childhood, once her son was born, work became a site of discomfort and confusion. Unlike other mothers who had grown up in upper-class households, Paula faced strong pressure from her husband and her husband's family to seek paid employment. As an Ipanema resident and member of the Carvalho Cardoso family, however, Paula felt she could not do some of the jobs she had done in her youth or young adulthood, like being a waitress or bartender, and that she lacked the skills and credentials to pursue more suitable jobs. At one point, in a deliberate and peculiar manner, Paula decided that she would "become a housewife," like a friend of hers had done after moving to Miami. She let go of their empregada. In Ipanema, where sometimes even the middle classes had domestic workers, the extended family's expectation that Paula either work (for pay) or let go of the empregada was highly unusual. When Paula described the moment when the extended family had discussed Paula's work-related future, I couldn't help but wonder if Dona Dirce, who frequently felt "taken advantage of"—by the maid, the clerk, the doorman, and, more abstractly, the "PT government" in the pre-2015 era—felt that Paula was "taking advantage" of the family. This was remarkable, considering that Mauricio had rarely held steady jobs and was supported by his parents' wealth.

Vera Ferreira de Oliveira was an example of how, in Ipanema, the hard work of the middle and lower classes was, initially, presented as a critique of the unmotivated wealthy but still fell short of serving as a broader social critique of the wide opportunity gap in Brazil between the wealthy and everyone else. Vera, whose mother had worked as a nanny in a working-class neighborhood in Niteroi for most of Vera's childhood, frequently noted that her husband, Thiago da Silva, simultaneously "lacked drive" on issues related to planning the couple's financial future and was "too inflexible" regarding their son Felipe's upbringing. Vera remarked:

My mother-in-law tells me: "Vera, you and Thiago need to connect better as a couple. Forget that discussion about buying joint property.

Focus on the marriage." But Ana, sometimes I get very frustrated because Thiago is very unconcerned about money. Deep down, he still believes that, if he makes a mistake, his family will bail him out. . . . He worries about Felipe dropping a bread crumb on the floor. I worry about Felipe's inability to achieve his potential in Brazil. I'm always telling Felipe, "What you have today is because your mom studied a lot and worked hard." Thiago can't say that to Felipe, because everything was given to him. The day that Felipe asked about a homeless person in the street, I told him, "Felipe, things get passed on from family to family. So, maybe [the homeless woman] comes from a family who didn't give her structure. You see how Vovó Lala [Vera's mother] used to live in a farm and her own mother had to work to give her a better life? And then she worked to give me a better life? There's continuity."

While Vera considered what she viewed as Thiago's lack of drive or general apathy toward developing a marital *patrimônio* (patrimony)—roughly, an arsenal of tangible goods and property they could leave for Felipe as inheritance—a main cause of marital tension, Thiago was constantly reassuring her that they should not focus on those *questões materiais* (material issues). His goal was to raise Felipe as "the kind of person who feels comfortable among different cultures" (chapter 5). For Thiago, who felt confident in his family's financial security and continued to feel that way notwithstanding the uncertainties Brazil was going through, opportunities were measured in terms of neoliberal forms of flexibility, cultural competency, social graces, manners, and ease.

Extended families, particularly in-laws, in the cases of Vera and Paula, played important roles in reframing concerns about material stability in terms of marital issues that needed to be addressed therapeutically. Both Vera's and Paula's parents-in-law had at some point remarked on "the level of anxiety over money" that their daughters-in-law had and viewed this as a cause of marital instability or even tensions in the extended family. Members of the same extended family often followed divergent class trajectories; relatives within the same upper-class family had different access to economic resources, as was true for Vera and Paula. The Ipanema and El Condado upper classes continued to rely on a totality of family strategies, including the significant financial involvement of grandparents and, in a few occasions, even ancestral trust funds, to ensure upward mobility or at least the preservation of their status. This financial involvement of grandparents at times enabled some upper-middle-class parents to orient themselves toward preserving noneconomic forms of social, symbolic, and emotional capital, and cultivating in their children skills and experiences linked to how the requirements of future labor markets were imagined. More frequently, though, the realities of extended family dramas came in conflict with parenting empires, as vigorous disagreements over money, inheritances, and spending choices acted against elite parents' affective expectations and austerity subjectivity.

The distinction between "self-made" as an individual enterprise versus the product of collective family lineage worked differently in Brazil and Puerto Rico. For instance, Zulema Nader, the executive director of an NGO and an Ipanema resident, had a niece who had pursued graduate studies at a university in the United States, ended up marrying a white American, and had settled in Leblon in 2010. Zulema and her mother, Dona Matilde, once commented on how the niece's American husband often remarked that he was "the first one in his family to have gone to college." Dona Matilde was puzzled, not so much by the statement, but by the fact that this was something that her grand-niece's American husband viewed as a source of pride. In her words: "I am proud of the fact that my mother, even back in her time, was an educated woman. All my siblings are educated. That's a source of pride, to come from that lineage of an educated extended family. But this is not his case. He mentioned that nobody else in his family was educated!"

In El Condado, the sense of pride in "being the first one in one's family to attend college," presumably an individual achievement rooted in personal effort, would have been legible. In fact, this was the way many of my interlocutors reacted to a close childhood friend of mine who had attended the same US graduate program as some of my interlocutors. This friend of mine, whom they knew was like a brother to me, had put me in contact with one of my earlier interlocutors. My friend had been raised in a working-class area of Puerto Rico, had held several low-wage jobs while attending college and graduate school, and had eventually occupied a prestigious job in the Obama administration. My friend was, indisputably, self-made; in most cases, my friend was the only person El Condado parents knew who had such a social trajectory. He was emblematic of something else, though: some interlocutors viewed him as reminder of how they could not raise their children to rely exclusively on inherited forms of capital but needed to provide academic, personal, and social skills valuable in a highly competitive cosmopolitan world.

Affective and financial entanglements provided the everyday relational context through which extended families confirmed for parents that material wealth was, in fact, immaterial. Family mobility sagas and experiences of entering into mixed-income marriages circulated among elite parents as evidence that financial resources, ultimately, were no match for values, personal struggles, and determination. It was through the extended family that a politics of austerity, of living minimalist and "debt-free," became a moral subjectivity.

AUSTERITY AS ELITE SUBJECTIVITY: DEBT-FREE
AND THE REFRAMING OF FAMILY DYSFUNCTIONS

Upper-class families in Ipanema and El Condado rarely understood economic activities in any narrow economic sense; rather, they viewed economic transactions within the extended family in terms of broader moral imperatives and intergenerational "lessons," not disconnected from the neoliberal austerity logic that characterized Brazil and Puerto Rico during the time of my fieldwork. Extended families claimed a moral economy of wealth around values like fiscal responsibility and living debt-free; perspectives on "gratefulness" influenced by Third World Catholicism and a distancing from popularized US consumption patterns; and a reframing of family dysfunctions. In this moral economy of extended family, austerity yielded an important form of neoliberal subjectivity.

Omar Tartak, in his midforties and a resident of El Condado, is gregarious, insightful, and personable, betraying, to a degree, what he described as a dysfunctional childhood. On a day we met at a frozen yogurt café near the highrise building where Omar and his wife, Evelyn, lived, Omar explained that he was trying to maintain "a decent lifestyle" despite the new expenses he was anticipating with the birth of the couple's third child. Initially, he had tried nudging his unwilling wife to go back to work, instead of becoming a stay-at-home mother, which she wanted to do. "That brewed so much resentment in her," he recalled. Rather than forcing the issue, Omar took on a part-time job managing his mother's lucrative medical supplies chain, while remaining the executive director of a for-profit educational organization. He explained, "I wish my mom would make up her mind about retiring. I don't want to be fighting with her all the time, about taking over the company. My mom helps us financially. She gives a monthly stipend to each one of us four [siblings]. Indirectly, she is paying tuition at St. John's, the most expensive school in Puerto Rico."

Omar was one of many El Condado parents who attributed most social ills and outcomes to "poor parenting." Regarding the students he came into contact with through his job, he once mentioned: "Many scholarship kids end up not finishing college after high school. I don't want to generalize, but even if some people get scholarships, there is an element of lacking a strong family unity. Parents who may not see education as a priority, who don't teach fiscal responsibility, partly because they can't, but partly also because there's no stability in the home." I was quite surprised by Omar's comment, given that his life was probably the epitome of instability. He had been neglected by his parents, to the point that he was living on his own at sixteen; his father had come in and out of the family multiple times, while his mother incessantly alternated between several abusive boyfriends and fundamentalist Pentecostalism; he had changed schools, and homes, almost every other year. I couldn't help but press him on this, given how candid and detailed he had been about what he considered his dysfunctional childhood. Nonetheless, he pushed back and insisted, "In my case, both parents were well educated and both insisted that I had the best education. But, what I think was key was that they taught us the value of saving, not living beyond our means, not being seduced by consumption."

As Omar began working for and depending more on his mother financially, he reframed his retrospective on her:

> Economically, she has always been super independent and wealthy, but emotionally she is very frail. She has always lived seeking those spiritual spaces. She's a very interesting woman. . . . All in all, I have to say that, my mother's spiritual, Pentecostal values, the positive values that religion brings, of acceptance and forgiveness, have stayed with me. Because I remember there were times when I was hanging out with thieves [*maleantes*]. Looking back, I realize that there was a trend for upper-middle-class kids to befriend kids from the housing projects [*caseríos*]. It's the bad, hard-core, tough boys from elite schools like Perpetuo, Marista, San Ignacio. They liked to fist fight. Back then, they were not carrying guns, thank God!

These contradictions—between elite family dysfunctions and the family dysfunctions of the poor—were common. There was a way to turn around what might in the case of the poor be viewed as "cultural" into something "moral" when in reference to the wealthy.

Among extended families, claiming to be "debt-free" was a family value and served to illustrate a family's ability to pull resources together. For instance, Roxana Valdejuli, a St. John's teacher and resident of El Condado, highlighted that "not living beyond your means" or "not having debt" was an important "value" that her parents had passed on to her. She explained, "When I got married, my father-in-law gave us a very comfortable sum, and the apartment in El Condado, which had been in the family for many generations. It was important for them that we began our lives without taking on any debt. No mortgage." When her father sold his company, Roxana's siblings began getting a percentage of the royalties. Yet, the main lesson she gathered was, "Debt is a huge problem in Puerto Rico. That's why we're in the situation we're in. People here live in debt [*se embrollan*] and can never get ahead [*no sacan los pies del plato*]!" These neoliberal subjectivities were precariously perched on the gaze of their even more affluent peers, as well as their subordinates (chapter 7).[7]

Important, if absent, in Roxana's view of being debt-free as a family value and part of the moral economy of extended families had to do with the very wealth on which she and her husband had come to depend to be debt-free. In fact, for most of the time of my research, Roxana's husband had been making "almost nothing" as a stockbroker, yet the family was doing "better than ever" even after 2015 because of their personal trusts and other family investments. At one point, Roxana acknowledged, "The people doing badly are those who made the money themselves, or put their money in Puerto Rico government bonds. Even physicians are screwed up. Unless you have inherited, you are really screwed here." And yet "personal debt" was legible through a broader narrative of national crisis and corruption in Puerto Rico (chapter 3, epilogue). National crises in Brazil and Puerto Rico contributed to a "shock doctrine of parenting" that increased financial intergenerational dependence, while widening the generational gap in terms of parenting practices; there was greater family dependency along with diminished intergenerational trust and perceived inability to meet new parenting cultural expectations.

The role of the extended family in enabling this debt-free life was considered a family value and evidence of family togetherness. The brunt of the blame for debt was squarely placed on those "financially irresponsible" Others—most notably the conspicuous consumers who contributed to the full parking lot at Plaza Las Americas mall in San Juan or individuals concerned with brands in Rio de Janeiro. One of the times when I formally interviewed Roxana, she mentioned that her parents had divorced when her sister and she were teenagers. "I imagine your life must have taken a turn at that time," I commented in reference to her description of the era as one of hardship. To my surprise, she responded that there had been some emotional hardship, but that she barely noticed a difference in terms of her lifestyle: her grandparents had set up one of the apartments they owned in Miramar so that their divorced daughter and grandchildren could live there. They had continued to pay for private school–related expenses and membership in the Caparra Country Club. Roxana stated, "Our extended family is very, very close. We have those values, you know?" This appeared as a recurrent story: what could have catapulted the family into downward mobility had been prevented by grandparents or aunts, uncles, and even siblings, who had come to the rescue. This was a story of wealth transference that cushioned social inequality in terms of morality and family values. In Roxana's words: "Our family pulls resources together. We don't view this as 'your money' or 'my money.' And, this is part of what we have learned from our parents or even our grandparents and what we also want to teach our children. In a sense, you could consider it a legacy. It is a perspective on money that is consistent with valuing our family, not owing anything, or being too susceptible to uncontrollable things, like the economy, the national debt, all that." These moral dimensions of social inequality operated through a fashioning of upper-class families as "austere," "unassuming," and harboring politically enlightened anticonsumption attitudes, in contradistinction to the consumption-focused (often poorer, darker, or lesser status) populations.

Drawing from US quantitative data and personal observations, Elizabeth Currid-Halkett argues that a newly emergent "aspirational class" in the United States (and Europe) has been "motivated by self-confident values and is actively choosing its way of life through an extensive process of information gathering and forming opinions and values, some of which involve money but many of which rest on cultural capital instead" (2017, 19). These upper classes show their status through certain behaviors and goods that do not cost a lot and are not ostentatious but still signal social position to others who have the knowledge to evaluate these behaviors and goods. The aspirational class's main currency, so to speak, is its self-regard as being more (or better) informed about health, parenting, and the environment, mostly, and engaging in consumer practices that reflect their values and cultural capital. Thus, their consumption choices, in a sense, are not inherently more expensive than the alternatives (e.g., almond milk versus cow's milk), and sometimes could be even cheaper (e.g., breast-feeding over formula feeding), but they are thought to be more informed and, eventually, become markers of status. Current discussions about the backlash against "conspicuous consumption" (Veblen 1899) and the replacement with other more acceptable forms of "inconspicuous consumption" (Currid-Halkett 2017) provide important framing for what would otherwise seem like ordinary child-rearing disagreement between doting grandparents and the parents in this ethnography.[8]

The history of the fortunes, heritage, and life trajectories in extended families, particularly those that could be traced to national economic endeavors and forms of social and political influence, were constructed against newer and less encumbered fortunes, whose sources are untraceable or disjointed from national and social contributions. Rather than viewing consumption practices exclusively as strategies of belonging, Ipanema parents viewed reducing (or reframing) consumption as a moral imperative and crusade in the context of national debt.

National, Ethnic, and Temperamental Productions of Whiteness

In the United States, inherited status or wealth is not as legitimate as status based on meritocratic achievement through hard work and cultural openness to a diverse world (Sherman 2017b, 12). This is very different in Latin America, largely because of the cultural fetishization of the extended family. The way to create moral wealth had to do with trying to anchor extended family resources in a common national or local history that resonated, politically and affectively, with a sense of a greater good. The Ipanema and El Condado upper classes produced perspectives on moral capital that condensed affective longing and a historical, nationalist, and even transnational sense of their power and prestige. Sometimes drawing on genealogies dating back to the national histories of mid-1900s Puerto Rico and turn-of-the-twentieth-century Brazil, the El Condado and Ipanema extended families I met produced and reproduced racial privilege through attachments to other regions of the world, whether through family migration sagas or contributions to national political developments.

PERSPECTIVES ON ELITE NATION BUILDING
AND ECCENTRICITY

El Condado residents Manolo Lastra and Nereida Carrión explained their family lineage in terms of their parents' and grandparents' "illustrious" role in the nation: one of their grandparents had been the right hand to Puerto Rico's first elected governor; the other one's mother was related to a former mayor of San Juan, and the father was connected to a member of the pro-statehood leadership at the time of my fieldwork. Most of the grandparents I met in Ipanema and El Condado were born in the 1940s and 1950s, and they inserted their individual and extended families' histories poignantly into a national period of rapid economic, cultural, and political change in Puerto Rico and Brazil. In Puerto Rico, the grandparent generation came of age during a period of massive government-sponsored Puerto Rican migration of the poor and working classes to US farms and inner cities, which produced a (largely white) middle class on the island (chapter 3). Two local elites emerged as a result of this US colonial project: the criollos, an elite that continued to be loyal to the previous Spanish colonizers, and that still located itself in the more autonomous side of the rapid industrialization and urbanization projects fostered under the new constitution, the ELA; and a new elite that affiliated itself with US imperialism, by seeking a closer affiliation, perhaps even a condition of statehood, with the United States, and that gained their wealth and power through their military and political alliance with the United States.[9] These Puerto Rican elites played integral roles in the colonization of Puerto Rico through their desire for sovereignty, bourgeoisie politics, and modern nation building. As in the rest of Latin America, criollos were part of a caste system that positioned them above mestizos, African descendants, and Indigenous people but below *peninsulares,* those born in Spain and Portugal (Donghi 1993).

Individuals like Manolo Lastra and Nereida Carrión could point to their relatives in school history books and even had genealogical charts, family books, and biographies of their relatives in their personal libraries. They often discussed feeling pressured to live up to their families' legacies and stated that they had a calling (*un llamado*) to do something for Puerto Rico. They also remarked on the challenges of realizing that vision or calling. In Manolo's words, "The issue we have in Puerto Rico is that we have grown up thinking of ourselves as unable to do anything without the US, *el mantengo* [being kept]. We don't have to work or be entrepreneurial because there's always that welfare check, you know." Manolo's extended family were very involved in both the pro-commonwealth and, to a lesser degree, the pro-independence parties, and they considered themselves pursuers of greater autonomy for Puerto Rico in relation to the United States. While in such families, upper classes were assumed to be pro-statehood, or *más americanos que los americanos* (more American than the Americans), the opposite was true for elite pro-statehood families; upper-class pro-statehood families, some financial contributors to the US Republican Party, viewed their own party as more pragmatic and beneficial for the lower classes, and they projected elitism onto the pro-commonwealth and pro-independence parties.

Political families were held together by everyday activities framed around historical and moral narratives, as well as a special investment in transmitting versions of those to children and grandchildren. They also carried, at times, an even more literal sense of lineage. For instance, Manolo's paternal aunts, in their late sixties at the time, had gone to a remote village in northern Spain after learning of some tenuous family connection with a family that shared their surname. "She knocks on these people's door and she's like 'Your grandparents and our grandparents were second cousins' or whatever," Manolo explained, with only a tinge of humor. And what did the Spanish family do? I asked. "I'm not sure, but they took pictures together, and got artisan work from the little village, which they see as our ancestral place."

Nereida stated that these politically influential families were unable to accept individual mediocrity; these individuals viewed their actions as political and national actions, not as the actions of individuals within specific families:

> In Puerto Rico we operate on a perpetually high level of social anxiety. My cousin was demoted from a government position, and the whole family mobilized, made public statements, declared the injustice of it all. The whole family takes this as a personal affront. Because this can't just be that this cousin is a lazy ass (*un vagonete*). It has to be that there is a massive conspiracy against the family, from the other political party or from the enemies within the same party. It is like no professional move is ever only about an individual; you bring your family lineage with you to the job.

Among El Condado parents who were members of political elites, the status of Puerto Rico in relation to the United States was central to their collective identity and lineage. Familial histories were forged and updated according to everyday national news and conditions, as well as passed on intergenerationally, constructing members of the family as historical subjects.

Both in El Condado and Ipanema, extended families narrated stories of their personal and familial connections to historical political figures, particularly to those who had been glorified in the national imaginary, like Luis Muñoz Marín and Luis A. Ferré in Puerto Rico, and Fernando Henrique Cardoso in Brazil. In certain instances, last names alluded to individuals who had participated in the creation of the modern nation, whose legacies continued to be, for the most part, cherished and positively compared to invariably "more corrupt" contemporary politicians. This was partly how the progressive elite distinguished itself from traditional elites and from new elites, by connecting their wealth to broader national political projects and figures. This allowed the Ipanema and El Condado upper classes to define themselves according to not only inherited forms of capital but also merit, social commitment, and patriotic duties.

There was prolific, clear evidence of how nepotism operated in extended families and around them, particularly in Puerto Rico. While this was often recognized among the interviewees, it was often dissociated from each subject's trajectory. After getting married, Tony Fortuño Vernet and Mariblanca Giusti moved from Puerto Rico to New York City to pursue master's degrees. They returned to Puerto Rico after 9/11 because Tony had already secured a job in finance. "We felt it was better to be the head of the mouse, than the tail of the lion [*cabeza de ratón y no rabo de león*]," Mariblanca explained. "We needed to come back to Puerto Rico, not to start over there in the US, where nobody knows you."

And in fact, Mariblanca's father spoke to a friend, and Mariblanca promptly secured a job: "My dad spoke with [prominent lawyer], and it turns out there was an opening in his law firm. I began working there and, not for anything, but I was the first one to arrive and the last one to leave. By the time I had my first kid, they wanted to keep me, so we agreed to fewer hours." There was a sense of serendipity or "being lucky" in these employment narratives—it so happened that there was an opening, almost miraculously—and there was some pride in the fact that one's family connections were strong enough to be able to provide these opportunities.

El Condado parents connected their wealth not only to old established political and banking families but, more frequently, to a lineage of families who were committed to "work hard for one's country" in the present. In El Condado, more so than in Ipanema, longevity in one's country oftentimes meant that one's family members had stayed on the island or had chosen to return after getting the appropriate credentials abroad. This was evidence of sacrificing for one's nation, since presumably it would have been more economically profitable to pursue careers in the United States. The #YoNoMeQuito hashtag, popular at the time of my fieldwork, alluded to this, the fact that no matter how difficult the economic and political situation of Puerto Rico was, one would not migrate. Situating oneself and one's family in terms of patriotic, national attachments, described in terms of emotional and social networks, was ultimately reflective of unacknowledged upper-class and white racial positions.

In Ipanema, the parents of some of my interlocutors, like Otávia in the epigraphs to the chapter, referred to their European heritage in terms of links to state, national, and migration projects from nineteenth-century Brazil, and they often drew their lineage to the landed upper classes from the interior of São Paulo, Rio de Janeiro, or Minas Gerais. The grandparents, and older extended family members I met, recalled the climate of optimism that gripped Rio in the late 1900s, as the city emerged from its colonial past to become a modern metropolis of 2.5 million inhabitants, with a strong international cultural identity rooted in its leading artistic exports of bossa nova, cinema novo, and globally circulating images of exotic tropical bliss (chapter 2). In the neighborhood that gave birth to the legendary "Garota de Ipanema," some parents mentioned their extended family's involvement in antidictatorship activism and postdictatorship democratic projects in the mid-1980s.

In addition to tracing deservingness and the morality of wealth through national contributions, as was a dominant case in El Condado, a few Ipanema families focused on intergenerational emotional and psychological similarities to explain not only family success, but also lessons learned that resulted in a family's higher moral ground (cf. Marcus 1992). The case of Fabiana Camargo Correa illustrates how, in certain instances, an individual's interiority was almost considered a genetic trait and was even reframed as a national character.

Fabiana Camargo Correa, the deceased younger sister of Otávia and Moacyr, had committed suicide when Cleide was just a child. "Fabiana's suicide" became an important symbol of elite family continuity beyond national or ethnic lineage; it was a tacit connection to a deeper, intergenerational family psyche. As Moacyr, the go-to family historian, remarked, "Fabiana was very sensitive to social milieu, to the problems of the world. This led her to depression, anxiety, a very complicated person. That is exactly like Cleide. That's what makes our family so unified and sensitive to the pain of others."[10] Fabiana's suicide was emblematic of a type of language that appeared in narratives of heritage and temperament among the wealthiest Ipanema families I met: it was an extended family narrative that combined the way in which money and materiality—including one's consumption habits, privilege, success, or phenotype—were rendered inconsequential in the face of concerns with heredity and mental health conditions.

Moreover, these were also narratives of how similarities in temperament, personality, and interiority could be found through family lineage. When I had the opportunity to ask Cleide, for instance, about Fabiana's suicide, she explained, "When I think of Fabiana, [the suicide's] impact on the whole family, even contemporary generations, it becomes clear material possessions do not matter. Our parents would never judge someone for what they have or don't have. Not only do they understand suffering, but they have felt it, intimately."[11] In Brazil, where the influence of any one political family would be more diffused and region specific, the extended family provides connections not only to the history of land-owning aristocracies and inherited access to land and property, but also to temperament and mental states. Fabiana was regarded as a brilliant individual whose mental condition had to do with taking over the problems of the nation or the world; what remains hidden here is that these were overwhelmingly European whites who benefited from their whiteness in lands that clearly placed whiteness at the top of rigid racial hierarchies in the Americas. These families of origin were, in a sense, described as white or "mixed," as Ipanema and El Condado interlocutors highlighted the foreign origins of ancestors (Spanish, Portuguese, Lebanese, Italian). Especially in Ipanema, when a family of origin was described as *misturada*, this focus on "mixing" was proposed in terms of various European or Middle Eastern nationalities but did not include the presence of African-descended individuals.

Migration Lineage, Whiteness, and Privileged Ethnicities

Margarita Berrocal and María Eugenia Tirado had been each other's maids of honor and were godmothers to each other's children. Margarita, María, and their close friend Viviana Fernández knew one another from their childhood days attending coming-of-age dances, participating in *comparsas* and coronations, volleyball tournaments, squash games, and family holiday parties at Casa Cuba, a beachfront social and sports club that was a primary socialization space and cultural center for Cuban exiles and their families in Puerto Rico. A few months into my fieldwork, I realized that not only did many of my interlocutors know one another, but also about a third of them were the children of at least one Cuban parent who had arrived to Puerto Rico in the aftermath of the Cuban Revolution and through the 1960s and 1970s. Margarita, María Eugenia, and Viviana belonged to Cuban extended families who owned successful advertising agencies.[12] Many of them credited Casa Cuba with the friendships and enduring networks they had maintained through the years. Margarita mentioned, "It was a much deeper level of attachment with the Casa Cuba friends than even with the Perpetuo friends, because our [Cuban] parents had common histories."

Casa Cuba was a physical and symbolic space around which notions of extended family and values were produced in relation to a politics of exile among the upper class in El Condado and the San Juan metropolitan area. Like other child-centered nodules of urbanism (chapters 2 and 3), Casa Cuba provided a sense of place closely related with the growing significance of reproduction, especially access to desired child-rearing, ideological anchoring, and cosmopolitan lifestyles. Not only did parents select neighborhoods, like El Condado and Ipanema, that most closely aligned with their sense of themselves and preference for certain ways of living, but they also chose supplementary spaces that solidified specific "extended family" identities and histories, like Casa Cuba.

About a dozen grandparents, in their late sixties or seventies, waited in the reception area on a summer afternoon for their grandchildren to come out of the Beach Fun Summer Camp in Casa Cuba. Photos of former Carnival queens were displayed on the wall, and a statue of Cuba's patron saint, La Virgen de la Caridad del Cobre, sat on a small corner altar. Summer camp leaders, ranging in age between late teens and early twenties, had themselves been campers and attended some of the elite schools in the San Juan metro area.

Although I had attended school not far from the Casa Cuba area, I had not set foot in the club, and it even carried a certain aura of mystery to me, until I matriculated my son in the club's summer camp in 2014. From my high school days, I knew that at these clubs, parties were organized, romantic relationships were fostered, and athletic tournaments held. So, when I went with Margarita and María Eugenia to check out the summer camp, I was actually surprised by the unremarkable ordinariness of it all, even though I could sense a lingering Cuban exile nostalgia in the décor and the ambience. "Here you still see that culture of *abuelas* coming to pick up their grandchildren," Margarita noted, maybe trying to highlight the specialness of the place. María Eugenia further remarked, "Something about Cubans is that, even if they have been here for fifty years, the extended family is still very important. This may be different than with American families . . . or even Puerto Ricans who are more Americanized."

Like Margarita and María Eugenia, and most of the children of Cuban exiles, Viviana Fernández expressed great attachment to her mother's exile saga; her mother and grandparents had arrived from Cuba penniless. "The little money they had sewn on their clothes was taken away," she explained. As if she had already been used to justifying the stereotype that many Puerto Ricans had of Cubans, Viviana added,

People say that Cubans are stuck up, snobbish, but what they don't understand is that Cubans have great psychological damage. I always keep that in mind when I'm hurt by my mother or by a family situation, of how they favor my sister. . . . My grandmother would tell me stories of how they had to abandon their house in Havana, with the maids who lived with them and their shih tzu, a dog that was like a family member. She would tell me: "I will never forget that last image of my house." They were always grateful toward Puerto Rico. How the neighbors gave them a fridge, a sofa, furniture. . . . My dad's [Puerto Rican] family also resented my mother, because she would always dress very well. Cubans are raised with a lot of pride, not because we think we're superior, but I feel great pride in having Cuban blood, and having that family closeness.

Like other parents, Viviana viewed the extended family as inseparable from her parents' individual mobility stories; her mother's dramatic exile story, in particular, constructed the family in light of endurance and hard work, of pain and resilience. She viewed the extended family in terms of moral geographies, which became part of a circuit of reproduction that helped code whiteness, racial anxiety, and class concerns common to El Condado parents.

Puerto Rican elites in El Condado and the neighboring area of Miramar of-tentimes claimed that Cubans were the "real racists," particularly against Puerto Ricans, and projected various notions of white supremacy onto Cuban exiles. According to Margarita Berrocal, a white Puerto Rican who was often con-fused for white American or European in the United States, and Carlos Andrés Pagán, a white, dark-haired, short Puerto Rican resident of El Condado,

> MARGARITA: Casa Cuba used to rent the pool to swimming instruc-tors who would then teach the classes. But the problem was that they couldn't really control who came in to take classes. Lots of black kids coming in, so the pool was full of blacks [*se llenó de negros*] . . . and, uh . . . Cubans can be very racist. So, they no longer teach swimming.

> CARLOS: My ex-wife's Cuban parents never really liked me, because I didn't have the racial profile they wanted: Cuban, white, cute, light eyes, you know? They never told me this, but one knows, intuitively. It is very difficult to be a Cuban from that generation and not be rac-ist. They were actually nice people, very respectful, not comemierda [snobbish or stuck up]. But they had a difficult time accepting me.

> MARGARITA: You really have three types of Cubans here: the Mira-mar Cubans, the Isla Verde–Casa Cuba Cubans, and the Cuban Jews in El Condado. The Casa Cuba Cubans are super Cuban identified, very heavy Cuban accents, as if they had arrived here yesterday. The Miramar Cubans also hated Fidel [Castro], but those Cubans inte-grated more into Puerto Rican society. The ones from Miramar are more comemierda,, like the Cuban stereotype. They were higher class and have married Puerto Ricans. Most of the Jews in Puerto Rico are actually Cuban, and most of those go to St. John's, marry among themselves. Those used to live in upscale Guaynabo suburbs, but now you also see them in El Condado or Dorado. They were the developers of all those buildings in Isla Verde. They are the owners of Pitusa, Kress, Capri, Caribbean Cinemas.

Among the parents I met in Ipanema, there were some references to family migrations from European countries, particularly Italy, Germany, and Spain; however, the more frequent references to family heritage related to Jewish or Lebanese-Syrian family traditions and contributions to Brazil. Zulema Nader is a Lebanese-Brazilian executive director of a national NGO that works closely with public schools in Brazil. She had lived in various apartments in Ipanema and Leblon, and her husband, a high executive for an international corporation, commuted to São Paulo for work. An engineer by training and the mother of three sons, Zulema explained that her extended family's wealth came from land ownership throughout Brazil:

> My grandparents were Lebanese and very aware of our family's history in Brazil. They did not think of business as a profit-making venture alone, but as a contribution to the nation where they were raising their family. This is radically different from Euro-American capitalism, where you have to make money, to consume, in order to be happy. I feel I'm continuing my family's tradition of helping Brazil reach its potential. Even if my sons are your typical Zona Sul guys [garotos da Zona Sul], they have that sense of heritage and the contribution my grandparents, and my parents, have made to Brazil.

While Zulema's Lebanese identification was more symbolic—largely circumscribed to frequenting specific restaurants and less salient than how she described her own cousin's involvement in Syrian-Lebanese cultural associations in São Paulo, for instance—the Lebanese background gained some currency in her parenting. She acknowledged that her sons were the typical privileged, upper-class young men born and raised between Ipanema and Leblon. Still it was important to her that her children understood her extended family's wealth in terms of national contributions that were "radically different from Euro-American capitalism." Her extended family's fortune gets repositioned from a narrative of capital and land accumulation, or an individualistic quest toward consumption, into one grounded in "giving back" to the Brazilian nation.

Among the Jewish-Brazilian families I met in Ipanema, there was an insistence in communicating that their secular Jewishness was in fact emblematic of an agnostic or even atheist quality that was considered cosmopolitan and intellectual. César Schumer's first marriage was to a Jewish-Brazilian woman, but his second marriage was to Silvana, one of the Ipanema residents more involved in a circle of parenting-themed lectures in the neighborhood and a "Catholic in name only." César and Silvana claimed that Judaism did not play an important role in their everyday life, even in terms of cultural practices. Nevertheless, César seemed to be familiar with the specific spaces associated with Judaism in Rio. He knew that the majority of Rio's Jewish population resided in the central neighborhoods of Copacabana, Ipanema, Botafogo, and Leblon, and that synagogues, day schools, and a few kosher shops were sprinkled throughout those areas. "Unless they are very Orthodox, you can't distinguish them [from the non-Jewish population]," César remarked. When I asked them if their son, in his early teens at the time, had any connection to this family background,

Silvana replied, "We've taken him a couple of times to the [Midrash] Centro Cultural in Leblon for events. There he sees how Jews in Brazil are very successful, and integrated fully, socially, culturally, in every way, into the nation." The lineages associated with extended families were privileged and accentuated the elite whiteness of upper-class Puerto Ricans and Brazilians in El Condado and Ipanema. These were identities that sustained positive images of merit, hard work, national contributions in ways that racialized populations did not have access to, even if their ethnic and migration sagas might suggest even more difficult challenges and obstacles.

Extended families played a critical role in the process of learning and assuming one's whiteness in Latin America (cf. Karam 2008). They were frequently the ancestral connections to more prestigious or cosmopolitan, deracialized ethnic identities.[13] These relations that spanned other countries gave a certain cosmopolitan character to these families, to counter the lineage of more traditional national elites; in Ipanema, where few individuals had pursued higher educational degrees abroad, the affective and familial relation to this international scene still provided that cosmopolitan character.

The family ethnic and migrant lineages discussed here emerge in contradistinction to other populations who are present in significant numbers in Rio de Janeiro and San Juan. Cleide's invocation of her grandparents' *fazenda* in the Brazilian state of Minas Gerais suggests identification between her own history and the national narrative, specifically the fazenda, with its specific social relations among classes, genders, and color groups, as a privileged site for the formation of all Brazil, both rural and urban. One of the aspects of this fazenda nostalgia, which surfaced in a few of my Ipanema interviews, has to be situated in one of the characteristics of racial violence, which lies precisely in limiting black populations' access to representation, including representations of domination itself (cf. Mathieu 1990). Likewise, Cubans (and Jewish Latin American groups) in El Condado, for instance, occupy higher echelons in a local and national racial hierarchy in which Dominicans are at the bottom; and, while César noticed the full integration of Jewish Brazilians, Brazilians from the Nordeste remained socially, spatially, and economically marginal, as examined in chapter 7.

Conclusion

Extended families, which gained importance in the context of contemporary parenting cultures in Latin America and the Caribbean, instituted a moral economy that was undermined by the fact that some family members were completely supported by trusts and funds, independent of productivity, and that some others remained outcasts regardless of how "self-made" they were. At the center of this moral economy was the fraught expectations, between parents and grandparents, about the value of material gifts versus spending time as forms of currencies in their interactions with children. El Condado and Ipanema parents often pushed grandparents to join in the labor of turning the material into the immaterial, of viewing their role as grandparents in exclusively (or primarily) affective terms, even when these younger generations were in fact depending on the very money they aimed to downplay.

In El Condado and Ipanema, parenting empires were sustained intergenerationally, as the upper- and upper-middle-class parents I interviewed oftentimes maintained their status and lifestyles in direct connection to their own parents' wealth, status, and prestige, while also forging alternative notions of "deservingness," "hard work," and "merit." Extended families were the main institution through which money and inequality were purified, and privilege and whiteness rendered legitimate. Perspectives on the extended family among the wealthy responded to the exigencies of a particular kind of moral economy. Extended families offered the intimate and institutional framing for a morality that involved monetary transactions ultimately viewed as based on goodness, generosity, and mutuality. Such moral economy, an interplay of upper-class cultural mores and economic activity, were built on the political cultures, expectations, traditions, and belief systems that draw market actions into the intimate world of the family.

The reliance of grandparents for financial support was oftentimes coupled with impressions that "grandparents are not what they used to be," as Violeta Ramírez de Arellano's daughters viewed her shortcomings as a grandmother. Similarly, Ipanema parents questioned their own parents' effectiveness in sustaining the social capital to which they had become accustomed growing up. As Silvana, an Ipanema parent, noted, "Up until my grandparents' generation, we knew where families lived and what each member was doing. Even if I hadn't talked to a friend for a long time, our families would stay in touch and preserved the relationship. I don't see that happening now." Nonetheless, extended families continued to provide the cultural, ethnic, and political lineages, which ultimately explained wealth in terms of service to the nation and being socially committed, rather than drawing from histories of land appropriation, inheritance, and other forms of wealth gathering often rooted in settler-colonialist projects.

"In our case, my parents pay for my niece's college tuition at Cornell," remarked Roxana Valdejuli, a resident of El Condado, as we headed to a Pilates class. "Extended families here think of money as a collective good. It's not as formal as the US trust fund babies, but it is like an informal version of that." I asked her if she, like other parents, felt that extended families played less of a role in childcare, and she explained, "Grandparents not only take care of the kid, but are basically the *ama de llaves* [butlers] for their children. They open the door for the workers that come into the house. They supervise the gardener, pool cleaner, delivery trucks." It is on these domestic workers, particularly the *niñeras* in El Condado and the *babás* (nannies) in Ipanema, that the tasks of parenting empires and childcare fall. I turn to them in chapter 7.

7

Affective Inequalities

Childcare Workers and Elite Consumptions of Blackness

On an early Thursday evening in July 2014, as I sat to take fieldnotes at an outdoor table at Mil Frutas, a boutique ice cream parlor in Ipanema, I noticed a slim, dark-skin babá talking on a cell phone, quite agitatedly. She was accompanying a stylish, white dark-haired Brazilian woman in her early forties. While the nanny resolved what seemed to be a disagreement with a romantic partner on the phone, the mother and her daughter, a four-year-old dressed in a pink tutu, sat at a nearby table. On a couple of occasions, the mother made recommendations to the nanny on what to say or ask of the person on the other end of the line. The mother, who eventually introduced herself to me as Claudia, urged the nanny: "Order something, Leandra. Go ahead!" Leandra said she didn't want anything, but Claudia insisted, as one would with a friend who needed a bit of nudging. Eventually, Claudia also turned to a valet parking employee who was working at an outdoors café adjacent to Mil Frutas: "Go ahead, order something!" Initially, the valet parking employee, a tall heavyset dark-skin man dressed in a three-piece suit, politely declined. Claudia kept insisting until he eventually gave in and went into Mil Frutas to look at the flavors. "Let him get samples," Claudia ordered one of the employees behind the counter, suggesting she would be treating the valet parking worker. "No, no, I don't need to sample. I am ready to get something," the valet parker insisted. "No, no. Try something first," and to the employees at the ice cream place, "Give him samples. He's a client."

Like many other El Condado residents, Maribel Seijo bemoaned, "Aquí no hay Mary Poppins" (There is no Mary Poppins here). A well-educated white Puerto Rican mother in her late forties, Maribel was trying to schedule a trip to Boston to meet up with former college roommates, but neither her mother nor her mother-in-law could stay with her kids. Other than for the occasional informal babysitting that Maribel's Dominican maid provided, Maribel only entrusted her children's care to family members. As she explained, she feared that the "bad habits" and "educational limitations" of nannies in Puerto Rico, most of whom, she noted, were "poorly educated Dominican immigrants," would "rub off" on her children. Mary Poppins would have been ideal but, alas, she didn't exist, at least not in Puerto Rico.

In this chapter, I focus on how the overwhelmingly light-skinned upper and upper-middle classes in Ipanema and El Condado viewed their relationship with darker-skinned immigrant women whom they hired to care for their children. In El Condado these women were usually immigrants from the neighboring Dominican Republic, while in Ipanema they were migrants from the Brazilian Northeast (*nordestinas*).[1] Perhaps counterintuitively, relationships with domestic workers, particularly nannies, underscored parents' self-concept as "progressive" or "liberal," even as these relationships clearly sustained the racial and class privilege at the core of parenting empires.[2]

Nordestinas in Ipanema and Dominican domestic workers in El Condado belonged to a global care chain. They were, overwhelmingly, women from poorer geopolitical regions who cared for children, elderly, and households in wealthier areas, as they themselves supported their own children in their regions of origin (Ehrenreich and Hochschild 2003). These internal and transnational migrants are essential to parenting empire practices that connect family life, household, and neighborhood cultural, civic, and spatial trends among liberal elites. Ipanema and El Condado parents frequently thought of domestic work in terms of their own affective and personal entanglements with specific domestic workers, rather than in broader sociological terms. In this chapter, I examine how wealthy white Latin American parents justified their own "structural oblivion" (McIntosh 2013) and selectively decided when and how blackness—particularly in the bodies of "their" nannies—became visible or remained invisible. This was facilitated by the profound levels of residential segregation and the fact that, in the course of an average day, white elites in El Condado and Ipanema encountered black people only in subordinate or altogether destitute positions. In relation to the working class and poor, Puerto Rican and Brazilian elites developed discourses around "a tendency to live beyond [their] means," "the need for all sectors of society to sacrifice," and the "need to keep costs of doing business low in order to maintain competitiveness," which were at the core of austerity subjectivities.

I consider four main ways in which Ipanema and El Condado parents produced racialized intimacy and difference—simultaneous affective attachment and sociological detachment—through the broader project of parenting empire. First, I examine how parents approached changes in the laws regulating domestic work, in Ipanema, and increased global pedagogical expectations, in El Condado; in particular, I consider the legal, pedagogical, and racial intersections underscoring the production of affective ambiguity in relation to subalterns (Berg and Ramos-Zayas 2015; Goldstein 2013). Second, I analyze how parents produced a collective morality and ethics of care, which drew from popular psychology concepts like being "hands on," even when they outsourced quotidian childcare tasks. Third, I deconstruct how parents projected agency onto domestic workers. In this case, I draw on neighborhood-based distinctions between Ipanema and El Condado, and the distinct cultures of domestic work in Brazilian and Puerto Rican societies. Finally, I demonstrate how in public performances of parenting empire in child-centered nodules of urbanism, like Mil Frutas above, the bodies of poor, dark-skin workers complemented the bodies of wealthier, white-skinned employers in choreographed interactions that were at times invisible and at times hypervisible (Costa 1983; Costa Vargas 2004). As a form of conclusion, I note how parenting empires were built on a complicated production of liberal self-fashioning among Ipanema and El Condado white elites while rendering individual nannies as stand-ins for race, regionalism, and migration (within the nation and across the Caribbean).

Affective Labor, Legislative Labor: Cultures of Domestic Work in Brazil and Puerto Rico

Many parents I met in Ipanema bemoaned the difficulty of finding good, reliable empregadas, particularly nannies, and they sometimes attributed this to changes in labor laws that the Workers' Party had implemented during its tenure. Toward the latter part of Lula da Silva's presidency and into the early part of Dilma Rousseff's term, before the country's economic setbacks and political and corporate scandals in 2015, the shortage of domestic workers actually made headlines in the Brazilian media (Greenwald, Fishman, and Miranda 2016; Pinho and Silva 2010; Saad Filho 2016). Because of Lula's programs of wealth redistribution, carried out largely through the Bolsa Família and Bolsa Escola, almost 40 million Brazilians left the lower classes and ascended into the lower-middle classes and middle classes (C. Amorim 2010). Upper classes frequently manifested some backlash against working classes, which, for the first time, had begun to have some purchasing power. These forms of social welfare, however modest, allowed members of previously marginalized groups to occupy spaces that had been, up to that point, off limits for them, such as airports, shopping malls, universities, and in a handful of cases, even some beachside neighborhood restaurants. What some elites internalized or performed as a "progressive" trait—rejecting consumerism as shallow and giving importance to the "immaterial" (chapters 4 and 5)—was at times connected to the conservative stance that the poor should not be "out of their place" by consuming goods and spaces that should remain off limits for them. These changes meant that, among other things, individuals previously employed as domestic workers had other employment options, at least until Michel Temer's takeover in 2016. Nevertheless, Brazil has been notorious for having the highest number of domestic workers in the world; 17 percent of all female workers (6.7 million) in Brazil were empregadas domésticas in 2010 (International Labour Organization 2010).

By 1872, sixteen years prior to the official abolition of slavery in Brazil, the line between slave and paid employee was beginning to blur; it became common among former slave-holding families to rent, rather than buy, house slaves. When the Consolidação das Leis Trabalhistas (CLT), a considerable labor rights victory for low-wage workers, was adopted in Brazil in 1943, domestic workers were excluded from its coverage because it was understood that they carried out "non-economic" labor (Mori, Bernardino-Costa, and Fleischer 2011; Pinho 2015). As Pinho notes, "By excluding domestic workers from its benefits, Brazilian legislators maintained the status quo of millions of poor (and mainly black) women, thus contributing to further naturalizing their position as 'less than' laborers" (2015, 107). It was not until seventy years later, in November 2013, that then-president Dilma Rousseff extended the legal benefits of CLT to domestic workers, including nannies.[3]

Silvana Villela Mattos, an Ipanema parent who often organized speaking engagements profiling prominent child development experts, and her lawyer husband, César Schumer, illustrated how other Ipanema parents viewed the domestic labor laws. "Hiring live-in workers has become more expensive and complicated," César told me. In Silvana's view, more people would be inclined to hire *diaristas* (workers who would come every day, but not stay overnight), or place their children in daycare centers, rather than "build relationships with" full-time live-ins. Harboring vestiges of the intimate, patriarchal world of the feudal household, while simultaneously evincing the desire for a more modern conception of the employer-employee relationship in professional terms, César remarked, "The regulation of formal employment can either decrease or increase benefits, because there are informal benefits that come with a long-term relationship between employer and employee."

César also noted, evoking a structure of feelings that he tightly attributed and circumscribed to preabolition Brazil and highlighting modernist aspirations, "Some regulation is needed, because we can't live in a slave society [*sociedade escravócrata*]. That's where domestic work comes from, the *amas de leite*. There's no developed country where everyone, even in the middle classes, has an empregada." Invocations of a history of slavery in relation to empregadas were common in Ipanema, though not in El Condado. As a rhetorical strategy, such invocations immobilized time, obscured differences with the colonial past, and, above all, prevented upper-class white elites from seeing themselves as subjects who continued to reproduce the very social relations they described; they oddly described a hierarchical and violent social structure, while remaining detached from their integral role in contributing to its reproduction. By contextualizing contemporary experiences within the frame of the colonial and slave-owning past, these white elites situated racial oppression outside time, eternal, already generated by history and therefore outside historical relationships (Ribeiro Corossacz 2015, 2018).

The expectation that employers, like Silvana and César, had of domestic workers, particularly of nannies, responded to a broader description of "affective labor," or the often invisible and affective qualities of work that are not so much intended to accomplish specific measurable tasks or levels of productivity but to produce or modify affective experiences in people (Hardt 1999; Hochschild 1979). Having a "good attitude," being "pleasant and polite," and having "social skills" are often associated with being adept at affective labor. At the time of my fieldwork, the relationship between domestic workers and employer was still characterized by the exchange of services not stipulated in work contracts; the exigencies of complicity and even affective dispositions between worker and employers; and emotional investments between a worker and her charges. These interactions were not necessarily inauthentic, but their authenticity was profoundly conditioned by radical inequalities and microaggressions.[4]

Parents in Ipanema and El Condado explained the "retrogressive attitudes" of domestic workers in reference to the "world views," or cosmologies, of these lower classes: how they fostered "poor eating habits," "poor hygiene," or "excessive TV watching" in their children, or how they "abandoned their children to be raised by others." More frequently, they alluded to their own view of parenting as a process of personal growth, which had "taught them" to be more "patient," allowed the child greater self-expression, and demanded consistent cultivation of their spiritual and psychological selves. Interest in pursuing personal projects of self-awareness among elite parents did little to transform their personal perspectives about nannies, whom they still viewed as inheritors of parental pathologies and, at times, even viscerally offensive.

Parenting empires rendered racial interactions as viscerally felt, including in terms of disgust, for instance: disgust toward bodies, toward manners, toward places of birth or residence, toward linguistic accents and diction, and, above all else, toward how the poor parented. Disgust indeed was "an immensely powerful indicator of the interface between the personal and the social" (Lawler 2005). In El Condado, Alejandra Rodríguez Emma, a stay-at-home parent with graduate training in psychology, had nanny "horror stories" that were stories of disgust. She had once placed an internet ad seeking a nanny and "what came here was atrocious!" (¡lo que vino aquí fue un desastre!). In addition to the objectification of the potential employees as indicated in the "lo" indirect pronoun (equivalent to the English "what" in the sentence), Alejandra's reaction was what one would expect of something that caused nausea. Disgust was visceral in a way that highlighted how space mattered in the ways in which upper-class parents in Ipanema and El Condado experienced relationships to nannies and domestic workers. Disgust hinges on proximity; when spatial or legal boundaries between racial or social groups are challenged, social hierarchy finds other ways of expression (Skeggs 2004). In the context of parenting empires, disgust—as threatening to children's health, for instance—was a morally sanctioned (and moralistic) endorsement of whiteness through parenting.

These forms of whiteness acquired materiality through parenting and were sustained through the historic, symbolic, and geographical conceptions of Ipanema and El Condado as sites of wealth, luxury, progressive outlook, and cosmopolitan "feel" (chapters 2 and 3). In the world of elite parenting, where few across-class and interracial spaces exist, the childcare worker becomes the closest individual onto whom visceral sentiments are projected. Disgust enabled an intimate, multiscale understanding of space and the everyday affective, material, and social interactions that produce and define it. Displays of wealth in countries of otherwise dire need and poverty, as in Brazil and Puerto Rico, have become commonplace in urban spaces around the globe. Importantly, the perception of inequality, more than raw measures of inequality, has deeper political consequences and more direct bearing on social well-being (Graham and Felton 2006). Parenting empires rendered disgust acceptable, even necessary, thus underscoring how sensorial, visceral hierarchies produced and sustained whiteness and experiential inequality, at times even beyond built environment and physical segregation, in Ipanema and El Condado (Alves 2014; cf. Dinzey-Flores 2017).

The culture of domestic work has been ubiquitous to Brazil, and most of Latin America, in a way that has not been the case in Puerto Rico. The structure of feeling associated with the institution of servitude is produced by the confluence of historical and material conditions and prevailing social organizations; these "cultures of servitude" (Qayum and Ray 2003) are shaped by specific configurations of race, class, gender, and spatial structural inequalities that traverse the domestic and public spheres. During the period of my fieldwork, Puerto Rico observed US minimum-wage laws; in theory, domestic workers, at least those who had work permits and were documented, were entitled to minimum hourly wages in US dollars, and they paid Social Security and taxes. While in Brazil, many middle-class families could afford full-time domestic workers, in Puerto Rico, only the wealthiest families employed full-time or live-in employees. Although financial issues played a role in decisions to hire live-in workers, an even more important consideration was a desire for privacy; the fact that most of the Ipanema and El Condado upper classes lived in apartment buildings, rather than the more spacious self-standing mansions that had characterized these neighborhoods at the turn of the twentieth century, made the presence of domestic workers ubiquitous, even when most apartments had a separate maid's room, service entrance, and forms of segregation in their architecture.

In Puerto Rico it was more common to have a weekly cleaning lady (*señora que limpia*) when the kids were older, and a daily worker who performed household tasks and provided occasional babysitting when the children were younger. El Condado parents often combined one of these paid care arrangements with help from grandparents. As Alejandra, the El Condado mother who expressed disgust at the nanny candidate, explained, "Having someone [a domestic worker] is more common now than it was even ten years ago. Even among moms who stay at home and don't work, there's always that *señora dominicana* [Dominican lady] working in the house." She added, "They may care for the children, but they are really paid to care for the house, and the babysitting would be in special cases. When I was still working, my mom helped pay for a nanny, but she would come by when the nanny was there, to supervise."

Studies of employer–domestic worker relationships in Latin America have critically examined "like one of the family" narratives that elites commonly deploy.[5] An accepted conclusion is that these relationships are (and always remain) inherently asymmetrical, notwithstanding the emotive shape or personal histories they involve.[6] And, in fact, domestic workers are frequent recipients of bourgeois discipline, and their bodies are considered polluting agents in the upper-class household. What complicates this picture is that domestic workers were also part of an everyday *convívio* (living, sharing) and became mirrors of how Ipanema and El Condado elites fashioned themselves socially, emotively, and internally. In societies with long unbroken histories of domestic servitude, such as Brazil, the institution of domestic work is central to understandings of elite selves and their self-conscious evolution. In their ethnographic study of Kolkata's feudal and corporate elites and their relationships with servants, Qayum and Ray (2003) argue that the change in the nature of domestic work—from live-in tenured to daily work contracts—is reflective of Indian elites' evolving interest in fashioning themselves as modern. These elites were caught in the contradiction of pursuing a modern self, with its democratic and Western undertones, while sustaining relationships of servitude they had come to see as indispensable in the upkeep of households; at the heart of this contradiction, one can examine the transformations and continuities in the institution of servitude in India.

Among the white upper classes of El Condado and Ipanema, who were dedicated to self-cultivation, psychological depth, and interiority projects, the class, racial, and regional subjectivities of domestic workers served as a critical and rare laboratory to test their level of racial learning and cosmopolitanism. For Ipanema and El Condado parents, whose lives unfolded in radically socially segregated spaces, black, poor, and migrant domestic workers provided one of the few contexts to engage with social difference in an ongoing, quotidian, and intimate way. The recasting of the relationship with childcare and domestic workers was one of the important elements of the complex projects of racial self-concept and moral self-fashioning behind parenting empires. El Condado and Ipanema white upper classes deployed narratives about the affective value of these relationships; these narratives were, indeed, required for the successful reproduction of whiteness among them. As most research on domestic workers and nannies has noted, even when children spend most of their time with these workers, they continue to internalize their parents' hierarchical social logic (Brites 2007).[7]

Neither El Condado nor Ipanema parents wanted their children to act like rich spoiled brats, and interactions between children and domestic workers or nannies were frequently viewed as a measuring stick for a child's own levels of interiority currency (chapter 4). While bratty upper-class children might have been (and continue to be) acceptable for traditional or conservative elites in Latin America or the Global South more broadly, this was not the case for Ipanema and El Condado parents, who viewed even their choice of neighborhood, schools, and friendships as evidence of their progressive, liberal social outlook. In this chapter, I show how relations of servitude, specifically in the realm of childcare, in fact strengthened how El Condado and Ipanema upper classes produced their own whiteness as inherently moral. A unifying question here thus becomes, How can positive affects, the felt emotional connectedness and intimacy that some parents described toward "their" childcare and domestic workers, coexist with, and even reinforce, the profound, enduring racial and class inequalities on which relations of servitude are premised? At the time of my fieldwork, debates around the politics behind "outsourcing" childcare and the racial, regional, and ethnic relations that white elite families engaged in through this process were central aspects of this question.

"Hands On" as Elite Parenting Ethics

Mariblanca Giusti raved about the advantages of living in El Condado, a pedestrian neighborhood, which shared many physical, economic, and cultural similarities with Ipanema. Like Ipanema, El Condado has a large lagoon to one side and the Atlantic Ocean to the other; it had an active tourism industry and an urban history of traditional mansions leading the way to contemporary luxury high-rises. Through a narrative of "wellness" common among El Condado and Ipanema parents alike, Mariblanca remarked, "Here you can encourage an active, healthy lifestyle for your kids. We do sports in the lagoon, kayaking, beach volleyball. It's not about video games and being stuck in front of a TV." Only one aspect of El Condado profoundly troubled Mariblanca—the nannies: "Unfortunately, many kids here are raised by nannies here. I know there is no perfect formula for all families. But, what values will kids raised by nannies have? The nanny may very well have good values, don't get me wrong. But how does a child feel when the person pushing him in the swings is not his mom or dad, but someone who's not from his family? This breaks my heart." Mariblanca's statement stood out, not by her stance on "kids raised by nannies," which I heard frequently in both El Condado and especially Ipanema, despite the ubiquity of nannies. Rather, it was the fact that Mariblanca was one of the few El Condado parents who not only had a full-time domestic worker in charge of cooking, cleaning, and frequent childcare, but whose domestic worker wore a uniform. While having domestic workers wearing distinguishing all-white uniforms was a source of popular debate during the time of my fieldwork in Ipanema, I rarely heard any reference to uniformed nannies in Puerto Rico (Barba 2016). Ironically, just as Mariblanca made the statement about "values" and "nannies raising kids," Tula, her nanny, had carried Mariblanca's younger child to another part of the apartment so that Mariblanca and I would not be interrupted. As I got to know Mariblanca and Tony Fortuño

Vernet, her husband, I learned that Tula, a dark-skin Dominican woman in her early fifties, had lived in Puerto Rico since the 1980s. She had been Tony's housekeeper for more than a decade and began providing childcare once the children were born.

Through a parenting ethics, Ipanema and El Condado elites determined, often quite arbitrarily, which tasks could be legitimately "outsourced" to the nanny versus which ones required "hands-on" parental involvement. With conviction, Mariblanca stated, "Tula knows when to help, and when to let me take care of my own children. With two kids, and a husband who travels quite a bit, of course I need the help. But I make sure I am the one who feeds them, bathes them, takes them to the park. They are clear on who their parents are." This perspective resonated with many Ipanema parents' expectations of a nanny and their concern with what in Brazil was referred to as *terceirização* (outsourcing), a popular psychology term used in reference to the displacement of parenting or child rearing onto nannies (Sgarioni 2014).

Silvana Villela Mattos, the Ipanema mother who discussed labor legislation in relation to domestic work above, mentioned that the nanny she hired was not a nurse: "We didn't want someone telling us what to do. 'Wash your hands! Use sanitizer! Take off your shoes!'" Eventually, they chose a nanny who "would do what we wanted her to do, not what she wanted to do." Since I knew Silvana well enough to know that she cared enough about coming across as thoughtful and diplomatic, I was taken aback by the forcefulness of her tone. She elaborated: "[The live-in nanny] was with us until Eduardo's tenth birthday. By then, Eduardo was embarrassed to be followed around by a nanny. She had a bunch of pictures of him [and would say], 'This is my son.' I would tell her, 'No, this is *my* son. My son is mine! Do you get that?' I got to overcome that jealousy. . . . In some cases, the mother gets home and the child doesn't want her. He wants to sleep with the nanny. If that had happened to me, I would still be in psychotherapy!" Silvana alluded to what Cameron Lynne Macdonald calls "shadow motherhood" (2010, 14) and Margaret Nelson refers to as "detached attachment" (1990, 76), the feeling rules concerning the emotional labor of family care providers. These rules require workers to suppress feelings in order to sustain the outward countenance that produces the proper state of mind in the mother (cf. Hochschild 1983). Nannies needed to display enough warmth and affection to make the child feel loved and the parents feel satisfied with the quality of care, while also being careful not to display too much love, to prevent the child from becoming overly attached and to avoid usurping the parent's place in the child's affections.

Mariblanca in El Condado and Silvana in Ipanema shared a common anxiety about an emotional power attributed to nannies, virtual strangers who could presumably co-opt maternal love by undertaking specific childcare tasks. More significantly, though, these hands-on elite parental ethics highlighted the parental "shortcomings" of other, often poor and working-class women. In Mariblanca's case, she would promptly attribute any life obstacle that Tula's dark, working-class adult children faced to Tula's "limitations"—her lack of hands-on presence—as a parent. Controlling the emotional dynamics between nannies and their charges was part of an elite ethics of being (selectively) hands on; this parental investment in controlling nannies and charges was integral to how concerns with parenting empires came together in forging Latin American whiteness.

Partly because of the difference in cultural approaches to nannies in Brazilian and Puerto Rican societies, the Ipanema and El Condado parents had somewhat different concerns about "outsourcing" childcare. In Brazil, parents did not question whether they would hire a nanny. The nanny being a given, Ipanema parents focused on the importance of being present parents, which usually meant that they would monitor and give detailed instructions to the nanny, while selectively participating in quotidian childcare tasks that they (quite arbitrarily) assumed where the most important ones. In El Condado most parents assumed that *la señora que limpia* (the cleaning lady) would only act as occasional babysitter, during her regular workday; for these parents, having a full-time nanny was not the default childcare option, as was the case in Ipanema.

Prefacing her comment with "maybe this sounds comemierda [snobbish]," Maribel, the El Condado parent who lamented the lack of a Mary Poppins, elaborated: "[In Puerto Rico] the only people available to take care of children are the same [lowering her voice, so the cleaning lady would not hear] *señoras dominicanas* that clean houses. Many are illegal, have a fourth grade education, you know? . . . I can't have my kids talking like *disque* o *estábanos*."[8] Among El Condado parents, "Dominican" was virtual synonymous with domestic worker, elderly caregiver, and nanny. "Tener una señora que limpia (having a cleaning lady) and "tener una dominicana" (having a Dominican woman) were objectifying phrases that Puerto Rican upper classes used interchangeably in reference to the domestic workers they hired. Nevertheless, many parents mentioned that, if given the choice, they would prefer having a nanny who was not Dominican. Colombian and Peruvian were mentioned as preferred nationalities, because these other migrant women presumably had higher educational levels, "a better accent," "speak Spanish better," or "had better manners." In Brazil, conversely, parents claimed to prefer nannies who were, in fact, from the Northeast rather than cariocas (from Rio). These parents claimed that nordestinas were "milder mannered," had "fewer connections to nearby fave-las," were "less tied down by family problems," and "did not speak like carioca de comunidade" or "favela Portuguese." Parents evaluated the nannies' classed, racial, and regional cultural "dispositions" in ways that produced a cosmology of the poor that went well beyond specific skills needed for adequate childcare. Unfolding in spaces of wealth, luxury, and privilege that were invariably child centered, projects of upper-class Latin American whiteness cognitively and af-fectively altered views of inequality and need, so that "inequality" and "need" often referred to perceived psychological inadequacies. Techniques of surveil-lance and disciplining, in child-centered contexts of "care," were foundational to parenting empires. These were affectively engineered techniques of shaming rooted in the power of whiteness, wealth, and parenting to determine the qual-ity, validity, and moral legitimacy of blackness, its invisibility or hypervisibility.

Separate conversations with Alejandra Rodríguez Emma and Mariblanca Giusti, El Condado residents who described their nanny stories in the previ-ous section, demonstrated how "Dominican," as a racialized category of care in Puerto Rico, acquired materiality through the cultural capital and national-ist claims intrinsic to parenting empires. The perceived linguistic "corruption" Dominicans posed on the already stigmatized "Puerto Rican Spanish" high-lighted this:

ALEJANDRA (STAY-AT-HOME; CLINICAL PSYCHOLOGIST): People actually prefer that nannies are not Dominican. [Why is that?] Because of the Spanish, mispronunciation of words, diction. Also because they are *mal acostumbradas* [having bad habits or poor man-ners]. These women lack an education. If they were cleaning only, OK. But taking care of children?

MARIBLANCA (YOGA INSTRUCTOR, BLOGGER): A friend whose child is in St. John's [a private school where English is the main lan-guage of instruction] told me that now even native Spanish-speaking kids are speaking more English, because they associate the Spanish language with being Dominican.

Although there is a dearth of work on the contemporary linguistic practices of the Puerto Rican upper classes, Jennifer Roth-Gordon's analysis of the prac-tices of linguistic discipline among Rio de Janeiro's middle class is pertinent here (Roth-Gordon 2017). Because Portuguese "slang" is associated with the physical space of the favela, a goal of middle-class Zona Sul parents is to enforce "proper" Portuguese as a form of socialization to whiteness. Roth-Gordon (2017) deploys

W. E. B. Du Bois's concept of "personal whiteness" to highlight the bodily discipline and forms of cultural capital that middle-class Rio residents use to explain their unequal access to resources.[9] People who fail to embody discipline, fostered by teaching their children grammar at an early age, for instance, are likely to be racialized, according to Roth-Gordon's study, as "non-white independently of phenotype" (Roth-Gordon 2017, 75–80).

Like Roth-Gordon, I also witnessed the significance parents placed on "proper" Portuguese in Ipanema and "proper" Spanish in El Condado, although the forms of racialization implicated in these linguistic evaluations were never independent of phenotype. Among the parents and teachers I met in Puerto Rico and Brazil, the insistence on "proper" native language almost always took place not only in relation to race and class, but also in relation to nativist (anti-Dominican) attitudes in Puerto Rico and geopolitical racialization practices, including the relationship to English.[10]

While Dominicans in El Condado and nordestinas in Ipanema shared a common position as a racialized or ethno-racial Other, critical issues interrupted this implicit Dominican–Puerto Rican versus Northeast–Rio de Janeiro comparison. As noted above, Ipanema parents in fact preferred nannies who were nordestinas, and not *cariocas de comunidade* (Rio-born individuals living in poor Zona Sul communities). In El Condado, perspectives on domestic work foregrounded anti-Dominican nativism and Puerto Rican cultural nationalism, which often triggered discussions about the lower status of *Puerto Rican* Spanish in a broader Latin American language hierarchy (Urciuoli 1991). In this broader sociolinguistic context, Puerto Rican elite parents felt they had to overcompensate with carefully articulated Spanish, as a way of challenging a global stereotype of Puerto Ricans. This Puerto Rican elite often believed that a homogenized "Dominican community"—of which nannies and domestic workers were a part—compromised the pedagogical and socialization goals they had for their children, as well as the national integrity of "their" (white, elite) country and language. Ipanema and El Condado parents were aware that domestic workers transmitted various forms of knowledge—social, emotional, ideological, and even linguistic—to their charges, oftentimes in a tacit way as a result of conviviality, and they were invested in controlling these processes.

Only two Puerto Rican parents used the "like one of the family" qualifier to describe their relationship with Dominican domestic workers, a qualifier that virtually every Ipanema parent deployed at one point or another. In both instances, the Puerto Rican parents were divorced mothers, and the Dominican worker had effectively become a stand-in for the missing parent, as well as a personal therapist and confidante to the postdivorce family, performing a great deal of emotional labor. In Brazil, the "like one of the family" referent was common, particularly in relation to specific domestic workers or nannies based on length of time serving the family or level of intensity in the relationship. In Ipanema, elite parents approached race and class through claims to an affective authenticity between themselves and their domestic workers or nannies. In El Condado, parents viewed themselves as instrumental in asserting a linguistic competency—and superiority to Dominican Spanish—aimed at counteracting global perspectives on Puerto Rican "culture of poverty" stereotypes long held in the US colonial context and often deployed against the so-called bad Spanish of Puerto Ricans.

Dominican migrants provided "teachable moments," or opportunities through which El Condado parents developed didactic instances to teach, compare, and evaluate their children's respect, compassion, and gratitude. The domestic workers stood in for how parents expected their children to relate not so much to the individual domestic worker that tended to them, but through a global logic of one's connection to the "Third World," particularly to countries that were "like the Dominican Republic," and the "less privileged" more abstractly. It was critical for upper-class El Condado parents to view Puerto Rico as more cosmopolitan, modern, and developed than the neighboring Dominican Republic. Dominican nannies sometimes allowed this discourse to gain materiality, relating it to how they made sense of their decision to migrate. Teachable moments in Ipanema shared some of the same impetus as those in El Condado—elite parents drew examples from their nannies' lives, regions of origin, and living spaces to encourage gratefulness in children. In El Condado and Ipanema, such a focus on "gratefulness"—like equivalent comments around "being lucky" or "being fortunate"—engendered perspectives on the sources of one's wealth or one's family wealth as almost mysterious and detached from the forms of inequality and oppression with which such wealth is historically encumbered. These parents viewed themselves as "lucky" and "privileged," but the political economy that in fact produced these drastic social inequalities—and the domestic workers' very humanity and personhood—remained concealed.

"Like One of the Family" and La Criada Malcriada:
Elite Productions of Subaltern Agency

In the Mil Frutas vignette earlier in this chapter, Claudia's public self-fashioning was emblematic of a cultivated informalidade, a privileged and practiced affective disposition that characterized elite relationships with subordinates in Ipanema; in the ice cream parlor, this cultivated informalidade was illustrated in

Claudia's relationship to Leandra and the valet parking worker (cf. Gaztambide-Fernández 2009; Khan 2012a).[11] First, half-jokingly, Claudia remarked, to no one in particular, that she was a good *patroa* (employer). After all, not only was she treating Leandra (and later the valet parking employee) to partake in the ice cream parlor experience with her and her daughter, but, more significantly, she was giving Claudia love advice publicly. As I learned later, Claudia was divorced, and Leandra had become a confidante in the world of dating and romantic entanglements. This was not because either Claudia or Leandra lacked friends of their same social status; in fact, both women were popular members of their respective segregated socioeconomic communities. While they viewed those other friends in terms of competition and performance, however, neither one of them had to compete with or perform niceties for each another. For Claudia, the relationship with Leandra offered a momentary "stepping out" of otherwise rigid social conventions, which was in itself a reflection of how she sustained her social and racial privilege. In her relationship with Leandra, Claudia could actually go beyond the "superficiality" that most of my Ipanema informants attributed to social relationships in their neighborhood; they could, in Claudia's own words, "build relationships that are not organized around showcasing one's conspicuous consumption."

Claudia had the power to orchestrate how privilege would be displayed and enacted—its very visibility or invisibility—in the space of the ice cream shop, by urging some to have an ice cream (Leandra), others to taste multiple flavors (valet parking worker), and yet others (the clerks) to treat people like "clients." Under ordinary circumstances (i.e., if the man had not been invited to approach the store counter by this obviously wealthy white woman), the dark-skin worker's status as a client might have been questioned. Instead, the valet parking worker was promoted, not only to client, but to one of "those clients" who could take their time (and the store clerks' time) tasting several flavors before deciding on one (quite pricey) treat. Deploying this Ipanemense cultivated *informalidade*, Claudia and other neighborhood residents addressed subordinates and service providers as they would their own friends and relatives. Mastering this cultivated *informalidade* was a clear sign of upper-class ease and public display of white interiority, and it did not preclude these parents from shifting out of the *informalidade* mode to giving orders. None of the parents who had grown up in upper- or upper-middle-class Ipanema households, as Claudia's did, expressed any ambivalence about giving orders and expressing requests, sometimes firmly, to their empregadas or nannies, even as they cultivated affective relationships with them; in fact, this exercise of control was praised as an important quality of being an involved hands-on parent. Such authoritarianism, as a characteristic of Brazilian society, has received significant attention from scholars who have explained it in terms of class; yet extremely little connection has been made between authoritarianism and whiteness (Pinho 2009).[12] This association between whiteness, affect, and authority was visible in daily interactions between domestic workers and their employers, producing a more tacit connection between dark skin color and obedience, as a strong indicator of good conduct and good habits.

In Claudia's case, a critical intention in her informalidade was that Leandra develop and express genuine emotional involvement with her and her daughter. The workers, in turn, needed to intuitively determine to engage (or not) in emotional self-sharing, while sensing when to be discreet about personal desires, aspirations, and expectations, all along remaining aware of the employer's emotional and personal needs above all else. More significantly, though, Claudia reflected what I came to notice as a leading tool of affective whiteness: the ability to decide when and the modality through which blackness gained or lost visibility. Ultimately, the power to highlight or silence the racial visibility of domestic workers and nannies was about the Ipanema and El Condado elites' attempt to highlight or silence their own whiteness, to decide when to render it irrelevant or salient.

Although this cultivated informalidade seemed specific to Ipanema and conditioned "like one of the family" narratives, in El Condado I witnessed a form of interaction that was somewhat equivalent and critical to Latin American whiteness, liberal parental ethos, and self-fashioning: the emphasis on the subordinate's agency. El Condado parents often commented, with ironic pride, how "their" domestic workers and nannies always "talked back," "challenged their instructions," and felt comfortable being "explosive" in their presence. A boutique owner and resident of El Condado, Camila Sandoval had been divorced for a few years from the father of her teenage daughter when I met her. She commented on the instrumental role that her señora dominicana had played, not only in terms of helping her with everyday tasks, like cleaning or picking up her daughter from school, but also by providing "therapy" to both Camila and her daughter during the difficult time following the divorce: "I would give Edelma [the domestic worker] instructions about what I wanted her to do with my daughter, but she would wipe her ass with those instructions [laughed]. Because she is a character. For me, what was most important was that my daughter had balanced meals, and that [Edelma] did not cuss and stayed calm in a crisis. But Edelma had a tendency to get hysterical anyway! She became my right hand, my therapist, and emotional support. She had a different perspective on relationships. Men couldn't be trusted, all that, based on her experience." Edelma's proclivity to "be herself" and challenge the employer's directions, rather than being viewed as a negative form of insubordination, was in fact co-opted as a cherished quality by Camila, as was the case among other El Condado parents I met. In both El Condado and Ipanema, upper-class parents viewed their own proclivity toward therapeutic language and popular psychology as evidence of a shared intimacy with subordinates; as long as these parents engaged domestic workers in discussions of "personal" subjects (romantic relationships, family conflict, or conflict resolution strategies), that was enough evidence of how they viewed domestic workers as their equals. Moreover, the ability to share folk theories of romantic relationships or psychological conversations with subordinates also suggested that elite parents had emotional competency across race and class lines; a developed sense of fairness and equality; and the ability to blur hierarchies through intimacy, as suggested in Claudia's relationship with Leandra and Camila's relationship with Edelma.

Verônica Igel Botelho, the Ipanema parent involved in children's theater and outdoor activities in the neighborhood, and an active member of IpaBebê, had a relationship with her domestic and childcare workers that was particularly revealing of the intensity of forms of intimacy under conditions of profound social inequality. When Verônica and I met for lunch, on an afternoon in July 2015, the first thing she relayed was that she had "adopted" the second daughter of Rafaela, an empregada who had worked for Verônica's family for almost two decades. Divorced when I first met her, Verônica had always sent me "Feliz Natal" (Merry Christmas) e-cards with a cover photo of herself; her biological daughters, Larissa and Renata; Rafaela; and Rafaela's two daughters. Verônica had convinced Rafaela to allow her daughters to live full-time at Verônica's home and had gotten them scholarships to attend a private Catholic school in Ipanema. Many neighborhood parents had gotten to know Rafaela, because Verônica would bring Rafaela's daughters along whenever she would meet other parents and their children at a beachside playground in Ipanema. For some of these parents, Rafaela represented the closest, most intimate window into the world of their own empregadas and nannies.

Verônica's intense familial connection with Rafaela coexisted with her pathologizing of Rafaela's life and parenting. Verônica blamed Rafaela's "pathology" on the regional ("being from Pernambuco, living in Cantagalo"), the religious (conservative, Jehovah's Witness), the psychological ("being abused," having many fears which she transmitted to the daughters, being "stubborn," "not knowing how things work"), and the moral ("four children, each by a different father"; "having left a child behind in Pernambuco"). These intimate-yet-pathological narratives had become public knowledge among the Ipanema families with whom Verônica spent most time. Yet, none of these families was surprised when Verônica, after marrying a man twenty years her junior and having a child at fifty, moved to Lisbon in 2018, leaving the rest of her Christmas card family behind.

For domestic workers with children, being a good mother meant financially providing for their children. For the employers who hired them, "leaving one's children for a job" was considered bad parenting; in fact, the deployment of such arguments confirmed, in their view, "culture of poverty" perspectives they harbored toward dominicanos in El Condado or nordestinos in Ipanema, or the poor and black more generally. Parenting empires produced morally sanctioned forms of whiteness that forbade any further discussion. After all, who can argue against the importance of parents being involved in their children's lives?

Parental expectations and the labor of racialized migrant populations in Ipanema and El Condado shared common perspectives on "security" and "insecurity," citizenship and rights, and locals and foreigners, and they aimed to produce more flexible perspectives on what constitutes "the family," particularly among elite individuals in nontraditional family structures. Elite parents positioned the labor of care workers in terms of a required intimacy, rendering intimate the labor and political economic conditions that enabled social inequality further forged the moral codes of whiteness on which parenting empires endured.

Invisible and Hypervisible: Race Narratives, Regional Geopolitics

Parenting empires support a language of feelings, sentiments, and cultivated forms of informalidade that frame relationships of unequal racial and social power in terms of self-awareness and trust. Ironically, genuine affection and power inequality coexist largely because employers viewed "their" employees as powerful subjects. Ipanema and El Condado parents harbored anxiety over a caregiver's power to disrupt family routines; instances in which the caregiver swiftly moved from "like one of the family" to being "threats and thieves" were common.

When I arrived in Vera Ferreira de Oliveira and Thiago da Silva's Ipanema apartment, Vera, one of the many parents I had come to know quite well over the time of my fieldwork, blurted out, "Ana, how do people in the US do it, how do they live without a maid?" In one of those odd moments of ethnographic synchronicity, I realized that it was the flip side of this question that had fascinated me for so long: "Why were upper-class Brazilians, in general, and Brazilian parents, in particular, unable to make any life decision without factoring in issues related to hiring (paid) domestic help?" Like the Indian elites in Ray and Qayum's ethnography, Brazilian elites harbored feudal expectations of a household largely upkept by servants and of lifelong affective and loyalty ties between employer and servant, while also believing that the lifestyles and aspirations of employer and servant were decidedly different. These expectations had been challenged by the increasing professionalization of domestic work under the PT government and the ensuing transition from live-in to daily employment contracts and an increasing democratic language of human rights and opportunities in state and civil society, at least in the pre-Bolsonaro era. Most Brazilian parents regarded their childcare experience as radically different from their own parents' experience and attributed this to the professionalization of domestic work and the loss of affective and loyalty ties due to an increasing reliance on work contracts rather than multigeneration connection to a specific employee. In this context, the catastrophic experience of losing an empregada is illustrative of the feeling of symbiosis on which this relationship is developed and, above all, of how parents viewed the agency of these caregivers (cf. Teixeira, Saraiva, and Carrieri 2015).

While quality childcare is arguably a leading concern among most parents worldwide, among the Ipanema parents I met, not having a "trustworthy" nanny determined critical life decisions—from the decision to have another child and the timing of IVF treatments to real estate and cosmetic surgery scheduling.[13] Vera and Thiago had decided against having a second child precisely because of the "nanny issue": "The issue of having to depend again on a nanny, so profoundly, made our decision. I felt guilty, because Felipe would cry about wanting a sibling. But it [the nanny-employer relationship] wears you down. I believe it is more difficult than a marriage. I know of a few families who have built beautiful relationships with the nanny, over generations, who ended up taking care of the nanny in old age, got her a house. Now nannies are just like regular employees, and the household becomes like a corporation." Vera was one of a few upper-middle-class Ipanema residents who had grown up in a lower working-class community, prior to experiencing tremendous upward mobility (see Walkerdine 2003). She subscribed to meritocratic discourses of "hard work" and "personal sacrifice" to explain her mobility and expressed profound disagreement with Workers' Party social welfare programs and ensuing domestic worker labor laws. Vera was also one of many Brazilian women who claimed that "empregada mantém o matrimónio, o casal" (the maid keeps the marriage going).[14]

On this particular day, Vera felt betrayed by Juju, a domestic worker who also served as Felipe's occasional nanny. She suspected that Juju had stolen from Vera's elderly mother. Vera suddenly switched from Portuguese to a labored English, so that her eight-year-old son, Felipe, would not understand. Vera explained that she had noticed money disappearing from her mother's purse and had proceeded to make some tenuous connections between the missing money, specific dates, and Juju. Still visibly upset, Vera stated, "We never treated her like a maid. Some people, like Thiago's own family, deal with these situations very rationally, as if this is just a service transaction. But I can't help getting involved. I would talk to her, but Thiago believes she will deny the whole thing. She lives in a slang [*sic* slum], and she knows where we live. I lose sleep over this. She loves Felipe. I began imagining, What if she kidnapped Felipe?" In many instances, the closest quotidian contact that upper- and upper-middle-class parents had with individuals outside their social group was in fact with domestic workers; for many of them, the empregadas' lives were considered a sort of "overflow of the favela" into their household, which was also played out in emotionally intense relationships and affective attachments. In November 2017, toward the end of my research, Vera, Thiago, and Felipe moved to Cascais, Portugal. When I Skyped with her from her new beachfront home, she was glowing. After years of marital struggle and Vera's disappointment about Thiago's dependency on his wealthy parents, she and Thiago were now "learning to be a couple, without depending on the extended family, and doing all the house chores ourselves."

On a stunning Ipanema beach day, as we wrapped our *pareios* to lounge chairs, Beatriz Pissollo Itamar, a single mother by choice, mentioned that, after numerous failed interviews, she had finally hired an empregada to take care of her apartment, her son, and her eighty-five-year-old father. When I asked what she knew about the domestic worker, she promptly answered, "I know way more than I care to know, to be honest, and it's only being two weeks! [laughed]. . . . I wanted to have a kind of relationship where she would be comfortable . . . and now she's too comfortable! Each Monday she comes in with an explosion of information about her weekend, her boyfriend, her friends, all of it." Most of the parents I interviewed believed they knew a lot (even "more than [they] wanted to know!") about their nanny's personal life, routines, and hardships. These parents' interest in the nanny's personal life was often a strategy to get a sense of the information exchanged between the empregada and the other family members she cared for, but was also a way to demonstrate their own openness to momentary intimacies across class and race.

Beatriz remarked that none of the nannies or domestic workers she had hired in the decades she had lived in Rio had lived in the adjacent comunidades, like Cantagalo or Pavão. They had all been originally from the Northeast, and Beatriz explained, "Nordestinas don't talk back a lot and are more discreet. They stay in the same position for a long time. It is also a bit complicated to have a person who lives so close by." Beatriz was among the most progressive Ipanema parents I met, if defined in terms of conventions about electoral political outlook, activism, and social consciousness. Nevertheless, she was still implicated in what was common among all the upper-middle and upper-class families I encountered: part of the process of defending her privilege consisted of sustaining, no matter how hesitantly or apologetically, the existence of separate moral worlds, which were always in danger of coming together.

While in El Condado the racialization of domestic workers happened through an equivalence between "domestic work" and "Dominican women," in Ipanema, this racialization was highlighted by projections of regional "differences" that attributed "passivity," "respectfulness," "adaptability," or "discreetness" to migrant women from the northeastern Brazilian states. Historically, Brazilian privileged classes have managed to convince themselves that their patronage is healthier for their servants than the lives available to them "on the outside" (Freyre 1933; Goldstein 2013, 89). In Ipanema, the domestic worker was presented as evidence of how intimacy and emotion soothed social inequality; in El Condado, where live-in domestic workers were rare, the function of the worker was different—it was a way to enforce national and perceived racial boundaries through discourses of difference (in education, ethnic background, language, moral values, etc.). Nevertheless, in both neighborhoods, the humanity of domestic workers was precarious and straddled a fine line between hypervisibility and invisibility, the cautious aspiration to completely trust and continuous fear of unforgivable betrayal.[15] "Betrayal" served as an emotive stand-in for a greater sociological reading that elite parents deployed to justify inequality on an experiential, visceral level. In this instance, parenting empires showcase fear and betrayal not only as intersubjective emotional experiences, but as the imposition of white affective and personal values on structures of inequality. Upper-class Ipanema and El Condado parents seemed to be in an ongoing crusade to "give the poor/black/foreigner a chance," and subsequently, showing how yet again their good-faith opportunity had led to personal hurt and betrayal.

The parents who employed nannies in El Condado, but especially in Ipanema, at times enabled these forms of happiness and even "cruel optimism," creating the possibility of being "like one of the family" and sometimes turning this possibility into a reality (Ahmed 2010; Berlant 2011). This affective promise, however, was not fully realized or realizable precisely because of the tacit requirements for domestic workers, particularly nannies or those who cared for children as part of their daily tasks, to navigate a firm invisibility/hypervisibility line. Jennifer Croissant (2014) suggests that affective labor may have a role in the development and maintenance of "agnotology capitalism," a capitalism that relies on a culturally induced ignorance or doubt, particularly the publication of inaccurate or misleading data. Her understanding of affective labor is concerned with its role as an enabler for a larger capitalist superstructure, where the reduction of alienation is a precondition for the elimination of dissent. Affective labor is part of a larger activity where the population is distracted by affective pursuits and fantasies of economic advancement. Although white uniforms and surveillance cameras were perhaps the most explicit ways of rendering an employee hypervisible, other relational expectations conditioned this hypervisibility. The requirement for invisibility was more forcefully noted in how Ipanema and El Condado parents perceived the role of nannies in framing their own parental identities as well as their sense of the nannies' educational and linguistic "limitations."

In both El Condado and Ipanema, parents seemed interested in the cosmopolitanism that an interest in "diversity" accrued in educational contexts, while undermining how whiteness, their whiteness and their children's whiteness, as well as a broader institutional and spatial whiteness, got reproduced in everyday interactions with people of color, with poor whites, and with nannies and domestic workers. The only diversity and inclusion that was in fact of pedagogic merit for their children was the one that could be contained in deliberately didactic settings—schools, community service, volunteerism, travel. Ipanema parents continuously remarked on the lack of Blacks in their neighborhoods and schools, while effectively rendering their babás and domestic workers—with whom they had the most continuous, intimate, and even affective relationships—invisible in these discussions.

Some of the parents I met lacked some basic knowledge about Brazilian racial relations; the fact that Brazil has the largest population of African descendants in the West, for instance, was a shocking surprise for Fernando Coutinho Leite, a father who was enthusiastic about sharing this knowledge with me when he learned I was interested in topics of race. In August 2015, I was having dinner with Fernando and his wife, Gabriela Braga Vellozo, in their Ipanema apartment, when Fernando all of a sudden—and maybe in reaction to several posts on my Facebook related to Black Lives Matter—asked, without any prompting, "Ana, you are an anthropologist, so you must know about Afro descendants in Brazil." I was wondering what part of this topic he was referring to, and knowing Fernando pretty well by now, I was certain he would go on to explain more, which he did. "Well, I saw a video on Facebook about the slave trade and how most slaves had gone to the Caribbean and to Brazil! Brazil has the second-largest African population in the world. Can you believe that?" At this point, what I was finding most unbelievable was that one of the most observant and deeply analytical people I had encountered in the time of my fieldwork had just learned what seemed to me a pretty broadly cited fact even in undergraduate Latin American studies courses in the United States.

I was also puzzled by the black bodies that seemed invisible to Fernando (and Gabriela), since there were so many of them in Ipanema: nannies, domestic workers, valet parking employees, security guards, store clerks, soccer coaches, personal trainers, ambulatory beach vendors, homeless men and women, and shoeless kids on playgrounds were overwhelmingly Black. The neighborhood's whiteness was only "interrupted" (before being promptly reconfigured) in moments of explicit social tension, policing, and surveillance, particularly when elite action in those instances was justified, and even advocated for, "in the name of the [elite] children." Thus, the daily conversations about the homeless, who were overwhelmingly Black men and women, coexisted with claims that there were no Blacks in Ipanema, because the production of personhood in this particular neighborhood was circumscribed to individuals who could engage in a cultivated informalidade, which was decidedly classed and raced. Ultimately, in/hypervisibility was about who one registered cognitively and affectively.

Discussions around family nannies, most of whom were Afro-Brazilian in Ipanema, could have gone in a number of directions; they could have been discussions about domestic work, child rearing, race, poverty, inequality. What I sensed more often, however, was an actual displacement of race onto political practices, cultural ideologies, sovereignty, and broader comments about who "we are" as a nation or a people. They prompted references to slavery in Brazil, not as a political and economic project of nation building, but as an informative sound byte needed to raise cosmopolitan children. In this sense, parenting empires required the consumption of certain forms of knowledge necessary to socialize children into a national elite.

Teaching racial fluency was central to the form of parenting empire that the Ipanema elite practiced.[16] Racial fluency focuses on how effectively one responds to perceptions of race; it does not anticipate an outcome that is antiracist but may be interested in identifying how racial strategies may intentionally reproduce racism (Hordge-Freeman 2015). Most of the Ipanema parents either downplayed or intellectualized race in ways that effectively undermined Brazilian everyday racism in favor of academic discussions about slavery. In El Condado, most parents codified race, so that blackness was associated with a lower class and/or migrant location, including in terms of Dominican workers and of young dark-skin Puerto Rican men living in housing projects nearby. Contemporary scholarship on racialization in Latin America has noted how blackness and whiteness are constituted in the relation between race as embodied experience that is exuded situationally and race as object of discourse (Roth-Gordon 2017), as well as an ethnicizing configuration with an emphasis on the "folkloric" and "exotic" (Godreau 2015). I argue here that the power of whiteness among Latin American upper classes in fact deepens discursive, embodied, and representational perspectives. It does this by alternatively cloaking and justifying privilege and locating white supremacy in sites that have traditionally been considered inaccessible to social practices and the material: inner worlds, affective dispositions, senses of self, and the quite literal "immateriality" of race operate in tandem under parenting empires. In a context where "racism" is increasingly acknowledged, even by elites, and where the ability to engage in sophisticated "race talk" is a sign of cosmopolitanism, racialization practices and projects have effectively become "processed" in the domains of the self and constructions of personhood. This does not negate that other forms of cultural capital and embodied and linguistic practices shape the legibility of such whiteness; rather, it complicates the assumption that "looking the part" of a white elite is enough.

Upper-class white parents determined the affective parameters of their relationship with nannies as an emotional underside of white supremacy. In these relationships, practices of parenting empire produced a whiteness free of moral stigma, notwithstanding the dramatic inequality gaps that characterize both Brazil and Puerto Rico, effectively removing inequality from sociological scrutiny. Nanny-employer relations were at the core of the production of a "benign" white self. I want to insist that the affect that parenting empire demands only privileges—that is, is only empowering—when it is cultivated and deployed by whites, through intersubjective patterns of cultivated informalidade; otherwise, the affective requirements of parenting empire become, in fact, a source of liability for racialized populations (Berg and Ramos-Zayas 2015).

Conclusion: Subaltern Hope as Mediative of the Affect/Power Inequality Scheme

"I do it out of love," Liz Silva firmly stated when I asked her how she became a nanny in Ipanema. Originally from Ceará, the capital of the northeastern Brazilian state of Fortaleza, Liz was in her early forties and had lived in Rio for twelve years when I met her at BaixoBebê, one of the beachfront playgrounds, in 2014. She had worked as a nurse for several years before becoming a nanny for the children of a Brazilian diplomat living in Paris. Once in Rio, Liz defined her work as a nanny in unusually professional terms: "I specialized in newborns, until about a year and a half. I work on six- to twelve-month contracts." Having such a timeline also allowed Liz to "control better the affection and attachment you develop for the babies." Liz always provided interesting perspectives on the Ipanema families she had met. She once noted:

> Parents, grandparents, the people who surround the child, compete for the kid's affection. To have a kid has become something glamorous, an investment, because it is so difficult to protect and secure their future in this country. . . . When you have conflict between the nanny and the mother, or the father, it's usually because the mother doesn't want to take time off from her career, and then realizes that the kid pays more attention to the nanny. Because "mother" is just a word from the child's perspective. What is significant is the affective bond that develops over time.

Liz had successfully cultivated the capacity to reflect on her own emotions and on other people's fears, excitement, desires, trust, and comfort, as the kiosk manager often remarked. Like other *babás top* (top nannies, sought-after nannies), she was "laboring to foster in herself and her clients a newly expressive therapeutic ethics. A wider array of affects, in particular those associated with care and empathy, feelings of trust and comfort, intimacy and concern" (Hordge-Freeman 2015, 181). Liz needed to be aware of parental anxieties about losing or keeping something as unmeasurable as a newborn's affection. Much negotiation and behind-the-scenes work went into producing the picture-perfect parent-child moments: moments when mother and child appeared mutually engaged, looking through books at a local upscale bookstore, like Livraria Travessa in Ipanema, were possible because of how the nannies crafted the backstage to these moments; how they would reorganize the books the kid left on the floor, making sure to step in when the child became rambunctious and impatient or when the mother found a book appealing and wanted to read a few pages without being interrupted. These nannies were critical in engineering this "quality time" in upper-class families.

During my graduate school years in the mid-1990s, I interviewed several Dominican domestic workers in Puerto Rico for a pilot project I thought would become my dissertation. Although no publication (or dissertation) came out of that project, I stayed in contact with some of the interviewees, including Yesenia Peña. Now in her midfifties, Yesenia had worked for two households of the same extended family, the Vidal family, for more than thirty years. Initially, Yesenia had cared for the children of Pablo Vidal and his wife, Andrea. While living with Pablo, Andrea, and their children, Yesenia had gotten pregnant and given birth to a son whom the family grew close to, adopted as their godson, put through private school, and included in their wills (cf. Romero 2011).

Once Pablo and Andrea Vidal's children left to attend college in the United States, Yesenia moved from the Vidal's Miramar house to an apartment she had purchased through a federal government subsidy in Santurce. She remained working for the family as a housekeeper. In her new role, Yesenia was one of several domestic workers who tended to the house and garden; took care of pets; cooked; decorated the house for special events, like Christmas parties and political fund-raisers; and occasionally babysat for other children in the Vidal extended family.

Yesenia described Pablo and Andrea as "wonderful, dedicated parents" and claimed to have learned how to "become a better parent, and learn to discipline [her son] by talking and considering his feelings," rather than in the more "authoritarian" way of her own parents. "Because you know how Dominican parents are," she stated. "No, what do you mean?" I probed. "Well, growing up in the countryside, my parents didn't care if I went to school, they don't ask me how I'm doing or how I'm feeling. All they want is for me to work, to send them money. Andrea told me 'It seems like your family only calls you when they want something.' But it is just a different way of parenting. Andrea doesn't see that, because she is all about her children."

Yesenia had grown much closer and increasingly torn about her relationship with the Vidals from the 1990s, when I first interviewed her, to the time of my fieldwork for *Parenting Empires*. She was grateful and awed by what she had accomplished, and she considered the Vidals instrumental in those accomplishments. As she explained, she had gone from being an undocumented immigrant who had survived a dangerous yola trip and sexual abuse in the first months after reaching Puerto Rico to being a green card holder, homeowner, and mother of a son who had graduated college and had a stable professional job. While her family in the Dominican Republic struggled to secure some basic needs, Yesenia had a retirement plan and health insurance, and she had sent enough money to build a two-story cement house close to her family in Gaspar Hernández, the northern coastal Dominican town where Yesenia had lived through her early twenties.

"I am closer to Andrea than I ever was to my own mother," Yesenia told me, as we sat at her kitchen counter. As our conversation continued, it became clear that this closeness was built on perspectives that Andrea and Pablo had cultivated about Yesenia's "exceptionalism," the fact that she was not "like most Dominicans," including the rest of Yesenia's family, as noted in Andrea's remark about Yesenia's mother only calling to ask for money. Yesenia served as intermediary between the Vidals and other hired staff of Dominican handymen, painters, and gardeners, because the employers "could not deal with the way Dominicans are." The employers considered these other workers lazy, unreliable, and mentally "slow," and they would let Yesenia know that this was the reason they preferred that Yesenia deal with them directly. The tight affective relationship the Vidals had developed with Yesenia's son, Pedro, had led in part to Pedro viewing himself as "completely Puerto Rican" and rejecting his Dominican heritage. Like the relationships described by other liberal parents, particularly in El Condado, Yesenia insisted that she had no problem telling Andrea or Pablo when they were wrong: "I have no qualms telling them when they are favoring one child over another or not setting clear boundaries in [their daughter's] romantic relationships." Nevertheless, these forms of intimacy were costly, as employers still demanded emotionally and physically taxing tasks. "I can't do certain tasks [because of a chronic pulmonary condition], but they don't respect that," Yesenia remarked.

Such forms of intimacy under deep oppression are nothing unique to the contexts of El Condado and Ipanema, nor to contemporary times, as they were virtually endemic of household arrangements during slavery and forms of patronage in the Americas. In some instances, nannies and domestic workers were reminders of enduring historical legacies and utmost social and racial inequality. In reflecting on the photo of the upper-class white Ipanema parents at the anti-PT march in this ethnography's introduction, one would be pressed to view it as very different from what Jean Baptiste Debret depicted in his mid-1800s painting *Um funcionário a passeio com sua família*. In Brazilian everyday parlance, the expression "casa de família," used by employers and empregadas alike, continued to serve as code for wealth and whiteness; such a family home was understood to be composed of the white wealthy family and one or more domestic workers. The core kin group was always normatively white; the employees black or a proxy for black, even if these were light-skinned nordestinas.

What is perhaps more notable about these contemporary forms of intimacy under profound inequality is the intensity, performative quality, and moral(istic) expectations they generate under parenting empires. Liz Silva and Yesenia Peña were emblematic of an increasingly segmented Latin American labor market of care, which categorizes individuals into "more" or "less" desirable workers based on the ideological, linguistic, regional, and emotive attributes that

FIGURE 7.1. Jean Baptiste Debret's mid-1800s painting *Um funcionário a passeio com sua família* (An employee on a stroll with his family).

might most effectively reproduce white privilege and social inequality under national crisis and interpretations of "corruption." Parenting empires framed the relationship between parent and domestic worker or nanny in ways that re-ignited narratives about the Brazilian and Puerto Rican poor as welfare dependent. These narratives have long genealogies traceable to slavery and patronage, to slave-based societies that continuously relied on relationships of favor and dependency between the poor (even if not black) and the well-off. Parenting empires effectively reanimated and assigned moral justifications to versions of those narratives, while repositioning them in a critique of any government project concerned with social welfare.

A government rhetoric of "waste" was deployed to explain a presumed breakdown of the moral social fabric and personal responsibility. This rhetoric effectively rewrote the crisis of capitalism as being caused not by the high-risk speculative financial sector, but rather by the "burdens" of the welfare state and the "dependency culture" it was blamed for creating. As dark and poor women were judged for their reproductive and spending practices, the wealthy claimed austerity subjectivities that circulated damaging visions of what caused poverty and social inequality, and what the response ought or ought not be. More-over, austerity narratives reanimated long-standing discourses of the poor's "dysfunctional" habits, dependence, and psychological traits in Puerto Rico, and of their flashiness, waste, and indebtedness in Brazil. In both Brazil and

Puerto Rico, policies associated with the welfare state had been imagined as a negative form of irresponsible government, blamed for creating a "welfare culture" and a sense of entitlement that needed to be purged. Parenting has become a form of subjectivity premised on ideologies of personal responsibility, self-regulation, mental resilience, spiritual growth, cosmopolitan yet austere lifestyles, and the enacting of alternative, localized forms of sovereignty that promised legitimate ways to purge a "welfare mentality" and invigorate the nation.

Relationships of servitude in El Condado and Ipanema tied the moral economy of privilege to a tacit belief that whiteness harbored a unique orientation toward self-knowledge, emotional depth, personal reflexivity, and communicative malleability; in their relationship to all domestic workers, but particularly nannies, these Puerto Rican and Brazilian elites corroborated an inherent connection between their wealth and morality, as they tied their relationships with employees to shifting cosmopolitan ideals around racial knowledge and multicultural ease. Domestic servitude provides a powerful lens to view social constitution and reconstitution over time, but also to view how these social transformations provide dynamic raw materials through which inner worlds get envisioned in social and racial ways beyond a blind desire for modernity or development, commonly attributed to the Global South. Relationships of servitude become important barometers to assess relations of subordination, and to tie these relationships between domestic workers and employers to a cosmopolitan desire to be racially open, progressive, and a good wealthy (and white) person. In contexts where Latin American upper classes are almost exclusively white, and where the gestures to transcend such racial segregation were minor and fleeting, the relationship between employers and childcare workers provided one of the few moments of reasonably intimate, meaningful, ongoing interracial and interclass communication. The moral economy of privilege and wealth, as a project behind parenting empire, challenged modernist ideals of increased technological and industrial development, the centrality of materialism and consumption, and a valuing of the West. While domestic work in Brazil and Puerto Rico, and throughout the world, has undergone significant transformations over the last century, its present social form in Ipanema, El Condado, and other elite urban centers is powerfully shaped by conceptions of the sovereign cosmopolitan subject. These aspirations to a cosmopolitanism in the Global South—an attachment to modernity in Brazil and to nonstate forms of sovereignty in Puerto Rico—become communicated through the language of parenting empire; these profoundly unequal affective relations rearticulate ideas and practices of slavery and colonialism through parenting in all its expectations of care, love, selflessness, child-centeredness, attachment, and a focus on socioemotional language and inner worlds.

In Ipanema and El Condado, parents produced self-knowledge and parental practices through their interactions with the black, poor, immigrant women who served as their nannies, babás, childcare providers, empregadas, or domestic workers. These interactions were characterized, simultaneously, by complicity and antagonism, and they unfolded in contexts of considerable affective depths and complexity. While the power and structural bases on which these relationships operated were profoundly unequal, this was an inequality of the most intimate, visceral, and ambiguous form. For Ipanema and El Condado parents, whose lives unfolded in radically segregated spaces, black, poor, and migrant domestic workers provided one of the few contexts of intimate difference. Moreover, while this could arguably also be the case for nonparents among the Latin American elite, practices of parenting empire recast the relationship with childcare and domestic workers—overwhelmingly black, poor, and migrant/foreign—as a project of racial self-concept and moral self-fashioning required for the successful reproduction of (liberal) whiteness. The literature on care work or domestic work often fails to recognize how the world of parenting empire has contributed to developing the highly unequal market of nannies, but also how those very individuals whose livelihoods happen around childcare highlight for employers some critical contradictions about their own self-fashioning, cosmopolitan aspirations, and whiteness.

Although this ethnography deliberately approaches social and racial inequality from the perspective of those who benefit from hierarchical arrangements, I conclude by highlighting how parenting empire is, ultimately, a project of white supremacy. Parenting empire becomes reified not only as a series of intensive parenting practices, but as the only admissible and morally acceptable way of caring for children. Through parenting empire, upper-class parents in Ipanema and El Condado showcased social (in)security instead of inequality, and thus legitimized neighborhood surveillance and policing of poor, dark bodies by making claims "in the name of the children." Under parenting empire, nannies and domestic workers were not only individuals engaging affectively and intimately with their employers, as scholars of domestic work in Latin America have noted; rather, they were actual stand-ins for how perspectives on race, regionalism, and migration (internal and trans-Caribbean) got circulated and communicated by white elite parents to meet their socialization goals and political visions.

Epilogue

We're supposed to be all about *Puerto Rico Se Levanta* [Puerto Rico Stands Up]. In reality, what we have here is collective PTSD.... We have Trump tossing paper towels at us. We have generators and batteries being stolen. That's not Trump.... We are witnessing what we've known since Darwin. Those who have learned to adapt and don't pretend to go on living beyond their means are the ones moving ahead. The [Miramar] food truck park is a clear example. You also have young people graduating from San Ignacio and Ivy League schools, studying agronomy, and becoming farmers, cultivating coffee, opening food truck parks. They are not part of that culture of corruption, of being a wiseguy (*cultura de ser ganso*), waiting for someone to do for them. People criticize the [US Fiscal Control] Board and privatization, but knowing the level of corruption we have and the irresponsible spending, what are the options?—Margarita Berrocal, El Condado

Ana, Brazil is a corrupt nation, a nation with a government that is ill equipped to provide quality education. How can we disregard a corporate takeover of schools under those conditions? We can't point fingers at others for our own corruption. The closing down of IpaBebê is a metaphor for how Rio is going, the crime, the violence. It is a metaphor for the triumph of violence in Ipanema, and the lies the government has been telling us over the last two decades.—Fernando Coutinho Leite, Ipanema

In December 2017, barely three months after Hurricane Maria, I ran into Margarita Berrocal, whose children attended Perpetuo, at Kasalta bakery near El Condado. She had lost her house to fraudulent lending. Her husband had been fired from his own family's business and was now a merchandise buyer for Me Salvé, a store that, ironically, is the butt of many classist jokes and is equivalent to a small Puerto Rican version of Walmart. At that very moment, at Kasalta,

Margarita was waiting to be interviewed for an entry-level administrative position working for a real estate agent in charge of selling John Paulson's real estate to foreigners. "These are the people benefiting now. They are buying up El Condado," Margarita explained.

IpaBebê, the beachside Ipanema playground, was removed in 2018. Like many other Ipanema parents, Fernando Coutinho Leite considered the closing of IpaBebê as Brazil's final curtain call, emblematic of the nation's political and social spiraling and its impending doom. As several of the key parents behind the everyday functioning of IpaBebê left Brazil, many settling in Lisbon and the adjacent town of Cascais, Portugal, the Ipanema beachfront play area failed to secure consistent sponsors. Fernando almost echoes anthropologist Suzana Maia's claim that fear is one of the most widespread emotions in Brazilian society: "More than just material privilege, comfort involves a certain way of being in the world, of inhabiting a house, a car, and a city. Owning a car is a sign of comfort, but driving anywhere in the Global South, one is constantly reminded that one owns a car against the poverty outside the car" (2012, 39). As Fernando's teenage daughter showed me the Korean pop band she had as her iPhone screensaver, Fernando bemoaned that he had never seen Brazil so divided, violent, and afraid. "We can see corruption more clearly now. Someone turned on the lights," he remarked.

Over the years of my fieldwork, the world has seen an expansive cycle of global protest, triggered by a combination of economic and political grievances that include austerity measures, unemployment, inequality, demands for public services, corruption, authoritarianism, police violence, and state repression; a unifying thread across many of these protests is a strong rejection of traditional party politics, with strong populist overtones, and a particular singling out of "corruption" as a leading cause of an array of social ills. Unfolding over the years leading up to Jair Bolsonaro's election in Brazil, and lasting through the aftermath of Hurricane Maria in Puerto Rico, *Parenting Empires* analyzes the lives of a segment of the population whose rhetoric and convictions around parenting, deliberately or inadvertently, were complementary to the electoral win of Brazil's far right and to the US Fiscal Control Board's tightening colonial grip on Puerto Rico.[1]

Parenting Empires documents how contemporary child-centered sociabilities, rather than benign or idiosyncratic novelties, are in fact quite damaging and enlist national elites to do the moral work of US empire in the Americas. Forms of imperial control through the dissemination of rigid and arbitrary ideas of what constitutes "good parenting" circumscribe personhood to specific aspirational and cosmopolitan ideals around the cultivation of interiority currency, often undermining structural hierarchies of race and class and fostering a moral economy of privilege that has become an endemic characteristic of Global North empires in the twenty-first century.

Parenting Empires, Local Corruptions

When John Paulson's assistant arrived at Kasalta to interview Margarita for the job, he introduced himself as Gary and described himself as a gringo; after knowing I lived in New York, he mentioned that he had lived in the East Village and in Williamsburg, and recently, attracted by El Condado real estate market, had moved to the neighborhood with his Cuban wife and young son. During the latter part of my fieldwork in Puerto Rico, the interests of wealthy bondholders had taken center stage, as draconian austerity measures demanded slashing $300 million from the island's public university and cutting 10 percent from the public retirement system. While the cost of the austerity policies' adjustments was shared by Puerto Rican workers, poor people, and small businesses, the "share of the pie going to the top of our society and external partners increases with the crisis and the adjustments" (Quiñones-Pérez and Seda-Irizarry 2016, 92).

On this December day in Kasalta, Gary and I were surprised when Margarita suggested that her job interview with Gary be conducted at the same long table where I was sitting with my opened laptop. This was an interesting ethnographic situation, in which I could not avoid listening to Gary the Gringo rave about how much John Paulson was doing for El Condado; how when he arrived, the nearby Ocean Park neighborhood was full of empty houses, but thanks to Paulson's investments, now this area had become high end. "What do you think about the situation in Puerto Rico?" Gary asked Margarita, as part of the interview. "There is money in Puerto Rico," she responded. With a confessional voice, she added, "The government may be broke, but the people have money." "Yes! That's exactly how I see it!" Gary the Gringo exclaimed excitedly, possibly imagining casting his real estate goals even wider. After about forty minutes, in which Margarita continued to assert herself as the businesswoman and entrepreneur she had been before she lost her job, her house, and her husband's family business, Gary the Gringo offered her the job, paying an hourly rate of $12.50.

"How do you think it went?" Margarita asked me after Gary the Gringo had left. I told her, truthfully, that she was probably overqualified for the administrative job she was about to accept. I repeated what most people have told me, about John Paulson pretty much buying up El Condado. Margarita, whom

I've known to share the pro-statehood inclination of many other Cuban exile families, smiled ironically: "We grew up thinking that, if it weren't for the US, we would be like a Third World country. Now even Panama City and Santo Domingo are doing way better than us! You know why? Corruption!" Just like Brazil, Puerto Rico was a fiscal paradise for the superrich; in fact, even the Brazilian and Puerto Rican upper-middle classes paid twice the level of taxes as the foreign superrich did in 2016 (Burton 2014), but the language of corruption trumped the validity of such a critique.

A language of state corruption, and the blind-faith belief in austerity, permeated most conversations I had with parents in Ipanema and El Condado toward the end of this study. "All governments are corrupt"; "All governments steal"; "We shouldn't be depending on the government, but on ourselves"; and "This level of social welfare is unsustainable" were comments I heard many times during my fieldwork, becoming particularly pressing in child-centered spaces. Haller and Shore (2005) view corruption as one of the ways in which people make sense of politics and of the state in the form of everyday life conversations and discursive rituals. Such narratives render corruption a semantic of governance that prevent nations from attaining the futures they desire.[2] Members of national elites, like Margarita Berrocal and Fernando Coutinho Leite, articulated corruption in ways that dovetailed with the goals of a hemispheric US war on corruption.

While contestation and congressional debate over the application of US law beyond its territory are enduring features of how the United States relates to the rest of the Americas, examining imperial and colonial reach through parenting expands the scope of analysis beyond legal, military, or financial control of borders. *Parenting Empires* analyzes how US hemispheric supremacy gets reproduced through the circulation of child-centered practices, expectations, and cultural norms—including those governing neighborhood built environment, moral economies, the cultivation of the self, and forms of personhood. *Parenting Empires* uncovers forms of US hemispheric control that reveal the Global North not as a collection of empires in distress, but as imperial polities and cultures in active realignment and reformation (Hardt and Negri 2004; Newkirk 2016).

This book is intended as a strong critique of contemporary parenting practices that, intentionally or not, solidify social inequality and hierarchies within nations and globally. These practices are not familial quirks or benign idiosyncrasies but transmutations of US empire and control and hemispheric ideological alliances among elites, which now seek forms of control that have moral grounding. Social and racial privileges and inequalities are justified in terms of "good parenting"; ideological fights against "corruption" and "crisis" are granted moral legitimacy "in the name of (some) children"; "austerity" as a national but also household and personal imperative is fostered as an aspirational identity.

Imperialism in the Americas and Its Affects

On May 18, 2016, the Colectiva Feminista en Construcción, a group of activists in Puerto Rico, organized a demonstration in front of the federal Supreme Court in San Juan. The event was promoted as "Puerto Rico contra el Golpe" (Puerto Rico against the Coup) and was described as an act of Latin American/ Caribbean solidarity against US imperial control of Brazil and Puerto Rico. "Ni Junta de Control Fiscal! Ni Golpe de Estado en Brasil!" was a slogan on posters circulated through social media to promote attendance.

Rarely are Brazil and Puerto Rico approached in explicit comparative terms. Nevertheless, the emotional registers associated with sovereignty and parenting in Puerto Rico and Brazil have never been disconnected from various strategies that the United States has used to orchestrate its colonial and imperial interventions in Latin America and the Caribbean since the turn of the twentieth century.

Imposed by US Congress and funded fully by a bankrupt Puerto Rican government, the Fiscal Control Board's main task in Puerto Rico was to demand more austerity by managing public institutions and services, including cutting funds for pension plans, public education, and public corporations on the island, while also reassuring hedge funds and creditors who had bought Puerto Rico's bonds that they would be paid.[3] The conflicts of interest implicating each of the seven members of La Junta, as the Fiscal Control Board is colloquially called, are too numerous to address here (see Dayen 2016); nevertheless, the tone of La Junta's existence rendered Puerto Rico, its government and citizens, as fiscally irresponsible overspenders.[4] In line with other privatization and public-sector reduction initiatives—and to make it easier for US billionaires to do business and get tax exemptions in Puerto Rico (chapter 3)—the Junta proposed transformation of the island's regulatory frameworks, including everything from shipping laws to occupational licensing.[5] In Latin America, the term "junta" evokes images of the CIA-backed military bodies that forcefully removed democratically elected South American presidents and replaced them with sanguine dictators; such juntas were responsible for the torture and disappearance of tens of thousands of dissenters in the 1960s and 1970s.

FIGURE E.1. Promotional material circulated by a feminist collective in Puerto Rico to encourage attendance at a demonstration against the US-imposed fiscal board and the impeachment of Dilma Rousseff in Brazil. Translation: No Fiscal Control Board [in Puerto Rico]! No Coup in Brazil! From Facebook.com/ColectivaFeministaPR

Ismael Villafañe, an El Condado resident whose children (with Maru Ramírez de Arellano) attended Perpetuo, declared, "There's not a perfect solution [to Puerto Rico's bankrupt government]. Everyone will have to buckle up, adapt to living with less. I don't love La Junta. And I realize it's imperialist, but . . . who else is going to do it?" Like Ismael, other El Condado and Ipanema residents articulated austerity as a lifestyle whereby citizens needed to learn to do without, to wait for what they wanted (the deferred gratification that elites have long deployed against consumption practices they projected onto the poor), and to be more efficient about resource allocation. As a cultural object, set of economic practices, subject-making discourse, and web of socio-historical fantasies, austerity became a powerful moral imperative. Austerity narratives coalesced around parenting. They reignited the moral and ethical value of "good parenting," as arguments and policies around managing "failed" denizen-parents emerged. Dominant austerity narratives were already in effect in less economically austere times, but in Brazil and Puerto Rico, they became bolder and more powerfully anchored across policy, surveillance, racialization practices, and urban projects in times of national governmentality and fiscal crises. Hemispheric articulations of corruption instigated an almost religious belief in austerity: as this rationale went, a retrenchment of inherently corrupt national governments along with less regulation of transnational economic and corporate interests was the route to increased economic growth in Brazil and Puerto Rico, respectively.[6]

Brazilian upper classes made a clear bet by removing the PT from power, initially by impeaching Dilma Rousseff and endorsing Michele Temer, and eventually by supporting (or at least adopting a "wait and see" attitude toward) Jair Bolsonaro. Despite the focus on Bolsonaro's election at the end of 2018, it is important not to forget how Dilma Rousseff's impeachment and its aftermath belonged to a longer history of US imperialism in the region. Structural adjustment policies imposed by Washington around trade liberalization, market deregulation, privatization of state enterprises, and downsizing of the state apparatus, as in other parts of the Global South, were critical to the reduction of wages and social benefits, a dramatic increase in poverty, and the general deterioration of middle-class living standards throughout Latin America (Veltmeyer, Petras, and Vieux 1997).

While Rio de Janeiro voted overwhelmingly for Bolsonaro in 2018, most of the Ipanema parents I met initially rejected the far-right candidate, and some even joined #EleNão demonstrations in the weeks leading up to the elections. After Bolsonaro's victory, however, many of these parents wondered if maybe the new government would be better suited to fight corruption, institute austerity measures and liberalization strategies, and foster economic growth than the previous PT one had been. Maybe Bolsonaro, despite his openly white supremacist, homophobic, misogynist, antienvironment, and pro-military policies, would be able to reassure the global financial sector about the fiscal predictability of Brazil's investment climate, some parents speculated.

Parallel to the "war on terror" in the Middle East and the "war on drugs" already present in the region, the more recent "war on corruption" had already become part of official US foreign policy toward Latin America at the time of Lula da Silva's presidency in the early 2000s. The war on corruption was embraced in Washington as a new method to force political-economic realignment and win back Latin American nations, which, at the time, seemed increasingly dedicated to social welfare and successfully becoming less vulnerable to US corporate greed and capitalist interests.[7] Yet only a handful of the Ipanema parents in this ethnography drew the connection between Dilma Rousseff's impeachment and the Workers' Party's efforts to circumvent US dollar dominance (through trade with Iran, for instance). Brazilian elites have historically sustained an illusion of developmental convergence between the United States and the white settler nations of the Southern Cone (cf. Salvatore 2016), and Ipanema residents were not an exception.

"Even to refer to Dilma's impeachment as a *golpe* [coup] generates tensions among friends and family, who you know were hitting those *panelas*, Vamos Pra Rua, all that circus, right here in Ipanema, right?" noted Beatriz Pissollo Itamar, one of maybe two Ipanema parents who remained firmly against Dilma's impeachment, Temer's coup, Lula's imprisonment, and Bolsonaro's election.[8] Beatriz often downplayed her political stances, fearing her son, a teenager by the end of my fieldwork, would be excluded from neighborhood social events and future professional opportunities in Rio's Zona Sul, where Brazilian clientelism was particularly entrenched. In Brazil, the privatization of local institutions and placement of national resources in US and foreign corporate hands, including selling offshore oil reserves for cents on the dollar to US Chevron and ExxonMobil, were not solely a response to a national fiscal crisis.[9] Rather, they were proposed as "anticorruption" measures. In fact, what was most dismaying in Bolsonaro's election in October 2018 was how Brazilian voters—in the name of fighting corruption, addressing street crime, and restoring an internationally appealing business climate—were willing to overlook the president-elect's possible violation of human, civil, and social rights and thus to ensure bloodshed, discrimination, repression, and environmental devastation (see Mische 2018; Pahnke 2017). Theirs was a forceful, visceral anti-PT hatred, considering the lack of proportion between the errors of the PT government and the human rights threats posed by a far-right Bolsonaro government. Some Brazilian parents genuinely worried about the future of their country in the immediate postelection weeks, but their lives soon fell back into quotidian routines and protected surroundings. Even the small segment of them who might have been conflicted about Bolsonaro continued to hope that a deal with the devil would yield the probusiness, deregulatory, anticorruption reforms they had come to associate with specific lifestyles, moral economies, and parenting practices.

Latin America is arguably the region of the world in which the United States has most closely experimented with the nature of empire. Underscoring this ethnography is the relationship between informal and formal empire. *Parenting Empires* reveals everyday intimate practices that continue to render the Global North, and particularly the United States, as a hegemonic site of exemplary governance and political superiority. In strategic, legal, economic, and political terms, Brazil (and South America as a whole) is very different from Puerto Rico and other parts of the Caribbean and Central America; whereas US tutelage, repeated interventions, and close supervision were the norm in

Puerto Rico and the Caribbean region, the United States never established territorial colonies in Brazil or South America. In this sense, Brazil has been arguably able to preserve its territorial integrity and governmental autonomy in a way that Puerto Rico never has. Nevertheless, the experience of US colonial control over Puerto Rico and the Caribbean region still influenced US conceptions of hegemony in relation to South America, including Brazil (cf. Salvatore 2016; Silva 2018).

The regional knowledge and cultural perspectives Latin American elites provide have been a precondition for the construction of US hemispheric influence and power. At the level of the neighborhood, a moral panic garnered support for the US war on corruption in Brazil and Puerto Rico. Upper-class parents in Ipanema and El Condado often took it on themselves to do the work of neoliberal governmentality in their neighborhoods, thus guaranteeing the success, or appearance of success, that super-parenting citizens could accomplish without need for government support or social welfare. And, thus, while many upper-class parents in this ethnography opposed Jair Bolsonaro, a candidate whose far-right evangelical conservatism was incompatible with Ipanema's structure of feelings, social history, and cosmopolitan vibe—just as most upper-class El Condado parents were opposed to the US Fiscal Control Board in Puerto Rico—their fear of an omnipresent, invisible hidden force preventing their social reproduction also led to an understated desire for a regulatory intelligence apparatus to combat the fear, a standard feature of imperial administration (Stoler 2006; cf. Grewal 2017).

Despite occasional cursory acknowledgment of US imperialism in Brazil or US colonialism in Puerto Rico, Ipanema and El Condado parents ultimately considered these forms of hemispheric control as natural, taken for granted, and even a necessary background that remained peripheral or altogether beyond the scope of analyses of national crises, austerity measures, and political corruption. Even for parents in Puerto Rico, where US control of the island's national territory, politics, and economy has been ubiquitous for more than a hundred years, the role of empire remained abstract at best. Being a colony was, from this perspective, Puerto Ricans' own fault. As an El Condado parent once mentioned, "If we really hated the US [involvement] so much, or if we had the competency to come up with an alternative, we would have done it already." The role of empire, in this sense, was always subject to the inability or unwillingness of the colonized or imperial subject to find viable alternatives.[10] Accusations akin to "blaming the Yanqui for everything" were the dusty rhetorical device through which both US pundits and Latin American elites deterred any criticism of the status quo or the policies that had historically protected their privilege. Such reframing of the problem clearly obliterated the fact that having the power to determine who is "corrupt" is in and of itself a fundamental source of elite status and white privilege, just as who can claim an austerity subjectivity is.

In the face of ever-widening global social inequality, Brazilian and Puerto Rican upper classes claimed moral legitimacy—and self-fashioned, perhaps counterintuitively, as anticonsumption, antimaterial, and invested in interiority currencies—by firmly positioning ordinary roles as parents and child-centered relationships at the intersection of neighborhood and city initiatives. These roles and relationships ultimately transformed the possibility for legitimate social mobilization into instances of democratic danger and despair. In Brazil, parents highlighted the security of their beachgoing families in opposition to the presence of Black young men from poor communities; in Puerto Rico, parents perceived their ability to walk with their children through their neighborhood to be threatened by the working-class demonstrators and university students who protested US-imposed Fiscal Control Board meetings held at El Condado hotels. Elites without children can and do share some of these political positions, of course. However, when (white and wealthy) children become central to discussions about who is allowed or not, of who is a good parent versus a parent denizen, of who belongs in which social networks and who is excluded, such discussions become unquestioned and unquestionable moral imperatives. As the social embodiment of innocence, children deploy ethico-moral narratives that have come to structure how we think about politics in contemporary Euro-American and white Latin American contexts, while also mapping political possibilities and impossibilities; importantly, only some people and some plights get noticed when innocence is what draws our attention to them (Ticktin 2017, 577–78). These ideas were fundamental to how elites in the Global South situated themselves locally, in their neighborhoods, but also in the nation and against their international peers. In Brazil and Puerto Rico, elites have been instrumental in deploying a language of corruption that showcases political dishonesty, failed democratic ideals, and an incomplete modernity as exclusively "Latin American" or Global South traits. Historically, Latin America upper classes have produced regional forms of knowledge that have provided US policy makers and business interests with enhanced visibility of the peripheries' problems. Latin American elite knowledge and local practices provide valuable services in the governmentality of colonial and neocolonial situations

(Salvatore 2016). Focusing on corruption exclusively as the source of crises, rather than as their manifestation or catalyst, misses dynamics of global restructuring, imperial influences, and colonial interventions.

Going Beyond Parenting Empires in Brazil and Puerto Rico

I have never believed that any one academic book can do the work that I have witnessed among grassroots activists during my life (e.g., Ramos-Zayas 2003), even though as academics we sometimes become wrapped up in our own importance. What books can accomplish is to provide a glimpse into someone else's reality, a way to hold inequality under intellectual scrutiny for a moment, of highlighting the contradictions in our thinking about a subject, and of offering one or several possible explanations for an observation. This ethnography sought to illuminate how elites in two neighborhoods in the Global South structured their intimate lives and exerted moral claims on their privilege at a time when child-centered sociabilities have become even more solidly entrenched in empire, colonialism, and modernity. *Parenting Empires* is premised on the notion that society must be defended in the name of one's children—children who are categorically and unquestionably more important than other people's children; this premise condones the moral outrage and legal right to surveil, incarcerate, and render expendable those "outside," overwhelmingly the poor and dark, frequently children and youth. This gestures to a search for a space of purity, outside corruption, violence, and contamination, a space emptied of the power that can ground both tolerance and action; yet, since "innocence is both mythical and ephemeral, we are constantly displacing politics to the limit of innocence in a never-ending quest, and in the process the structural and historical causes of inequality get rendered invisible" (Ticktin 2017, 578). The articulation of empire through parenting produces not only state-sanctioned disenfranchisements, persecutions, and internments, but dangerous overproduction of popular profiling of who is actively working on her/himself to be a "good parent" and who is not.

Parenting has been targeted globally as an arena in which states create new generations of subjects who embody ideals integral to the success of the new capitalism: individualism, risk taking, and entrepreneurship (Faircloth, Hoffman, and Layne 2013, 4).[11] Parenting frames the limits and possibilities of nation in everyday life and the modalities through which social inequality enters the most intimate domains of experience. Upper-class parents are not subordinate pawns of states; rather, they are individuals who viewed their countries as inherently "corrupt" entities, and who viewed themselves—in their role as parents, entrusted with the nation's future—as uniquely positioned to step in for the government's inability to do its job. The upper-class parents whose lives are documented in this ethnography were invested in deciding when laws were suspended and when they were not. They operationalized who enjoyed the right to have rights at any specific moment, in the neighborhood, in the city, in their interaction with household workers and marginalized populations in adjacent communities. Their production of a deep grammar of racialized distinctions and profiling replayed historical anxieties of who is really "us," who gets to be really "white," and who is just "passing," and in terms of who would be drawn into affective entanglements or who raises social concerns and moral panics.

Global parenting cultures reanimate the potency of moral categories of deservingness, belongingness, and citizenship, and determine when race, class, and neoliberalism become visible, hypervisible, or invisible, legitimate or immoral. In Ipanema and El Condado, upper-class parents forged parenting empires that demonstrated strong stakes in the proliferation of ambiguities— ambiguity about who is white (chapters 5), about which paid workers are considered "part of the family" (chapter 7), about who is a legitimate citizen of the neighborhood and the nation (chapters 2 and 3), about whose heritage and wealth are moral (chapter 6), and about which forms of currency are material and which ones don't matter or are, in fact, immaterial (chapter 4). In affluent neighborhoods like Ipanema and El Condado, parenting became political because it was intimately connected to the power of some to determine what was good and best for others and, by implication, what was deemed inadequate and in need of various types of surveillance, correctives, and institutional interventions. By recasting neighborhoods in terms of child-centered forms of sociability and relatedness, the Global South elites in this ethnography deployed practices, spaces, and ideologies associated with child rearing to foster the moral, affective, and quotidian conditions that framed sovereign aspirations and supported empire building as everyday projects of the self.

A goal of this ethnography has been to trace the interconnected nature of contemporary parenting and empire in the Americas. It examines how this interconnection supplies the moral basis for multiple languages of crisis, corruption, austerity, and fear, by thinking about parenting and its problems through a broad interpretive framework of parenting empires. If the nation has invariably been imagined through metaphors of the family (what Étienne Balibar calls "the nationalization of the family"), those periods in which familial bonds and aspirations seem to be fraying often lead to worries about the stability, political landscape, and future of the nation. Under the neoliberalization of the Global South, the modern state has played a significant role in the production and promotion of certain kinds of families and parents. While location and context clearly matter, states around the world have sought to produce and promote certain types of parenting and have enlisted certain elites as vessels in the everyday disciplining of those popular classes who fail to "measure up" to increasingly absurd and arbitrary expectations about child rearing.

There are several academic, theoretical, and political interventions *Parenting Empires* has aspired to make. It has examined how upper-class parenting perspectives connect with the great themes of US foreign policy and hemispheric control (e.g., the role of the United States in the hemisphere, economic interests and corporate expansion, undermining anti-US sentiments, the proper conduct toward US tourists/billionaires/entrepreneurs).[12] This is not to suggest that upper classes in El Condado and Ipanema never dealt critically with the question of empire or questioned the validity of the United States as exemplary of democratic values. Significantly, as Ricardo Salvatore (2016) demonstrates, over most of the twentieth century, members of the South American intelligentsia questioned the good intentions of the United States because of its repeated military interventions in Central America and the Caribbean. Nevertheless, national elites in Brazil and Puerto Rico still favored modern forms of imperial engagement, forms of empire that provided access to public goods and general welfare to their subjects, as well as to cosmopolitan cultural phenomena, including narratives around "multiculturalism" (chapter 5) and the cultivation of inner worlds (chapter 4).

Parenting Empires has also aimed to complicate portraits that present elites as caricatures of materialism and superficiality, blinded by glamour or family lineage. The *dondoca* (in Brazil) or *dama cívica* (in Puerto Rico)—and other akin gendered images of the "ladies who lunch" that have popularly represented Latin American upper classes—are limiting at best, and obscure much more about the elite than what they might reveal. Rather than a judgment on specific individuals, or even necessarily an exposé on the wealthy, this ethnography is a critical portrait of what we miss by viewing Latin American elites solely at the level of macro political spheres or stereotypes, or uniquely in terms of their most obvious self-segregationist or exclusionary practices. The focus here is on how mundane, well-intentioned, and even thoughtful actions of elites in Latin America and the Caribbean have an amplified impact on the lives of everyone they come into contact with; upper-class parents subscribe to moral economies of privilege and processes of self-cultivation that still yield unequal spatial configurations, superficial relations to racism and prejudice, and profound social inequality. In a sense, my goal was to examine how exactly the road to hell is paved with (elites') good intentions.

Parenting Empires examines the local manifestations of global phenomena—shifts in what it means to be cosmopolitan in terms of specific "progressive" perspectives on race and wealth, the cultivation of interiority practices, the rise of austerity politics, political distrust, and a cosmetic reframing of colonial and imperial control. These global phenomena have powerfully shaped how adults relate to one another in child-centered ways. These new forms of relatedness have altered adult solidarity, social networks, and investment (or disinvestment) in the outcome-focused (rather than the feel-good, intention-focused) pursuit of social justice and equality. Historian Nancy Cott argues that "turning men and women into husbands and wives, marriage has designated the way both sexes act in the world" (2000, 3). As *Parenting Empires* demonstrates, by turning men and women into fathers and mothers, parenting has not only recast gender politics but also the rising inequalities of class and race. Concerns with the public face of parenting, how adult sociabilities unfold in child-centered nodules of urbanism, play a pivotal role in how countries assess their domestic and international status in moments of economic and political change. While marriage is no longer the only socially acceptable way of making families among cosmopolitan elites, parenting has stepped in as the foundation of modern social norms, white supremacy, and geopolitical hierarchies that endure across increasingly diverse family configurations.

Disentangling class and race in the Latin American and Caribbean context has been recognized as largely an academic exercise, rather than a reflection of the lived experiences of a majority. Nevertheless, in this ethnography, I contribute to Critical White Studies by demonstrating how, at the upper echelons of the class hierarchy, elite status (if not exclusive income level) becomes available to individuals who are closer to a European ideal, to the virtual exclusion of all others. Importantly, as I also show, there was considerable variation in what constituted "looking white" versus "being white," as well as significant cosmetic efforts to move through the gradations of whiteness that would place various white people closer to a European aesthetic ideal (chapter 5).

The moral economy of privilege laid out throughout this ethnography—the undermining of materialism in favor of presumably immaterial forms of currency, anticonsumption ideals, and neoliberal forms of personhood that focus on self-cultivation—underscores how affects and intimacies unfold in contexts of radical class and racial inequalities, giving the impression of mutuality and emotional connection. As examined in relation to domestic workers, particularly nannies, white privilege endures, requires, and even gets solidified through affective relationships with subordinates. The "cruel optimisms" (Berlant 2011) that affects often produce perfectly coexist with, and in fact are enabled by, the social, psychological, emotional, and physical proximities that have been traditionally associated with progressive, liberal contexts. These affects, nurtured within relationships of drastic social and racial subordination, demonstrate how, in context of racialized affective entanglements, morality becomes legible only when white privilege is a precondition.

The South-South comparative methodology in *Parenting Empires* deliberately decenters the United States as the default comparative reference, while retaining the framework of US hemispheric control of the region as integral to the analysis of both parenting and sovereignty. Methodologically and epistemologically, I have remained careful not to overstate or oversimplify commonalities across place and time. Nevertheless, perhaps unexpectedly in a South-South ethnographic comparison of Brazil and Puerto Rico is the recurrence of certain themes around parenting and its connection to sovereignty, as these resonate in a comparative context. The US colonial experience in Puerto Rico and the Caribbean required the United States to become instructor of self-government in control of financial advising, military involvement, and policing, while Brazil and other South American countries were laboratories of US financial expansion, foreign policy interventions, and a way to measure the impact of US democracy, modernity, and development. This South-South comparison, methodologically unmediated by the United States yet analytically grounded on US hemispheric imperialism, enabled a reframing of the problem not as one between a far-right and democratic liberalism, or even as one between sovereign populism and global elites.

Parenting, and the forms of sociability and relatedness it fosters, demonstrates how affects—in all their racialized logics (cf. Berg and Ramos-Zayas 2015)—operate in the service of empire. Among Global South elites, parenting provides the moral language through which fear, hatred, confusion, and admiration for whoever has power and promises order or proposes austerity solutions to national "crises" get produced, endorsed, and circulated. As Spinoza would claim, these passions reduce collective power and enable individuals to "shrug" in the face of even the most tyrannical regime. Conservative ideas about the moral (child-centered) life and the transformation of privilege and wealth into ethical criterion and evidence of interiority currencies are perfectly compatible with even the most liberal and progressive forms of self-fashioning. Rather than signaling exceptional historical moments, crisis and ontological insecurity in Brazil and Puerto Rico are ordinary, quotidian, and systemic, and better examined in ordinary, quotidian, and systemic levels for which relations and practices around parenting are particularly well suited. It is important to remain attentive to historical distortions and the political reading that even liberals deploy to defend, justify, or adopt a "wait-and-see" attitude toward fascist or colonial governments, as well as how they approach liberalism's classist, racist, and colonial histories. Contemporary parenting is a critical site to rethink the affects and imaginations on which the concept of empire and colonialism gets refashioned and strengthened.

Parenting empires inherently halt any possibility for social justice and equality, since such possibility requires a recognition that our children are not more important than other people's children, and certainly not more important than the children of those who don't have access to protect or advocate for their children as much as we do. These moral dilemmas, embodiments of privilege, and forms of self-fashioning often provide, in this sense, the impetus for civic neighborhood action, privatization, and exclusionary practices along race and class, even in the absence of gates and country club memberships.

notes

1. PARENTING EMPIRES

1. Zephyr Frank's work, for instance, uses inheritance records to flesh out the life of Antonio Jose Dutra, a slave sold from Angola who proceeded to build an impressive personal fortune in Rio de Janeiro in the 1830s and 1840s. Dutra was typical of middle-wealth holders, individuals of modest means who had gradually accumulated wealth by investing their capital in slaves. With the cessation of the slave trade and subsequent abolition of slavery in 1888, these middle-wealth holders were hit harder than the wealthiest inhabitants of Rio de Janeiro, who had invested instead in stocks and bonds and in urban real estate. Thus, as Frank demonstrates, while the abolition of slavery undermined the position of the middle groups and curtailed the social mobility of free blacks in Brazil, it did not have severe repercussions on the wealthier populations, whose wealth could be better assessed through ownership of urban real estate, not ownership of slaves. Julian Go argues that when the United States took control of the Philippines and Puerto Rico, in the wake of the Spanish-American War in 1898, it particularly targeted the wealthy, educated political elites in both colonies as collaborators. In both territories, US colonial officials built extensive public school systems and set up American-style elections and governmental institutions. Colonial officials aimed their lessons in democratic government at the political elite: the relatively small class of the wealthy, educated, and politically powerful within each colony. While they retained ultimate control for themselves, the Americans allowed the elite to vote, hold local office, and formulate legislation in national assemblies. Go assesses complex processes of cultural accommodation and transformation, which reveal how elites in both the Caribbean and the Pacific sought to "domesticate" the novel forms and language of the occupying power and redefine them as different from its Spanish colonial predecessor. Thus, Go calls attention to the various registers at which US colonialism operated; ultimately, the success of the US empire depended on how successfully its agents were at colonizing local culture and inducing cultural change.

2. Teresa Caldeira explains that, in São Paulo, particularly after the end of the Brazilian dictatorship in the late 1980s, there has been an increase in "crime talk" and fear of

violence among the upper classes. This preoccupation with crime has, in fact, changed the urban landscape, built environment, and notion of public space, while fostering the growth of gated communities, surveillance industries, and even a new aesthetics of securitization among elites. The São Paulo upper and middle classes in Caldeira's study have all but abandoned the detached house for high-rise apartment complexes in the center and gated communities on the periphery. The newer gated communities, or *condominios fechados*, are all-inclusive spaces, which provide an array of social, professional, and educational services and parallel institutions. On the infrequent occasions when São Paulo elites venture outside their walls, the very rich do so in helicopters and bulletproofed cars with armed bodyguards and specially trained drivers. Caldeira considers the challenges that these forms of social and spatial segregation pose to the consolidation of democracy and human rights in Brazil, while also noticing how the gated community has indeed become a global phenomenon. Zaire Dinzey-Flores describes the rise of gates in the Puerto Rican city of Ponce since the early 1990s. As the integration policy of the New Deal reform movement of the 1940s and 1950s failed, writes Dinzey-Flores, gates and fences emerged as mechanisms through which the wealthy could self-segregate in *urbanizaciones* (middle- and upper-class neighborhoods). More significantly, and departing from Caldeira's study of São Paulo, Dinzey-Flores shows how, in the Puerto Rican case, the government—through policies like Mano Dura contra el Crimen (Heavy Hand against Crime) in the 1990s—places walls around public housing complexes (*los caseríos*), where poor and racialized populations live. These low-income families see their access to and from the outside world shaped and limited by an architecture of exclusion and surveillance, designed not so much to protect them from crime, but to protect others from the crime that, for many Puerto Ricans, the government, and the media, low-income people have come to represent. The *urbanización* and the *caseríos* become emblematic of "types" of people—the hardworking or deserving versus the social welfare dependent or undeserving, the good citizen versus the denizen, and so forth. These types and culture wars, Dinzey-Flores demonstrates, are established on a tacit racial and racist logic that implicitly codes the space of the *caserío* as a space of blackness and crime.

3. Other important scholarship that explicitly deals with the question of whiteness in Brazil includes Iray Carone and Maria Aparecida Silva Bento's *Psicologia social do racismo: Estudo sobre branquitude e branqueamento no Brasil* (2002), Valeria Ribeiro Corossacz's *White Middle-Class Men in Rio de Janeiro: The Making of a Dominant Subject* (2018), and Vron Ware's 2004 edited volume on *branquidade* (whiteness) in Brazil. From an ethnographic perspective, Suzana Maia (2012) has examined the connection between Brazilian body aesthetics, national images, and whiteness. Also crucial to discussions of whiteness in Brazil is Guerreiro Ramos's 1957 article "Patologia social do 'branco' brasileiro," possibly the earliest academic approach to the subject in the Brazilian context. To my knowledge, there is no comparable ethnographic literature on whiteness in Puerto Rico, though scholars of race allude to the linguistic and political valorization of white skin on the island (e.g., Godreau 2000, 2015; Vargas-Ramos 2005).

4. Not coincidentally, Souza argues, the middle- and upper-class demonstrations against the incumbent Workers' Party, which were visible in Ipanema in the months leading up to Dilma Rousseff's impeachment, attributed the country's corruption exclusively

to the national government. Under Rousseff and her predecessor, Lula da Silva, Brazil witnessed the implementation of social welfare programs that had lifted tens of millions out of poverty, begun addressing racial discrimination through racial quotas in universities, and extended labor laws to protect domestic workers, including nannies.

5. A growing ethnographic literature focuses on the subjective aspects of middle-class belonging. While the focus of this research is the middle class, and even the global middle classes, they enable important, if indirect, comparisons to equivalent work that has focused on elites. See Rachel Heiman, Carla Freeman, and Mark Liechty's anthology, *The Global Middle Classes: Theorizing through Ethnography* (2012).

6. In *The Production of Space*, Lefebvre (1991) views space not as "context" in which events and relationships unfold but as the very process of production of these relationships and social practices.

7. Elsewhere (Ramos-Zayas 2012), I argue that an emotion-based theory of practice renders aspects of individual interiority legible, while recognizing that such "interiority" is entangled in the power hierarchies of a political economy. Ipanema and El Condado parents, rather than viewing themselves as subordinate to the state, as was the case among the Newark working-class and immigrant populations, framed their "interiority currency" in light of racial and class privilege, which contributed to their production of everyday forms of sovereignty and valuing of austerity politics.

8. Although adults who do not have children are often as involved (if not more) in such deliberate "inner quests," parenting provides a socially uncontested morally privileged grounding, imagined along the lines of "altruism," "selflessness," and "sacrifice" in a way that not having children rendered difficult.

9. I realize that conspicuous consumption persists, and that the distinction between "conspicuous" and "inconspicuous" is by no means rigid, but I center on how elites tend to change their habits once the masses gain the ability to copy them.

10. Pierre Bourdieu expands understandings of social inequality by providing a broad theory of elite reproduction through tastes (consumption), associations (social capital), and dispositions (cultural capital). A focus on inculcation, articulated in the concepts of "doxa" (Bourdieu 1977, 166; 1984, 68) and "body hexis" (Bourdieu 1977, 124), accounts for conscious and unconscious bodily practices that become unquestioned. Michèle Lamont (1992) notes that marks of social distinction among the French and US upper-middle classes are based not only on socioeconomic and cultural practices, as suggested by Bourdieu, but also on moral ones "centered around such qualities as honesty, work ethic, personal integrity, and consideration for others" (4).

11. Norbert Elias (1994) examines how internalized "self-restraint," imposed by increasingly complex networks of social connections, develops the "psychological" self-perceptions that Freud recognized as the "super-ego." Elias shows that habitus was the outcome of long-term historical process, rather than the natural constitution of the nation or cultural group. He calls these distinct sociological, historical, and intimate connections between a macro structural level and contemporary modes of conduct and emotional disposition "the process of civilization." Elias does not address how individuals get to control their emotions, or how the lack of successful control of emotions has different consequences for different populations (cf. Berg and Ramos-Zayas 2015). I owe

this reflection on elite futurity to a conversation with anthropologist Edgar Rivera Colón (personal correspondence, February 8, 2019).

12. Adam Howard (2010) moves beyond a conception of privilege as a commodity, which has dominated the body of scholarship on elite education, to understanding it as an experience more intrinsic of who a person is or has become.

13. Joseph Tobin (1995) argues that contemporary bourgeois approaches to early childhood education stress the substitution of techniques of verbal expression for other more genuinely child-centered emotionality. Contemporary "therapeutic culture" of child rearing is in fact deeply ambivalent about emotions, by emphasizing the value of emotional expression while demanding strict emotional control.

14. Carla Freeman's study (2014) of middle-class Barbadian entrepreneurs, while not directly *about* parenting, notes a recent emphasis on children as "projects," requiring not only strict discipline, good manners, and proper behavior, but also the cultivation of new modes of expression and creativity, open communication, warmth, and care. This shows a radical revision of the affective culture of child rearing that Freeman's interlocutors recalled from their own childhoods.

15. The process of making the child through "concerted cultivation" is part of a broader neoliberal project that emphasizes individual responsibility and self-management alongside a focus on managing risk. As sociologist Annette Lareau (2002) shows, children in upper- and upper-middle-class families are taught to question authority, engage in constant negotiation with their parents, and, through their various engagements, become socially adept. More recently, "intensive parenting has been associated with depression in mothers, suicide in teenagers, and overall deficiencies in raising self-reliant, independent young adults (even linking this to the boomerang effect, college graduates returning to live with their parents [e.g., Marano 2008; Rosenfeld and Wise 2010]). "Intensive motherhood," a term Sharon Hays introduced in 1996 to describe an emergent ideology urging mothers to "spend a tremendous amount of time, energy and money in raising their children" (1996, x), had been spun off in almost comedic renditions. In journalistic, autobiographical, and the new genre of "mommy" literature, terms like "hyperparenting," "Tiger Moms," and "helicopter parenting" provide imaginative counterparts to Margaret Mead's culturalist perspectives on child rearing in Samoa and around the globe.

16. As Argeo Quiñones-Pérez and Ian Seda-Irizarry (2016) note, the 2015 "Fiscal Stabilization and Economic Growth Plan" for Puerto Rico proposed various neoliberal prescriptions dating from the time of the Tobin Report, while adding others like negotiating debt restructuring with bondholders, obtaining federal concessions with more Medicare and Medicaid, and obtaining exemption from cabotage laws. They conclude, "The Puerto Rican economy has become a model of extreme capitalist wealth extraction. . . . Meanwhile the share of profits and interest [is increasingly] going to local extractive elites, mostly intermediaries of global financial capital and other fractions of capital" (97–98).

17. The United States was instrumental in staging the 1964 military coup against a democratically elected left-wing Brazilian government devoted to the distribution of wealth for social welfare. Regional interference practices in response to domestic crises in Latin America gained legitimacy in the post–Cold War era (Coe 2015). For

the next twenty-one years, the United States continued to support a military dictatorship that served its economic interests, while vehemently denying that it played any role in the coup.

18. The peculiar ways in which US white male academics relate to Brazil and all things Brazilian, including Brazilian (female) spouses, deserves attention, but this is beyond the scope of this project.

19. After India and the United States, Brazil had the highest number of Facebook users at 90.11 million in 2016 (Young 2013).

20. Sally Falk Moore makes a plea for a comparative anthropology that does not insist on synchronic societal ethnographies or the production of typologies (2005, 2). She proposes a time-conscious, process-oriented approach to comparison to bring both context and cross-cutting themes into focus (10).

21. As part of the *Informe sobre desarrollo humano: Puerto Rico 2016*, a government study of human development and income distribution in Puerto Rico since 1990, Puerto Rican economist Marcia Rivera Hernández demonstrates that Puerto Rico has the fifth-greatest social inequality in the world, with a 2014 Gini index of .547, significantly above the US average of .481 (Instituto de Estadísticas 2017; Pacheco 2016; Toro 2008; cf. Mora Pérez 2015; Quiñones-Pérez and Seda-Irizarry 2016). Anecdotal references to the irony of a fiscal crisis, on the one hand, and "an abundance of luxury cars," on the other, were in fact backed up by statistical studies declaring that "more Porsches are sold in Puerto Rico than in the US, Brazil, and Argentina . . . in reality, more are sold in Puerto Rico than in any other country of America" (Pacheco 2016). Comparatively, the Gini index in Brazil fell from .607 in 1990 to .526 in 2012, a significant reduction in inequality that took place during the first decade of this century. At the time of my fieldwork, the most notable concentration of a new Brazilian middle class was in the Northeast of the country (43 percent). Brazil remained among the most unequal nations, occupying the eighteenth most unequal country in 2014 (Rockman 2014).

22. As Rubén Gaztambide-Fernández (2015) states, ethical responsibility to the (elite) participants should not override ethical responsibility to society. Throughout this project, I remain attentive to how research ethics are never innocuous to social standing; in fact, "the question of accountability is complicated by the fact that the rights of some groups to remain anonymous might conflict with the rights of others to know the processes involved in the reproduction of inequality" (Gaztambide-Fernández and Howard 2012, 298; see also Galliher 1980).

2. THE FEEL OF IPANEMA

1. Although the entire Zona Sul is considered a prestigious social area in Rio de Janeiro, within this area, Ipanema and Leblon are neighborhoods viewed as able to prevent problems related to modernization in ways that the neighboring Copacabana could not; hence, Ipanema residents live in constant fear that their neighborhood will become like Copacabana. They are keenly aware of these street-by-street or block-by-block distinctions and oftentimes described their own social position based on where they stood on this spatial status grid. See Velho (1978) 2013.

2. In Brazil, the term "subúrbio," and its derivatives, like "suburbano," is not equivalent to the US "suburb" or "suburban." In fact, it is almost the opposite: the subúrbio is a poor, stigmatized area noted for its poverty and marginality, at the outskirts of the more desirable inner neighborhoods.

3. Concern with violent crime in Rio, as in other large Brazilian cities, first emerged in the public consciousness in the early 1980s, during the transition from military dictatorship to electoral democracy (Caldeira 2000). Although statistics show a rise in violent crimes—such as murder, kidnapping, and armed robbery—from the early 1980s through the mid-1990s, recent crime records are more mixed. As Garotinho (1998) argues for Rio, and Caldeira (2000) for São Paulo, "talk of crime" is not directly related to crime statistics. Garotinho points out that the middle classes in Rio felt particularly secure in 1994, despite the spike in the crime rate.

4. According to the Instituto Brasileiro de Geografia e Estatística (IBGE), the Brazilian government statistics agency, Ipanema had a population of close to 43,000 residents in 2015, a decline from 46,800 in 2000. Almost 67 percent ranged in age between fifteen and sixty-four years old; 22 percent were over sixty-five years old; and about 11 percent were fourteen or younger (IBGE 2011). In Rio de Janeiro, the skyrocketing real estate prices, particularly in the Zona Sul and traditionally wealthy neighborhoods, as well as limited space downtown led more and more people to move to the Zona Oeste, including both the nouveau riche areas of Barra and Recreio as well as the working-class suburbs of Jacarepaguá and Campo Grande. Nine out of the ten most expensive apartments in Brazil were located in Rio de Janeiro's Zona Sul, within four kilometers of one another, in 2014. Seven of those were beachfront apartments in Ipanema or Leblon (see Barros 2014).

5. Roughly two-thirds of the white upper- and upper-middle-class Ipanema parents I interviewed had been firmly anti-PT since the beginning of my fieldwork, the summer of 2012. The events of 2015 had only reaffirmed, not created, their anti-PT sentiments. There was perhaps another third of my research sample that had been firmly committed to the PT and felt genuine pride in what Brazil had been able to achieve under the PT. By 2015, about half of those original PT supporters, a group largely consisting of an intellectual elite of journalists and artists, claimed to still support the PT, even if not necessarily the party's leadership. While these PT supporters were also white and upper- or upper-middle-class Ipanema residents, they felt isolated, judged, and excluded from many of the social parenting circles they had developed over the years. All original PT supporters noted the irony of how the PT had become the "corrupt party," when in reality corruption had never been so prosecuted in Brazil.

6. What changed in the political moment that provided the context for the last years of my fieldwork was that PT opponents had successfully channeled broad social discontent against corruption, connecting the impeachment proceedings with the Petrobras scandal. This fostered a collective antigovernment stance among most of the Ipanema parents in this ethnography.

7. "O bairro era a capital cultural do Rio, e, portanto, a capital cultural do Brasil" ("Ipanema," 2004, 34).

8. In Rio, the success of the import-export economy galvanized the elites, who came to see the poor as irrational and those who would speak on their behalf as dangerous. In

1904, manual workers and the unemployed, goaded by educated professionals, rose up and rioted against an obligatory smallpox vaccination imposed by political elites. Here, for the first time in the republic, poor people appeared on the stage of politics, not at the mercy of their patrons, but as a group loosely referred to as "the people" (Owensby 1999, 43).

9. Toward the end of the nineteenth century, Brazil saw the first kindergartens, which were private institutions for the children of the wealthy. Although Getúlio Vargas's legislation obligated workplaces to provide nurseries for breastfeeding mothers to care for their infants at work, these were not closely monitored, and penalties for noncompliance were low (Freitas, Shelton, and Tudge 2008). Not until the 1960s did Brazil witness increased demand for higher quality services for young children because of the entrance of middle- and upper-middle-class women into the workforce.

10. While the Zona Norte had been important to Rio's colonial past as the seat of the Portuguese royal family, by the second half of the nineteenth century, new working-class subúrbios formed along rail lines, near factories, and close to a booming seaport, and favelas proliferated; currently, about half of Rio's residents live in the densely populated Zona Norte (Herzog 2012, 123). The Zona Norte became characterized as "purgatory," and the Zona Sul as "paradise." Importantly, though, even in the early fifties, the Zona Sul was not everyone's "paradise." Rather, it was also "a hell of perdição, where Copacabana dictates immorality, erosion of costumes, a frivolous and bohemian life" (P. Gomes 1953).

11. To increase the capital imperatives of landowners and realtors, Copacabana and Ipanema began to be marketed not only or even primarily for their residences, but for their "lifestyle" (Cardoso 2010, 84).

12. Two racial discourses developed almost in tandem with each other: (1) Blacks and *mestiços* were criminalized, and public policies around racial whitening were put in place, and (2) the myth of racial democracy became an ideological national identity, as suggested by Gilberto Freyre's "cadinho da raças" (Huguenin 2011, 29). In José Edward's article "Quem somos nós?" (Who are we?), the magazine *Veja* acknowledges that it has become fashionable for affluent white Brazilians to stress possible race mixture in their backgrounds (Dávila 2003, 233–35).

13. By the 1940s several tunnels had accelerated urban growth through the hills. A flux of wealth and capital toward the Atlantic beachfront region, along with a commitment to an *estética civilizatória*—that is, an interest in curtailing any possible expansion of living quarters for the poor—encouraged Pereira Passos to grant developers and French planner Alfred Agache absolute freedom of construction.

14. O'Donnell (2013) argues that Copacabana and Ipanema were represented in terms of a "beach-civilizing project," a specific model of modernity, rooted in the development of a model of distinction, with specific locations in an economic and symbolic hierarchy.

15. The high-rise in Rio de Janeiro, marketed to and associated with elite families and foreigners, emerged as an *arquitetura domiciliaria* (housing architecture) alongside an imaginary of modernity. According to Lilian Vaz (2002), until the 1930s, the expression "casa de apartamentos" was indiscriminately used for hotels, boardinghouses, and apartment buildings for families, particularly in reference to rental properties. To distinguish elite family buildings from other forms of collective residence, advertise-

ments for Atlantic beachfront apartments highlighted "luxurious bathrooms," "beach views," "telephones in all rooms," "proximity to the Copacabana Palace," and the "highly rigorous criteria to select residents" as the main marketing strategy. Note that casas de apartamentos appeared concomitantly with a significant growth of favelas in the hills around the city; these poor neighborhoods were stigmatized precisely for a presumed promiscuity attributed to the proximity among residents. From an advertisement noted by Lilian Vaz: "The entrance has the same aspect of the ordinances of the great and luxurious hotels. Severe control allows tenants to get rid of undesirable people who can be dispatched with an acceptable excuse. There is no hassle in the corridors. Order and silence. . . . To become a tenant of the building, the applicant fills out an application, stating his marital status, that he must be married, living with his wife. No single or widowers allowed" (2002, 123–24).

16. The growth of a Zona Sul class of professionais liberais (professionals in the areas of teaching, law, engineering, and other occupations typical of an industrializing economy) in the 1920s and 1930s also guided real estate offerings. These upwardly mobile populations, still excluded from the old elite society, sought residence in areas considered attuned to their social goals, accomplishments, and aspirations. By the 1950s, mid-level bank employees could aspire to be within a common "sphere of familiarity," or "intimidade," with their employers, "notwithstanding the protocols of hierarchy" and the duty of "serviceability" (Owensby 1999, 67).

17. In *A utopia urbana*, anthropologist Gilberto Velho notes the significance of Atlantic beachfront neighborhoods, like Copacabana in the 1950s, for this new professional class: "The creation of the Copacabana myth, as well as Ipanema or Barra, is only possible in a type of society in which there is an identification between place of residence and social prestige in such a way that the simple change of neighborhood can be interpreted as social mobility, even without a change in the occupation or income" ([1978] 2013, 30).

18. Several advertising campaigns explicitly sought to arouse anxiety and guilt in parents by calling their attention to the frightening possibility that their sons could just as easily end up shining shoes as being secure professionals. A 1930s ad shows a young, ragged, barefoot boy hunkered down to shine the shoes of a knee-stockinged boy in shorts, jacket, and tie, with books under his arm. The text reads: "Which of them is your son? One of them has everything: books, nice clothes, entertainment . . . boots to be shined. The other, an unfortunate one, often does not even get a crust of bread. This kind of thing happens every day on the street corners, always with different characters! A life insurance policy would have made the other child happy, if only his parents had taken precautions. Anyone can afford this policy. By economizing just a little bit at a time, you can guarantee your son's education and future" (*Revista Commercial dos Varejistas* 1, no. 6 [April 1932]: back cover, cited in Owensby 1999, 93).

19. During the turn of the last century, Botafogo, a neighborhood associated with a foreign elite and high-class local bureaucracy, would also become the main commercial center for the new residents of the *bairros praianos*, but two decades later there was no longer a need for this.

20. These class formations had already been the subject of discussion a few decades prior, particularly in relation to LGBTQ populations of various class backgrounds.

Toward the late 1960s, the strip right in front of the Copacabana Palace became a preferred meeting site for LGBTQ people. According to Fábio Bila (2009), at the time, this area was considered socioeconomically mixed. Upper-class gay beachgoers experienced some tension with groups of young middle-class youth and Copacabana residents who also wanted to exert claims over the area. With the economic decline of Copacabana in the 1970s, this area would eventually be associated with a gay populations from lower classes and peripheral Rio areas (in Huguenin 2011, 175–92).

21. The internationalization of Brazilian musical production had a longer trajectory than this, including the promotion of Brazilian-born Portuguese Carmen Miranda's presence in Hollywood and other US "good neighbor" strategies during the New Deal.

22. When Ruy Castro (1999) used the term "provincialism cosmopolita" to refer to life in Ipanema, he was alluding to the neighborhood's history of being grounded on key intellectuals, artists, and political figures who all seemed to know one another. Some of the leading "characters" in Ipanema's narrative of origin had not been born in the neighborhood: Vinicius de Moraes lived in Gávea; Antônio Carlos Jobim was originally from Tijuca; and João Gilberto lived in Jardim de Alah, near the Ipanema-Leblon border. Nevertheless, they would become leading figures of bossa nova, a musical genre whose creation and themes would introduce Ipanema to the international stage.

23. Although many favelas were eliminated to expand the space that would come to be occupied by the new elites in the 1960s, the 1980s and 1990s saw growth in the number of residents in all Rio de Janeiro's favelas (Carneiro Lemos 2003).

24. Wilbert Gesler (1993) coined the term "therapeutic landscapes" to describe places that have "an enduring reputation for achieving physical, mental, and spiritual healing" (1993, 171; cf. Conradson 2005). This focus on the interconnections between place, identity, and health, however, has tended to disregard power dynamics, such as how the affluent may have more access to places of healing, or how the same place may provide healing to some and be an unhealthy context for others.

25. Ruy Castro stated that he could not deliver an academic lecture in Ipanema because that would only be possible if Ipanema were in São Paulo; he preferred to call his participation a *bate-papo* (chit-chat session). Space, in relation to this "imperialism ipanemense" (de Barros Queiroz 2012, 17), is a category of thought that structures representations and social practices.

26. Velho (1978 [2013]) coined the term "vanguarda aristocratizante" to describe the bohemian intellectual and artistic scene in Rio de Janeiro in the 1970s; as he notes, despite a "liberal," "progressive," and "avant-garde" identity, the upper- and upper-middle-class carioca elites ultimately continued to protect their class and racial privilege. As Huguenin states, "It seems like the [Ipanema] beach and the neighborhood itself, through the years produce a marketing of openness, assimilation, and incorporation of difference and of those who are different. However this is not about any kind of difference. Each time the neighborhood or specific areas of the beach face the possibility of becoming open to a popular crowd, there is also a displacement. Bossa nova seems to experience more dissonance when mixed with the sounds of pagoda or funk" (2011, 134).

27. Between 1968 and 1980, editors of the newspaper *O Pasquim* produced satire and social critique of the military regime, and drew writers to the Bar Zeppelin, a meeting site

for what came to be known as the "esquerda festiva" (festive Left). This image continues to distinguish segments of Ipanema's upper-class from elites in other parts of the city.

28. In 2010, the observation deck, named Mirante da Paz, was inaugurated near the General Osório metro station. A year later, the Instituto Atlântico endorsed what was called "princípio de auto-regulamentação" to expedite the granting of forty-four property titles to Cantagalo's residents. The initiative aimed to foster a new perspective on what constitutes citizenship among residents; generate economic profit if the area rose in value; increase self-esteem; and provide access to a mailing address and banking services that require a property title.

29. In the 1990s and early 2000s, the Zona Sul upper classes mobilized to advocate for lofty goals, which included respect for human rights, "peace" in the city, and "justice for those who suffered the arbitrary and violent actions of the State" (da Cunha 2012, 211). This mobilization, however, was premised on the idea that these issues could be achieved by reducing the separation between inhabitants of different areas of the city and public safety authorities, like the civil and military police, two bodies notorious for their racist and classist practices. In 2009, the fifth Unidade de Polícia Pacificadora was established in Cantagalo, and nearly two hundred trained police officers were assigned to the area (da Cunha 2012, 212).

30. While a June 21, 2015, Datafolha poll showed that 87 percent of Brazilians were in favor of the age reduction, child development experts, community activists, and parents in poor and working-class neighborhoods, including #SouMãeContraAReducão, mobilized against the proposal. Within a twenty-four-hour period, the Brazilian Congress had first rejected and then approved the reduction of age of criminal responsibility ("Within 24 Hours," 2015).

31. In "Policiais não são máquinas de segurança: São homens e mulheres que, como nós, sofrem, amam, desejam, têm medo, mas arriscam sua vida para nos proteger" (Minayo 2013), the author highlights the main conclusions from "Anuário de Segurança Pública de 2013," a study of the challenges, life conditions, and stressors faced by police officers in Brazil.

32. Most residents viewed the 1970s as a golden age of the Ipanema Left and artistic intelligentsia. As James Freeman notices, public spaces in Ipanema and Copacabana "thrive despite the polarization of the city and the worldwide trend of elites avoiding uncontrolled public spaces" (2008, 538). An enduring carioca perspective was that the beach, as a public space that inspired great local and national pride, was the most democratic area of Rio de Janeiro and, perhaps, of Brazil as a whole.

3. PARENTING EL CONDADO

1. Like Puerto Rico, Brazil was a fiscal paradise for the superrich, partly because a large portion of the tax structure of the country is based on indirect taxes (taxes on the consumption of goods and services), and not in the form of property taxes. According to data from the Receita Federal in 2014, about 71 million Brazilians made R$200 billion, received as profits and dividends, without paying any *imposto de renda de pessoa física* (IRPF). Brazil has one of the lowest taxes on inheritance in the world at 3 percent.

2. Between 2010 and 2014, the average number of people leaving the island each year was fifty-three thousand. Between April 2014 and March 2015, the number was closer to eighty-seven thousand (at the height of Puerto Rico's massive emigration in the 1950s, the yearly average was about forty-seven thousand). The island's public debt is more than 100 percent of its GNP, not counting net liabilities of the public pension system at $43.4 billion (Quiñones-Pérez and Seda-Irizarry 2016).

3. In 1950, the US Congress allowed Puerto Rico's voters to elect a constituent assembly to write a constitution, which was ratified by a plebiscite in 1952. Although the Estado Libre Asociado de Puerto Rico was presented as a "compact between Puerto Rico and the US" (BERNABE 2007), the US federal government retained all its prerogatives; the ELA had jurisdiction only over insular matters, while all issues related to Puerto Rico–US relations remained off limits. Puerto Ricans, who had been given US citizenship in 1917, could not elect US presidents, and island imports remained entirely controlled by the United States under the 1920 Merchant Marine Act. In true neoliberal fashion, unrestricted trade between the United States and Puerto Rico remained, and the island's government lacked power to protect the island's market from well-established US competitors.

4. From the late 1970s through the mid-1990s, new tax exemption incentives enacted under Section 936 of the US Internal Revenue Code proved attractive to high-tech operations, especially pharmaceuticals, and Puerto Rico became the largest exporter of legal drugs into the United States. By 2006, however, Section 936, the centerpiece of the Popular Democratic Party's industrial policy, had been eliminated, as the US Congress looked to close the loophole that had allowed corporations to avoid paying taxes. As a result of phasing out Section 936, about forty thousand jobs were lost, and billions in corporate funds deposited in island banks left Puerto Rico, without ever having been effectively channeled into economic development projects. Each successive administration borrowed money to maintain its spending level or to keep from cutting it more. This spiraling down led to the downgrading of Puerto Rico's government bonds to "junk" status on Wall Street (Quiñones-Pérez and Seda-Irizarry 2016, 94).

5. Like US states, Puerto Rico cannot file for chapter 9 bankruptcy; the possibility for the country to seek chapter 9 bankruptcy protection was discreetly eliminated by the United States in 1984 (Walsh 2016; Wolff 2016).

6. Under US colonialism, Puerto Rico has never even come close to full employment. Even at its peak, Operation Bootstrap never got unemployment under 10 percent, and massive emigration was encouraged by Puerto Rico's government to alleviate population pressure. The government's reliance on tax exemptions to attract outside investment to bring jobs to the island works in a perverse way: unlike manufacturing operations, which create jobs both directly and indirectly through linkages to local firms, retail chains like Walmart drive small local stores out of business, putting as many people out of work as they hire but still getting tax credits for "creating jobs."

7. On June 9, 2016, the US Supreme Court ruled in *Puerto Rico v. Sanchez Valle* that the "double jeopardy" clause, by which two defendants could not be charged and prosecuted for the same crime at the state and federal levels, did not apply to Puerto Rico. This was considered a landmark case in relation to Puerto Rico's sovereignty (or lack thereof).

8. In 2015, the Congress-appointed seven-member fiscal board—each member on Puerto Rico taxpayers' payroll—was charged with overseeing all the financial and political actions of the Puerto Rico government, under the acronym PROMESA, which many considered particularly cynical, given it means "promise" in Spanish, and few can see the promise of privileging the payments of bondholders and hedge funds above providing even the most basic educational and subsistence services to the island middle class. The oversight board has sovereign power over the government, with the ability to overrule and veto decisions made by elected officials (H.R. 5278, 114th Cong. [2015–16]; Fortuño-Bernier 2016).

9. During the latter part of my fieldwork in Puerto Rico, the interests of bondholders had taken center stage, as draconian austerity measures slashed $300 million from the island's public university and cut 10 percent from the public retirement system. The island, particularly San Juan, had experienced the largest population losses (including the loss of doctors and other upper-middle-class professionals) between 2010 and 2015 (Coto 2017).

10. Even by the late 1800s, under the Spanish colonial regime, El Condado and Miramar had already been tacitly or explicitly designated areas for wealthy and influential populations. During Spanish colonization, Miramar consisted of private land that the Spanish Crown had given to elite San Juan families who sought a healthier and more hygienic place to live, outside the islet that is now Old San Juan.

11. In 1920, the Behn brothers organized the International Telephone and Telegraph Corporation (IT&T), a name they used to deliberately confuse investors (especially foreign) with AT&T. But the development of the Condado area was even more crucial to their success as telephone entrepreneurs.

12. The grand hotel was an enterprise packaged and placed in the Caribbean with all the luxuries and amenities that US visitors expected, particularly distinct for being a "family experience." The idea of tourism in the Caribbean was radically divided as a result of Prohibition. Places like Cuba and Mexico received visitors that sought a more "dangerous experience": not only did the hotels in these places offer alcohol, casino gambling, and vaudeville-style entertainment, but these destinations were also associated with political instability and required traveling parents to assume some degree of risk. According to Theodore Roosevelt Jr., governor of Puerto Rico from 1929 to 1932, the island of Puerto Rico was the "Switzerland of America" ("Grand Condado Vanderbilt" 2009). In a letter to Governor Roosevelt, dated January 28, 1931, the Association of Hotels and Restaurants of Puerto Rico demanded legal protection because boardinghouses on the island were challenging the hotel industry. The association's secretary requested that the governor order a revision of the sanitary guidelines of 1915 for the industry and that those boardinghouses be included among the restrictions, since many did not have to comply with most regulations ("Grand Condado Vanderbilt" 2009). After insinuations of possibly unsanitary and hazardous conditions, the boardinghouses became dissociated from family travel, just as hotel living was becoming more family friendly.

13. Through the 1950s and 1960s, mainstream newspapers like *El Imparcial* would frequently publish articles with the clear mission of the need to "clean" San Juan of what was viewed as a growing homosexual and *transvesti* population, warning that not doing so would turn San Juan into another Greenwich Village (Laureano 2016, 105). Already

in the 1970s, Puerto Rico was inserted into circuits of transvesti shows, which would also receive artists and performances from Europe and Latin America, especially Brazil.

14. In August 2000, the Association of Hotels and Tourism of Puerto Rico held a panel titled "El Condado: Merecedor de un Mejor Futuro," where the tourism industry and government and municipal agencies discussed revitalization plans for an area that, according to the association's executive director, had undergone severe decay (Santiago 2000). "Illegal businesses" and "vendors that lack permits" were partly blamed for El Condado's "decay," as were "poor lighting" in the parks and "traffic" and parking issues. In 2004, the Stella Maris Church in El Condado was demolished to the dismay of many; at that point, few outsiders knew that an "upscale" elderly home, a "high quality residential facility for the elderly," along with a new church would be built in the same lot. Although nobody was very clear about the funding for the $30 million project, some speculated that the Archdiocese of San Juan would provide financing to be then repaid by the wealthy elderly residents in the form of rent. In addition to the ARCC, another resident organization emerged in El Condado in 2007, with the mission to improve El Condado "as an example of economic and social value for the country," and with the vision of "leaders that love Puerto Rico, that integrate diverse people and communities for transforming the quality of life of the Condado as a window for global impact" (Casellas 2004).

15. See Asociación de Residentes de Miramar meeting minutes, Asociación de Residentes de Miramar, San Juan, PR.

16. Asociación de Residentes de Miramar meeting minutes, May 31, 2014, Asociación de Residentes de Miramar, San Juan, PR.

17. Middle-class ideas about achievement and taste, which contribute to the positioning of leisure and "enrichment" in private or semipublic spaces, are not accessible to every child. Childcare is a booming business in both Puerto Rico and Brazil, but it is also characterized by heavy segregation along class, race, and regional lines; affluent areas have childcare facilities that integrate care, leisure, and education/instruction, thus leading to a greater institutionalization of childhood culture.

18. Van den Berg (2013) analyzes how the Netherlands urban planning program to turn the area of Rotterdam into a "child-friendly city" in fact entailed replacing existing urban dwellings with new, larger, and more expensive homes in what the author calls "urban regeneration." Middle-class families become, in the eyes of urban administrators, the silver bullet destined to solve various urban problems. Children, teens, and parents are thus a focal point of gentrification policies: they are considered stellar gentrifiers. Yet, children and teens are also most often looked down on as urban problems and undesirable subjects (Lees 2008). In this sense, while middle-class children and highly educated parents are imagined as the solution to urban problems, poorer urban youth are mainly seen as the cause of those problems and as "illegitimate subjects" (Watt 2006, 777). The unequal character of this "child friendly" type of gentrification thus brings forth the unequal construction of the category of "children" as either "opportunity rich" (having potential) or "opportunity poor" (being "at risk").

19. Problems of density were viewed as responsible for the "production of a wall of buildings in El Condado as well as in Miramar, without any consideration for the loss of views, privacy and ambience. Of the several proposals to handle traffic in El Condado,

one that stood out involved demolishing the Puente Dos Hermanos, so that El Condado's peninsula would be disconnected from the El Escambrón area of San Juan. An outcome of this, according to the proposal, would be 'a greater local feel (*ambiente* local) [that] would render El Condado streets less exposed to the comings and goings of interests foreign to good neighborliness [*intereses ajenos a una buena vicinal*]. The commercial emphasis would be reduced as traffic declines in a superior-quality zone in sync [*a tono con*] with the cultural level of residents and tourists'" (Amador 1968, 65). Perhaps the main reason, ultimately, that the bridge was not demolished was that it would also cut out direct vehicle access between Old San Juan and El Condado, as well as pedestrian access between El Condado and El Escambrón, where a social club had been established. Some significant accomplishments were attained in the short term, however, including cleaning the lagoon water from an oil spill and trash, forbidding motor boats, removing graffiti painted by "*vandalos*" (thieves), eliminating the pier where the clandestine fishermen settled, and initiating plans so that the terrains occupied by the US Navy, between Munoz Rivera Park and Condado Ensenada, would "be returned to the people" (Asociación de Residentes de Miramar 2014, 78). Some other main goals to be undertaken, to various degrees of success, throughout the 1970s and into the 1980s included acquiring a disputed territory north of Ashford Avenue and turning it into a public beach project, to be called Ventana al Mar; forbidding "inappropriate" commercial advertisement, and increasing police surveillance in the lagoon zone.

20. In Guaynabo, gating coincided with a government-led city marketing campaign, and neoliberal policies of the municipality have been articulated through the public funding of private enterprises. By the early 2000s, Guaynabo City exclusively catered to middle- to high-income residents and had reasserted the position that Guaynabo occupies in the Puerto Rican class imaginary, through the creation of new and trendy magazines, the opening of a flea market, and the writing of a musical satire, *Estoy en bici en Guaynabo City* (Riding my bike in Guaynabo City).

21. As Willem Boterman states, "The field of parenthood is a social arena wherein trade-offs are required among social networks, labor market position, housing demands and various forms of consumption . . . and the field of parenthood is the arena wherein the concept of good parenting is negotiated" (2012, 2400). One thing Boterman notes is that households that tend to have high shares of both economic and cultural capital are likely to stay in the city because they have invested in the city in a symbolic sense, but they also have the financial means to make relatively few compromises in terms of housing (2401).

22. *Miramar Siempre!*, August 2014, Asociación de Residentes de Miramar, San Juan, PR.

23. The first time I realized that Kasalta is an informationally dense space for the upper-middle and upper-class Condado elite seems like a fluke of fieldwork. I went to Kasalta early one morning to get a coffee before heading off to meet one of the fathers I was going to interview that day. Inadvertently, I sat at one of the long tables next to a group of mothers whose children attended St. John's. Always curious about the politics of fieldwork when it comes to eavesdropping, I really felt I couldn't avoid overhearing their conversation, particularly when they mentioned the names of a couple who had become

central to my fieldwork. The conversation wasn't particularly damning; they were simply commenting on how this particular couple, who had some social prominence or local celebrity status, had matriculated their child in St. John's. Nobody said anything objectionable, or something that would damage the couple's reputation, but I did realize that it could have gone that way, based on people's "hmm"s and "ahh"s. If probed a bit, everyone appeared to have common points of reference in overlapping social networks. As another parent once mentioned, "I stopped going to Kasalta, because every single time I would go, I'd end up sitting next to a group who was gossiping about someone I knew. . . . This is a village, not even a city, and Kasalta is the village's communication center."

24. Only about a third of the women in my sample had full-time jobs (in finance, law, medicine, or as chefs and/or entrepreneurs). The overwhelming majority, probably the remaining two-thirds, worked part time or as freelancers (as psychologists, legal consultants, fitness/yoga instruction). Puerto Rico does not have a strong tradition of wealthy "women who lunch," as Brazil does. In Puerto Rico, even many of the wealthy women in older generations (the grandmothers) tended to be involved in paid work.

4. WHITENESS FROM WITHIN

1. In "Interior Horizon: An Ethical Space of Selfhood in South India," anthropologist Anand Pandian analyzes the domain of selfhood as an arena of transformative labor rather than one of discovery. He focuses on the ethical practices of the self, as "elements of a Nietzschean 'genealogy' of interiority, attesting to the contrary forces, histories, and accidents of experience through which selves may be invested with durable and workable depths." Pandian argues "that the constitution of an interior domain of selfhood in modern South India can be understood in relation to three overlapping and moralizing forces: the colonial experiences that imposed Western modes of self-engagement," the vernacular vocabularies of selfhood (long-standing literary traditions), and "the practices of quotidian life through which these and other forms of exterior experience may be 'folded' (Deleuze 1988) into an interior horizon of ethical selfhood" (2010, 65–66). I argue that the constitution of an interior domain of selfhood among a Puerto Rican elite can be understood in light of similar overlapping and moralizing forces, including a complicit and complex relationship with US colonialism and perspectives on economic instability; a vernacular imagery and relationship to a hierarchical private schooling system; and everyday parenting acts, practices, and spaces.

2. Although in its beginnings, Latin American psychology relied on European and North American psychology's hegemony, original Latin American theories and paradigms have surfaced since the 1960s (Salas 2014). Liberation psychology is an example of Latin American psychology that is centered on the specific social realities of Latin America and involves a call for action, asking psychologists to engage in changing conditions of social injustice among the underprivileged (Martín-Baró, Aron, and Corne 1994).

3. Christian Ingo Lenz Dunker (2008) examines the cultural dissemination of psychoanalysis in Brazil and argues that cultural syncretism and incomplete assimilation of liberal ideology contribute to the specificity of how psychoanalysis was culturally assimilated in Brazil, particularly during the 1970s and the periods leading to the redemocratization of

the country. Dunker argues that a Brazilian sociability is condensed in *cordialidade*, politeness without ritual, and a political economy that is "a succession of counter-imperialist practices" intended to maintain imperialism or formal rulings in terms of informality (Prado 1994). Moreover, this sociability rooted in social and belief syncretism allows psychoanalysis to be absorbed as an element in a polymorphic belief system, along with the implementation of a sociopolitical structure of liberalism and a high level of self-irony, where rules and rituals are not followed for their face value. The cultural syncretism of Brazil allows a reduction of pathologization associated with psychoanalysts in other countries. Because of this general fluidity, in this chapter I view popular psychology, religious/spiritual, and other emotional wellness practices as fluid dimensions of overlapping projects of interior world making.

4. Cristiana Facchinetti and Rafael Dias de Castro (2015) analyze the background of the historiography of psychoanalysis in Rio de Janeiro, from its introduction in the 1920s as a new form of therapy. During the 1970s, there was a significant spread of psychoanalysis among the urban middle classes, with a growing demand for individual, group, and family psychotherapy. According to G. C. Filho (1982), not only did the number of people accessing psychoanalytic treatment expand during the 1970s, but there was also an increase in the "social prestige" or status conferred on those practicing or attending psychoanalytic treatment. In response to perceived economic downturns, there has been a resurgence of New Age versions of self-improvement, offering transcendental rewards (karmic clearing) to attain the fantasy of self-making. Micki McGee (2012) argues that turning critical and scholarly attention to self-help culture in the Global South in cross-cultural perspective will help shed light on how new forms of authority and (self) policing are practiced.

5. By the 1980s, wellness and well-being in Brazil and Puerto Rico referred not so much to physical health but to the search for happiness (positive psychology) and quality of life. This intensified in the 1990s with a boom in the study of happiness, optimism, and positive emotions (Galinha and Ribeiro 2005). According to N. Rose (1996b), the fact that subjects in democratic modern societies are "obliged to be free" (17) has meant that the self has acquired increased salience: its subjectivity has come to be enhanced by those practices that encourage autonomous individuals to strive for "self-realization." Key here is to what extent cultures of individual self-improvement in the Global South are setting the ideological stage for either new forms of governmentality or new forms of social resistance (McGee 2012, 687).

6. For Foucault, the self is coerced into existence not to become an agent but as a mechanism of control, where systems of discourse work from the inside out by creating a self-regulating subject. Likewise, Stuart Hall (1996) stresses that there is no true "self" hiding "inside" or behind the superficial, because self and identity are "constructed within, not outside discourse" (22–23). But this deconstruction of the self does not lead to a social structure and personality approach about how different eras produce humans with different psychological characteristics, emotions, beliefs, or pathologies. Instead, Rose (1996a) advocates for a "genealogy of subjectification" (128) concerned with localized attempts to produce meaning as this occurs through professional vocabularies and the technologies and practices of science, medicine, government, and the workplace.

Most research in the symbolic interactionist tradition has focused on self-understandings, self-meanings, and self-concepts as the social products of interest; the emphasis being on the social production of the personal self. Yet the social construction of selfhood is also about meanings and understandings associated with the public self, the self that is visible and known to others and encompassed by what we come to accept within the cultural category of personhood.

7. Kardecismo is a spiritual doctrine that follows the teachings of French scientist Allan Kardec, branching out into various Brazilian interpretations of the French doctrines, most notably those developed by Chico Xavier in the 1970s. Around the time when Kardecismo was losing followers in France, in the 1920s, it gained followers among the European upper classes in Brazil. Kandercistas were among the fastest growing religious segments in Brazil, with 1.3 percent of the population as followers in 2001, making the country one of the "greatest spiritual nations in the world" (India Brazil Chamber of Commerce, accessed June 5, 2019, http://www.indiabrazilchamber.org). There are numerous histories of Kardecismo and many ethnographic studies on Brazilian hospitals that integrate this doctrine along with Western medicine. The relationship between Kardecismo and Umbanda, or Candomblé, an African spiritual practice, has a long history, and racial associations, beyond the scope of this work (D. Amorim 1988; Pires 1984). Interestingly, while Puerto Rico espiritismo is relatively outside mainstream religious life and is associated with the racialized working classes, Brazilian Kandercismo (also considered espiritismo) was a popular practice among the white upper and upper-middle classes (see Moreira-Almeida and Koss-Chioino 2009).

8. As I noticed in past work among Newark "street therapists" (2012), and again in this project among the Latin American elite, there is a global, evolving interface of therapeutic language and neoliberal economic rationalities. Psychological language, and various everyday forms of therapeutic governance of the poor, influenced local common sense and discourse, confounding how people understood a country's social structure and their positionality within that structure. The framework of "racialized affect" (Berg and Ramos-Zayas 2015) offers a useful set of tools to approach upper-class Latin American affective dispositions, as these are definitively entrenched in power structures.

9. This perspective is actually sustained in a study that measures subjective wellness in Brazil. See Albuquerque and Troccolli 2004.

10. In "Changing Models of Parenting in Contemporary Urban Families in Bulgaria" (2010), Nevena Dimova shows that in comparison to the family models in socialist Bulgaria, the post-1989 period has been characterized by the emergence of competitive as well as gender-equality models within Bulgarian urban families. Dimova identifies the appearance of new models of masculinity—"superman," "equal partner," and "active father"—that Bulgarian men have come to associate with a more active participation in the private space of the family. These changes, which Dimova attributes to decreased accessibility to quality state nurseries and kindergarten along with increased exposure to Western parenting ideologies, ironically has resulted in more equitable gender relations and parenting patterns.

11. Adults of different social classes relate to their children with expectations shaped both by present circumstances and by envisioned future adult roles in society. According

to Diana Hoffman (2013), while in the Global North, good parenting has become a skill set to be learned, and the relationship between parents and children is one of mastering expert knowledge, in the Global South, individual parents' biographies reflect anxieties about the self in relation to class and racial configurations associated with notions of deservingness, citizenship, and cosmopolitanism.

12. In *Distinction: A Social Critique of the Judgment of Taste* (1984), Pierre Bourdieu shows how judgments of taste are related to social position and are in and of themselves acts of social positioning. He highlights the class distinctions between tastes that are internalized through socialization in childhood versus those that have to be learned later, and that appearing second nature is a critical element of the status accrued to a practice.

13. On April 4, 2014, Brazil's National Council for the Rights of Children and Adolescents published Resolution 163, which renders abusive and illegal any marketing directed at children with the intention of persuading them toward consuming any product or service, thus clarifying existing laws.

14. In "Perto da magia, longe da politica," Reginaldo Prandi (1996) attributes the lower class's movement away from Catholicism to the church's trend toward secularization and the exclusion of the disenfranchised from Brazil's modernity projects.

15. In "Disgusted Subjects: The Making of Middle-Class Identities," Stephanie Lawler (2005) shows how expressions of disgust among the middle class are in fact perceptions of violations of "taste." As Lawler shows, disgust is an underexplored emotion; while the classed dimensions of taste have been widely discussed, little attention has been given to the disgust that is aroused when "good" taste is seen to be violated.

16. "Moreno" is a term used constantly among whites to describe both tanned or dark-haired whites and some nonwhites in Ipanema. Praised by Gilberto Freyre in relation to a presumably expanding intermediate racial category, the term "moreno" was originally employed by the Spanish to describe the "wheat-colored" Moors (Santana Pinho 2009, 46). While in other Latin American countries, including Puerto Rico, moreno is sometimes a class-cum-race term used in reference to upper-class blacks, in Brazil it stands for a great variety of skin colors, from the darkest black to light-skinned brunettes.

17. Racial fluency is a term that draws comparisons between the management of racial symbols and how humans develop language; in Hordge-Freeman's study, it seeks to answer how socialization teaches Afro-Brazilians (in Bahia) to confront their position in a racialized system with creative strategies that can manage, reinforce, and contest their placement in the racial order. Thus, racial fluency is "as much about the diverse strategies people use to identify and manage racial situations as it is a reflection of the different ways that people define themselves and others" (2015, 138).

18. In "Person and Psychologization in Brazil: A Study of Moral Regulation," Luis Fernando Dias Duarte (2000) traces how the moral role of the person requires an understanding of how the process of moral regulation happens among an elite who are often themselves the moral regulators. Moral regulations constitute one of the most structuring political mechanisms in the construction of social and cultural borders, and they delimit a specific zone of action dedicated to the construction of human subjects, that is, of one or more varieties of persons that behave in a way that is considered to be appropriate to the profiles of the larger political collectives of which they are a part (citizens). In Brazil,

Dias Duarte argues, "psychologization" has been persistently proposed and discussed as one of the criteria for recognizing "modernity," "rationalization," "civilization," and "disciplinization" (148). In an ironic reframing of what Brazilian scholar Florestan Fernandes called "escravidão dentro dos homens" (slavery within men; 1978, 92), interiority currency allowed El Condado and Ipanema elites to render their whiteness, if not inconsequential, certainly immaterial. The language to articulate inner qualities, personal growth, and spirituality was prolific and scientifically supported, and it resonated with individuals' child-centered lives, an equivalent sophisticated and popular way to articulate that racial privilege did not exist in their world.

5. SCHOOLING WHITENESS

1. The elite status of these schools, while enduring, is not static. New elite schools, particularly international schools in Brazil and more secular private schools in Puerto Rico, have emerged over the past two decades. Nevertheless, while the elite status of these new schools has to be constantly proven, the status of traditional elite schools is well established.

2. The identification of social networks and their political and economic importance has been well documented. What is less known is how these networks vary when they are based on friendships rather than other types of relations (Pahl 2002, 420). As Pahl argues, friend-type relations are more likely than other networks to provide the basis of enduring trust, and, thus, it is imperative to see friendship as a powerful form of social glue.

3. The role of schools in economic and symbolic processes of social reproduction has been a central concern of sociological theory. See Gaztambide-Fernández 2009 and Khan 2012a, for instance.

4. The exception to this was a handful of public school "gifted and talented"–type programs—at the time of my fieldwork, the University of Puerto Rico High School and Brazil's Escola Pedro II were the only ones that fell in this category. One parent each in Puerto Rico and in Brazil had studied in these schools themselves in the 1980s (cf. Maxwell and Appleton 2016).

5. Nevertheless, despite promises of economic benefit, Ryuko Kubota (2014) finds (in the case of Japan) that linguistic instrumentalism does not necessarily guarantee financial rewards, but rather, may be associated with creating and maintaining systems of hierarchy. In 1902, the US commissioner of education noted in reference to Puerto Rico: "Colonization carried forward by the armies of war is vastly more costly than that carried forward by the armies of peace, whose outposts and garrisons are the public schools of the advancing nation" (cited in Hsu 2015, 134). The commission's heavy endorsement of English displayed the entangled relationship between colonially imposed English, Americanization, and the goals of economic subjugation that undergirded American imperial conquest of Puerto Rico.

6. Educational advantages associated with cultural capital, including English fluency, are highest for students from advantaged families, whose children therefore attend high-quality and, particularly important in Brazil and Puerto Rico, private schools. In "The

Educational Achievement of Brazilian Adolescents: Cultural Capital and the Interaction between Families and Schools," Leticia Marteleto and Fernando Andrade (2013) note that most studies examining the effects of family cultural capital on educational achievement have focused on countries with a large middle class and high levels of income. In highly unequal societies, like Brazil (and Puerto Rico), Marteleto and Andrade find that academic gaps associated with cultural capital are in fact magnified. In Brazil, schools mediate the association between family cultural capital and educational achievement; thus, the wide gap in school resources that characterize low-income, highly unequal countries yield even greater differences in student achievement, and this is exacerbated by differences in quality between public and private school sectors. High-quality private schools act to further inequalities found at the social level, and research has shown a strengthening of the inequality in private school access in Brazil (Marteleto and Andrade 2013).

7. English is both bound with neoliberalism and exerts claims to global neutrality that belie, in the case of Puerto Rico and the Philippines, the historical colonial inequalities, which created the conditions for its existence. Hsu locates the current global growth of English within the framework of "coloniality"—that is, the "long-standing patterns of power that emerged as a result of colonialism, but that 'define culture, labor, intersubjective relations, and knowledge production well beyond the strict limits of colonial administration'" (Maldonado-Torres 2010, 77)—to highlight two relationships in regard to neoliberalism and second language: first the connection between English and neoliberalism, focusing on the idea of English as a global language and the linguistic instrumentalism of English as a necessary tool for economic viability in the globalized market, and second, tracing English in the neoliberal context to the history of English as an element of overseas colonial rule.

8. English instruction in the classroom enforced the bonds of colonial capitalism and prepared Puerto Ricans to accede to their new dependent relationship under the paternal guidance of the United States (Hsu 2015, 135). After various attempts to undertake public instruction exclusively in English in Puerto Rican schools, a momentous shift occurred in 1949 when Spanish was instituted as the medium of instruction at all levels (Hsu 2015, 136).

9. In past work among working-class Puerto Ricans in the United States, I have written extensively about the racialization and criminalization of Puerto Ricans as US colonial subjects, and the myriad everyday practices of virtue and reform through which US Puerto Ricans have thought to collectively transform these "conduct" and "inclinations" projected onto them, including classed and regional linguistic practices (cf. Ramos-Zayas 2003, 2012).

10. Among Ipanema parents, only after an incident concerning Escola Parque did some parents discuss the possibility of sending their children to the Escola Pedro II, a public school that required testing and luck to get into. As Bridget Byrne highlights in her study of south London middle-class parents, choosing public school can be viewed as an "ideological commitment," while still maintaining a racialized and classed commitment to whiteness. In Brazil there were two seemingly contradictory tendencies in elite school choice, particularly among Sao Paulo's elites, at the time of my fieldwork: (1) there was an increase in international private schools, including a campus of the NYC for-profit

school Avenues, as well as an interest in US boarding schools (Maxwell and Aggleton 2016); and (2) more elites were beginning to seek public education with the explicit intention of poking their children's social bubble (Bedinelli and Mendonça 2017).

11. Most examinations of "social envy" have focused on the poor envying the wealthy. Envy arising from perceived unjust inequalities of educational opportunity has been seen by many as a paradigm instance of where the sentiment of envy may in some sense be legitimate (Ahier and Beck 2003, 323). Thus, envy can provide a potential framework for developing understandings of the emergence of new forms of social discontent (Hughes 2007).

12. Drawing on Adam Smith, Andrew Sayer uses the term "moral sentiments" in reference to those evaluative judgments, manifested in particular emotional responses, that have their basis "in our vulnerability and our physical, psychological and emotional dependence on others" (2005, 162). Sympathy, benevolence, compassion, envy, a sense of justice (or fairness), mutual indifference, shame, and humiliation are the moral sentiments informing relations with people of other classes as well as the "immoral" sentiments of class contempt and "othering." Hughes (2007), in turn, is concerned with the relationship between these lay sentiments and abstract principles of distributive justice. Focusing on envy, Hughes suggests that whether the discontent over inequality is framed as (legitimate) rage or as (immoral) envy depends largely on the discourses made available by particular classed and gendered social locations.

13. The Brazilian white elite, immediately after the end of slavery, declared the country uniquely equal. The first census after the end of slavery, in 1890, did not ask about race but about color, and over the next years, racial identity was steadily replaced with considerations of color. In 1976, a survey from the National Statistics Institute came back with a list of 136 color categories. Although some considered this a progressive ideology, since it allowed for nuance instead of clear-cut indicators of racial purity, there was an ineluctable hierarchy of what were considered racial traits; the whiter one was, the more of these "valuable" (European) characteristics one possessed. The white elite, just like the individuals whom I met in Ipanema, were ultimately the builders of such mythologies of a *democracia racial*. As in Brazil, early researchers characterized Puerto Rico as a "racial democracy" (Babín 1958; Barbosa 1937), and economic causes have historically been cited as conditioning a racial continuum (Hoetink 1967).

14. Isar Godreau (2000) refers to this as "la semántica fugitive de la raza" (the fugitive semantic of race) to ethnographically demonstrate the everyday currency of the racial continuum, as opposed to the racial binary, in Puerto Rico. The continuum continues to have traction, even though as far back as the 1960s, scholars like Eduardo Seda Bonilla (1968) and Rogler (1944) provided evidence of how black Puerto Ricans experienced lower socioeconomic levels and access to political institutions, were perceived to be unattractive, lived in segregated housing, and were discriminated against in daily life. Renzo Sereno (1947) indicated the tendency of Puerto Ricans to assert their whiteness in the midst of a fear of being seen as black. More recently, a new generation of scholars of Latin America and the Caribbean, particularly in Brazil, have adopted racial binary models in the census to address inequality (e.g., Costa Vargas 2004; Telles 2004). See also Cerón-Anaya's (2018) theorization of "the racialization of class."

15. Ipanema parents and even many El Condado parents did not consider going abroad to college or having international academic credentials as indispensable for the goals and aspirations they had for their children. In some cases, a few individuals noted that doing so could be a disadvantage. Studies in law, for instance, were viewed as something one had to do in Puerto Rico, at the University of Puerto Rico Law School. In part this was because there was a strong connection to gaining expertise in the particularities of Puerto Rico's legal system if one aimed to pursue political or corporate careers on the island. In Brazil, an equivalent was studies of education or psychology—mental health, for instance, was viewed as context specific—a degree from a European or US university would not provide the knowledge required to practice in Brazil. These perspectives were more common among families who belonged to a more traditional local bourgeoisie, where parents and relatives were influential and entrenched in the country's economy and politics.

16. While several El Condado parents had spent a portion of their undergraduate lives at colleges in Puerto Rico, every single one of them had attended a US college for at least a year. Among those who did complete a bachelor's degree in the United States, some key commonalities were that they maintained and sometimes strengthened Puerto Rico elite school networks, even at a distance. The connections among the most elite colleges, which in the 1980s and 1990s tended to select students primarily from a handful of elite schools on the island, were even stronger and more enduring.

17. One the most evident outcomes of this debate in Brazil, for instance, has been the growing number of Brazilians who self-identify as black and *pardos* (50.7 percent), exceeding the percentage of those identifying as white in the most recent census (47.7 percent; IBGE 2011).

18. Beatriz mentioned a private secular school in the artistic-bohemian Santa Teresa neighborhood. Several parents even mentioned Dom Pedro II, a public school that requires an entrance exam and lottery for admission, as a possibility. Students at Dom Pedro II, in fact, had occupied their school in protest over the cuts in public spending, which stipulated that no public spending would occur in Brazil for twenty years. This was despite the fact that the 1988 Constitution states that the state had to allocate 18 percent of its income on education, given the historical deficit in this area.

19. Likewise, one of the directors of another such foundation, Jorge Paulo Lemann's Fundação Estudar, was involved in Vem Pra Rua, another group behind the anti-Dilma demonstrations.

6. THE EXTENDED FAMILY

1. Historically, families in Brazil and Puerto Rico were characterized by a diversity of individuals: parents, children, grandparents, sons, daughters, uncles, in-laws, religion-related members, servants, and close friends (Buarque de Holanda 1941; Freyre 1933). The belief was that family solidarity and personal connections were more relevant than class interests (Frank 2001); that the family or the allied families of the ruling class appear as networks formed not just by blood relatives, but by godfathers and godchildren, as well as supporters and friends. The affective logic and the dynamic of favor binding this fictive

kin permeated Latin American and Caribbean social relations from their beginnings and into the present. In fact, as La Rosa (2013) argues, the fact that corruption appears widely accepted in Brazil is related to the unequal distribution of power and social status cultivated through family membership.

2. Inspired by Margaret Nelson's concept of "doing family" (2006), I view grandparenting as an active arsenal of practices built on interactional work and activities that sustain familial ties, define family boundaries, and establish appropriate behavior for specific family members. This perspective provides a resignification of the work of "care" and nurturance, as well as a challenge to romantic perspectives on support and positive attributes by considering conflict in the context of the family. Rather than viewing the family as a self-contained unit, therefore, I emphasize the relevance of social processes, regional specificity, and national and global forces that condition interpersonal, affective relations in Ipanema and El Condado.

3. Despite changes in the structure and character of the Peruvian elite over the years, Liuba Kogan (2009) notes that gender relations had transformed at a much slower pace. While Peruvian elite women, like those in Kogan's study, were generally unconcerned about the economic and personal costs of having many children, they were still subject to femininity ideals and social pressures partly inculcated by the traditional Catholic schools they had attended. The combination of material resources and traditional ideals yielded concepts like *sentirse bien* (to feel good about oneself), which rendered the body a leading source of self-esteem. The men in these families "believed that a father's duty was to advise, guide, and 'shape' their children." Kogan's finding, about a general lack of affection, limited communication, and emotional distance between parents and children among Lima's upper class did not resonate with what I found among the Ipanema and El Condado elites, although the connection between parenting and everyday "wellness" practices did. As Kogan notes, "[Peruvian elite] women dedicate a significant amount of time to caring for their physical appearance: they had to spend at least 'a bare minimum' [of dedication to this]. Some find the beauty salon as a place to 'relax and find entertainment' while . . . engaging in various procedures to 'maintain yourself well' [*mantenerse bien*]. . . . Not becoming overweight was presented as the basic requirement to 'feeling good about oneself'" (2009, 66). These gendered perspectives were particularly noticeable in the grandparenting expectations that Ipanema and El Condado mothers had of their own mothers, but not of their fathers.

4. Conflicts in upper-class families often had direct repercussions on the reproduction of material and symbolic capital, as S. J. Yanagisako (2002) argues. In Italy, treason and mistrust are necessary sentiments to the fragmentation of the domestic economy and capital expansion and diversification. Rather than viewing trust and treason as contrasting moral commitments or actions, Yanagisako acknowledges both sentiments as integral aspects of the continuous process of generation and regeneration in the family economic projects of the elite.

5. The Euro-American parenting culture literature has convincingly identified a series of parenting practices that have become politicized; most notable are the breastfeeding versus formula feeding debates (others include co-sleeping, sleep training, birthing options, etc.). I went into the field expecting these issues to be salient among the progressive Brazilian

and Puerto Rican elites too. Although there were occasional comments by women who felt pressured either to breastfeed or to bottle feed, these were not salient enough, nor the cause of strong emotions among mothers and their families. People talked about the "women who marched to have the right to take their *teta* [tit] out anywhere," and they also recalled physicians and nurses who had pushed breastfeeding "too much." They talked about grandmothers who were baffled by how strongly their daughters insisted on breastfeeding their kids.

6. After several months of doing fieldwork, I had yet to actually meet anyone coming close to that image, nor had I met a Puerto Rican equivalent of the phenomenon, so cleverly portrayed in the satire YouTube and theater show *The Housewife of Miramar*.

7. Clarice Peixoto and Françoise Clavairolle (2005) examine intergenerational adult cohabitation in contemporary Brazil to show the sources of stress and even domestic violence that unfold when a married couple lives with their parents or in-laws, or when the grandparents move to the couple's home. As the authors note, as a way of context, in the 1980s and 1990s, there were social policies in Brazil that facilitated the purchasing of residential real estate, allowing middle-class couples to buy their own house, gain independence and autonomy from their extended families, and ensure authority over family dynamics (e.g., children's education, division of tasks, etc.). Nowadays, however, an increase in unemployment and low salaries has increased the reliance on family networks for support in moments of crisis (divorce, becoming a widow/er), which also made it more difficult for families to acquire and maintain a nuclear family home.

8. In *The Theory of the Leisure Class* (1899), Thorstein Veblen coined the term "conspicuous consumption" to express the relationship between material goods and status at the peak of the Gilded Age and in the wake of the Industrial Revolution, when an individual's place in society became determined by her or his consumption patterns, ability, and how others regarded those observable consumption habits. By the mid-1900s, however, many more people could afford the luxury goods previously only available to the wealthiest individuals. As John Kenneth Galbraith observes in *The Affluent Society* (1958), once luxury goods were no longer a mark of distinction, the display of wealth was deemed "passé" to a point that conspicuous consumption was associated no longer with the very wealthy, but rather with everyone else. In the absence of an American aristocracy, C. Wright Mills observed in *The Power Elite* (1956), having money gave entrance in ways that forced the truly elite to find more implicit marks of status than wealth and consumption habits. Pierre Bourdieu's *Distinction* (1984) is the seminal work on the source, cultivation, and reproduction of such more implicit marks of status, or what the French sociologist called "cultural capital." Currid-Halkett concludes that the aspirational class can be even more pernicious than the superrich because their spending, behavioral, and value choices are more subtle, viewed as more benevolent, and yet still shore up their and their children's distinct sociocultural (and often economic) position of privilege, leaving everyone else out.

9. In the wake of US colonization, a local white elite projected themselves as illustrious leaders of a racial democracy and came to essentialize *puertorriqueñidad* as a fusion of Indigenous, Spanish, and African mixture to prove Puerto Rico's capacity to renegotiate its relation with the United States as equals (Rodríguez-Silva 2004). Since the elite's

plans for industrialization necessitated political stability and the compliance of the Puerto Rican masses, the government used overpopulation on the island as an excuse to export cheap labor to the United States (i.e., the migration of thousands of Puerto Rican workers) and to support a massive sterilization campaign (Briggs 2002). In the 1990s, the Puerto Rican elite sought to support the US war on drugs through the implementation of policing policies aimed at surveilling and occupying public housing and poor communities (Dinzey-Flores 2013). During the political protests in the late 1990s and early 2000s, which demanded the removal of the US military from Vieques, Puerto Rican elites also collaborated with President Clinton to forcibly remove activists and their encampments from the island.

10. In *Lives in Trust: The Fortunes of Dynastic Families in Late Twentieth-Century America*, George Marcus shows how psychotherapy of whatever variety is frequently resorted to within rich families and is perhaps the key conditioning discourse that offers a set of systematic ideas and concepts about the content of family relations. As Marcus observes, whether eccentricity becomes the prideful collective narrative of (wealthy) families, or whether its importance as rebellion has been magnified as the focal concern of official dynastic narrative, "it constitutes the most subtle vehicle, based on discourses about the person, that invades the otherwise independent and self-ordered psyches and bodies of contemporary dynastic descendants. Stories of character with heavy moral tones are easy to cast off; good-humored and somewhat mysterious stories of eccentricity, which still construct selfhood in a way that presumes the continuing power of collective dynastic identity, are much more difficult for descendants to distance themselves from" (1992, 165).

11. From his research experience among American dynastic families, Marcus found that the most intimate and effective control of persons is embedded in the pervasive evaluative discussions that parents develop about their children based on how children's personalities are like or unlike key members of the parents' or an earlier generation. Thus, the "gradual recognition among adult descendants that their own identities are bound up with, and are even repetitions of, specific personalities of the family's past is both quite common and disturbing for [members of the upper classes]" (1992, 196).

12. Although there has historically been a significant Cuban community in the Isla Verde area surrounding Casa Cuba, of the parents I met, only María Eugenia and Margarita had grown up in Isla Verde. Viviana and the other Cuban parents had grown up in El Condado, Miramar, upper-class Guaynabo suburbs, or moving across them.

13. For a history of Cuban exile to Puerto Rico, see Duany 1995; for Middle Eastern migration to Brazil, see Lesser 1996.

7. AFFECTIVE INEQUALITIES

1. In Rio, and perhaps in the rest of Brazil, the "nordestina/o" category operated as both a geopolitical referent and a racialized category; the racialization of the category could exist independent of region of origin or even phenotype and could even apply to white nordestinas. When Ipanema parents used "nordestina" in reference to their own babás, however, I felt there was compelling evidence to suggest that these workers were

in fact from towns and cities in northeastern states, even if they had been in Rio for many years. Upper-class white Ipanema parents often declared a preference for babás who were "noncariocas" *and/or* who didn't live in the nearby Ipanema "favelas," fearing these individuals would "bring the favela into their homes." Some excellent studies focus on domestic workers in Brazil and Latin America more broadly; however, here I focus on the employers, as the materially powerful, dominant side of these complex power dynamics. See Preuss 1990. For context on Dominican migration to Puerto Rico, see Duany 2005.

2. "Progressive" was defined in terms of social dispositions (e.g., concern for the environment), not necessarily in relation to specific political party affiliations.

3. Details of the revised labor laws can be found in Domingues and Barreiro de Souza 2012.

4. This is not to suggest an equivalency in the kinds of expected nonmonetary, frequently violent transactions involved in domestic work. In Ribeiro Corossacz's (2014) study of wealthy white men in Rio de Janeiro, she notes the concept of "pregar empregada" (to [sexually] possess an employee) to allude to a common practice of a young wealthy white man's sexual initiation with a female domestic worker often classified as "black," "mulata," or the racialized regional term "nordestina." She mentions that this was a phenomenon that her upper-class white male interviewees were familiar with since childhood and that was often treated as a stereotype or a cultural feature of Brazilian society, almost like an element of folklore.

5. The relatively limited existing scholarship on domestic labor in Brazil contrasts sharply with the commonness of the presence of domestic workers in Brazilian homes, including in middle-class families (Pinho and Silva 2010, 91–92). As Pinho and Silva claim, this is due to the ordinariness of having a maid to do everything in Brazil, which renders invisible the power relations between maids and the families for whom they work. A notable exception to this void is Ribeiro Corossacz's (2018) full-length ethnography on the relationship between domestic workers and middle-class white men in Rio de Janeiro.

6. As Miriam Preuss (1990) notes in her ethnographic study of Brazilian empregadas, none of these domestic workers referred to their *patrõas* (employer) as their "sister," even if they were close in age. The relationship also registers movements toward proximity and detachment; in Preuss's study, the empregadas would sometimes copy their patrõas's way of talking and dressing, while the patrõas would resent those imitations, perhaps fearing that they would lose their symbols of distinction ("Quem ela pensa que é para sair por aí usando o mesmo perfume que eu uso?"). Another characteristic that has been examined is the hostility of employers, based on their mutual condition as women, in terms of the men in the domestic sphere. Many of the empregadas in Preuss's study related experiences of sexual harassment by the men in the house, though they showed greater indignation over exploitation in other areas (salary, work hours). The circumstances surrounding domestic work are imbricated into powerful social differences accentuated by an ever-increasing gap between wealth and poverty. Taking this into account, I also view the employer-domestic worker relationship, in the context of parenting, as a relationship that produces powerful didactic forms of social learning along race, class, ethnic, and even nationality lines.

7. As Brites (2007) notes in her ethnographic research, while employers may not be as intimately linked to the cultural universe of domestic workers, the children often spent quite a bit of time listening to an empregada's stories, listening to their same music, asking them personal questions, and so on.

8. "Disque" and "estábanos"—viewed as mispronounced versions of "dice que" and "estábamos"—have come to serve as common references to Dominican speech in Puerto Rico and are deployed as "evidence" of Dominicans' "inferior" levels of education.

9. Roth-Gordon (2017) noticed a financial anxiety among her informants that was due to the social mobility of the working and poor classes and the middle class's inability to distinguish themselves from those "below them" who were presumably catching up. This context changed in the post-2015 years, as Dilma's impeachment also led to the dismantling of social welfare programs.

10. Ipanema and El Condado elite understood "proper" Portuguese and "proper" Spanish in relation to symbolic, imperial, and colonial perspectives about the United States and the English language. English was a language that both carried professional advantages and was no longer exclusively associated with elite status, particularly in Puerto Rico.

11. *La criada malcriada* in the subhead, translated as "the bad-mannered maid," was the title of a popular TV comedy sketch that ran in Puerto Rico from the 1960s through the 1980s. The main character was the iconic Azucena, a feisty maid who lacked formal education and manners but was "street smart" and ended up getting her way. My perspective on *cultivated informalidade* benefits from the works of Shamus Khan (2012a, b) and Rubén Gaztambide-Fernández (2009, 2015), whose respective ethnographies of US elite boarding schools note how socialization involves a process of appropriating cultural practices from those above *and* below oneself, and being at ease in multiple contexts.

12. For instance, Roberto da Matta (1997) argues that Brazilian social relations unfold within a seemingly contradictory scheme in which a well-established hierarchy grounded on social inequality operates alongside a form of modernist individualism. The ritual of "Você sabe com quem está falando?" and the "jeitinho," according to da Matta, are emblematic of an extremely relational society, whose personality confers a place to each individual within a notably hierarchical system.

13. Teixeira, Saraiva, and Carrieri (2015) document the nonmonetary transactions between Brazilian domestic workers in Belo Horizonte and their employers as a dominant moral code between domestic workers and patrões that dated back to turn-of-the-twentieth-century Brazil. Employers were expected to provide protection, food, housing, and clothing in exchange for the worker's obedience and loyalty. Among many of the domestic workers interviewed, nonmaterial aspects, like affection, tended to complicate evaluations of who was a "good employer"; notably, these assessments were often rooted in the empregada's perception that she was not being "treated as empregada" but as a member of the family. These relations often conditioned the worker's (in)ability to demand labor rights.

14. Ipanema and El Condado fathers were not required to interact with paid child-caring adults as much as the mothers were. These gender divisions of labor have been studied extensively and convincingly (Ehrenreich and Hochschild 2003).

15. In "Eu sou os olhos dela," Liane Silveira (2015, 96;) begins her ethnographic study of nannies at various Zona Sul squares by asking: "Who, among us, was exclusively raised by their parents?" The "us" in this question is obviously a fragment of the Brazilian middle and upper classes, including the academics most likely to be the audience for her article and who may share her interest in understanding the lives of "the most intimate stranger in a house: the nanny."

16. Although Robin Sheriff (2001) highlights Brazilian hesitation about "race talk" in her ethnographic study of a poor comunidade in Rio de Janeiro, Hordge-Freeman's examination of race in Bahia, conducted several years later, noted that "in Brazil, contemporary developments, including growing research on racial inequality and the black movement, have emphasized the social significance of race in society" (2015, 142). See also Costa Vargas 2004.

EPILOGUE

1. See Llaneras 2018. Bolsonaro gained 95 percent of the votes in wealthy municipalities, while Fernando Haddad earned nine out of ten poor municipalities. Likewise, racial divisions were also evident in the first round of the elections: Bolsonaro won in nine out of ten predominantly white municipalities; Haddad won seven out of ten predominantly nonwhite municipalities. Importantly, though, Bolsonaro's supporters are everywhere in Rio, not just among the upper-class white males enamored of his Christian "family values," which constitute Bolsonaro's traditional base.

2. Sharma and Gupta (2006) likewise show how ordinary citizens commonly denounce the state as "profoundly corrupt" in public talk. Despite this, Gupta shows that corruption is the space in which the state dissolves at the local level and is replaced by various sociocultural practices and relations. As Gupta argues in the case of India, corruption became a narrative, or at its extremes, a metalanguage through which anxieties, concerns, and ideas of the ideal world are communicated. As a social practice, corruption contributes to enhancing emotional ties of belonging, conviviality, sharing, and common identity.

3. This is especially relevant to the government's announced plan to privatize the Puerto Rico Electric Power Authority (PREPA), the island's public electric utility. By auctioning off parts of the utility to private bidders, the plan would leave different pieces of the utility's operations up to different companies. If all goes according to plan, that process would happen with as little regulatory oversight as possible, leaving a slew of corporations free to set their own rules regarding everything from rates to reliability to power sourcing.

4. The imposition of the Fiscal Control Board was a reminder of the colonial legal framework devised by the US Supreme Court at the turn of the twentieth century. At the time, several cases, known as the insular cases, resulted in decisions that affirmed Puerto Rico as "foreign in a domestic sense" (Burnett and Marshall 2001); that is, full constitutional rights did not automatically extend to all places under US control, including Puerto Rico. See also Sparrow 2006.

5. The plan further includes generous tax incentives for corporations to do business on the island and invest in public-private partnerships. Fleeing what they see as

the impending taxation of their newfound fortunes, wealthy cryptocurrency investors are heading en masse to Puerto Rico, with their hearts set on building a crypto utopia—named Sol—run solely on cryptocurrencies and blockchain technology. Crypto millionaires (and billionaires) are buying up property left and right in historic Old San Juan. Puerto Rico charges no federal personal income tax or capital gains tax, and it offers favorable business taxes. Even more enticing is the fact that Americans need not renounce their citizenship. The Puerto Rico governor planned to speak at the Puerto Crypto blockchain summit in El Condado in March 2017 (cf. Swartz 2017). See also Kleiner (2018), who has written about bitcoin becoming entwined in speculative capitalism.

6. In Puerto Rico and Brazil, this approach has led to punishingly deep cuts to the public sphere, including shuttering more than two-thirds of Puerto Rican governmental bodies, closing more than three hundred public schools, and putting huge swaths of the island's public infrastructure up for sale. "The record is unambiguous that austerity does not lead to economic growth. It leads to contraction," Nobel Prize–winner and former chief World Bank economist Joseph Stiglitz told the *Intercept* when asked about the plan. "What is deeply disturbing is that when you have cuts to things like health care, education, and infrastructure, that's inevitably going to have implications for long-term economic growth" (Aronoff 2018). He and twenty-five other economists recently released their own fiscal plan for Puerto Rico as the new official one was being drafted. Slower growth would mean even less ability for the government to pay back its creditors.

7. Following Lula's reelection in 2007, with the new US war on corruption displacing clumsy attempts to spread its spurious war on terror to Brazil, Sergio Moro, the judge that gained prominence for the Lava Jato investigation, would visit the United States on an official State Department fellowship, connecting with US agencies and institutions responsible for combating money laundering. Then, in 2009, Judge Moro appeared in leaked State Department cables, speaking at a joint event with the US Department of Justice (DOJ) under the banner "Project Bridges" in Rio de Janeiro. Outlining an operation similar in configuration to the future Lava Jato—ostensibly set up to investigate illicit funding for terrorism—the event coordinators talked about creating a partnership between the US DOJ and the Brazilian judiciary to investigate corruption. The cable talks about how task forces could be set up in cities such as Campo Grande or Curitiba, which they identify as having a strong fervor for action on corruption. Those cities were known for their conservatism and default opposition to the then-governing Workers' Party. See Brasil Wire Editors 2018; Mahler and Confessore 2015.

8. A panela is a form of protest in which the residents of Copacabana, Ipanema, and Leblon would make noise with metal cooking pots out the windows of their apartments, usually at night, when Dilma was giving a message on TV.

9. The influential US-Brazil Business Council, a group founded in the late 1970s by Citigroup, Monsanto, Coca-Cola, Dow Chemicals, and other US multinationals, detailed the privatization list on their website, which included four airports, two port terminals, five highways, one rail line, six electric power distributors, three water treatment facilities, and offshore oil development blocks.

10. Discussions about corruption drew, for instance, from a language of the Brazilian *jeitinho* as a cultural trait (da Matta 1997) and of *el mantengo* as a Puerto Rican "culture of poverty" narrative (cf. Diaz Quiñones 2000).

11. Inderpal Grewal (2017) suggests that motherhood has become an object of control and a technology of the security state in twenty-first-century United States. The confluence of antiterrorism practices, existing social divisions, emerging social media, economic inequalities, and wars in the Middle East all contributed to the making of the insecure US "security mom." In the United States, motherhood not only governmentalizes the security state but also articulates and recuperates its anxious desires for security and surveillance.

12. Inderpal Grewal (2017) discusses the emergence of the "security mom" and the "security feminist" as figures of motherhood and female empowerment who attempt the work of state security in the aftermath of 9/11 in the United States. These figures embody the exceptional individual as one who governmentalizes security in the private realm of the family, leading to a rearticulation of family and gender relations. Motherhood becomes more about surveillance than about other tasks of parenting, aided by a technology industry that creates and markets products that enable such surveillance. Grewal shows how these figures emerge through the intersectionalities and contradictions of twenty-first-century security and surveillance in two intertwined institutions: the American (US) family and American counterterrorism.

references

Abreu, Mauricio de A. 1987. *Evolução urbana do Rio de Janeiro.* Rio de Janeiro: IPLANRIO/Zahar.

Ahier, John, and John Beck. 2003. "Education and the Politics of Envy." *British Journal of Educational Studies* 51 (4): 320–43.

Ahmed, Sara. 2010. *The Promise of Happiness.* Durham, NC: Duke University Press.

Albuquerque, A. Salazar, and B. Torres Troccolli. 2004. "Desenvolvimento de uma escala de bem-estar subjetivo." *Psicologia: Teoria e Pesquisa* 20 (2): 153–64.

Alm, James. 2006. "Assessing Puerto Rico's Fiscal Policies." In *The Economy of Puerto Rico: Restoring Growth,* edited by Susan Collins, Barry Bosworth, and Miguel Soto-Class. Washington, DC: Brookings Institution.

Almeida, M. N. S. 2016. "Desenvolvimento e dependência no capitalismo sob hegemonia norte-americana: Reflexões sobre o caso brasileiro." PhD diss., Universidade de São Paulo.

Alves, Jaime. 2014. "From Necropolis to Blackpolis: Necropolitical Governance and Black Spatial Practice in São Paulo, Brazil." *Antipodes* 46 (2): 323–39.

Amador, Gabriel Ferrer. 1968. *Mejoramiento ambiental de la Laguna del Condado.* San Juan: n.p.

Amorim, Celso. 2010. "Brazilian Foreign Policy under President Lula (2003–2010): An Overview." *Revista Brasileira de Política Internacional* 53:214–40.

Amorim, Deolindo. 1988. *O espiritismo e as doutrinas espiritualistas.* São Paulo: C.E. Léon Denis.

Aponte-Parés, Luis. 2019. "The Imperial Gaze: Tourism and Puerto Rico—A Review Essay." *CENTRO Journal* 31 (1): 103–41.

Araújo, Vera, and Guilherme Remalho. 2017. "Revistar passageiro de ônibus não é uma acção ilegal, diz PM." *O Globo,* January 13. http://oglobo.globo.com/rio/revistar -passageiro-de-onibus-nao-uma-acao-ilegal-diz-mp-20770538.

Aries, Philippe. 1960. *Centuries of Childhood: A Social History of Family Life.* Translated by Robert Baldick. New York: Vintage.

Aronoff, Kate. 2018. "Hedge-Fund Driven Austerity Could Come Back to Bite the Hedge Funds Driving It in Puerto Rico." *Intercept*, February 3. https://theintercept .com/2018/02/03/puerto-rico-debt-fiscal-plan.

Asad, Talal. 2009. *Genealogies of Religion: Discipline and Reasons of Power in Christianity and Islam*. Baltimore: Johns Hopkins University Press.

Babín, María Teresa. 1958. *Panorama de la cultura Puertorriqueña*. New York: Las Americas.

Barba, Mariana Della. 2016. "Babás de branco: Promotora vê conflito de interesse e pede anulação favorável a clubes." *BBC Brazil*, January 14. https://www.bbc.com /portuguese/noticias/2016/01/160113_baba_promotora_mdb.

Barbosa, José Celso. 1937. "Problema de razas." In *Problema de razas: Documentos para la historia*, edited by Pilar Barbosa, 131. San Juan: Imprenta Venezuela.

Barreto, Amílcar A. 2001. "Statehood, the English Language, and the Politics of Education in Puerto Rico." *Polity* 34 (1): 89–105.

Barros, Mariana. 2014. "Dos dez apartamentos mais caros do Brasil, nove ficam numa mesma cidade, a maioria em um trecho de apenas quatro quilômetros: Conheça os valores e as metragens dessas preciosidades." *Veja*, May 13. http://veja.abril.com.br/blog /cidades-sem-fronteiras/2014/05/13/edificios-mais-caros.

Bedinelli, Talita, and Heloísa Mendonça. 2017. "Estudantes de classe média vão à escola pública por economia e para sair da 'bolha' social." *El País Brasil*, July 2. https://brasil .elpais.com/brasil/2017/06/23/politica/1498232692_929257.html.

Berg, Ulla, and Ana Ramos-Zayas. 2015. "Racializing Affect: A Theoretical Proposition." *Current Anthropology* 56 (6): 654–77.

Berlant, Lauren. 2011. *Cruel Optimism*. Durham, NC: Duke University Press.

Bernabe, Rafael. 2007. "Puerto Rico's New Era: A Crisis in Crisis Management." *NACLA Report on the Americas* 40 (6): 15–20.

Bila, Fábio. 2009. "Cidadania Sob o Sol de Ipanema: Os gays da Farme de Amoedo e suasestratégias de afirmação." Master's thesis, Universidade Estadual do NorteFluminense.

Bonilla-Silva, Eduardo. 2013. *Racism without Racists: Color-Blind Racism and the Persistence of Racial Inequality in America*. 4th ed. New York: Rowman and Littlefield.

Bonilla-Silva, Eduardo. 2015. "More than Prejudice: Restatement, Critical Reflections, and New Directions in Critical Race Theory." *Sociology of Race and Ethnicity* 1 (1): 1–15.

Boterman, Willem. 2012. "Residential Mobility of Urban Middle Classes in the Field of Parenthood." *Environment and Planning A: Economy and Space* 44 (10): 2397–2412.

Bourdieu, Pierre. 1977. *Outline of a Theory of Practice*. Translated by Richard Nice. Cambridge: Cambridge University Press.

Bourdieu, Pierre. 1984. *Distinction: A Social Critique of the Judgement of Taste*. Translated by Richard Nice. Cambridge, MA: Harvard University Press.

Brasil Wire Editors. 2018. "Hidden History: The US 'War on Corruption' in Brazil." *TruthDig*, February 4. https://www.truthdig.com/articles/hidden-history-u-s-war -corruption-brazil.

Briggs, Laura. 2002. "La Vida, Moynihan, and Other Libels: Migration, Social Science, and the Making of the Puerto Rican Welfare Queen." *CENTRO Journal* 14 (1): 74–101.

Brites, Jurema. 2007. "Afeto e desigualdade: Gênero, geração e classe entre empregadas domésticas e seus empregadores." *Cadernos Pagu* 29:91–109.

Buarque de Holanda, Sergio. 1941. "Prefácio do tradutor." In *Memórias de um colono no Brasil (1850)*, edited by Thomas Davatz, 5–35. São Paulo: Martins Fontes.

Burdick, John. 1998. *Blessed Anastácia: Women, Race, and Popular Christianity in Brazil.* New York: Routledge.

Burnett, Christina D., and Burke Marshall. 2001. *Foreign in a Domestic Sense: Puerto Rico, American Expansion, and the Constitution.* Durham, NC: Duke University Press.

Burton, Katherine. 2014. "Puerto Rico: Tropical Tax Haven for America's Super-Rich." *Business Week*, June 26.

Byrne, Bridget. 2006. "In Search of a 'Good Mix': 'Race,' Class, Gender and Practices of Mothering." *Sociology* 40 (6): 1001–71.

Caldeira, Teresa P. R. 2000. *City of Walls: Crime, Segregation, and Citizenship in São Paulo.* Berkeley: University of California Press.

Callero, Peter L. 2003. "The Sociology of the Self." *Annual Review of Sociology* 29 (1): 115–33.

Cardoso, Elizabeth D. 2010. "Estrutura urbana e representações: A invenção de um novo processo de segregação espacial no Rio de Janeiro nas rimeiras décadas do século XX." *GeoTexto* 6:73–88.

Cardoso de Oliveira, Luis. 2002. *Direito legal e insulto moral: Dilemas da cidadania no Brasil, Quebec e EUA.* Rio de Janeiro: Relume Dumará.

Carneiro Lemos, Luiz Henrique. 2003. "A zona sul como padrão locacional do grupo detentor de capital simbólico e a sua influência sobre a localização das Lojas de Alto Prestígio na Cidade do Rio de Janeiro." PhD diss., Universidade de Lisboa.

Carone, Iray, and Maria Aparecida Silva Bento. 2002. *Psicologia social do racismo: Estudo sobre branquitude e branqueamento no Brasil.* Petrópolis: Vozes.

Carvalho, Bruno. 2007. "Mapping the Urbanized Beaches of Rio de Janeiro: Modernization, Modernity and Everyday Life." *Journal of Latin American Cultural Studies* 16 (3): 325–39.

Carvalho, Laura. 2017. "Globalização financeira eleva desigualdade." *Folha de S.Paulo*, December 28. http://www1.folha.uol.com.br/colunas/laura-carvalho/2017/12/1946105-globalizacao-financeira-eleva-desigualdade.shtml.

Casellas, Carmen. 2004. "Edad de oro en el Condado." *El Nuevo Día*, May 12.

Castro, Ruy. 1999. *Ela é carioca—Uma enciclopédia de Ipanema.* São Paulo: Companhia das Letras.

Cecello, Kristin, and Kanan Kholoussy. 2016. *Domestic Tensions, National Anxieties: Global Perspectives on Marriage, Crisis, and Nation.* New York: Oxford University Press.

Cerón-Anaya, Hugo. 2018. *Privilege at Play: Class, Race, Gender, and Golf in Mexico.* New York: Oxford University Press.

Coe, Brooke. 2015. "Sovereignty Regimes and the Norm of Noninterference in the Global South: Regional and Temporal Variation." *Global Governance: A Review of Multilateralism and International Organizations* 21 (2): 275–98.

Collins, Susan, Barry Bosworth, and Miguel Soto-Class. 2006. *The Economy of Puerto Rico: Restoring Growth.* Washington, DC: Brookings Institution.

Conradson, David. 2005. "Landscape, Care and the Relational Self: Therapeutic Encounters in Rural England." *Health and Place* 11:337–48.

Costa, Jurandir Freire. 1983. "Da cor ao corpo: A violência do racismo." In *SOUSA, neusa santos: Tornar-se negro*. Rio de Janeiro: Graal.

Costa Vargas, João. 2004. "Hyperconsciousness of Race and Its Negation: The Dialectic of White Supremacy in Brazil." *Identities* 11:443–70.

Coto, Danica. 2017. "Board: Puerto Rico to Be Hit with Painful Austerity Measures." *US News and World Report*, February 21. https://www.usnews.com/news/business/articles/2017-02-21/board-puerto-rico-to-be-hit-with-painful-austerity-measures.

Cott, Nancy. 2000. *Public Vows: A History of Marriage and the Nation*. Cambridge, MA: Harvard University Press.

Croissant, Jennifer. 2014. "Agnotology: Ignorance and Absence, or, Toward a Sociology of Things That Are Not There." *Social Epistemology: A Journal of Knowledge, Culture, and Policy* 18 (1): 4–25.

Crystal, David. 1997. *English as a Global Language*. Cambridge: Cambridge University Press.

Curet Cuevas, Eliezer. 2003. *Economía política de Puerto Rico: 1950 a 2000*. San Juan: Ed. M.A.C.

Currid-Halkett, Elizabeth. 2017. *The Sum of Small Things: A Theory of the Aspirational Class*. Princeton, NJ: Princeton University Press.

da Cunha, Christina Vital. 2012. "A cidade para os civilizados: Significados da ordem pública em contextos de violência urbana." *Dilemas: Revista de Estudos de Conflito e Controle Social* 5 (2): 211–32.

da Matta, Roberto. 1997. *Carnavais, malandros e heróis: Para uma sociologia do dilema Brasileiro*. 6th ed. Rio de Janeiro: Rocco.

Davies, William. 2015. *The Happiness Industry*. New York: Verso.

Dávila, Jerry. 2003. *Diploma of Whiteness: Race and Social Policy in Brazil, 1917–1945*. Durham, NC: Duke University Press.

Dayen, David. 2016. "Protests Greet Puerto Rico Control Board." *American Prospect*, October 4. http://prospect.org/article/protests-greet-puerto-rico-control-board.

de Barros Queiroz, Andréa Cristina. 2012. "A *República de Ipanema* da cidade maravilhosa." In *Anais do XV Encontro Regional da História de ANPUH-Rio*. Rio de Janeiro: ANPUH. http://www.encontro2012.rj.anpuh.org/resources/anais/15/1330344606_ARQUIVO_TextoANPUH-RIO2012-ARepublicadeIpanemadacidademaravilhosa.pdf.

Del Rio, Vicente, and William Siembieda, eds. 2009. *Contemporary Urbanism in Brazil: Beyond Brasília*. Gainesville: University Press of Florida.

Dias Duarte, Luis F. 2000. "Person and Psychologization in Brazil: A Study of Moral Regulation." *Journal of Latin American Anthropology* 4 (2): 142–71.

Diaz Quiñones, Arcadio. 2000. *El arte de bregar*. Río Piedras: Editorial Huracán.

Dimova, Nevena. 2010. "Changing Models of Parenting in Contemporary Urban Families in Bulgaria." *Anthropology of East Europe Review* 28 (1): 98–118.

Dinzey-Flores, Zaire. 2006. "Between White Privilege and Black Disadvantage: The Moving Binaries of Racial Inequality in Puerto Rico." Presented at the PRSA Conference, Cornell University, Ithaca, New York, October 5–8.

Dinzey-Flores, Zaire. 2013. *Locked In, Locked Out: Gated Communities in a Puerto Rican City*. Philadelphia: University of Pennsylvania Press.

Dinzey-Flores, Zaire. 2017. "Spatially Polarized Landscapes and a New Approach to Urban Inequality." *Latin American Research Review* 52 (2): 241–52.

Domingues, Edson Paulo, and Kênia Barreiro de Souza. 2012. *The Welfare Impacts of Changes in the Brazilian Domestic Work Market*. Brasilia: International Policy Centre for Inclusive Growth. http://www.ipc-undp.org/pub/IPCWorkingPaper96.pdf.

Donghi, Tulio H. 1993. *The Contemporary History of Latin America*. Durham, NC: Duke University Press.

Duany, Jorge. 1995. *Los Cubanos en Puerto Rico: Economía étnica e identidad cultural*. Río Piedras: Editorial de la Universidad de Puerto Rico.

Duany, Jorge. 2005. "Dominican Migration to Puerto Rico." *CENTRO Journal* 17 (1): 242–69.

Dunker, Christian I. L. 2008. "Psychology and Psychoanalysis in Brazil: From Cultural Syncretism to the Collapse of Liberal Individualism." *Theory and Psychology* 18 (2): 223–36.

Edmonds, Alexander. 2010. *Pretty Modern: Beauty, Sex, and Plastic Surgery in Brazil*. Durham, NC: Duke University Press.

Ehrenreich, Barbara, and Arlie Hochschild. 2003. *Global Woman: Nannies, Maids, and Sex Workers in the New Economy*. New York: Holt.

Elias, Norbert. 1994. *The Civilizing Process*. Translated from the German (1939/1969) by Lilienthal Markus. Oxford: Blackwell.

Elias, Norbert. 1997. "Towards a Theory of Social Processes." *British Journal of Sociology* 48 (3): 355–83.

Facchinetti, Cristiana, and Rafael Dias de Castro. 2015. "The Historiography of Psychoanalysis in Brazil: The Case of Rio de Janeiro." *Dynamis* 35 (1): 13–34.

Faircloth, Charlotte, D. M. Hoffman, and L. L. Layne, eds. 2013. *Parenting in Global Perspectives: Negotiating Ideologies of Kinship, Self, and Politics*. London: Routledge.

Fernandes, Florestan. 1978. *A integração do negro na sociedade de classes*. São Paulo: Ática.

Ferré, Rosario. 1996. *The House in the Lagoon*. London: Abacus.

Figueroa, Alex. 2018. "Condado toma las riendas de su seguridad." *El Nuevo Día*, October 10.

Filho, Andre. 1934. *Cidade maravilhosa*. Musical editor: Henrique Machado. London: Decca Records.

Filho, G. C. 1982. "Instituição Psicanalítica no Rio de Janeiro." In *Crise na psicanálise*, edited by G. C. Filho, 118–40. Rio de Janeiro: Graal.

Fortuño Bernier, Francisco. 2016. "Fighting Puerto Rico's Federal Coup." *Jacobin*, September 13. https://www.jacobinmag.com/2016/09/puerto-rico-debt-promesa-crisis-colonial/.

Foucault, Michel. 1977. *Discipline and Punish: The Birth of the Prison*. Translated by Allan Sheridan. New York: Vintage.

Frank, Zephyr. 2001. "Families and Oligarchic Politics on the Brazilian Frontier: Mato Grosso, 1889–1937." *Latin American Research Review* 36 (1): 49–74.

Frank, Zephyr L. 2004. *Dutra's World: Wealth and Family in Nineteenth-Century Rio de Janeiro*. Albuquerque: University of New Mexico Press.

Freeman, Carla. 2014. *Entrepreneurial Selves: Neoliberal Respectability and the Making of a Caribbean Middle Class.* Durham, NC: Duke University Press.

Freeman, James. 2008. "Great, Good, and Divided: The Politics of Public Space in Rio de Janeiro." *Journal of Urban Affairs* 30 (5): 529–56.

Freitas, Lia B., Terri Shelton, and Jonathan Tudge. 2008. "Conceptions of US and Brazilian Early Childhood Care and Education: A Historical and Comparative Analysis." *International Journal of Behavioral Development* 32 (2): 161–70.

Freyre, Gilberto. 1933. *Casa-Grande e Senzala: Formação da família brasileira sob o regime da economia patriarcal.* Vol. 1. Rio de Janeiro: J. Olympio.

Galbraith, John K. 1958. *The Affluent Society.* Boston, MA: Houghton Mifflin.

Galinha, Iolanda, and Pais Ribeiro. 2005. "História e evolução do conceito de bem-estar subjetivo." *Psicologia, Saúde and Doenças* 6 (2): 203–21.

Galliher, John. 1980. "Social Scientists' Ethical Responsibilities to Superordinates: Looking upward Meekly." *Social Problems* 27 (3): 298–308.

Garotinho, Anthony. 1998. "Uma política de segurança para o Rio de Janeiro." *Arché* 7 (19): 139–57.

Gaztambide-Fernández, Rubén A. 2009. *The Best of the Best: Becoming Elite at an American Boarding School.* Cambridge, MA: Harvard University Press.

Gaztambide-Fernández, Rubén A. 2015. "Elite Entanglements and the Demand for a Radically Un/Ethical Position: The Case of Wienie Night." *International Journal of Qualitative Studies in Education (QSE)* 8 (9): 1129–47.

Gaztambide-Fernandez, Rubén, and Adam Howard. 2012. "Access, Status, and Representation: Some Reflections from Two Ethnographic Studies of Elite Schools." *Anthropology and Education Quarterly* 43 (3): 289–305.

Gesler, Wilbert M. 1993. "Therapeutic Landscapes: Theory and a Case Study of Epidauros, Greece." *Environment and Planning D: Society and Space* 11 (2): 171–89.

Gessaghi, Victoria. 2010. "Trayectorias educativas y clase Alta: Etnografía de una relación." PhD diss., Facultad de Filosofía y Letras, Universidad de Buenos Aires.

Giddens, Anthony. 1991. *Modernity and Self-Identity: Self and Society in the Late Modern Age.* Palo Alto, CA: Stanford University Press.

Gindre, Gustavo. 2015. "Os protestos de domingo e a estratégia da Globo." *Carta Capital,* August 17. https://www.cartacapital.com.br/blogs/intervozes/os-protestos-de-domingo-e-a-estrategia-da-globo-8793.html.

Go, Julian. 2008. *American Empire and the Politics of Meaning: Elite Political Cultures in the Philippines and Puerto Rico during US Colonialism.* Durham, NC: Duke University Press.

Godfrey, Brian J. 1991. "Modernizing the Brazilian City." *Geographical Review* 81 (1): 18–34.

Godfrey, Brian J., and Olivia M. Arguinzoni. 2012. "Regulating Public Space on the Beachfronts of Rio de Janeiro." *Geographical Review* 102 (1): 17–34.

Godreau, Isar P. 2000. "La semántica fugitiva: 'Raza,' color y vida cotidiana en Puerto Rico." *Revista de Ciencias Sociales* 9:52–57.

Godreau, Isar P. 2015. *Scripts of Blackness: Race, Cultural Nationalism, and US Colonialism in Puerto Rico.* Urbana: University of Illinois Press.

Goldstein, Donna. 2013. *Laughter out of Place: Race, Class, Violence, and Sexuality in a Rio Shantytown*. Berkeley: University of California Press.

Gomes, Ana Cristina, and Vicente del Rio. 1998. "A outra urbanidade: A construção da cidade pós moderna e o caso da Barra da Tijuca." In *Arquitectura: Pesquisa y projeto*, edited by Vicente del Rio, 101–20. Rio de Janeiro: Universidade Federal do Rio de Janeiro.

Gomes, Pedro. 1953. "Dois mundos opostos do Rio." *O Cruzeiro*, March 1.

Gómez Espino, Juan Miguel. 2012. "El grupo focal y el uso de viñetas en la investigación con niños." *Empiria: Revista de Metodología de las Ciencias Sociales* 24:46–65.

Gottiniaux, Pierre. 2016. "Puerto Rico's Neocolonial Debt." CADTM, December 3. http://www.cadtm.org/Puerto-Rico-s-Neocolonial-Debt.

Graham, Carol, and Andrew Felton. 2006. "Inequality and Happiness: Insights from Latin America." *Journal of Economic Inequality* 4 (1): 1569–1721.

"Grand Condado Vanderbilt." 2009. San Juan, PR: State Historic Preservation Office, US Department of the Interior. http://www.agencias.pr.gov/oech/oech/Documents/Propiedades%20en%20el%20Registro%20Nacional/San%20Juan/Hotel%20Condado%20Vanderbilt.pdf

Greenwald, Glenn, Andrew Fishman, and David Miranda. 2016. "'We Are Repulsed by This Government': Brazil's Wealthy Are Fleeing the Country." *Intercept*, March 18.

Grewal, Inderpal. 2017. *Saving the Security State: Exceptional Citizens in Twenty-First-Century America*. Durham, NC: Duke University Press.

Grusec, Joan E. 2011. "Socialization Processes in the Family: Social and Emotional Development." *Annual Review of Psychology* 62:243–69.

Guerreiro Ramos, A. 1957. "Patologia social do 'branco' brasileiro." In *Introdução crítica à sociologia brasileira*, 215–40. Rio de Janeiro: Editorial Andes Limit.

Guimarães, Cleo, and Isabela Bastos. 2013. "Mães usam paus de barraca para proteger os filhos de princípio de arrastão em Ipanema." *O Globo*, November 15. https://oglobo.globo.com/rio/maes-usam-paus-de-barraca-para-proteger-os-filhos-de-principio-de-arrastao-em-ipanema-10792377.

Hadot, Pierre. 1995. *Philosophy as a Way of Life: Spiritual Exercises from Socrates to Foucault*. Oxford: Blackwell.

Hall, Stuart. 1996. "Race, Articulation, and Societies Structured in Dominance." In *Black British Cultural Studies: A Reader*, edited by Houston A. Baker Jr., Manthia Diawara, and Ruth H. Lindeborg, 16–60. Chicago: University of Chicago Press.

Haller, D., and C. Shore, eds. 2005. *Corruption: Anthropological Perspectives*. London: Pluto Press.

Hardt, Michael. 1999. "Affective Labor." *boundary 2* 26 (2): 89–100.

Hardt, Michael, and Antonio Negri. 2004. *Multitude: War and Democracy in the Age of Empire*. New York: Penguin.

Hays, Sharon. 1996. *The Cultural Contradictions of Motherhood*. New Haven, CT: Yale University Press.

Heiman, Rachel, Carla Freeman, and Mark Liechty, eds. 2012. *The Global Middle Classes: Theorizing through Ethnography*. Santa Fe, NM: School for Advanced Research Press.

Herzog, Lawrence. 2012. "Barra da Tijuca: The Political Economy of a Global Suburb in Rio de Janeiro." *Latin American Perspectives* 40 (2): 118–34.

Hewitt, John P. 1998. *The Myth of Self-Esteem: Finding Happiness and Solving Problems in America*. Contemporary Social Issues. New York: St. Martin's Press.

Hochschild, Arlie. 1979. "Emotion Work, Feeling Rules, and Social Structure." *American Journal of Sociology* 85 (3): 551–75.

Hochschild, Arlie R. 1983. *The Managed Heart: Commercialization of Human Feeling*. Berkeley: University of California Press.

Hochschild, Arlie R. 2016. *Strangers in Their Own Land: Anger and Mourning on the American Right*. New York: New Press.

Hoetink, Harry. 1967. *Caribbean Race Relations*. London: Oxford University Press.

Hoffman, Diana. 2013. "Power Struggles: The Paradoxes of Emotion and Control among Child-Centered Mothers in Privileged America." In *Parenting in Global Perspective*, edited by C. Faircloth, D. Hoffman, and L. Layne, 229–43. New York: Routledge.

Hordge-Freeman, Elizabeth. 2015. *The Color of Love: Racial Features, Stigma, and Socialization in Black Brazilian Families*. Austin: University of Texas Press.

Howard, Adam. 2010. "Stepping Outside Class: Affluent Students Resisting Privilege." In *Educating Elites: Class Privilege and Educational Advantage*, edited by A. Howard and R. Gaztambide-Fernández, 79–95. Lanham, MD: Rowman and Littlefield.

Howard, Adam. 2013. "Negotiating Privilege through Social Justice Efforts." In *Privilege, Agency and Affect: Understanding the Production and Effects of Action*, edited by C. Maxwell and P. Aggleton, 185–201. Hampshire: Palgrave Macmillan.

Hsu, Funie. 2015. "The Coloniality of Neoliberal English: The Enduring Structures of American Colonial English Instruction in the Philippines and Puerto Rico." *L2 Journal* 7 (3): 123–45.

Hughes, Christina. 2007. "The Equality of Social Envies." *Sociology* 41 (2): 347–63.

Huguenin, Fernanda Pacheco da Silva. 2011. "As praias de Ipanema: Liminaridade e proxemia a Beira Mar." PhD diss., Universidade de Brasília.

IBGE (Instituto Brasileiro de Geografia e Estatística). 2011. *Censo demográfico 2010*. Rio de Janeiro: IBGE. http://www.censo2010.ibge.gov.br.

Illouz, Eva. 2007. *Cold Intimacies: The Making of Emotional Capitalism*. Cambridge: Polity Press.

Illouz, Eva. 2008. *Saving the Modern Soul: Therapy, Emotions, and the Culture of Self-Help*. Berkeley: University of California Press.

Instituto de Estadísticas de Puerto Rico. 2017. *Informe sobre desarrollo humano: Puerto Rico 2016*. San Juan: Instituto de Estadísticas de Puerto Rico. https://estadisticas.pr/en/Informe_Desarrollo_Humano.

International Labour Organization. 2010. *World of Work Report*. Geneva: International Institute for Labour Studies.

"Ipanema, 110 anos na vanguarda." 2004. Caderno Zona Sul, *O Globo*, April 22.

Jackson, John L. 2010. "On Ethnographic Sincerity." *Current Anthropology* 51 (2): 279–89.

Jensen, Tracey. 2010. "Warmth and Wealth: Re-imagining Social Class in Taxonomies of Good Parenting." *Studies in the Maternal* 2 (1): 1–13.

Jensen, Tracey, and Imogen Tyler. 2012. "Austerity Parenting: New Economies of Parent-Citizenship." *Studies in the Maternal* 4 (2). http://doi.org/10.16995/sim.34.

Karam, John Tofik. 2008. *Another Arabesque: Syrian-Lebanese Ethnicity in Neoliberal Brazil*. Philadelphia: Temple University Press.

Karsten, Lia. 2002. "Mapping Childhood in Amsterdam: The Spatial and Social Construction of Children's Domains in the City." *Journal of Economic and Social Geography* 93 (3): 231–41.

Keefe, Susan E., Amado M. Padilla, and Manuel L. Carlos. 1979. "The Mexican-American Extended Family as an Emotional Support System." *Human Organization* 38 (2): 144–52.

Khan, Shamus. 2012a. *Privilege: The Making of an Adolescent Elite at St. Paul's School*. Princeton, NJ: Princeton University Press.

Khan, Shamus. 2012b. "The Sociology of Elites." *Annual Review of Sociology* 38:361–77.

Kleiner, Dmytri. 2018. "The Face Value of Bitcoin: Proof of Work and the Labour Theory of Value." *P2P Foundation* (blog), February 1. https://blog.p2pfoundation.net/face-value-bitcoin-proof-work-labour-theory-value/2018/02/01.

Kogan, Liuba. 2009. *Regias y conservadores: Mujeres y hombres de clase alta en la Lima de los noventa*. Lima: Fondo Editorial del Congreso del Perú.

Kubota, Ryuko. 2014. "The Multi/Plural Turn, Postcolonial Theory, and Neoliberal Multiculturalism: Complicities and Implications for Applied Linguistics." *Applied Linguistics* 37(4): 474–94.

Lacan, Jacques. 1997. *The Ethics of Psychoanalysis, 1959–60: The Seminar of Jacques Lacan, Book VII*. Edited by Jacques-Alain Miller. New York: Norton.

Lamont, Michèle. 1992. *Money, Morals, and Manners: The Culture of the French and American Upper-Middle Class*. Chicago: University of Chicago Press.

Lareau, Annette. 2002. "Invisible Inequality: Social Class and Childrearing in Black Families and White Families." *American Sociological Review* 67 (5): 747–76.

La Rosa, Thais. 2013. *Cultural Behavior in Post-Urbanized Brazil: The Cordial Man and Intrafamiliar Conflict*. Portland, OR: Portland State University.

Laureano, Javier E. 2016. *San Juan Gay: Conquista de un espacio urbano de 1948 a 1991*. San Juan: Instituto de Cultura Puertorriqueña.

Lawler, Stephanie. 2005. "Disgusted Subjects: The Making of Middle-class Identities." *Sociological Review* 53 (3): 429–46.

Lee, Ellie, Jennie Bristow, Charlotte Faircloth, and Jan Macvarish, eds. 2014. *Parenting Culture Studies*. London: Palgrave Macmillan.

Lees, Loretta. 2008. "Gentrification and Social Mixing: Towards an Inclusive Urban Renaissance?" *Urban Studies* 45 (12): 2449–70.

Lefebvre, Henri. 1991. *The Production of Space*. Oxford: Blackwell.

Lefebvre, Henri. 2014. *Toward an Architecture of Enjoyment*. Edited by Lukasz Stanek. Minneapolis: University of Minnesota Press.

Lesser, Jeffrey. 1996. "(Re)Creating Ethnicity: Middle Eastern Immigration to Brazil." *Americas* 53 (1): 45–65.

Levy, Teresita. 2014. *Puerto Ricans in the Empire: Tobacco Growers and US Colonialism*. New Brunswick, NJ: Rutgers University Press.

Lewis, Oscar. 1966. *The Culture of Poverty*. New York: Scientific America.

Lispector, Clarice. 1978. *Um sopro de vida*. Rio de Janeiro: Nova Fronteira.

Llaneras, Kiko. 2018. "Bolsonaro arrasa en ciudades blancas y ricas: Un mapa del voto en 5,500 municipios." *El País*, October 25. https://elpais.com/internacional/2018/10/23 /actualidad/1540291997_116759.html.

Long, Heather. 2016. "There's a Big Sale on Puerto Rican Homes." *CNN Money*, February 21.

Lund, Joshua. 2012. *The Mestizo State: Reading Race in Modern Mexico*. Minneapolis: University of Minnesota Press.

Mahler, Jonathan, and Nicholas Confessore. 2015. "Inside the Billion-Dollar Battle for Puerto Rico's Future." *New York Times*, December 20. https://www.nytimes.com/2015 /12/20/us/politics/puerto-rico-money-debt.html.

Maia, Suzana. 2012. *Transnational Desires: Brazilian Erotic Dancers in New York*. Nashville: Vanderbilt University Press.

Majhanovich, Suzanne. 2013. "English as a Tool of Neo-Colonialism and Globalization in Asian Contexts." In *Critical Perspectives on International Education*, edited by Y. Hébert and A. Abdi, 249–61. Rotterdam: Sense.

Maldonado-Torres, N. 2010. "The Time and Space of Race: Reflections on David Theo Goldberg's Interrelational and Comparative Methodology." *Patterns of Prejudice* 44 (1): 77–88.

Marano, H. E. 2008. *A Nation of Wimps: The High Cost of Invasive Parenting*. New York: Broadway Books.

Marcus, George. 1992. *Lives in Trust: The Fortunes of Dynastic Families in Late Twentieth-Century America*. Boulder: Westview Press.

Marteleto, Leticia, and Fernando Andrade. 2013. "The Educational Achievement of Brazilian Adolescents: Cultural Capital and the Interaction between Families and Schools." *Sociology of Education* 87 (1): 16–35.

Martín-Baró, Ignacio, Adrianne Aron, and Shawn Corne. 1994. *Writings for a Liberation Psychology*. Cambridge, MA: Harvard University Press.

Mathieu, N.-C. 1990. "When Yielding Is Not Consenting: Material and Psychic Determinants of Women's Dominated Consciousness and Some of Their Interpretations in Ethnology (Part II)." *Feminist Issues* 10 (1): 51–90.

Maxwell, Claire, and Peter Aggleton, eds. 2013. *Privilege, Agency and Affect*. Basingstoke: Palgrave Macmillan.

Maxell, Claire, and Peter Aggleton, eds. 2016. *Elite Education: International Perspectives*. New York: Routledge.

Mayer, John D., Peter Salovey, and David Caruso. 2000. "Models of Emotional Intelligence." In *Handbook of Intelligence*, edited by Robert J. Sternberg, 396–420. Cambridge: Cambridge University Press.

McGee, Micki. 2012. "From Makeover Media to Remaking Culture: Four Directions for the Critical Study of Self-Help Culture." *Sociology Compass* 6 (9): 685–93.

McIntosh, Janet. 2013. "Structural Oblivion and Perspectivism: Land and Belonging among Contemporary White Kenyans." Paper presented at African Dynamics in a Multipolar World: 5th European Conference on African Studies, Lisbon, Portugal, June 27–29.

Medina, Francisco A. 2016. "The Promise of Colonialism in Puerto Rico: Decolonization in Unsettling Times." Unpublished paper, CUNY Graduate Center.

Mendez, Fernando, and Micha Germann. 2018. "Contested Sovereignty: Mapping Referendums on Sovereignty over Time and Space." *British Journal of Political Science* 48 (1): 141–65.

Merleau-Ponty, Maurice. 2004. *Maurice Merleau-Ponty: Basic Writings.* Edited by Thomas Baldwin. London: Routledge.

Millán Pabón, Carmen. 2004. "Inicia la primera fase del Parque Laguna del Condado." *El Nuevo Día*, October 30.

Mills, C. Wright. 1956. *The Power Elite.* New York: Oxford University Press.

Minayo, Maria Cecília de Souza. 2013. "Policiais não são máquinas de segurança: São homens e mulheres que, como nós, sofrem, amam, desejam, têm medo, mas arriscam sua vida para nos proteger." *O Globo*, November 16. https://oglobo.globo.com/opiniao /policiais-nao-sao-maquinas-de-seguranca-10785971.

Mische, Ann. 2018. "Protest, Anti-Partisanship, and the Trajectory of Democratic Crisis in Brazil," *Mobilizing Ideas*, November 4. https://mobilizingideas.wordpress.com /2018/10/24/special-featured-essay-protest-anti-partisanship-and-the-trajectory-of -democratic-crisis-in-brazil/.

Moore, Sally Falk. 2005. "Comparison. Possible and Impossible." *Annual Review of Anthropology* 34 (1): 1–11.

Mora Pérez, Némesis. 2015. "Puerto Rico entre los países de mayor desigualdad social en el mundo." *Puerto Rico Te Quiero*, June 10. http://puertoricotequiero.com/puerto-rico -entre-los-paises-de-mayor-desigualdad-social-en-el-mundo/.

Morawski, Erica N. 2014. "Designing Destinations: Hotel Architecture, Urbanism, and American Tourism in Puerto Rico and Cuba." PhD diss., University of Illinois at Chicago.

Moreira-Almeida, Alexander, and Joan Koss-Chioino. 2009. "Recognition and Treatment of Psychotic Symptoms: Spiritists Compared to Mental Health Professionals in Brazil and Puerto Rico." *Psychiatrist* 72 (3): 268–83.

Mori, Natalia, Joaze Bernardino-Costa, and Soraya Fleischer, eds. 2011. *Tensões e experiências: Um retrato das trabalhadoras domésticas de Brasília e Salvador.* Brasília: CFEMEA.

Morrison, Toni. 1992. *Playing in the Dark: Whiteness and the Literary Imagination.* Cambridge, MA: Harvard University Press.

Motta, Roberto. 2013. "Insegurança pública Brasileira: O debate inexistente." *Instituto Liberal*, November 14. http://institutoliberal.org.br/blog/?p=8476.

Munem, Bahia M. 2014. *Expulsions and Receptions: Palestinian Iraq War Refugees in the Brazilian Nation-State.* New Brunswick, NJ: Rutgers University Press.

Nader, Laura. 1974. "Up the Anthropologist—Perspectives Gained from Studying Up." In *Reinventing Anthropology*, edited by Dell Hymes, 284–311. New York: Vintage Books.

Nash, J. C. 2008. "Re-Thinking Intersectionality." *Feminist Review* 89 (1): 1–15.

Neate, Rupert. 2016. "Puerto Rico Woos US Investors with Huge Tax Breaks as Locals Fund Debt Crisis." *Guardian* (London), February 14.

Nelson, Margaret K. 1990. *Negotiated Care: The Experience of Family Day Care Providers.* Philadelphia, PA: Temple University Press.

Nelson, Margaret K. 2006. "Single Mothers 'Do' Family." *Journal of Marriage and Family* 68 (4): 781–95.

Newkirk, Vann, II. 2016. "Puerto Rico Belongs to Congress." *Atlantic*, June 10.

Norvell, J. M. 2002. "A brancura desconfortável das camadas médias brasileiras." In *Raça como retórica: A construção da diferença*, edited by Y. Maggie and C. B. Rezende, 245–68. Rio de Janeiro: Civilização Brasileira.

O'Donnell, Julia. 2013. *A invenção de Copacabana: Culturas urbanas e estilos de vida no Rio de Janeiro (1890–1940)*. Rio de Janeiro: Zahar.

O'Dougherty, Maureen. 2002. *Consumption Intensified: The Politics of Middle-Class Daily Life In Brazil*. Durham, NC: Duke University Press.

Owensby, Brian P. 1999. *Intimate Ironies: Modernity and the Making of Middle-Class Lives in Brazil*. Palo Alto, CA: Stanford University Press.

Pacheco, Istra. 2016. "Puerto Rico es uno de los cinco países con más desigualdad social." *Primera Hora*, May 14.

Pahl, Ray. 2002. "Towards a More Significant Sociology of Friendship." *European Journal of Sociology* 43 (3): 410–23.

Pahnke, Anthony. 2017. "The Brazilian Crisis." *Monthly Review*, February.

Pandian, Anand. 2010. "Interior Horizons: An Ethical Space of Selfhood in South India." *Journal of the Royal Anthropological Institute* 16:64–83.

"Patroa de foto polêmica em manifestação faz desabafo: 'Caso ela queira, irá novamente.'" 2016. *Extra* (Rio de Janeiro), March 15. http://extra.globo.com/noticias/rio/patroa -de-foto-polemica-em-manifestacao-faz-desabafo-caso-ela-queira-ira-novamente -18880130.html.

Peixoto, Clarice, and Françoise Clavairolle. 2005. *Envelhecimento, políticas sociais e novas tecnologias*. Rio de Janeiro: FGV.

Piller, Ingrid, and Jinhyun Cho. 2013. "Neoliberalism as Language Policy." *Language in Society* 42 (1): 23–44.

Pinçon, Michel, and Monique Pinçon-Charlot. 2007. *Les ghettos du Gotha: Comment la bourgeoisie défend ses espaces*. Paris: Le Seuil.

Pinho, Patricia de Santana. 2009. "White but Not Quite: Tones and Overtones of Whiteness in Brazil." *Small Axe* 13 (2): 39–56.

Pinho, Patricia de Santana. 2015. "The Dirty Body that Cleans: Representations of Domestic Workers in Brazilian Common Sense." *Meridians: Feminism, Race, Transnationalism* 13 (1): 103–28.

Pinho, Patricia de Santana, and Elisabeth Silva. 2010. "Domestic Workers in Brazil: Legacies and Horizons Latin American." *Research Review* 45 (2): 90–113.

Pires, José Herculano. 1984. *Mediunidade: Vida e comunicação*. Sao Paulo: Edicel.

Piza, E. 2000. "Branco no Brasil? Ninguém sabe, ninguém viu." In *Tirando a máscar: Ensaios sobre o racismo no Brasil*, edited by A. S. A. Guimarães and L. Huntley, 97–126. São Paulo: Paz e Terra, SEF.

Prada, Paulo. 2016. "White Male Cabinet Raises Fears of Backsliding in Diverse Brazil." *Reuters*, May 16. https://www.reuters.com/article/us-brazil-politics -diversity/white-male-cabinet-raises-fears-of-backsliding-in-diverse-brazil -idUSKCN0Y71KH.

Prado, Caio, Jr. 1994. *Formação do Brasil contemporâneo*. São Paulo: Editora Brasiliense.

Prandi, Reginaldo. 1996. "Perto da magia, longe da politica." In *A realidade social das religiões no Brasil*, edited by Antônio Pierucci and Reginaldo Prandi, 93–105. São Paulo: USP/Hucitec.

Preuss, Miriam R. G. 1990. "Emprego doméstico: Um lugar de conflito." *Cadernos do CEAS* 128: 41–45.

Pugh, Allison J. 2009. *Longing and Belonging: Parents, Children, and Consumer Culture.* Berkeley: University of California Press.

Qayum, Seemin, and Raka Ray. 2003. "Grappling with Modernity: India's Respectable Classes and the Culture of Domestic Servitude." *Ethnography* 4 (4): 520–55.

Quiñones-Pérez, Argeo T., and Ian J. Seda-Irizarry. 2016. "Wealth Extraction, Governmental Servitude, and Social Disintegration in Colonial Puerto Rico." *New Politics* 16 (2): 91–98.

Ramos-Zayas, Ana. 2003. *National Performances: Class, Race, and Space in Puerto Rican Chicago.* Chicago: University of Chicago Press.

Ramos-Zayas, Ana. 2004. "Delinquent Citizenship, National Performance: Racialization, Surveillance, and the Politics of 'Worthiness' in Puerto Rican Chicago." *Journal of Latino Studies* 2:26–44.

Ramos-Zayas, Ana. 2012. *Street Therapists: Affect, Race, and Neoliberal Personhood in Latino Newark.* Chicago: University of Chicago Press.

Ribeiro, Luiz C. 1998. *Dos cortiços aos condomínios fechados: As formas de produção da moradia no Rio de Janeiro.* Rio de Janeiro: Civilização Brasileira.

Ribeiro Corossacz, Valeria. 2014. "Cor, classe, gênero: Aprendizado sexual e relações de domínio." *Revista Estudos Feministas* 22 (2): 521–42.

Ribeiro Corossacz, Valeria. 2015. "Whiteness, Maleness, and Power: A Study in Rio de Janeiro." *Latin American and Caribbean Ethnic Studies* 10 (2): 157–79.

Ribiero Corossacz, Valeria. 2018. *White Middle-Class Men in Rio de Janeiro: The Making of a Dominant Subject.* Lanham, MD: Lexington Books.

Robinson, Andy. 2016. "Brazil's New Government Shows Its Colors: All-White, All-Male, Ultraconservative." *The Nation*, May 18. https://www.thenation.com/article/brazils-new-government-shows-its-colors-all-white-all-male-ultra-conservative/.

Rocha, Cristina. 2006. *Zen in Brazil: The Quest for Cosmopolitan Modernity.* Honolulu: University of Hawaii Press.

Rockman, Roberto. 2014. "Como a ascensão da classe C causou uma revolução social." *Carta Capital*, November 12.

Rodríguez-Silva, Ileana. 2004. "A Conspiracy of Silence: Blackness, Class and Nation in Post-Emancipation Puerto Rico, 1850–1920." PhD diss., University of Wisconsin, Madison.

Rodriguez Valle, Marisol. 2005. *A província da ousadia: Representações sociais sobre Ipanema.* Rio de Janeiro: UFRJ/PPGSA.

Rogler, Charles. 1944. "The Role of Semantics in the Study of Race Distance in Puerto Rico." *Social Forces* 22:448–53.

Romero, Mary. 2011. *The Maid's Daughter: Living inside and outside the American Dream.* New York: New York University Press.

Rose, Nikolas. 1996a. "Identity, Genealogy, History." In *Questions of Cultural identity*, edited by Stuart Hall and Paul du Gay, 128–50. London: Sage.

Rose, Nikolas. 1996b. *Inventing Ourselves: Psychology, Power and Personhood*. Cambridge: Cambridge University Press.

Rosenfeld, Alvin, and Nicole Wise. 2010. *The Over-Scheduled Child: Avoiding the Hyper-Parenting Trap*. New York: St. Martin's Griffin.

Roth-Gordon, Jennifer. 2017. *Race and the Brazilian Body: Blackness, Whiteness, and Everyday Language in Rio de Janeiro*. Berkeley: University of California Press.

Rouse, Carolyn. 2004. "'If She's a Vegetable, We'll Be Her Garden': Embodiment, Transcendence, and Citations of Competing Metaphors in the Case of a Dying Child." *American Ethnologist* 31 (4): 514–29.

Saad Filho, Alfredo. 2016. "Salários e exploração na teoria marxista do valor." *Economia e Sociedade* 10 (1): 27–42.

Safa, Helen I. 1974. *The Urban Poor of Puerto Rico: A Study in Development and Inequality*. New York: Holt, Rinehart and Winston.

Salas, Gonzalo, ed. 2014. *Historias de la psicología en América del Sur: Diálogos y perspectivas*. La Serena, Chile: Nueva Mirada.

Salvatore, Ricardo. 2016. *Disciplinary Conquest: US Scholars in South America, 1900–1945*. Durham, NC: Duke University Press.

Santiago, Yaritza. 2000. "A revitalizar la calidad de vida del Condado." *En Nuevo Día*, August 18.

Saunders, Peter. 1985. "Space, the City and Urban Sociology." In *Social Relations and Spatial Structures*, edited by Derek Gregory and John Urry, 67–89. Basingstoke: Macmillan.

Sayer, Andrew. 2005. *The Moral Significance of Class*. Cambridge: Cambridge University Press.

Seda-Bonilla, Eduardo. 1968. "Dos modelos de relaciones raciales: Estados Unidos y América Latina." *Revista de Ciencias Sociales* 4:569–97.

Semán, Pablo Federico, and Nicolás Viotti. 2015. "El paraíso está dentro de nosotros: La espiritualidad de la Nueva Era, ayer y hoy." *Nueva sociedad* 260:81–94.

Sereno, Renzo. 1947. "Cryptomelanism: A Study of Color Relations and Personal Insecurity in Puerto Rico." *Psychiatry* 10:260–72.

Serrano, Isabela de Almeida. 1945. *Minha casa*. Rio de Janeiro: Vozes.

Sgarioni, Mariana. 2014. "A criança terceirizada: As confissões das babás." *N Magazine: Para a Nova Geração de Pais*, March 6.

Sharma, A., and A. Gupta, eds. 2006. *The Anthropology of the State: A Reader*. Malden, MA: Blackwell.

Sheriff, Robin. 2001. *Dreaming Equality: Color, Race, and Racism in Urban Brazil*. New Brunswick, NJ: Rutgers University Press.

Sherman, Rachel. 2017a. "Conflicted Cultivation: Parenting, Privilege, and Moral Worth in Wealthy New York Families." *American Journal of Cultural Sociology* 5 (1–2): 1–33.

Sherman, Rachel. 2017b. *Uneasy Street: The Anxieties of Affluence*. Princeton, NJ: Princeton University Press.

Silva, Luiz Inácio da. 2018. "US Doesn't Want a Strong and Independent Brazil Backing Latin America." *RT Question More*, March 31. https://www.rt.com/news/422861-brazil -lula-latin-america-us/.

Silveira, Liane. 2015. "'Eu sou os olhos dela': As babás nas imagens, na praça ou uma etnografia do olhar." *Sociologia, Problemas e Práticas* 77:95–111.

Simonds, Wendy. 1992. *Women and Self-Help Culture: Reading between the Lines*. New Brunswick, NJ: Rutgers University Press.

Skeggs, Beverley. 2004. *Class, Self, Culture*. New York: Routledge.

Skidmore. Thomas. 1974. *Black into White: Race and Nationality in Brazilian Thought*. London: Oxford University Press.

Sonntag, Selma K. 2003. *The Local Politics of Global English: Case Studies in Linguistic Globalization*. Lanham, MD: Lexington Books.

Souza, Jessé. 2017. *A elite do atraso: Da escravidão à Lava Jato*. Rio de Janeiro: Casa da Palavra/LeYa.

Sovik, L. 2010. *Aqui ninguém é branco*. Rio de Janeiro: Aeroplano.

Sparrow, Bartholomew H. 2006. *The Insular Cases and the Emergence of American Empire*. Lawrence: University Press of Kansas.

Stack, Carol B. 1974. *All Our Kin: Strategies for Survival in a Black Community*. New York: Harper and Row.

Steil, C. A., ed. 2006. *Cotas raciais na universidade: Um debate*. Porto Alegre: UFRGS Editora.

Stoler, Ann Laura. 2006. "Degrees of Imperial Sovereignty." *Public Culture* 18 (1): 125–46.

Strasser, Franz. 2015. "Puerto Rico's Population Swap: The Middle Class for Millionaires." *BBC News*, May 5. http://www.bbc.com/news/magazine-32344131.

Suárez Carrasquillo, Carlos A. 2011. "Gated Communities and City Marketing: Recent Trends in Guaynabo, Puerto Rico." *Cities* 28 (5): 444–51.

Swartz, Lana. 2017. *Paid: Tales of Dongles, Checks, and Other Stuff*. Cambridge, MA: MIT Press.

Taylor, C. 1989. *Sources of the Self*. Cambridge, MA: Harvard University Press.

Taylor, Janelle S. 2005. "Surfacing the Body Interior." *Annual Review of Anthropology* 34 (1): 741–56.

Teixeira, Juliana M., Luiz S. Saraiva, and Alexandre P. Carrieri. 2015. "Os lugares das empregadas domésticas." *Organizações e Sociedade* 22 (72): 161–78.

Telles, Edward. 2004. *Race in Another America: The Significance of Skin Color in Brazil*. Princeton, NJ: Princeton University Press.

Ticktin, Miriam. 2017. "World without Innocence." *American Ethnologist* 44 (4): 577–90.

Tobin, Joseph. 1995. "The Irony of Self-Expression." *American Journal of Education* 103 (3): 233–58.

Tolosa, Hamilton. 1996. "Rio de Janeiro: Urban Expansion and Structural Change." In *The Mega City in Latin America*, edited by Alan Gilbert, 203–23. New York: United Nations University Press.

Toro, Harold. 2008. "Facing the Challenges." *ReVista*, Spring. https://revista.drclas .harvard.edu/book/inequality-puerto-rico.

Trouillot, Michel-Rolph. 2002. "North Atlantic Universals: Analytical Fictions, 1492–1945." *South Atlantic Quarterly* 101 (4): 839–58.

Urciuoli, Bonnie. 1991. "The Political Topography of Spanish and English: The View from a New York Puerto Rican Neighborhood." *American Ethnologist* 18 (2): 295–310.

van den Berg, Marguerite. 2013. "City Children and Genderfied Neighbourhoods: The New Generation as Urban Regeneration Strategy." *International Journal of Urban and Regional Research* 37 (2): 523–36.

Vargas-Ramos, Carlos. 2005. "Black, Trigueño, White . . . ? Shifting Racial Identification among Puerto Ricans." *Du Bois Review: Social Science Research on Race* 2 (2): 267–85.

Vaz, Lilian E. 2002. *Modernidade e moradia: Habitação coletiva no Rio de Janeiro, séculos XIX e XX*. Rio de Janeiro: 7 Letras.

Veblen, Thorstein. 1899. *The Theory of the Leisure Class: An Economic Study in the Evolution of Institutions*. New York: Macmillan.

Velho, Gilberto. (1978) 2013. *A utopia urbana: Um estudo de antropologia social*. Rio de Janeiro: Zahar.

Veltmeyer, Henry, James Petras, and Steve Vieux. 1997. *Neoliberalism and Class Conflict in Latin America: A Comparative Perspective on the Political Economy of Structural Adjustment*. London: Palgrave MacMillan.

Wade, Peter. 2004. "Images of Latin American Mestizaje and the Politics of Comparison." *Bulletin of Latin American Research* 23 (3): 355–66.

Walkerdine, Valerie. 2003. "Reclassifying Upward Mobility: Femininity and the Neoliberal Subject." *Gender and Education* 15 (3): 237–48.

Walsh, Mary Williams. 2016. "Puerto Rico Fights for Chapter 9 Bankruptcy in Supreme Court." *New York Times*, March 22.

Ware, Vron, ed. 2004. *Branquidade: Identidade branca e multiculturalismo*. Rio de Janeiro: Garamond Universitária.

Watt, Paul. 2006. "Respectability, Roughness and 'Race': Neighbourhood Place Images and the Making of Working-Class Social Distinctions in London." *International Journal of Urban and Regional Research* 30 (4): 776–97.

Wee, Lionel. 2003. "Linguistic Instrumentalism in Singapore." *Journal of Multilingual and Multicultural Development* 24:211–24.

Williams, Raymond. 1977. "Structures of Feeling." In *Marxism and Literature*, 128–35. Oxford: Oxford University Press.

Windle, Joel, and Maria Alice Nogueira. 2015. "The Role of Internationalisation in the Schooling of Brazilian Elites: Distinction between Two Class Fractions." *British Journal of Sociology of Education* 36 (1): 174–92.

"Within 24 Hours, Brazil's Congress Rejects Then Approves Reduction of Age of Criminal Responsibility." 2015. *Rio on Watch*, August 26.

Wolff, Jennifer. 2016. "Debtors' Island: How Puerto Rico Became a Hedge Fund Playground." *New Labor Forum*, March. https://newlaborforum.cuny.edu/2016/03/29/debtors-island/.

Wright, Erik Olin. 2015. *Understanding Class*. New York: Verso.

Yanagisako, S. J. 2002. *Producing Culture and Capital: Family Firms in Italy*. Princeton, NJ: Princeton University Press.

Young, Kirsty. 2013. "Adult Friendships in the Facebook Era." *Webology* 10 (1). http://www.webology.org/2013/v10n1/a103.html.

index

Pandian, Anand, 104, 110–11, 245n1
Parenting Culture Studies (Lee et al.), 11
Partido dos Trabalhadores (PT; Workers' Party), 1–2, 41–45, 187, 203, 221, 232n4, 259n7. *See also* Rousseff, Dilma
Paulson, John, 66–67, 216–18
Pentecostalism, 120, 170. *See also* religion
Pereira Passos, Francisco, 46–48, 237n13
persona humilde (simple person), 103
persona sencilla (down-to-earth person), 34, 67, 92, 99, 103–6, 115
personhood, 20, 34, 55, 246–47n6; neoliberalism and, 4–7, 15–18, 228–29; parenting and, 107, 216–18; subordinates and, 198; self-fashioning and, 6, 94, 97–98, 207–8, 228
Piller, Ingrid, 135
Pinçon, Michel, 5
Pinçon-Charlot, Monique, 5
Pinheiro, Helô, 51
Pinho, Patricia de Santana, 123, 147, 188
piruas, 26
play areas, 37–38, 54–55. *See also* child-centered nodules of urbanism
Plaza Las Américas (shopping mall), 91, 171
Policia Militar (military police). *See* policing and surveillance
policing and surveillance, 140, 220, 225–26; hemispheric control and, 229, 246n4, 254n9, 260nn11–12; neighborhoods and, 11–12, 15, 38–41, 61–64, 85, 89, 206–7, 214, 231n2, 243n19
political parties, 70, 174. *See also specific political parties*
Popular Democratic Party (PPD), 70
postos (Ipanema beach posts), 39, 57, 100
Presbyterian Community Hospital (El Presbiteriano), 67, 72–73
professionais liberais (liberal professionals), 49, 238nn16–18
Projeto de Segurança de Ipanema (Ipanema Security Project). *See* policing and surveillance
projeto praiano-civilizatório (civilizing beach project), 47, 50, 63, 238n19
PROMESA. *See* financial crises, in Puerto Rico
provincial cosmopolitanism, 51, 131, 239n22. *See also* cosmopolitanism
psy-sciences: *atenada/o*, 102; influence of, 95–97, 245nn2–3, 246n5; life coaching, 16–17, 95–98, 123–24; personal growth, 10,

15, 80–81, 105, 108, 111–12, 248n18; popular psychology, 129, 139–41, 155, 163–65, 177, 179, 187–94, 201–2; psychoanalysis, 233n11, 245n3, 246n4; psychological narrativity, 18; self-awareness, 17, 98–99, 116, 120; self-help, 98, 112, 246n4; street therapists, 17; therapeutic culture, 234n13; traditions of, 99–100, 247n8, 248n18. *See also* wellness
public housing (*caseríos, residenciales públicos*), 81, 86–88, 93, 170, 231–32n2, 255n9
public transit, 60–62
Puerto Rico Se Levanta (Puerto Rico Stands Up), 215
Puerto Rico v. Sanchez Valle, 241n7
Pugh, Allison, 139–40

race: as aesthetic project, 130, 143–52; Afro descendants and, 147, 206–7; color and, 56–57, 148–49, 151–52; discourses about, 14, 43–45, 150, 202–8, 237n12, 248n17; racial choice, 143–52, 207; racial democracy, 7, 15–16, 59, 123, 143–44, 145, 152, 237n12, 251n13, 252n17, 254n9; racialization, 59–60, 146–47, 197, 205, 208, 220–21, 255n1; racialized affect, 104, 106, 247n8; racial relations, 206–7, 258n16; self-fashioning and, 146, 152, 187, 192, 198, 200, 214, 229–30; skin color, 56–57, 149, 151–52, 248n16; slavery, 188, 231n1, 251n13; white privilege, 7, 16, 101, 130, 133–34, 146, 224, 228–29, 232n3, 237n12. *See also* whiteness; white supremacy
The Real Housewives of Miramar, 254n6
Rede Globo, 44
regional geopolitics, 202–8
religion: in schools, 21, 61, 76, 131–33, 138–39, 201, 253n3; spirituality and, 14–17, 34, 56, 95–98, 103–11, 116–19, 131–34, 170, 189, 213, 239n24, 245n3, 247n7, 248n18. *See also specific religions*
residenciales públicos. *See* public housing
Rivera Colón, Edgar, 96–97
Rodrigues de Freitas Lagoon (Lagoa Rodrigues de Freitas), 14, 46, 57
Rodriguez Valle, Marisol, 51–52
Rosselló, Pedro, Sr., 70–71
Rosselló, Ricardo, 68–69
Roth-Gordon, Jennifer, 7, 196–97
Rousseff, Dilma, 1–2, 41–43, 52, 68–69, 187–88, 221–22